NELSON ALGREN

NELSON ALGREN

A LIFE ON THE WILD SIDE

Bettina Drew

G. P. PUTNAM'S SONS / NEW YORK

Published by G. P. Putnam's Sons,
200 Madison Avenue, New York, NY 10016
Published simultaneously in Canada.

The text of this book is set in Times Roman.

Library of Congress Cataloging-in-Publication Data

Drew, Bettina, date.
Nelson Algren : a life on the wild side / Bettina Drew.
p. cm.
Bibliography: p.
Includes index.
ISBN 0-399-13422-0
1. Algren, Nelson, 1909–1981—Biography. 2. Novelists,
American—20th century—Biography. I. Title.
PS3501.L4625Z67   1989   89-10299 CIP
813′.52—dc20

Printed in the United States of America
1   2   3   4   5   6   7   8   9   10

FOR PETER BRICKLEBANK
AND FOR THE MEMORY OF
ALYCE DREW

For their help on this book I would like to thank Anne Geismar, who convinced me I could do it; Peter Bricklebank, for spending so many days and evenings poring over the manuscript with me; Roger Groening, for his encouragement and lifesaving editorial advice; and Art Shay, for his unfailing help and affection.

I am especially grateful to Robert Tibbetts, Curator of the Ohio State University Division of Rare Books and Manuscripts, who allowed me such unhindered access to Algren's personal papers and helped me so amiably in so many ways, and to his assistant, Jennifer Songster-Burnett, who guided me through the extensive collection with expertise and insight. I would also like to thank my editor, Faith Sale, her assistant, Jennifer Barth, and my agent, Georges Borchardt, for all that they have done on behalf of the book. To the many scholars and librarians who provided me with invaluable information, I remain indebted. Most of all, I am grateful to the scores of Algren's friends, lovers, relatives, and acquaintances who shared with me so generously.

Contents

IV

I

With heart at rest I climbed the citadel's
Steep height, and saw the city as from a tower,
Hospital, brothel, prison, and such hells,
Where evil comes up softly like a flower.

—BAUDELAIRE

1.

Chicago Childhood

ALGREN'S GRANDFATHER NELS AHLGREN was "good on the con," but in the late 1850s, when the eighteen-year-old son of a Stockholm shopkeeper found a cache of Hebrew prayer books among his dead father's possessions, his fanatical conversion to Judaism was sincere. Renaming himself Isaac Ben Abraham, he sailed for America and became a fur trader in a Swedish community in Minnesota. His trading post was burned out in the last Indian raid east of the Mississippi, and, having drifted to Chicago, he married a German-Jewish servant girl named Yetta Stur and with her established a country store in Black Oak, Indiana. Here, Nelson's undoubtedly embellished account continues, Isaac made change with Swedish pennies worth two-thirds of an American cent, and when the pennies ran out, he minted his own from tin; but the customers turned away, and he turned to farming as a squatter. Another tale recounts how, upon learning the government could tax only stationary property, Abraham made a tin hut on wagon wheels, then rolled and straddled it across the county line in an effort to avoid taxation in either county. When both jurisdictions demanded payment, he returned to the plow.

Dissatisfied, he left his family for San Francisco, presenting himself as a rabbi. But he soon found the city's Russian, Polish, and European Jews insufficiently orthodox, and they in turn wished this conceited converted Swede would go elsewhere, even if he did know the Bible word for word. Yetta, leaving the children, came west to find him, and was soon pregnant. Nelson Algren's father, Gershom Abraham, named for the son of Moses, was born in San Francisco around 1868. A year or so later, having somehow raised passage money, Isaac sailed with his wife and son for Palestine.

The first things Gershom remembered were camels ridden by Arabs, a memory Algren thought odd for a man who would spend his life working for the screw works and Yellow Cab Company in Chicago. But however exotic, life in Jerusalem was easy only for Isaac, who once again refused to work and lounged around discussing the Scriptures with other prophets. An intellectual above manual labor, he was an authority, a patriarch. He prophesied. He read the Torah. He was happy.

But Yetta had "to cook and sew and take care of all these other bums," Nelson said, and she soon tired of it. Obtaining money for the trip home from the American Consulate, she gathered her son and summarily left her husband. "Hey!" he shouted after her, comprehending the departure of his meal ticket, "I'm coming with you!" His fare was somehow found, but to Isaac, the pictures of the presidents on their passage money were blasphemous, graven images, and while the other passengers watched in horror, he threw it all overboard. ("But it's always interested me," Nelson said later, "that he didn't take the money and *say,* 'I threw it overboard last night.' It was done publicly.") Pitying Yetta, the story goes, the passengers took up a collection so the Abrahams could cross the ocean.

Yetta soon found herself again deserted in Indiana. Gerson, who had Americanized his name, grew up on the farm in Black Oak, and later the family moved to Chicago, where, after sixteen or seventeen years, Isaac showed up again, a wizened old man with blue eyes and a long white beard. He'd abandoned Judaism for socialism and traveled the world, a sort of mercenary missionary who'd adopt any faith that would send him somewhere and pay his expenses. He stayed the winter but in spring felt he should go; his family insisted he could stay, but he refused. "He always put it in a pious way," recalled Nelson, who had never met the old man. "Actually I think he wanted to go." He accepted half a dollar and left town, no longer believing in any religion or truth.

Gerson seemed to regret ever having left Black Oak. Certainly his plodding, noncompetitive temperament seemed more suited to farm life than to the teeming city where he survived by becoming a mechanic. Algren saw his father as a hick farm-boy drawn to the 1893 Chicago World's Fair by Little Egypt's dancing, a naive man enjoying simple pleasures—musicians like "McGuire's Ice Cream Kings" and dances where shy youths were introduced to ladies sophisticated enough to know the Speedy Three-Step. The uneducated Gerson was not the most suave or worldly of men, so when he reached thirty without having taken a wife, it was undoubtedly a relief to meet, probably through Yetta's German-Jewish Chicago connections, the eminently marriageable Goldie Kalisher.

Her parents, Louis and Henrietta Kalisher, were of the merchant class. They had a large three-story home with a little old-world cottage out back, and Algren recalled that in retirement jolly Grandfather Kalisher, with a big mustache and thick wavy hair, made cigars in his basement. The Kalishers were German above all; they did not practice the Jewish faith. Nelson claimed they were as anxious to assimilate in America as they had been as Jews in the Fatherland, and in this they were fortunate to be fair-haired and blue-eyed. Louis, a rather patriarchal Prussian, decreed they would speak German in their house and English outside: Yiddish was a mongrel language. Of his three sons, one became a Government man in Washington, D.C., one took to the sea, and the other ran off to the wars. The six daughters, none of them beauties, were less adventurous. Most married, had several children, and grew stout.

And Gerson the garage mechanic, so innocent of the laboring man's true lot that he worked for double wages at McCormick Reaper until the picketers threatened to kill him, took the twenty-one-year-old Goldie to see the Bismarck Gardens. And married her, with a rabbi presiding, in June of 1899.

Their first child, Irene, was born a year later, followed by a second daughter, Bernice, in 1902. The family had moved to Detroit, where Gerson worked at the new Packard Motor Company. Its cars a symbol of automotive luxury, Packard was a benevolent company where workers took pride in their craftsmanship, and life was good for the Abrahams. The energetic and ambitious Goldie ran a corner candy and cigarette store, acquiring "Goldie's Cottage," a little summer house on Flax Creek near Detroit.

Goldie was still a young woman. Buxom and full, she posed for a studio photograph with her daughters, proud and at ease among them, her thick hair in flattering waves. Her face had not yet fallen into the set lines of middle age, but when her two daughters were seven and nine, more independent and less trouble, she became pregnant again. Her son, named Nelson Algren Abraham after the old man, was born on March 28, 1909. Photographs taken after his birth show that Goldie, with her big, practical hands, sleeves rolled up to the elbow, and thick hair side-parted plainly over her broad, unadorned face, had become the picture of the German hausfrau, with only a rare smile that was not one of joy.

Nelson was a beautiful child who took after the favored Bernice. His bright, wavy blond hair grew long and shaggy when he was a toddler, and by age three his features were well defined, self-aware and somewhat petulant. In 1912, all the aunts agreed that he looked grand posing with his two sisters on the front porch of Goldie's cottage, a wooden two-story structure reminiscent of an old trading post, whose steps went right down to the river's edge. There a row-boat waited to take them for idyllic turn-of-the-century afternoons on the sleepy river flanked by leafy trees. Goldie and the children and the aunts spent much of the summer there—Gerson apparently working in the city—and the women vied for little Nelson's attention. On the back of one photograph, a relative wrote that they had been "calling him and he in return is thinking shall I answer or not. He thinks it a great joke to have everyone running around looking for him."

Once, around age three, he found himself lost in Detroit. He was looking for his Uncle Theodore, Goldie's favorite brother. A Great Lake sailor on the *Chicora,* Theodore Kalisher had been ordered ashore after a fistfight with the ship's cook. On the *Chicora*'s next trip out, she went down with all hands. Uncle Theodore, miraculous survivor, hero of family legends, had become alive to Nelson through his mother's incessant tales. So, enlisting a tiny friend, Nelson had set off in search of him. They were gone the whole day, and a half-century later Nelson could still remember the newly laid sidewalks at the end of town. At a railroad track, he saw an engineer leaning out of a train and, devising an end for the adventure, told his friend that was Uncle Theodore. The wanderers were finally picked up by a Jewish tailor, taken to the police station, and fed ice cream until their mothers came to retrieve them.

In 1913, Nelson's family returned to Chicago, making a down payment on a house in a South Side Irish Protestant neighborhood near 71st Street and Cottage Grove. It was the era of the street vendor, the organ-grinder and his red-capped monkey, and the ped-dler who yelled "Rags and old iron!" along the streets, Algren re-membered nostalgically in *Who Lost an American?* and *The Last*

Carousel. The milkman made rounds, and in summer kids stole frozen chunks from the iceman's wagon. Evenings, the lamplighter came riding up the street on his bike, turning the streetlamps' filaments from a "green gem" into a "blue flutter." In Nelson's memoirs it was a childhood of "roll-a-hoop" and "fly-a-kite" springs: he treated his bossy Catholic girlfriend Ethel to ice-cream sundaes, saw Punch and Judy shows and Saturday-afternoon movies, mourned the loss of pet dogs, and appeared in theatrical productions at the Park Manor School. With the neighboring Lindholm boys, he scoured the Saturday streets for tinfoil and old beer and soda corks. He roasted potatoes, stolen from the basement, on a nearby patch of land still wild enough to be called a prairie.

But behind the Abrahams' door lay a different life Algren chose only to hint at in memoirs. Goldie was dissatisfied. Unemployed, unhappy with the neighborhood, she was in competition with her sisters. She wanted Gerson to be richer, more aggressive, like the other relatives; all he wanted was to hoe in the prairie Victory Garden on his day off. They argued. Nelson's cousin Clarence, who witnessed Goldie hurling insults and shouts at Gerson, recalled how Nelson would confide sadly that Ma and Pa had been fighting again. " 'You're so damned smart, how come you don't get to be foreman?' was my mother's ceaseless accusation," Nelson described it,

> until it seemed to me that the highest condition of man was being "Foreman." I would hear her going at him when the bulb that lit our kitchen and the lamp that lit our door were the only lights foretelling the beginning of the winter workday.
>
> "*Some* men make theirselves Foreman"—a rattle of kettles was his reply, made in serving himself breakfast to show her how little kindness remained in the world.
>
> "If you're so damned smart—"

Goldie was hard to live with. Though she got along with Bernice and was remembered fondly by her granddaughter Ruth Sherman, her grandson Robert Joffe recalled her as cold, domineering, and cruel to children; and in Nelson's memoirs she nearly always appears as the source of humiliation or discord. It took him fifty years to admit that she beat him with her hands and fists—not once or twice but as a consistent expression of her rage. Once, he said many years later, she had yelled at him to get out of the house and go ice skating, and he, unwilling to defy her but refusing to obey, hid for hours in a large piano crate on the back porch, a small prisoner of fear in the midwinter cold.

Although Algren dutifully supported Goldie when she was old, he never seemed to really feel comfortable with her. She was an ignorant woman who ate without manners, called his writing trash, and yearned for a fur coat. As a grandmother, Goldie was a critical and abusive dream-smasher. She tormented Bernice's son Robert Joffe when he was a child: That baseball he kept on his dresser, the one his parents said had been hit by his hero? It had only been scuffed with dirt, she informed him cruelly. And in summers at the Indiana dunes, Goldie would chase the little boy and beat him with a broom while his mother went out to the store. Decades later, over lunch with Robert, Nelson, noting that age had forced her into using a weapon, remarked wryly, "But you got her when she was an old woman. I had her when she was in her prime."

In those early years, Gerson was his ally. Nelson loved his father, who was proud to have given his son the home Isaac Abraham had been so incapable of providing. Gerson fabricated toys out of scraps of machines and once, Algren's memoirs reveal, he taught Nelson to make a pushmobile from orange crates and roller-skate wheels: Nelson rode it evenings to the 71st Street trolley to meet his father returning from work, holding his hand or his lunchbox all the way home. The pushmobile induced neighboring Mr. Kooglin to offer him a newspaper route; but the neighborhood bully made sure Nelson would deliver no *Abendpost*s. Algren told stories of the bully taking the pushmobile and leaving it on the tracks; another time he scattered all of Nelson's papers. The small, thin Nelson "chased up and down the alley, crying in the wind, and finally, in a fright, abandoned paper, pushmobile, and all. When my father heard the story, at the supper table," Nelson remembered, "his only word was for me to finish my supper. Then he took me back down the alley, picked up the pushmobile with one hand and, holding my hand with the other, assured me that Mr. Kooglin wouldn't fire me, and Mr. Kooglin didn't."

But Gerson couldn't fix everything. The simple fact that he labored for a wage made him vulnerable. If his role as a breadwinner was shaken, the rest of the house shook with him:

> My father was a working man in a day when the working hour was from 6 A.M. to 6 P.M. He left the house before daylight six days a week, year in and year out.

He worked for McCormick Reaper and Otis Elevator and Packard and the Yellow Cab Company in a time when there was no sick leave, no vacations, no seniority and no social security. There was nothing for him to do but to get a hold as a machinist and to hold as hard as he could for as long as he could.

He was a good holder but he was unable to keep any one job for more than four or five years because he couldn't handle other men. He could handle any piece of machinery; if left alone. But he was as unable to give orders as he was to take them. He was a tenacious holder; but after four or five years he would hit a foreman. This would happen so blindly that he would be as stunned by it as the man he had hit.

When he walked into the kitchen at noon with his tool chest under his arm my mother knew it had happened again. The first time this happened I was frightened, because I had never seen him, during the week, in the middle of the day. I had the feeling my mother was going to go for him like never before.

This was one time she didn't go at him at all.

Then for days we lived under an oppression of which only the tool chest in the corner of the kitchen spoke. On the morning I rose to find the tool chest and the old man gone to work together, the sense of ominousness lifted; and life began once more.

There were other forces in the world that could create chaos; from an early age, Nelson was also aware of death. The summer before he started school, Goldie had taken him to see the wreck of the pleasure boat *Eastland,* which had listed at the dock and then fallen on its side in the thirty-foot-deep Chicago River, drowning 981 Western Electric workers bound for a Michigan City picnic. Then the Black Diphtheria took only forty-eight hours to kill three children at the Park Manor School. But in Algren's memoirs the most significant death was that of John the Greek, who ran the wonderful ice-cream store where Nelson took Ethel for sundaes. One day the shop didn't open, and the police broke in and cut John down from where he had hanged himself. The young Nelson, impelled by an unsatisfied curiosity, stared in through the windows of the abandoned store and saw that the strawberry syrup, frozen and burst from its container, hung suspended like a strip of bloody meat.

The Great War seemed hardly to affect nine-year-old Nelson, but after the armistice, Bernice took him downtown to see the homecoming Prairie Boys in parade. It was special to be included with Bernice. Nelson never got along with his older sister Irene, a rather unattractive office worker, but Bernice was the bright spot in the otherwise gloomy family. Happy, popular, outgoing, she was known around school as "a physics shark, historian, poet, n'everything." She was athletic too, a star swimmer nicknamed "Pretzie" for her long and agile body. Bernice was also a freethinker and politically liberal, but surely what attracted Nelson most was her love of drama and literature. She had seen almost every movie at the Park Manor Theater, acted in school plays, written poetry, and loved reading aloud so much that she read *Silas Marner* to her appreciative younger brother. She also brought him books from the library, first Stevenson's *A Child's Garden of Verses* and later Dickens. Perhaps in imitation of her, Nelson began to write. At age eleven, he created a newspaper, complete with weather reports, entertainment listings, pictures, want ads, and science fiction stories, that showed a marked interest in politics: "NEVADA COWBOYS FORM UNION—SAID TO BE FIRST OF ITS KIND IN AMERICA," announced one headline, and a political cartoon suggested that the Bolsheviks were incapable of reaching an "intercourse with the world."

In 1920 the Abrahams spent part of the summer in Princeton, Illinois, an idyllic town that was the picture of untroubled midwestern life. Nelson rode ponies and played with goats and geese and other children, wearing a sailor's hat, knickers, and a serious expression. Earlier that summer he had sneaked into Comiskey Park to see the White Sox and Swede Risberg, and by now he had taken for himself the nickname Swede.

But violence and madness were always close at hand. Algren recalled that when he sold *Saturday Evening Blade*s with his friends, he watched open-mouthed the stupid, bloody fistfights at the bar across the street from his hawking-place, "feeling nothing save some sort of city-wide sorrow." For the years following the war brought loss. Irene, over eighteen, moved permanently to New York, and good-natured Grandfather Kalisher, who'd made a bellows-breathing clown blow smoke for Nelson, died. Nelson's cousin Carlisle Ansorg, who was close to Bernice, who loved books and had written poetry from the front, had been gassed in France; soon after his return home he was institutionalized at the state psychiatric hospital at Elgin, Illinois. The specter of the mentally ruined war veteran would haunt Algren for years. Carlisle may have been treated for a few years and released, but Bernice's son remembers that much later, he would periodically escape to Bernice's house, where he babbled on incoherently until carted back to Elgin, harmless but completely crazy.

In the spring of 1921 the Abrahams moved to 4834 North Troy Street on the Northwest Side. Gerson opened a tire and battery shop a block away, and Bernice, now graduated from high school, was studying at Chicago Normal College for a career as a schoolteacher. Nelson, still thin and small, was the new kid on the block. At first the neighborhood seemed rough, and he had to suffer the local kids' disdain for the White Sox, since by virtue of nearby Wrigley Field, the National League's Cubs held sway over the territory. The news that Swede Risberg had been one of the players to throw the 1919 World Series was a blow to Nelson's tenuous position. A truer test of his manhood came two years later in a Kedzie Avenue poolroom, where only guys in long pants could play rotation. Nelson, forbidden by Goldie to wear longies till he was fourteen, waited against the wall until he saved money for long pants by working for the iceman; then he slipped them on in the poolroom bathroom and stepped out a man at last.

At the same time he kept reading and admiring Bernice, who was seeing musicals, operas, classical concerts, and the Ballets-Russes in downtown Chicago. In his early adolescence Nelson rapidly developed his own judgments about books and plays. For Christmas 1923 he gave Bernice a book of poetry called *In American,* by John V. A. Weaver, a Mencken protégé who wrote in American slang. The poems were small portraits—a dull man spurned by a woman who sees more of life than he can ever hope to, a gambler watching in disgust as a destitute man won't play a winning tip—and the book was permeated by loss: a suicide, a lover killed in France, a tavern keeper aware that Prohibition would destroy his "family" at the bar. Everyday people betrayed by life, speaking in their own language, they were strikingly similar to Algren's later characters; it was as if his aesthetic had already begun forming by age fourteen.

But friends noticed nothing about the Swede that marked him for literary greatness. By 1925, he and his three buddies, Jerome Hanock, Ralph Zwick, and Ben Curtis, were playing basketball several times a week, pooling their money and eating dinner at each other's houses. They organized the Uptown Arrows basketball team, which played other Albany Park social and athletic clubs throughout the 1925–1926 season. They also engaged in small-time gambling, flipping baseball cards and once pitching pennies in a duel that lasted two miles to the movie theater. They occasionally gathered for poker games in Swede's basement, but if they did play for money, it wasn't serious. They never got into any trouble, Ben Curtis recalled. "We were very conservative. We did things the way they were supposed to be done. Our big aim in life was to make the high school basketball team." But when Nelson recalled his adolescence, he usually remembered the poolroom.

Nelson was bright, inclined to practical jokes and quick with a comeback. "He always managed to top me—but never in any harmful way," said Ben. "He just had a great imagination." Despite failing geometry, Nelson did fairly well at Hibbard High School, but his love of books and poetry was something he shared only, if at all, with Bernice. Slim, elegant, sensitive, and nothing like his mother, she yearned for something more than the life of the Abrahams. With her schoolteacher friends, she bought a summer cabin on the Indiana dunes. Nelson admired her: she knew what to do with her money— go to plays, buy houses on the beach—she knew that life was to be enjoyed. He looked to Bernice, never to his parents, for guidance. No longer physically vulnerable to Goldie, he refused to heed her or submit to her authority. He withheld his affection. He was rebellious, and he didn't take orders. When he began smoking in the house, only Bernice could convince him to stop. "Anything Bernice said was right," he said later. "She knew everything."

By age twenty-four, Bernice had been dating Morris Joffe, a chemical engineer two years her senior, for a few years. A round, bespectacled man, dapper but somewhat comic in his white duck pants, he often hired a rig when he took Bernice out. They decided to marry in 1926. To Nelson it must have seemed incomprehensible that a freethinking atheist like Bernice would fall for the conventional, almost prissy Joffe. He had thought he and Bernice understood each other, and he seems to have been disappointed by her marriage, though afterward Bernice made sure to see him often. For the next ten years his fiction would be dominated by themes of betrayal; in college stories brother-sister relationships were prominent, and in his first novel the redemptive love between the hero and his sister would be completely severed.

Life seemed boring to the teenage Nelson. Unemployed in the summers while Ralph Zwick worked at the hardware store and Jerome Hanock was proving his loyalty to Sears, Roebuck, Nelson and Ben Curtis bounced balls against the steps of the deserted school and discussed their possibilities in the Chicago heat. They pooled their money and bought an old jalopy so they could escape to Bernice's cabin on the dunes, where they swam, luxuriated on the expanses of white sand and grasses, and indulged themselves in the belief that life was passing them by.

With Bernice gone, Nelson was even more isolated from his ignorant, poorly read parents. It especially bothered him the way his mother mispronounced words, said "moon" for "noon," "pregrant" instead of "pregnant." "El-ec-tro-cuted, Ma," he'd say in exasperation when she told him someone had been "elexecuted." Wanting her to be more dignified, he couldn't stand it when he came home from school and found her in the middle of the floor with a scrub bucket—especially if he'd brought home a friend whose mother was more sophisticated. And he had grown impatient with Gerson's simple ways. The only thing that gave the old man pleasure was fixing. "Other men wished to be forever drunken," Nelson would say later. "He wished to be forever fixing." Beyond that he seemed limited, telling the same dumb jokes year after year, unable to understand a movie without having the plot explained. And it seemed to Nelson, already reading about socialism, that the old man, running his own business, had no concept of a profit. He charged only for his labor, making no markup on materials, and he grew angry when his son suggested he do otherwise. Nelson reminded him that the grocer sold for more than he paid, but Gerson just didn't get it: "That's different. He's a *business* man."

Though Nelson loathed physical work and conversation with Gerson was impossible, on weekends he helped out in the shop. One flight above, a "dancing academy" operated as a front for a gambling joint that Ben Curtis remembers being run by "*the* gamblers of the city—possibly by a Capone group." Gerson's shop changed a lot of tires for the upstairs neighbors, and because he was known in the neighborhood, Nelson had made his way up to the forbidden gaming rooms. His father had little idea of what it was all about. When Nelson told him cops used to go up there, Gerson balked: "That's crazy. A cop can't do that; they'd put him in jail." Nelson said, "Cops, pa, cops take money, cops steal." "I don't want to listen to crazy talk like that," Gerson said, flaring. "A cop, a policeman is made to defend the law! . . . If he doesn't do that, then he gets put

into jail." In the face of such naiveté, Nelson began to feel contemptuous of his father:

> Contemptuous of his hands, whose crevices were so deeply packed
> with rubber they would never be clean again. . . . Contemptuous
> of his little rubber-blackened book in which, every Sunday after-
> noon on the back porch, touching a pencil to his tongue, he would
> add up the quarters and halves of the past week and always come
> out with five or ten dollars missing. . . . Contemptuous too of the
> old man kneeling in the winter gutter, his big hands naked to the
> cold with his wrench and jack, while the twenty-year-old car-owner
> waited, inside the warmth of the tire shack, his hands gloved and
> hair pomaded, restlessly waiting for the old man to get the job
> done. . . . It was always "Hurry up, Abe, I got a date," or worse,
> when the job was done, "The old man'll be in to pay you,"—and
> then, in a whiff of exhaust and a soft whirr of snow, wheel off with
> that dollar and a half saved to spend on his date. . . . Contemp-
> tuous too because I was a High School junior in a red and gold
> sweater that was sure to have a letter on it and the old man's lips
> moved when he tried to read a newspaper.
>
> Yet my allowance consisted of how much I could earn running
> the shop by myself on Sunday. Until, one Saturday night, I won
> forty dollars shooting crap and woke up feeling like a millionaire.
> My mother was calling me, telling me it was almost nine o'clock,
> that if I was going to open the shop I [should] get a move on. I
> rolled over and went back to sleep.
>
> Half an hour later my father came in and woke me.
>
> "Are you going to open the shop?"
>
> "Open it yourself."
>
> He did. He never reproached me. Simply took his weekday lunch
> bucket, put in a full day on his day of rest, and didn't ask me the
> next Sunday.
>
> After that we scarcely spoke again.

Ben Curtis had been upstairs with Nelson to the horseshoe bar,
which was probably where he won the forty dollars that cemented
his start as a gambler. "There was a man downstairs and he kept an
eye out," Ben recalled. "No one could go up without passing this
man. If it looked like anything was bad, he'd call upstairs. Nelson
knew the man and we got by him. At the top of the stairs we got to
a little room and the doors closed. A man frisked us. Inside I saw
money, cash like I had never seen. They didn't play for chips but
for silver dollars and bills." Nelson was also aware that every once

in a while a truck would pull up and some big men would go upstairs, come down with the safe, and move everything to another place across the street; an hour later the now empty gambling hall would be raided.

In those Prohibition years Nelson knew where to go, say "Joe sent me," and be admitted to have a stein of beer. Even at seventeen, he seemed to know his way around the underworld without fear. Alone, he explored Chicago, and though he remained friendly with Ben, Jerome, and Ralph, he felt different from them. Ralph Zwick remembers him as somewhat aloof: he didn't often call them; they had to call him. And he didn't seem very interested in girls. Though Nelson later said he lost his virginity at seventeen, he never had a girlfriend his friends could recall. Women, if he had any, were something else he kept from them.

For he had begun to realize that he didn't share his friends' view of life. He had no desire for the safe existence Jerome Hanock was making for himself as a Sears, Roebuck employee. The idea of trading fulfillment in life for staid security made him angry and resentful, and he felt his friends didn't share his feeling that life should be rich and fulfilling, "more than just a guarantee of respectable survival."

He wanted to do something meaningful—and that was writing. In his last two years at school, he had done consistently well in English and Oral Expression. While Ben was lucky to scratch out a theme, Nelson could easily produce essays that were read in class. In his senior year, he took a journalism course and began writing small articles for the high school paper, little pieces on school happenings, and character sketches. And he may have begun to write the juvenile poems found among his papers. "Even in high school, he wanted to be a writer—he was going to be a journalist," said Ben Curtis. "Without letting us know, he had laid out his plans for the future."

Ben, closest to Nelson, wasn't surprised, as Ralph and Jerome were, when Nelson announced he was going to college, though very few working-class kids from Chicago's Northwest Side got a university education in those days. His decision created, as Nelson realized later, a class difference between himself and his friends, widening an already existing gulf of expectations. Nelson's later assertions that he graduated in the bottom tenth of his class after five years in school, that his hero was the baseball player who had been left back, were not true so much as designed to obscure the fact that as a young man he was upwardly mobile, though his search was for self-fulfillment, not money.

Bernice, also ambitious through her marriage and career, thought Nelson should go to the University of Illinois, and persuaded Joffe to help pay the tuition while Nelson worked his way through. Gerson, "staggered" by the idea of a four-year education, feebly suggested that he ought to get a job as a draftsman or something, but Bernice declared firmly that Nelson was going to college. And that was it. "The old man never went against anything she said," Nelson remembered. "He had the same feeling the rest of us did: that Bernice knew what was right. If the other sister had said it, they would have had a fight, but if Bernice says I go to college then I go. My mother always went along with Bernice. So I went."

2.
Urbana–Champaign

IN SEPTEMBER 1927, fraternities and sororities at the University of Illinois, Urbana, planned football parties, mixers, and fancy-dress galas, but Nelson's first stop was a long line at the YMCA to look for a job. Soon mowing lawns or selling sandwiches, he rented a single room in a boardinghouse close to campus. "I never knew anybody down there," Nelson said later of his four years in college. As an independent, he wasn't invited to frat parties, and he had no money for the occasionally available wood alcohol. But he didn't care. He felt he had nothing in common with the ten thousand other students. He never joined any college clubs or teams, and worked for the campus paper because it was required for the journalism degree. Instead he savored his isolation and independence. With plenty of time to think and read, he tended toward the humanities and at the end of his first year had a B average with As in rhetoric and journalism and Cs and Ds in zoology and chemistry.

His first summer home he seemed to Ben and Ralph strangely busy, and he returned for his sophomore year even more aloof. He landed work as a waiter in a small fraternity, a job he kept until graduation. With fixed hours, free meals, and thirty dollars a month, he organized his life into a routine and entered what he called a "spiritual phase." Books were everything. After work he devoured Chaucer, Byron, Shelley, Keats, Browning, and Shakespeare. He read essayists Walter Pater, Charles Lamb, and Thomas Carlyle; and the poets continually amazed him. He read Matthew Arnold's "Dover Beach" again and again, and went about reciting poetry in his head. Studying literature became a moral imperative: "To be a man was not to excel physically, not to dominate anyone, but simply to live nobly. In order to live nobly one must think of nothing but poetry and philosophy."

A program of austerity dominated his daily life. At six A.M. he rose, took a cold bath, and went to work by the shortest route. There he ate plain oatmeal with no milk, cream, sugar, or fruit: any food not necessary for survival was self-indulgence, though hunger was tolerated only if it didn't interfere with thinking. While waiting on tables, it was better to be reflecting on some of Shakespeare's lines than to join in some silly breakfast small talk. He said "Good morning," but discouraged further conversation. If someone spoke to him, he would decide whether the question was worth answering, and he didn't waste time.

This asceticism—a mixture of Marcus Aurelius, the Latin Stoics, and Pascal—seemed justified, since his grandfather Nels Ahlgren, for whom he now had developed a strong affinity, had also lived this way. But sticking to a repressive moral code was not easy. An occasional bet was permissible, but more complicated desires, like the need for women, he tried vainly to suppress, even with cold showers. He knew few, if any, university women, but dating them would mean time away from books, money for fancy meals, and frivolous entertainment with no guarantee of sex. Later he remembered looking for prostitutes, "walking down Walnut Street, you know, but with a very oppressive sense of sin." But after knocking on several doors in a likely district without finding the right place, he went back to his books.

His voracious reading encouraged him to question the structure of organized society. In a course with sociologist Donald Taft, he read the nineteenth-century philosopher Max Nordau, author of *Contemporary Lies of Civilization* and a socialist and Zionist like Nels Ahlgren. Nelson had never read anybody so critical of existing society as the revolutionary Nordau. He had already read Ramsay MacDonald's *The Socialist Movement* and talked about socialism at home in Chicago, but Nordau opposed even the draft. That year Nelson's grades in the mandatory ROTC artillery drill plummeted— probably attributable as much to Nordau as to his own aversion to lining up in a baggy uniform and shooting off guns. Demoted for his clumsiness with firearms, he later claimed that his new job during exercises was to lead out the drill division's mascot: an ass.

In the spring he took "Social Factors in Personality" and "Social Control." Professor Taft, a criminologist, undoubtedly fueled Nelson's interest in criminals and prisons. Taft believed crime had to be studied in relation to society and, like Havelock Ellis, saw crime as an index to progress: there was naturally more crime in a democracy than in an autocracy. So while Herbert Hoover called crime the greatest evil facing America, Taft warned that a preoccupation with robbers and murderers blinded Americans to people far more threatening. "Outside the ranks of criminals are men whose acts, though technically not crime, threaten our lives and welfare in much more important ways," Taft stated, citing war profiteers and shipbuilders who urged the country into war for personal gain. The term "criminal" was a label excluding legal brutalities; and insincerity, while not usually a crime, could be far more devastating. Nelson may have surmised that capitalism presupposed exploitation and relied on insincerity by selling unnecessary items to an impressionable public. He soon agreed that, while criminals as a class were dangerous, the class itself contained many far from dangerous types: illiterate losers, dim-witted kleptomaniacs, scapegoat blacks, and unlucky street girls. To think about these issues rationally, free from cultural prejudices, was enough for a life's work if one had, like Taft, a forum in which to expound them. That year he decided to become a sociologist.

By now, Ben and Ralph, who saw Nelson at yearly Urbana football games and during vacations, had noticed a definite change in him. When he was home he was exploring poor Chicago neighborhoods—mostly dumps, as Ralph Zwick recalled, "taverns and clubhouses." "We kind of drifted a little bit apart," said Ben Curtis. "That's when I found out that he had begun traveling among the poorer people, the downtrodden. . . . He started talking in different terms. He became left-wing and very compassionate." There were immigrant and Polish neighborhoods east and south of North Troy, and at some point Nelson visited the Great Lakes Memorial Veterans' Hospital and wrote, in the first person, a long poem about a Great War veteran enduring a hospital life of pills and spells. Another moody prose piece suggests he sought out "the shamed women," "vast legions and endless ranks of marching women with bowed-down heads." He seems to have continued to haunt the pool halls and to have worked setting pins in a bowling alley.

Though he approached these forays as a sociologist, his family assured him that field was out of the question. He would need a master's degree, and there was simply no money for it. In his junior year, he officially entered the journalism school while continuing with economics, French, and expository writing. Undoubtedly disappointed and perhaps caring less, he relaxed a little. He found a room in a house owned by a cheerful widow in her thirties, and, abandoning his puritanical regime, began eating better. During the three terms he lived there, he said once, they became lovers; pleasure was not necessarily evil, after all. But if the drive that had earned him As in sociology and English was gone, with it went his obsessive need for repression.

In the fall of 1929, the *The Daily Illini*'s scare headlines were reserved for football victories, and naiveté about the increasingly precarious state of the stock exchange prevailed. "Huge barriers of buying orders, hastily erected by powerful financial interests, finally checked the most frantic stampede of selling yet experienced by the securities market which threatened to bring about an utter collapse in prices," a one-column article did report following Black Tuesday, October 29, 1929, but two days later the headlines assured readers that the capitalists had everything under control: "STOCK PRICES RALLY, AIDED BY FINANCIERS; HYSTERICAL SELLING IS CHECKED BY MORGAN AND ROCKEFELLER FORCES."

Two weeks later, on November 13, when a fresh collapse sent nearly three hundred issues on the New York Stock Exchange crashing to new lows, the bankers had no comment. Already, food prices were dropping, less merchandise was being shipped, and predictions that the market might not hit its lowest point for another eighteen months began to be heard. "The stories of the bankers are rather fictitious," Urbana economist H. M. Gray stated bluntly. "It would be foolish of them to support a definitely undetermined market that is sure to come down."

Effects of the slump soon reached the Midwest. Banks with heavy investments in stocks began failing, and a run on Urbana's University State Bank was halted only after it one day paid out more than $75,000 in cash. Increasing joblessness and a bitterly cold winter encouraged social unrest that had been simmering since the early 1920s. The radical National Miners' Union was gaining strength in central Illinois, and demonstrations in the coal-mine town of Taylorville brought out the National Guard. Twenty-two people were injured when twelve hundred jobless stormed Cleveland's City Hall, and a demonstration of hundreds of Chicago unemployed demanding work, characterized by *The Daily Illini* as "a Communist mob," was broken up by riot squads and mounted police.

The world outside the university seemed chaotic. That spring the local news was dominated by a fire that swept through the Ohio State Penitentiary in Columbus and killed 318 locked-up prisoners. No general fire precautions had been taken at the severely overcrowded prison, and probably all could have been saved if let out at the first alarm. In a local front-page newspaper story, Professor Taft remarked that the blaze merely brought attention to the long-standing overcrowding of Midwest prisons. Incarceration as a means of social control fascinated Nelson, and the life inside captured his imagination: tiers of ringing steel and concrete, the lack of sunlight and sex, the fitful violence of a locked-up rage. The inherent drama of all that human energy in the negligent hands of an indifferent state was not lost on him.

Throughout the fall of 1930, stocks continued to drop. Banks urged customers to be patriotic and buy, and everywhere there was news of suicides, lynchings, and clashes between the unemployed and armed riot police. Now in his senior year, Algren covered the city jails and courts as a reporter for *The Daily Illini,* where local reporting reflected the national malaise and confusion. No bylines identified his articles, but such a beat meant contact with homeless transients, stewbums, and petty thieves; crimes of adultery, drunkenness, vandalism, burglary, and murder. Cases filed before the city court in an endless parade, and Nelson, seeing yet another aspect of the underworld, enjoyed the assignment.

In the spring of 1931, he wrote his first surviving fiction, sketches for Rhetoric 4 that drew heavily from the pool halls, bowling alleys, tenement houses, and immigrants of Chicago. His first story, "Fifty-fifty," about a well-connected Chinese-American pimp who terrorizes the neighborhood, is one of his few stories with an evil protagonist. He preferred writing about the *victims* of oppression, and he continued in this for the rest of his life. The stories that followed, always about the defeated, largely concerned disillusionment and loss of innocence. One such piece was "I Was a Farm Boy," about a rural man corrupted by vague forces of urban sin. In the more successful "A Woman Called Mary," a female prisoner, days from completing her sentence, trembles with the possibilities of the outside world, only to be crushed when a jealous inmate plants a gun on her, and she is sentenced to five more years. His professor gave him an A. "You have an insight into characters and a sense of drama. Try a longer composition." In his next, perhaps more autobiographical effort, the innocence of eleven-year-old Christopher, out swimming with his friends, is shattered when he is taunted for being a Jew. This provoked even further praise: "This is one of the most vivid sketches I have seen. I am eager to see you continue with it."

A series of loosely connected stories followed, about a family of Chicago Poles living in a house that "stands on the prairie like an accidental box," built on a developer's promise of economic prosperity that never came. From this "economic accident" of a family springs Nick, the protagonist of "Nick," "Nick's Brothers," "A Child," and "The Vendreyevs." Nick grows up increasingly alienated from his family: watching his brawny, violent, piggish brothers eat dinner is an ordeal. He works setting pins in a bowling alley and, when his father dies, quits school to hang out at the pool hall. In another story, his betrayal of his sister Blima, the only person he loves, seems complete when he spends the night with a prostitute. Inevitably, he takes to the streets to panhandle. In a *Dr. Zhivago*–like ending, he and Blima pass on the streetcar without seeing each other, each merely surviving without their old, uncorrupted love.

As in many of Algren's early stories, here the male hero's only pure feeling is for a sister who, much like Bernice, is the embodiment of love. But though his inspiration had autobiographical sources, the basis for Algren's fiction was always rooted in the outside world. His characters were usually immigrants—outsiders—and often destitute. These were stories of betrayed dreams, of Eastern Europeans once in search of a better life and now adrift in an alien country. In "Little Mr. Gorshkov," a once respected Russian civil servant, now a widowed umbrella mender, is cruelly evicted from his depressing rented room, not even permitted to retrieve his wife's mug, the only remnant of his once dignified life. At twenty-two Algren, with his sociological perspective and emphasis on economic and social forces, leaned spontaneously toward literary naturalism, which, exemplified by writers like Zola, Dreiser, Crane, and Norris, held that man was largely the product of his environment.

Writing came easily that spring; sometimes he handed in themes within two days of each other, receiving encouragement almost every time he did so. Writing was a way to distinguish himself, to find out who he was. He tried consciously to be "a writer in the literary sense," yet it did not occur to him as a career. "It was just something that I never thought of not doing . . . you know, the way a race horse runs." He would write as a newspaperman. Confident of his abilities and more than willing to conform and succeed American style, in June 1931 he borrowed money for a dark, formal suit so he could look like the hundreds of other University of Illinois graduates. He had passed a test of the Illinois Press Association for certification as a journalist and planned to find work as soon as he left school.

3.
Drifting into a Career

BEARING A CARD that identified him as a qualified "editor, columnist . . . headline writer . . . et cetera," and armed with faith and his graduation suit, Nelson Abraham began looking for work in the most stagnant year since the crash. By the summer of 1931, more than eight hundred Chicago families were being evicted for nonpayment of rent; thousands more had already lost their jobs, savings, and homes; breadlines, soup kitchens, street-corner orators and demonstrations could be found throughout the city. Nelson tried all the Chicago newspapers with no success. After untold weeks of discouragement, coupled with pressure from Gerson and Goldie's newly mounting financial troubles, he decided to look outside the city. Any place was bound to be better than Chicago.

He hitchhiked through the Midwest, living in cheap hotels, winding up in a whorehouse in Minneapolis. There, a young Swedish prostitute came to his room to borrow some whiskey for her cold. Having no glasses, Nelson bid her drink from the bottle and, fearful of disease, inwardly vowed to dispose of it when she left. Conversation was awkward. He affronted her by asking if she ever went home, and when she told him that in fact she lived at home, that her parents thought she was a nice girl, Nelson's reply betrayed his middle-class orientation.

"I think you're a nice girl," he said. "I don't have sympathy with people who just start condemning before understanding—preachers—you know." But her expression stopped him. She quickly left. "I had been overly eager to prove I had no contempt for her," he realized later, "while she had never once assumed that I could be contemptuous. I had betrayed myself, and she wouldn't be patronized."

A naive but confident young man out discovering the world: he had a stroke of seemingly incredible fortune when a man at the *Minneapolis Journal* told him to sit down and work if he could write headlines. He took a room at the YMCA and worked, by his own recollection, ten days or three weeks. But when he asked for his paycheck, he was obligingly told there wasn't one: he was just being given experience and filling in for a man out of town. "Well, then I have to leave," he said inadequately, and his sister Irene, taking her turn at helping him out, sent him the bus fare home. Exploited and angry, he seemed to give up looking for work at all.

Spending the summer at home and probably making trips to the Indiana dunes, he turned again to writing stories. But he soon moved from adolescent sketches of Nick Vendreyev to the prison settings that would always haunt him. Disillusionment with the status quo would bring Algren back to lost people time and time again.

Stories like the sentimental and hopelessly contrived "News Flash" introduced what would become a familiar Algren theme: the criminal forced to choose between two undesirable options; though in contrast to later stories, here the convicted man did not choose life. He resolved a similar conflict more realistically in "Escape—or the Woman," in which a convict must choose between escape and making love to a woman prisoner he's adored from afar for years. A preposterous plot, but here the convict chooses freedom: altruism and love are unaffordable luxuries. Nelson took his writing seriously enough to send stories to the fiction editor at the *Chicago Daily News*, and he was increasingly able to judge his own work. He realized that "A Woman Called Mary" was one of his better stories, and another, "Sweat," about a dying man loathed by his cellmate to the point of a vengeful cruelty, he liked enough to use three years later in his first novel.

Writing, he was no longer the unemployed, useless kid brother, son of Gerson and Goldie. He was powerful, unashamed, opinionated, and to go along with this identity, he began tinkering with his name. Nelson Abraham didn't sound right for a writer, so he tried variations. There was Nelson A. Abraham, Nelson Algren Abraham, even Nelson ben Algren after his grandfather—this last, with its echoes of sagacity, he placed atop his manuscripts, but sometime later he scratched it out. Too Jewish? He had already repudiated religion, and, though almost all his friends were Jewish, he considered himself "neither Jew nor Gentile, neither Aryan or Semite."

Another possibility for a name, which he had used before, was N. A. Abraham—the initials at least lending the leaden Abraham an air of mystery—and he wrote this name above the scratches on the stories. Just as he had chosen the name Blima for its "flat, ugly sound," there was definite poetic consideration in the choice of a new name, but it was not until later, when he dropped Abraham for the more Swedish-sounding Algren, that the name would allow him to separate from both his family and his Jewish origins.

Like many people coming of age in an era of mass unemployment, Nelson may have already been seeking out the radical left. A notation in his not always accurate FBI file suggests he may have been associated with the Communist Youth League as early as 1931, and he was certainly meeting literary people sympathetic to the left. It was probably now that he met the poet Lawrence Lipton, who held literary salons and had been part of the 1920s Chicago circle of Ben Hecht, Carl Sandburg, Edgar Lee Masters, Sherwood Anderson, and Harriet Monroe. To judge from Algren's poems, he had also become infatuated with the dark-haired, bohemian sculptress Barbara Bein, who wrote poetry and may have visited him on the dunes, where her family had a summer house.

But Chicago could not have been pleasant. In July, Gerson and Goldie mortgaged the house, which had apparently been paid off, and later that month consolidated another outstanding debt into the loan—perhaps the tire and battery shop was failing. And there was Nelson, the only son and living off them—proof of his parents' belief that he'd have been better off getting a job straight out of high school. Ben Curtis thought Nelson harbored resentment toward his parents, who seemed to appreciate neither his education nor how hard he'd worked for it. It must have become clear that staying in Chicago meant nothing more than dependence and joblessness and the cold weather coming on, and so sometime in the fall of 1931, perhaps as late as December, he took to the road, heading south to continue his search for newspaper work. Most likely he did not know, as he left the house with good clothes on his back and, presumably, some of the family's money in his pockets, that he would soon be living as a vagabond, a drifter among tens of thousands.

Amid the multitudes hitchhiking along the highways in 1931, Nelson, traveling along the road in his suit, did not find work. The newspapers in the small towns suggested he try the big cities; the big cities told him to try the small towns. By now he must have known that the card from the journalism school was just a gimmick. What did they care if he carried it in his pocket like a fool, waiting at the edge of Route 66 with his thumb stuck out? He drifted south, through "Little Egypt," where the Mississippi meets the Ohio River in southern Illinois.

By boxcar or highway, through East Texas or due south along the Mississippi, he made his way to New Orleans, a city known to tramps as the cheapest in the nation. It was a port that beckoned the jobless: men who came to ship out to sea and women who came to be prostitutes without hope of anything better. If flat broke they slept in the parks, and in the day walked past balconies with curved iron railings and large windows shuttered against the sun, courtyards alive with flowering vines, the laughing babble of Creole and French. Despite its poverty, there was a sophistication about New Orleans that could never stomach the fanaticism of Huey Long, a European atmosphere that had long attracted writers and painters.

It was a sensual city and nothing like Chicago. On the wharves, enormous bunches of bananas and huge crates of lemons were unloaded daily, scenting the air and splashing the dockside with color. An aroma of coffee wafted from a now declining market. There were restaurants "acrawl with the living smells of lobster and shrimp, steaming with simmering oyster stew and awash with gumbo." Nelson remembered eating a poorboy sandwich at the old French Market while watching a muscled black man, naked to the waist, decapitating huge snapping turtles for soup. He looked on in amazement as the executioner stacked the still-moving bodies into a huge, headless pyramid; elsewhere in the city radios played "Walking the Wild Side of Life." Another recollection, of buying a Coke in a New Orleans store: a very lovely girl came out to serve him—topless. Stunned, he just kept staring, managing to mumble that he'd drink his Coke there: it was a whorehouse.

It was impossible not to notice all the whores in New Orleans in 1932, in bars and alleys, behind shuttered doors on darkened streets. From farms or cities and ever replaceable, they went for almost nothing and lived in constant fear of incurable venereal diseases. Prostitution was acknowledged, institutionalized: the Depression had put the once legal red-light district of Storyville back into use. In those days, before they were destroyed so that the city might deny its past, there were tiny shuttered stalls in rows, almost like cages, built along the front of low, cheap wooden buildings. These were the territory of the cheapest whores, those too diseased or too skinny or too black or too drunk or just not lucky enough to work in a house. "Honey! Come on over here!" they might beckon passing men from the shadows. Notes written many years later, in thick marker in a random notebook, hardly legible, slurred, as if taken from a dreamlike memory of an old, old time: "I remember a girl . . . blood-red light on a girl naked to the waist . . . and the Southern Pacific stars in New Orleans . . . a Negro dance hall . . . the girls were so hard-pressed that if you bought one a pork sandwich for ten cents you could sleep with her."

When the newspapers as usual yielded nothing, Nelson was willing to do any reasonable work, but there wasn't any. Was he carrying a suitcase? It could always be pawned. He too could sleep on the park benches, but in the morning they were cold and wet with dew. If he hit rock bottom there was a mission serving chicory coffee and coleslaw, but though he may have lived for days on bananas in those early weeks of 1932, the optimism of his college education, while somewhat tarnished, had not worn off.

And then he did find work that seemed worthy of his suit and education: he became a door-to-door salesman, one of a growing army during the Depression. They worked on commission; the company could then pay them not an hourly wage but a percentage only when a sale was made. At first Nelson made the rounds for Standard Coffee, luring housewives with a brightly colored percolator. But sales were slow, and he switched firms to become a Watkins man, with a suitcase full of powders, lotions, and hairbrushes.

But there was no job to which he could have been more poorly suited than sales. He just couldn't *believe* in a product. Years later, he wrote that the head salesman told him to listen to the housewives talk—just stand there and listen because they all wanted somebody to talk to. So one day he stood in the shade of a woman's porch and listened to her interminable jabber:

> It was hot. . . . I wanted to groan but I couldn't. I wanted to sit down but I couldn't. I wanted her to stop and buy but she wouldn't. So I passed out.
> Not from hunger. But from boredom.

In the spring he met two other drifters, both named Luther. One was a Texan with a steel plate in his skull from a World War I injury.

He was willing to work now and again, but the other, a tall Florida cracker, was "just a promoter," constantly dreaming up schemes to make money. They were hustlers, ex-cons, small-time shysters, and they probably sized Nelson up by his suit and accent: a legitimate-looking front, maybe money, and certainly someone to help share the rent on their cheap Camp Street room. Nelson's sales job paid next to nothing. In dire need of their hustling skills and probably curious, he moved in.

They were an odd trio. To judge from Nelson's remarks, the Luther with the steel skull—apparently nicknamed Fort after a long prison stint at Fort Myers—was violent, manipulative, and not always friendly, while his partner talked Nelson into schemes with a sly confidentiality. Yet their desperate circumstances connected them, and they worked together to collect the few dollars' rent and keep food in their stomachs. Once Nelson remembered "sitting around a little kitchen in New Orleans with three other guys . . . one was an old man, I was the youngest, and then two middle-aged men. Sitting around a little, a little kind of night bulb, with four bowls of some kind of soup somebody had cooked up with this one little piece of meat in it, and the man who cooked the soup was distributing it. . . . We assumed that he was going to keep that piece for himself. When he poured mine, I noticed that he just tilted that ham just enough so that the meat didn't slip out and he did it for the other guys, but he slipped with the old man. . . . I don't know what the old man was doing there except for a free meal or something. And he slipped. Overconfidence I guess, and the meat went into the old man's plate. We just looked at it there. We couldn't take it back but it just seemed such a shame that it was only one piece of meat."

But then, without warning, good times came to the Camp Street room: Luther the promoter had a plan. One day he came in carrying a stack of papers. "We've just done turned that corner," his fictional counterpart in *A Walk on the Wild Side* announced. The papers were bogus certificates to a downtown beauty salon entitling the bearer to a marcel wave and shampoo. As Luther saw it, what woman in N'Awlins wouldn't want a marcel wave and shampoo for free?

Not many, it seemed, and selling these certificates for a twenty-five-cent "courtesy charge" sure beat lugging around the store-at-your-door suitcase. When a skeptical woman read the small print and saw that the permanent was actually $3.50, the salesmen explained that they were giving it away free as a new promotion. "So

she says, 'Well, I don't understand why it should be for nothing,' "
Nelson remembered. "And we say, 'Well, we don't know any more
than that about it, but you know you can call up.' We always checked
the house. There was only about one phone to a block. You can tell
if it's wired. And then we'd say, 'Just call up, but we'll give it to
your next-door neighbor.' That always got them—the other woman.
None of them had had a finger wave since they'd been married." It
became quite a successful operation. The salesmen made themselves
ten dollars a day for two days, Nelson recalled. "We had our pockets
full of quarters, jingling."

But those salad days were short-lived: "One of these fools went
back and a couple husbands were waiting for him. They beat the
shit out of him. So we got out of there. We went down to the Rio
Grande Valley with about eleven bucks between us, which was like
a thousand."

In the midsummer of 1932, he traveled by boxcar toward the
grapefruit fields of southern Texas. Time passed without meaning
under a blistering sun; no routine could measure the passing days
and weeks. Memories of these days merged into a blur, were faded,
lost. He got off a train in East Texas, where the legendary H. L.
Hunt was making his fortune buying oil-rich land at Depression
prices. On August 16, an oilman named Isidor Achinofsky gave him
a handwritten introduction to a nearby newspaper. "Please try and
get this young man, Nelson Abraham, a job on your newspaper as
a heavy advertiser I believe you can help him a lot. Anything you
can do for Mr. Abraham will be appreciated." "It was just his way
of shaking me off," Nelson said later; there were no jobs to be had.
So he got on yet another train, past Fort Worth and San Antonio
to the Rio Grande Valley, where one of the Luthers knew someone
who owned a packing shed.

"And so we got down to the Rio Grande Valley and picked oranges
and grapefruit there for a while—made about seventy-five cents a
day at the most and tried to get work in a packing shed—that was
the best job you could get, it seemed the ultimate thing, the most
fortunate thing that could happen to anybody. I didn't get that."
Somehow, the Florida Luther had promoted or borrowed a Studebaker, and the three of them traveled around the Valley, staying in
different places. But Nelson was becoming uncomfortable. "I was
always getting conned by these guys. They conned me out of a watch.

I don't know. I was always putting up security for these guys." It must have seemed better than being alone, until the steel-skulled Luther acquired a gun and suggested they stick up a supermarket; and Nelson realized that the man was nuts.

Fortunately, Nelson and the Florida Luther took off in the Studebaker and left the steel-skulled man behind. They were looking for a better way than grapefruit picking or robbery to make money and were so desperate that an abandoned gas station between Rio Hondo and Harlingen looked like a real opportunity. The plan was to persuade the Sinclair agent in Harlingen to let them live at the station in exchange for fixing it up. This made the agent look good; he could write up to Dallas and say he'd got the station going.

"It was all falling apart," Nelson said in an account he would shamelessly and repeatedly embroider. "There were no windows in it. It was a jungle . . . there were also deer and wild hogs. There were giant mosquitoes in droves. We fixed it up. We dug the pits [for gas]. . . . Of course there was no gas to *be* sold, you understand. . . . We had to walk a ways down the road to get water, but we existed. . . . [Luther's] idea was that I would be there in charge of the station and he'd run around the Rio Grande Valley picking up produce."

But Nelson's version of later events differs sharply from the truth and the far grimmer reality of the 1932 Texas Fruit Belt. For, though as Nelson tells it he lived alone with Luther at the station, in fact, he soon invited his friend Ben Curtis down from Chicago—probably because he was lonesome for someone intelligent and familiar and also because Ben, whose father had run a mechanic's shop and who knew something about cars, would bring money with him. Ben did indeed go down to Texas to live at the station, which he remembered as a normal, unremarkable gas station with windows. And Ben remembers Nelson not as the foolish innocent Nelson later invariably portrayed, but as a very serious young man well aware of what he was doing.

Optimistically, Nelson did think the gas station could earn them a livelihood. It was on a main thoroughfare, and he seems to have reasoned that, with their combined knowledge of cars, he and Ben could indeed make the station function. But he could hardly have thought the station would earn them a fortune, just as he was no longer the naive young man who believed he had a future in newspaper work. Instead, the sociologist in him had become fascinated by the migrant camps and the down-and-out transients called fruit bums. "They would move from area to area along the Valley wherever anything matured—they went to pick tomatoes or grapefruit or whatever they had to," Ben recalled. "They had no regular home life." Nelson wanted to stay there, Ben felt, because he could observe the lives of the truly destitute.

"He surprised me with the way he talked about things and about people," Ben continued. "I was an innocent . . . [but] Nelson was sharp. He knew what was going on all the time. . . . We were down there for several weeks and never had a bath. Nelson said, 'Come with me, I know a guy in town, he's got a bathtub.' The man had a hard-working wife and a family, and we each had a bath. I said, 'How come this guy's got a house?' And Nelson said, 'Well, black people used to live there. Now they can't rent it to white people unless they get rid of the idea that anybody black lived there, so they let this white family live there for a year . . . and then they let it to white people.' All these things he knew about, he told me." Ben was shocked to learn of incest between one of the migrant workers and his twelve- or thirteen-year-old daughter, but "Nelson had taken it for granted. He had seen a lot of this, even at that early age." As well as seeing him as a source of food, Nelson seemed to regard the bony, hollow-chested, chain-smoking Luther with a curious detachment, as if he were studying him under a microscope. Still, Nelson seemed to find his intense scrutiny of Valley life more fascinating than enjoyable.

Business at the station was practically nonexistent. They sold two or three gallons of gas a day, fuel apparently not obtained on Nelson's credit, as he would later claim, but with money Ben Curtis had brought from home. Ben confided in Nelson that he had some funds left over, but life was so bleak Nelson didn't even want to hear about it. "Don't *ever* show me that money, don't ever show *any*body that money," Nelson warned Ben sharply. It was tomato season, and through Luther's grace, their diet consisted mainly of tomatoes. "We ate 'em raw, we ate 'em cooked, we ate 'em boiled, we ate 'em chopped," said Ben, who soon tired of the fare. "We'd been eating this junk here, and I said, 'Let's go out and eat something good.' Nelson said, 'Forget it. If anybody discovers you've got any money, they'll kill you for it.' "

It was Nelson's awareness of the repressed violence surrounding them that finally ended these dismal weeks at the station, and it all began with Luther and a huge load of black-eyed peas. "This Luther went to a Mexican and bought all his black-eyed peas," Ben recalled. "I don't remember the exact figures, but . . . let us say that the stores in town were selling them for sixteen cents a pound. Luther went and sold [the peas] to them for twelve cents a pound and he promised the poor farmers twenty cents a pound. He didn't care what he promised them because he wasn't going to pay them. The stores were glad to buy them because they were cheaper than they could buy them elsewhere." And as Nelson packed the peas into Mason jars, Luther was planning to move on. "I'm packing black-eyed peas until I'm blind and this guy don't show up," goes Nelson's account. "Then I hear a car drive up in the middle of the night." It was Luther, come to fill up his car's tank and take off. "[We] had all this gas at the station—we had two tanks with about ninety gallons in each out there—and now he wants to get out of this station deal . . . so he's going to leave me there, you know, picking and packing black-eyed peas." And waiting for a posse of angry Mexican farmers looking for their money.

Ben Curtis: "That's when Nelson said to me, 'We better get out of here. We're known to be with him, and we'll wake up with a knife in our backs.'

"So that's when I left, but he kept on traveling."

For years, when asked how he started writing, Nelson would invariably tell the story of the gas station, with some of the details changed, characteristically, to accommodate his fiction and his intense need for personal secrecy. It was a turning point in his life, but he never revealed the extent of his disillusionment. He never mentioned Ben's presence in Texas—not in a *Paris Review* interview, not in *Conversations with Nelson Algren,* not in his fiction: he preferred to present himself as a lone wanderer, more innocent than he really was, to keep the depth of his comedown unexposed. To describe Luther's scheme might have revealed that his disillusionment came not just from being swindled for gas, as he told it, but from being set up for a beating or worse. For those who cared to read it, he would recount what happened, after a fashion, in "So Help Me," a story about a naked exploitation which ends in death.

For all his sociological observation, he hadn't realized until now how the grim poverty he was witnessing could lead, inexorably, to death. Perhaps he had once thought of Fort's plans to stick up the

Jitney Jungle as the crazy scheme of a demented individual, and he knew that a stranger might be killed for his money, but after living with Luther for several months, he had probably thought the man would see him as more than a mark who could take the rap whenever it became convenient. To realize that Luther would sacrifice him as willingly as Fort had, just to make a little money, was to see a world for which even he was not prepared: a world where relationships meant nothing, where money was more important than life, and life was so cheap as to be valueless. There was no humanity in such a world. He too could have lain dead and dumped on a desolate Texas road like any other too trusting loser.

At the gas station he had found horror: he had seen the truth, and realized now that he'd been lied to all his life. "Everything I'd been told was wrong. . . . I'd been told, I'd been assured that it was a strive and succeed world. What you did: you got yourself an education and a degree and then you went to work for a family newspaper and then you married a nice girl and raised children and this was what America was. But this is not what America was. America was not socialized and I resented very deeply that I'd been lied to. I'd not only been lied to morally, I'd been lied to even insofar as the information that I had about journalism. I'd been told how to write headlines for newspapers . . . but the way you'd been taught, this got you fired immediately from a newspaper. You had to reverse everything you'd been taught, mechanically as well as morally."

He would continue on the road by himself. In a world of duplicity and falsehood, each man went alone.

Wandering around the Valley, perhaps near La Feria or farther up the Southern Pacific tracks toward Hebbronville, he found himself with a dozen or so unemployed people in a big old house with a sign out front saying HOTEL. Here the people seemed decent. "It was a curious hotel because it was made up of people who were taken in, who had no money, and whom the proprietor hoped would get some. He himself had a job in the grapefruit shed. His wife cooked in the kitchen and everybody lived in the hopes that someone would get some money." These hopes seemed fulfilled when a passing county fair took Nelson on as a carnival shill.

The carnival was the epitome of duplicity and falsehood, but all his jobs on the road had been like that, and all he wanted was not to be conned; the phony chance wheel may have also appealed to his love of gambling. By his own account, it was a big horizontal wheel rigged by a crude wire system the New York operator worked with his foot, while his partner, a big Texan, looked out for trouble. Nelson and the other shills stood around the wheel with a half-dollar or so apiece, ready to kick up a commotion when a mark came sauntering down the midway. "Then almost everybody would win . . . the guy would say, 'Another winner, another winner,' and then you would get five half dollars back or five silver dollars back for the one, and whenever that happened one of the more trusted shills would hit you in the side to get the money back and then you'd play it again " The mark, seeing how easy it was, would play and win until the barker told him, "I wouldn't pick that money up because . . . now is your chance to win a hundred," and, betting the two dollars to play the hundred, the mark would have a fantastic amount of money coming and then suddenly he'd lose. He might owe three or four hundred dollars, and the operators accepted checks, so he could write out a check for his losses right there. You couldn't win. A Navajo blanket back of the wheel was meant to be a prize, but it was nailed up, so Nelson knew they weren't expecting any winners.

Unfortunately, Nelson's nightly take at the wheel just didn't stand up to the big bucks the operators were raking in. Sure, he made enough to buy a couple of hamburgers and coffee every night, and sometimes the shills could get free hot dogs at the concession, but that was it. Every night silver dollars and five-spots, tens, singles, and plenty of change passed through his hands, enough money to get out of Texas—but then he'd get that punch in the side. If the other shills were willing to work for hot dogs, fine; but he was tired of being taken. Luther had been enough. He wanted a raise.

By his own undoubtedly embellished recollection, one night he saw the sheriff making his nightly tour of the fair and then won six or twelve dollars in halves. When the other shill hit him he shoved the winnings deep in his pockets. They couldn't say he hadn't won it fair in front of the sheriff, and after a frozen moment he backed off. He strolled with the sheriff down the midway, then melted into the crowd, slipping through a fence in the darkness to head for the railroad tracks.

Now he entered what Eric Sevareid called "a new social dimension, the great underground world, peopled by tens of thousands of American men, women, and children, white, black, brown, and yellow, who inhabit the jungle, eat from blackened tin cans, find warmth at night in the boxcars, take the sun by day on the flat cars, steal one day, beg with cap in hand the next, fight with fists and often razors, hold sexual intercourse under a blanket in a dark corner of the crowded car, coagulate into pairs and gangs and then disintegrate again, wander from town to town, anxious for the next place, tired of it in a day, fretting to be gone again, happy only when the wheels are clicking under them, the telephone poles slipping by."

He went along from city to town, sometimes held overnight on a vagrancy charge, in the morning just told to keep moving. "He moved, moved, everything moved; men either kept moving or went to jail." He wandered into Mexico and back through Texas, through Waycross, Carzozo, Fort Worth, La Feria. Maybe he worked in exchange for food; maybe he ate in a jungle or mission. But whatever he did, he was alone. Once, he later told Dorothy Farrell, while crossing a shallow river dotted with islands, a flock of birds swooped down to attack him. They dove at his head, screeched into his ears, and he beat them away, flailing wildly with his hands.

He remained angry over the gas station fiasco. He had been betrayed, and maybe he'd been set up for the fall guy all along, even before Fort's robbery plans or Luther's pea swindle. But the only place to direct his rage was on paper. Somewhere, he said later, he stopped and wrote a long letter to a friend in Chicago, probably Larry Lipton, complaining about the South from Perdido Street to La Feria.

He remembered gambling once, hoping for the win that would change his luck or get him out of Texas. He went broke in a crap game in what he remembered as El Paso—though it may have been Brownsville—and was walking down the street when a cop accused him of breaking a nearby window. In the county jail with eight drunks, he walked out the open cell door and past the sleeping turnkey, on the front steps running into the same cop who'd put him in—who this time made sure the door was locked, then offered to get him off for two hundred bucks. Nelson waited for the judge and was fined five dollars for vagrancy. Maybe he got off on time served.

He was always at the mercy of the law, it seemed, and it was not a fair law that fined a man for being broke or took him off a train for the railroad company's reward. They were in cahoots, the railroad companies and the police, and boxcar riding, the only way across the endless expanse of Texas, could be a dangerous game. Freight-hoppers could be shot off trains or fall between the moving cars. Even getting to the tracks was a problem because they didn't want the homeless on the highways; and once there the trains might be speeding by with all the doors closed—and hobos had to get on with nobody noticing. Officially unrecognized, transients had to pretend they didn't exist. Stay out of sight—and be able to duck in and out to get water when the train stopped.

As winter came on, he passed through Tulsa, Oklahoma. "I remember eating at a kind of a home . . . Army Veterans' God's Blessing Station, or something like that. . . . I remember it must have been around Christmas and that it was awful cold." It was snowing, and he was just another bum. But he was drifting toward Chicago, where he could have, at least, a roof over his head and a sense of stability. He was also drifting, with a newfound sense of purpose, to literary and intellectual circles—like the John Reed Club—where he could make sense of what had happened and channel his opposition to a system that had created the devastation he'd witnessed. Everything he'd seen convinced him that the brutalities of that system had to be exposed at all costs. In a world swimming with deceit, to be able to speak the truth was the only thing that mattered.

4.

So Help Me

H E BEGAN WRITING when he reached his parents' house in Chicago. Not long afterward he saw an ad for the Writers' Circle at the Jewish People's Institute on Douglas Boulevard and took the streetcar down. It was an interesting choice of organizations for a young man whose first published story would portray anti-Semitism and who would shortly drop his Jewish name for a Swedish one; yet it provided just the encouraging atmosphere he sought. The Circle was run by Murray Gitlin, a young writer who had recently had a story in *Esquire.* Gitlin remembered the twenty-three-year-old Nelson as mild and modest, "a fine, gentle person. He didn't put on an air. . . . He had a sensitive face, a good, interesting face, and he spoke softly. . . . I liked him immediately." When Nelson showed him the manuscripts he'd been working on, Gitlin saw he had no need to join the group. "The man could already write. I said, 'You're a writer. Just go to it.' "

But unemployment and the humiliations of the road had damaged his self-confidence. The Abrahams, reshuffling loans and liens in an effort to hang on to their house, had taken Nelson in, but they could hardly have been proud of him or pleased about his decision to write, which showed so little promise of providing a living. Though Morris Joffe vehemently denied it, Nelson claimed he wasn't allowed to use his brother-in-law's typewriter, and whatever the truth of this, Nelson felt uncomfortable enough about using it to ride an hour by trolley to a typewriter in Gitlin's office, working on the machine consistently for several weeks. "He didn't feel he had it in him," Gitlin recalled. "He didn't have a high opinion of himself. . . . He was on the edge. Had I said, 'Well, I don't think you'll make it,' he might have accepted it." Instead, Gitlin assured him that his work was both good and publishable. When the stories Nelson began sending out came back rejected, Gitlin told him, "That's just the way it is. Keep going."

His new fiction was more polished. Developing the theme of betrayal that now preoccupied him, "Forgive Them, Lord" was the story of a black man who witnesses a lynching and then confides the story of the murder to a prostitute he sees each week, unaware that she has little feeling for him. She betrays him to the white murderers, who are also her customers, and ensures his death. This story seems contrived, but "The Brothers' House," a throwback to his college prison stories, was far more successful. In it, a young man released after twenty months in a county jail makes his way home on foot, sleeping in fields and walking eighteen days through the American countryside. Though his mother is dead and his brothers have beaten him cruelly in the past, he yearns for them and the community they represent. But his hopes of family love are swiftly, brutally crushed by one brother's complete indifference. Central here is the failure of love, a theme that would mark not only many Algren stories but also Algren's life.

Still missing in his fiction, however, was an intense and direct application of all he had seen and heard. Then Larry Lipton, whose literary gatherings Nelson was probably attending, apparently suggested that the long complaining letter Nelson had written about the South could be rewritten into an effective story. The result was "So Help Me," an imaginary reworking of the steel-skulled Luther's plan to rob the Jitney Jungle. As in "The Brothers' House," the hero's name is David, and the villain, as in "Forgive Them, Lord," is named Luther. Strongly autobiographical, the story is a fictional evocation of Nelson's travels with the Luthers, with David constantly being conned by the pair of vagrants. Separated from them by a huge gulf in values and expectations, David is also Jewish.

In the story, told in monologue, the drifter Homer is giving an account of events to a "big-league lawyer." His tale begins in New Orleans, where he and Luther, an ex-con from the state farm at Wetumpka, meet the innocent "Jew-kid" David, fresh out of high school and come south to find work so he can marry his pregnant girlfriend. Homer, who has a hunch he can "wrangle a meal out of him," assures David there is plenty of work picking fruit in the Rio Grande Valley, so the trio travel by boxcar to southern Texas. But only David is willing to work in the fields. The others, under the guise of friendship, pawn his watch and suitcase, later convincing themselves with tequila that he can grab the money while they hold up a drugstore. With David sweating at gunpoint, they narrowly avoid capture and escape by train. As they sleep fitfully in the moving car, David's recurring screaming nightmare returns, and the steel-skulled Luther, edgy and frightened, shoots him dead. At least that is the story the narrator Homer, hoping to avoid a murder rap, tells the district attorney.

Completely different from anything he had written before, "So Help Me" evoked an entire world of outcast people with its own customs and values. In an American cracker idiom replete with the slang terms of the criminal bum, Homer reveals his story against the background of his life: floating from prison to city street to railroad jungle, staying in migrant camps, eating in missions. Circumstances have obviously stunted his humanity; and he is aware of his lack of morality only to the extent that he realizes he needs to sound reasonable and respectable to the lawyer. His desperation to clear himself and blame his partner becomes obvious; his vulnerability is completely exposed: he is a powerless, penniless loser and, whether or not he murdered, he stands accused of it with only his inevitably unsatisfactory wits to clear himself. But however pathetic, Homer is frightening. His striking characteristic, as the young Chicago author of *Studs Lonigan,* James T. Farrell, saw it, was "his lack of sentiments and value for love, his almost complete divorcement from the middle-class conceptions of success, and his lack of substitution of any other concepts for them."

The theme of anti-Semitism runs deeply through the story. Homer never thinks of David as anything but the "Jew-kid" and refers to him that way, or as the Jew, constantly, mentioning his name only once. David is considered inferior solely because he is Jewish: "O' course, I wouldn't never have picked up with him if I'd knowed," Homer explains easily. As a Jew, David is to be exploited, starved, victimized, and finally, one suspects, deliberately killed: "Now . . . maybe you will even think that Fort really wanted to get rid of the Jew-kid so's we would oney have two ways to split instead of three," Homer stupidly suggests to the lawyer. The abundance of these references suggests strongly that Nelson was preoccupied with David's ethnic background, and on top of one draft he wrote "jew kid," twice, in exceptionally large handwriting.

In sending out stories, Nelson had already dropped the name Abraham for the more lyrical and Swedish Algren. Using his middle name was an easy switch, comprehensible to his family: pen names were not unusual, and even they had noticed Nelson's affinity for Nels Ahlgren and his "*socialisme.*" But he was also casting aside his family's hold on his writing identity, separating himself from them, as the year on the road had already done. The new name also masked his Jewish origins, protecting him from painful anti-Semitism, a theme that would later almost completely vanish from his fiction. Abraham was itself an assumed name, and it brought with it a burden he saw no point in bearing: he had no religious leanings or desire to be typed as a Jewish writer. Writing "So Help Me" was apparently a new, deeply satisfying experience; he had visions of literary greatness, and Abraham was a name he "didn't figure . . . could get on a theater marquee."

Probably Larry Lipton, who knew Martha Foley and Whit Burnett, suggested Nelson submit his work to *Story* magazine, then publishing young artists such as William Saroyan, Erskine Caldwell, J. D. Salinger, and James T. Farrell. Nelson had never heard of *Story,* but he sent off "The Brothers' House," "Sweat," "A Woman Called Mary," and the new, lengthy "So Help Me." On May 22 he got a letter from Whit Burnett: "We have been very favorably impressed with the longest of the four stories you sent us a few days ago and we are considering the possibility of using it in *Story,* possibly in the next issue." Burnett was also hanging on to "The Brothers' House," and a twenty-dollar check would be forthcoming. One can only imagine Algren's joy. His vision of the world had been redeemed; he was no longer a bum but a writer, risen from the anonymity of thousands of vagrants. When "Forgive Them, Lord" was accepted for publication in *A Year* magazine, he had definitely found a career—and on his own terms. Nothing was more satisfying than writing, and the idea that he might now make a living took hold of him.

Thinking of himself as a writer brought a sense of purpose and much-needed self-esteem, for though he ate regularly at his parents' house, he still had no job. By the fall of 1932, Chicago had almost as many unemployed people as workers, and though Roosevelt's March 1933 bank holiday had restored some confidence in the business community, it made little difference to the unemployed. Social unrest continued throughout the city: breadlines and demonstrations remained despite the establishment of federal relief. In May 1933, anarchist bombs shook the downtown offices of five Chicago companies.

As if to further alienate the jobless, the Chicago World's Fair opened that May to commemorate "A Century of Progress." Promoted by mottoes like "Business Is Booming" and "The Worst Is Over," the fair sported a large "No Help Wanted" sign at its front gates. The commercial extravaganza usurped the one black beach in Chicago, readying it for white patrons by removing rocks and other "unsafe" conditions heretofore, apparently, safe enough. Just outside the grounds, prostitution flourished, and miserable Hoovervilles of packing-box houses sprang up nearby, their citizens scavenging for food in garbage cans.

Amid such poverty and contradiction, with a government that never seemed to be helping fast enough, the left, with the American Communist Party at its forefront, at least offered a coherent analysis of the economic situation and promised to destroy the kind of system that brought about such deprivation. Along with its efforts to unionize workers, fight discrimination, and educate people to the gross disparities between rich and poor under capitalism, the Party was also organized on the cultural front, considering art an important weapon of class warfare. Established writers favoring revolution published in *New Masses* and gathered at an International Writers' Congress held in the Soviet Union in 1930. Now the Party encouraged younger working-class artists and writers through a nationwide network of John Reed Clubs. These clubs arranged art exhibits, wrote strike pamphlets, sponsored speakers at union meetings, and arranged other events to protest racism, war, Fascism, and imperialism.

The Chicago John Reed Club met on the second floor of 1427 South Michigan Avenue, where Nelson was soon dropping by. There were both visual artists and writers in the club. The young black writer Richard Wright, future author of *Native Son,* was a mainstay of the writers' group, which oversaw the publication of *Left Front,* a revolutionary magazine of art, literature, and politics. There was something alive in the club's unpretentious atmosphere. Long benches served as seats and cigarette butts were crushed out on the floor; along the walls colorful murals depicted huge victorious workers raising streaming banners.

Well-known writers like James T. Farrell came in to speak. *New Masses,* on sale at the club, introduced members to Kenneth Fearing, Langston Hughes, and Archibald MacLeish. Though most of the club's writers came to socialize and rarely brought manuscripts to meetings, members read aloud John Reed's "America 1918," criticized the works of William Carlos Williams, discussed—and probably repudiated—T. S. Eliot (Nelson thought him elitist), and dissected the revolutionary message of Walt Whitman, whose work affected Nelson deeply.

In addition to Wright, Nelson met Abe Aaron, a young radical from the Pennsylvania coal mines working his way through the University of Chicago. Aaron, like Wright, was one of the more serious members of the club. He had won prizes for his political essays and had published in Jack Conroy's magazine for proletarian writing, *The Anvil.* And, while holding down three jobs, he worked actively for social justice, often sacrificing writing time to put furniture back into the homes of people thrown into the street for nonpayment of rent. He was articulate, well-read, sensitive, and highly moral. Also Jewish, Abe was one of the few people Nelson trusted enough to invite to his parents' house, and he came over half a dozen times to breakfasts served by Goldie in the dining room. Abe had the vague impression Nelson was getting help from his family, especially from his sister Bernice; and yet he saw Nelson as a loner.

"Nelson was a tall, gangly, shuffling sort of guy," Abe recalled, "amused by life, amused by the idiosyncracies of humanity around him, about how people were not what they seemed to be, and we would constantly, he for the most part, be conjecturing about what a person actually meant when he said something." Sometimes they went to a hash house and sat all night talking about writers over a cup of coffee. Nelson loved Carl Sandburg and Maxim Gorky and the Englishman George Gissing, all of whom wrote about the lower depths. He also liked Jack Conroy's just-published novel *The Disinherited,* and was impressed by both the realistic portrayal of the unemployed transient and the title "American Gorky" which a critic had bestowed upon its author.

Given Nelson's subject matter and disillusionment with society, it was almost inevitable that he found himself working within the Communist movement, though his ambitions were far more literary than political. Abe and Dick Wright, by contrast, were inclined to see their writing as an instrument for social change. In Abe's view, he and Dick were political writers, but Nelson was just the opposite: "He was a poet more than a political animal, and he had a vision of the truth." But if Nelson was unsure of an imminent Communist triumph, his vision of the world was very similar to that of the left. That there was a class system at work in the United States he had seen with his own eyes, had seen the injustice of it in the misery of the thousands of homeless stumbling around the country, of the black vagrants carted off to chain gangs, of the maimed discarded veterans unable to work. He knew that this system, based on acquiring profits rather than providing for human needs, was immoral; it was a system that kept people's faith by constructing an intricate system of lies, such as those of the University of Illinois journalism school or the Chicago World's Fair. If the Communists wanted to overthrow this system and its racism, misery, and greed, then he was all for them.

The political community nourished him, allowed him a place to think and breathe. And yet, while he always felt himself a man of the left, his dedication was to his art before the revolution; his ambition was to be a great artist, like Gorky. Through his political friends he was meeting literary people who could help him, like Jim Farrell and Jack Conroy. He and Conroy liked each other right away. Jovial, hard-drinking, of Irish descent, Conroy was a self-taught workingman whose brother and father had died in the mines, and there was no doubt about either his politics or his commitment to literature about oppressed people. *The Disinherited* had established him as the leader of the emerging genre of proletarian literature, and *The Anvil* was to publish the unknown Richard Wright, Frank Yerby, and Nelson Algren. Conroy knew talent. When Nelson began writing to him, it was the beginning of a friendship that was to last more than twenty-five years.

In those days, Abe Aaron was one of the few club members who could afford his own place. He worked as a desk clerk in exchange for his room at the Troy Lane Apartments hotel, and on Friday nights his writing friends dropped by for a salon of sorts. Abe's friends Harvey Kier and Harold Jacobson came regularly, along with Nelson and Dick Wright, who was just beginning to publish poems in small leftist magazines. They took up a collection for coffee and potato pancakes and then talked deep into the night, lounging on the bed that served as a sofa. The debates concerned politics, the black underclass, Roosevelt, the World's Fair, literature. Here Nelson felt enough at ease to talk about what he'd seen on the road. Dick, who had fled racist oppression in the Deep South and was now working in the post office, wanted to write about poor, uneducated blacks and shared Nelson's interest in the lumpenproletariat.

But Abe suddenly lost his job, though he never told Dick and Nelson why. After the first few meetings, Abe's boss had taken him aside. It wasn't himself, he assured Abe, but someone higher up who objected. It just didn't look right having a black man come into the hotel. Might give the place a bad name. Why not just move the meeting or tell the man not to come? But Dick was a published writer, a serious man, Abe protested. Still the boss was unmoved. Friday came again and so did Dick. The following Saturday the boss warned Abe again: "One more time and I'll have to let you go." Since Abe couldn't forbid Dick to come or capitulate to racism by ending the meetings, he held another the next Friday night. On Saturday he was looking for a place to live. "I would never have told Dick," Abe said later, "because he would have been furious that I had lost my job over him." A job was something nobody gave up lightly in 1933.

Those summer evenings, if Nelson wasn't at a literary or political meeting, he seems to have been out exploring the city, sometimes taking Ben and Jerome Hanock and Ralph Zwick to places Ben, who'd lived in Chicago all his life, had never heard of. One was a dime-a-dance hall of the variety Nelson would later describe in *Somebody in Boots*. "You'd buy a string of tickets for ten cents each," said Ben, who, along with Nelson, mostly watched from the sidelines. "The girls wore very sleazy dresses and when you danced they'd hold you very close," the music lasting only a few seconds before the girl would want another ticket. Among Algren's writings from this time is a sketch of a tattoo man waiting for the girls who came in "because of the pain the needle gives"; another of a man scorned while trying to make a human relationship with a hooker. But whether he went to tattoo parlors or brothels is unclear. It is certain that he spent time with Barbara Bein, the shy, moody "flower child" who understood vagabonds turned writers: her brother was Albert Bein, a road-hewn playwright and novelist just beginning to have success on the New York stage. But something went wrong in their relationship. Shortly before leaving for New York, Nelson wrote her a long, bitter letter; and whatever the trouble between them, she was, it seems, more than partly to blame: a mutual friend lectured her mightily about it, "bearing in mind Nelson's experience." But his emotions over this must have been swallowed up in his enthusiasm for his new role as a revolutionary artist. He later joked, somewhat seriously, that the appearance of his first story, "So Help Me," in August 1933 was one of the greatest influences of his literary career. There was something magical in the success of his writing that seemed to over-come all disappointments and hurts. His self-confidence seemed to soar almost overnight to new heights. Writing gave him a future.

In early September, Algren recalled, "I was twenty-four and I got this letter from Vanguard Press: 'Are you working on a novel? We are interested in a novel on the basis of this piece in *Story* magazine.' I had nothing else to do so instead of answering the letter, I rode to New York. I was so used to hitchhiking by that time, I was so used to walking out the door and getting on Route 66—it was just as easy as getting into a car, and although I never knew exactly what route I was going to take, I never had any trouble. By that time I was a professional transient so I knew all the places to go. . . . Some kids— two guys with lots of bedding in the car—picked me up and they were going to New York by way of Niagara Falls." He'd never seen the falls. What he found was the reality behind the romance: "the colored spray of Niagara, the rapids and the roaring, the Maid of the Mist and the rats by those rapids."

But what to tell Vanguard? Maybe he could go back to Texas and do something similar to "So Help Me," and maybe there'd be some good money in the deal. In the plush, paneled Madison Avenue office of Vanguard's president, James Henle, he realized there probably was.

The novel? Well, he had one in mind about the Southwest and would like to go down there to write it.

"How much would you need?" Henle wanted to know.

As much as he could get, but he couldn't tell Henle that, and he knew nothing about the going rate for advances. He calculated his expenses in the Rio Grande Valley: ten dollars to get down there, twenty dollars a month for room and board, ten dollars for tobacco and whatnot. He put the stakes as high as he dared:

"One hundred dollars."

An agreement was, needless to say, reached. He would finish the novel in six months and show Henle what he had in three. Both men were pleased. Henle had commissioned a book from an obviously talented young writer at little or no risk to his company, and Nelson had gotten a cool hundred bucks, more money than he'd seen in ages, just by throwing out a title and some vague details. He couldn't believe his luck. A contract for "The Gods Gather" was typed and signed. Henle gave him a ten-dollar bill from his wallet and a handshake; later Nelson would receive thirty dollars a month for three months and a hundred dollars more if Henle liked what he saw. He also got a letter saying he was employed by Vanguard Press, a document he planned to use when pulled off trains.

He left the office congratulating himself and, according to one memoir, broke the bill in Hubert's Wax Museum. Then he paid a call on Barbara's brother in the Bronx. Albert Bein had lost a leg riding the rails and published a novel about the reform school where he'd spent five years for trespassing; his play *Little Ol' Boy* had received favorable reviews in New York. To the apprentice Nelson, Bein, seven years older and a leftist, must have seemed like a master. The name of Maxim Gorky came up frequently in their conversation, amid tales of Bein's life and travels. But, Bein recalled, "It soon developed that he was uncertain of what to write about and we spent most of the time trying to hit upon story ideas for his promised book." They weren't successful, but the meeting ended cordially, and after seeing a few other friends in New York, Nelson once again took the long American road to Texas, this time no longer broke or purposeless.

As George Orwell had just done in England, Algren traveled through the country as a sociological observer. He moved almost entirely by boxcar, openly friendly with the hobos, asking questions as he went, getting thrown in jail with them, recording their stories and expressions with an observation sharpened by political perspective. He wrote down what he saw in a back-pocket notebook. It was a harrowing and exhausting experience, perhaps worse than he'd remembered tramp life before. Sometimes, if there were no boxcars, he rode the rail rods—rows of pipes aong the underside of trains that supported a man who could hold himself rigid, careful not to fall asleep and drop through the bars to the moving wheels.

These tramps he met were powerless, and whatever rights they once possessed had long since been abrogated by the police and railroad companies. The railroad bulls had hose length, bat, rope, or gun; they might beat a man for nothing, but mostly they just wanted money: bums brought twenty-five cents a head in some places, two dollars in others. Bums who refused to come out and hid in the boxcars could be locked inside; they could burn their way out or be picked up in the next town. Bulls became legend from city to city: avoid "Hook" Kelly and Texas Slim; beware "Hobo" Brown, dressed like a bum. Penalty for riding the manifest—the fast freight— from Washington to Florida, 61 days; 90 days on a pea farm if caught in Beaumont, Texas. Penalty for breaking a seal: twenty years or so.

But in most places you got through with no trouble: there were so many 'bos the bulls just got you for the head count and took you off the trains for a while. In Greenville, North Carolina, they drove up and took everyone off. "The colored guys, I think they separated them and sent them on to the labor camps," Nelson remembered later. "The white guys they let go to the Salvation Army and warned them that if they caught them trying to get out of town on the train again, they would pick them up." How you got out of town was your problem. Your problem; and if you went to jail it was a cell of green sheet-iron with a kangaroo court that extorted money from newcomers to buy edible food.

The physical wretchedness of day-to-day life was overwhelming. In late September it was already cool, and there were days of lying in the "jungle"—transient camps by the tracks—cold and hungry, others without rest when you hurried to move the enormous boxcar doors. If kicked off a train, freezing, you took shelter in the depot until ejected, and when kicked out of restaurants you climbed into the first waiting train—even if it was just a switch engine. There were jungles in the South that were swarming with mosquitoes, but if you moved off by yourself away from the fire, you might wake to find you'd slept on poison oak. And keeping clean—it was harder than eating: baths were twenty-five cents. Bums could sometimes bathe in animals' water—but they were not allowed to sully it with soap.

There were men whose eyes were dust-rimmed, their mouths covered in sores; a man's foot might be so callused that if a nail from his thin-soled shoes pierced his foot, he withdrew it with neither pain nor blood. And the hunger, the endless hunger of the men: "Ah'm so hungry if you put a ham sandwich mah mouth'd slap my brains out trying to get it," somebody might say, and Nelson watched a fair-haired boy vomit from emptiness above Monroe.

When the Crescent Limited went by, people were eating in the warm cars, with silver on clean, linen-covered tables.

Worse than anything were the accidents. You might watch a kid make a try for a train going just a little too fast, and he'd miss and suddenly all the blood in his body was pouring out, running black in the sun from a sliced-off arm. Nelson never forgot how a boy with a blue bandana ran for a train and flung himself into a coal car, not seeing that its bottom was open to the wheels. Nelson, on the car's outside ladder, stepped on the boy's hand in the dark. And how long did they ride like that, a boy clinging to life by fingertips smashed under a shoe until the train finally, mercifully stopped?

Only brief friendships could be made in such a world. For a while he traveled with Jennings, a sixteen-year-old, possibly the boy whose life he'd saved. Dodging a warrant, Jennings had once gone home to stand by his girl in church. He had apparently stolen a chicken, was caught, and for his crime received five months and two days working dawn to dusk in a labor camp, getting fifteen cents and a plug of tobacco a week. "For fools and the unfeeling, this is all well enough," Nelson wrote in his notebook. Jennings was destined to endlessly flee the authorities. Once a Marine recruiter tried to sign him up to fight Sandino in the Nicaraguan jungles, and the boy, knowing that even the road was preferable to armed combat, said he had a deformity, though he had none. In his novel, Nelson would describe the bayonet-slung recruiter who got a price for every head he signed up.

Nelson saw men who followed him abjectly, like dogs, others who lived on the road because they were too deformed for "civilized" society. "A Negro, 29," he noted, "stricken with typhoid when one, goes about on all fours about the land, like an animal. Enormous chest and head." Another man, jumped in Greenville, South Carolina, by a brass-knuckled trio, had a history of bad luck reaching back much further than the mugging. "This man was twenty-three, had been ten years on the road. Ran away from reform school when he was thirteen—there three years. Brother killed in an accident when he was ten."

As Algren moved within the murky complexity of this underground world, the novel began to take shape in his mind. He might call it "The Gods Gather," "Native Son," or any of a dozen titles he listed in his notebook. He would describe the life of a man like John Jennings, who lived no place but the road. Called Cass McKay, his hero would be a harmless youth moving blindly within a world of violence, a man of no skill, ignorant and illiterate. He would be, as Algren later described him, "utterly displaced, not only from society but from himself, unable to tell what to love or to hate, what to cling to and what reject, adrift in a land that no longer had any use for him. Where crossing bells announced the long freight moving past lonely stations in the Georgia Pines, I had seen him riding shoeless on a boxcar roof. I had seen him holding onto cell-bars in the El Paso County Jail; I had seen him taking charity in a Salvation Army pew: a man representing the desolation of the outlaws as well as the disorder of the great cities, expatriated within his own frontiers as well as exiled from himself. . . . A man of no responsibility, even to himself . . . a man who might belong to [the] revolution one day and the reaction the next—it wouldn't matter, as through it he might, however blindly, save himself . . . he cannot endure his life, yet he shall endure it, moving within the great city's aimless din, in perpetual search of something to belong to, in order to belong to himself." He would be the final descendant of crackers forced west from the plantations as slavery expanded, with no stake in cotton, cattle, or oil; who put their backs against the cabin wall, brought out the fiddle and jug and spat on both the Confederacy and the Union; who now had no cabin wall at all; nothing but the swarming cross-current of humanity along the rails.

Deciding to bypass the already too well-known Rio Grande Valley, he headed west through San Antonio and picked rocks out of sacks of dried beans to pay for a beanery meal. He wound up in El Paso and crossed the bridge to Mexico, saw a bullfight and wandered through Juarez to the red-light district; he may have seen a cockfight in a clearing. Perhaps he started his novel here; years later he wrote that he stayed, free of charge, at a small hotel run by a woman who called herself the Angel of the Americas. In this account, the angel seemed to like him, for it seems she gave him breakfast too.

5.
Alpine, Texas

FROM EL PASO, Nelson caught an eastbound freight, riding on a boxcar roof as the train worked its way into the rocky Davis Mountains. Texas stretched ahead, an endless, desolate country in itself: if he was too choosy about where to go he'd lose two days crossing the state again, and he needed to start on the novel. Passing through a town called Alpine, he saw the spires of what looked like a college on top of a hill; then the train descended through the Glass Mountains to the dry Texas plains, toward Sanderson. The freight pulled to a stop in the small town, he remembered, and the bulls scrambled up the ladder to pull down the hobos. Nothing to do but go along peaceably and hope they didn't throw you in jail, feel grateful, just as they wanted you to, when the train pulled out and left you standing, free and unhurt, to wait for the next one. That was what awaited him in Texas. Ninety miles back, at that college, if it was one, there might be a typewriter and something to read, so he stuck out his thumb and hitchhiked back to Alpine.

This town of several thousand people lay in a valley surrounded by craggy mountains; the air was refreshing and cool, the land extremely arid. The strong mineral content of the grasses and its location at the junction of the Santa Fe and Southern Pacific railroads made Alpine the center and shipping point for a large ranching area known as "Cows' Heaven." In the 1930s, legendary cattle barons of the Old West still reigned over vast ranches. Their cowboys labored long hot hours in the pastures and shipping pens and thronged the streets on weekends in Stetson hats and high-heeled boots.

The town had sprung up around the railroad. It had only one

paved street, with a barbershop, a post office, and two or three stores, cafés, and banks. The Southern Pacific ran through the center of town, flanked by the omnipresent Texas water tower. To the east was the hilltop campus of Sul Ross State Teachers College; to the south, on the other side of the tracks in the shadow of a large mountain, lay Mexican town—not really a bad place, Alpine told itself, but simply the other, poorer side, with a number of businesses arranged around a Catholic church.

By the time Nelson arrived, Alpine was no stranger to hobos. The town was the switching point for those who made the Great Depression migration by rail because it was the cheapest way to go. Thousands of homeless vagabonds headed for the golden fruitfields of Arizona and California, and then, finding themselves little more than slaves if they could get work at all, headed back again. At times there were a hundred and fifty on each train that passed through Alpine, a caravan of souls outlined against the sky like sparrows on a telephone wire, or riding with their feet hanging out the open boxcar doors. They descended from the trains begging, and the townsfolk generally fed them: they were far more pathetic than frightening. A year or two earlier the town had converted an abandoned food warehouse into a shelter, in an attempt to contain the poverty, for the vagrants were taken off the trains and led to the shelter to keep them out of town. Inside, by a fire in a tin drum, each was given a blanket, a can of beans, and a loaf of bread. But by the fall of 1933, the shelter no longer seemed necessary. Roosevelt had been in office the good part of a year, and the fear that motivated the vagrant migration had somewhat subsided.

Nelson Algren's fortunes had also improved: now he could afford his own room. Still, when he looked for a place to live, his hobo instincts led him away from the center of town and toward the Santa Fe tracks to what he described as "a deteriorated ranch." Actually, Mrs. Nettleton's was a working-class boardinghouse for railroad men, cowboys, stray transients, and high school students whose folks lived out of town. A rambling wood structure in need of some paint, it had a couple of cows in the backyard that provided milk for the guests and a bit of regular income. The landlady was a matter-of-fact widow who took Nelson's word for it, perhaps upon seeing Vanguard's letter, that he had money coming. Room and board would be twenty a month; and he moved into a small room with a stove, a cotlike bed, and a table for writing. A bare electric bulb hung on a wire from the wooden ceiling.

When he walked up to the Sul Ross campus, he found not one but a whole room full of typewriters, unused except for an occasional typing class, for enrollment was down because of the Depression. The sight of all those typewriters in a forgotten West Texas town, when he'd traveled over an hour by streetcar to use one in Chicago, must have angered him. Did Dick Wright or Abe Aaron or any of the others in the John Reed Club who wrote seriously and with vision have a typewriter? And yet here were all these machines for people who didn't even need them.

"I would simply walk in and use one of the typewriters. Nobody else was using it," Nelson recalled in an interview, speaking as if Alpine had been a ghost town. In memoirs of this time he often portrayed himself as the aloof, freethinking anarchist, rarely revealing his vulnerability or innermost feelings, so that these writings are both a fiction and a measure of the extent to which he really did not, whether consciously or unconsciously, recognize the authority of the people in charge. Actually, he had the permission of the school's president to use both the typewriters and the library, and he probably obtained it by once again flourishing the letter from Vanguard.

Once settled, he found himself faced with a seemingly insurmountable task, stuck in a foreign and apparently barren culture. Aside from the ease with which he'd set himself up, the town had little to recommend it. There was nobody to talk to; politics, as familiar to Nelson—as a direct response to the environment—didn't exist here. People hardly mentioned the Depression, seeing it as a burden to be borne without complaint. For companionship he wrote to political friends in New York and Chicago, venting his hatred of Texas as his personal, cultural, and political alienation, unfettered by self-analysis, reached new heights. Referring to the Texans as "burros and Baptists," he was disgusted by Alpine's hypocrisy: the town was segregated but self-righteous. Angrily, he banged out poems on the typewriter. One, "As Walt Might Have Put It," he dedicated to the "ten ranting millions of pimply-souled patrioteers, those effervescent boils called Legionnaires." "I sing my country, and the thing Democratick," it began, parodying Whitman. But the poem's smug, superior tone alarmed Nelson's friends who had more perspective. On October 15, less than two weeks after his arrival in

Alpine, he received a letter so inspiring he would keep it for the rest of his life. From a Brooklyn comrade named Milton, it urged him to drop his city sophistication and Menckenite snobbery: if he found the Texans indescribably boring, it was only because he didn't know them well enough. One could make a novel from anything, and Nelson would do well to remember that his job as a materialistic artist was to teach the ideas that he and "millions are fighting for, are being tortured for. On to the great American revolutionary novel!"

Chastised so encouragingly, he began his work in earnest, enthusiastically believing he would wrest from Jack Conroy the title of "American Gorky." He set out to write a "proletarian novel," a type of work that, informed by Marxist analysis and exemplified by Conroy's *The Disinherited,* was considered an important weapon of class warfare, actively encouraged by the John Reed Clubs and the Communist Party. Most proletarian novels of the thirties, however, focused on the plight of the working classes, who would lead America into the light of a classless society. But after living on the road as a vagrant, Algren had at least partially come to see himself as an outsider in relation to society, and while he was acutely aware of the exploitation inherent in the capitalist-worker relationship, for him this theme was only a gateway to exploring the lumpenproletariat, the "social scum" even lower than the working class.

He set the novel in Texas, New Orleans, and Chicago, allowing him to draw on his knowledge of transient boxcar life and the cities he knew best. He also used incidents from the recent trip from New York: his main character would burn his way out of a boxcar, see arms severed by moving trains, nearly lose his life by jumping into an open-bottomed coal car, and learn a cross-country constellation of towns to avoid and safe places to sleep.

Algren made hero Cass McKay a naive and illiterate Texas cracker, raised motherless in a shack where "poverty, bleak and blind, sat staring at four barren walls." A sensitive child, Cass lives amid violence but never becomes immune to it. Gawky and unattractive, afflicted with an almost idiotic Texas twang, he has neither enough looks, brains, nor luck to enter any social class higher than that of the hobo and criminal he eventually becomes. Nelson set Cass's childhood in Mexican town, along a "broad dust-road . . . with gas lamps leaning askew above lean curs asleep in the sun, where brown half-naked children played in the ruts that many wheels had made."

Wandering through Alpine, Nelson watched the railroads shipping cattle and sheep, saw the town's poor gather at the stopped trains in the hope of stealing coal there. He saw the maintenance crews in the section houses and listened to the railroad men at the Nettleton House. Around the shipping pens or in the streets he heard of the great cattle ranches and their barons. He wrote a number of scenes from the cowhands' viewpoint, emphasizing the economic disparity between the hands and a powerful rancher named Boone Terry. But this disparity was not a schema that Algren had to impose on his fiction. It was a glaring reality everywhere he turned.

Fascism was also on his mind those autumn days of 1933. He now wrote "An American Diary," an unpublished story of a frustrated unemployed worker who becomes a Bible-thumping, anti-Communist anti-Semite as easily as he could have become a Communist firebrand, illustrating Algren's belief that political affiliation required a stability the lumpenproletariat could rarely attain. He also began a poem called "Nazi." By late 1933, Communist circles were well aware of Hitler's tyrannical, racist, union-busting policies, as the left in general took the Nazi threat more seriously than did mainstream America. Obviously feeling strongly about Fascism and still using the name Abraham except for publication, Nelson also continued to write and think about anti-Semitism.

He worked furiously on the novel. He was constantly on the typewriter at Sul Ross and rarely had time for the occasional students who wandered in to talk or ask questions. He had the setting and the main character now, and as he wrote, the story began to emerge. But he was tough on himself. By the middle of November he jotted in his notebooks that the novel he now called "Native Son" had a feeling of haste to it, that the story turned jerkily and lacked the humor of Conroy's *The Disinherited*—the humorlessness due in part to his lack of folk knowledge. The characters needed to speak more, and the novel needed restraint and work. He had four months until his deadline of March 15.

Some people in Alpine weren't so bad after all. Mrs. Nettleton invited him to Thanksgiving dinner, and Nelson recalled that an eighty-year-old lady named Mrs. James also arrived to eat. She was the widow of Jesse's infamous brother Frank, dead since 1915. "She ate more than any three people there," Nelson would exaggerate later. "If she could eat like that at eighty, I could see why Frank had turned outlaw when she was young." He loved nonconformists, and his memoirs indicate that he was proud to know her.

He was also becoming a celebrity at Sul Ross. Students began dropping by the typing room, drawn to his dedication, knowledge of literature, matter-of-fact opinions, and unwillingness to engage in small talk. He didn't discourage them, and before long three or four students started coming by the Nettleton House once a week or so to talk about writing. Nelson "craved companionship," said Paul Forchheimer, at sixteen one of the youngest members of the group. "He enjoyed the role of being looked up to." He seemed very, very intense. His hardened face told them that he had lived through what he was writing about, and he had a certain reserve along with shrewd powers of observation. He talked about the things he'd done and seen without bragging, discussing only how a writer might react to them. "He was really as much of a sociologist as a writer," Paul noticed.

"From a personal standpoint he was very reticent, but he had no hesitation in talking about what he wanted to do, and of course the writing of this novel was uppermost in his mind." Algren used the grateful students as a sounding board, asking their opinions on parts of the novel he was submitting to small magazines in the hope of being paid. They might occasionally bring him their own writings to criticize, but they were quite willing to be an audience for his views. "We were the aspirants and he was the real thing," Paul recalled.

These informal gatherings soon led to more formal associations with the college, and he was invited to speak to a freshman literature class. Asked for an example of social realism, he looked out the window to a gang of laborers at work on the railroad tracks. "If one of those workers hits his hand with a hammer," Nelson said, "I'm not going to have him say 'Goodness gracious!' He's going to say 'Sonofabitch!' " His frankness was disarming, and from then on he was included in the activities of the college's Writers' Club. At one meeting at the Forchheimers' house, he talked about proletarian writing to a small, rapt group of students and adults. An article in the Sul Ross *Skyline,* summarizing the substance of a later talk, "The Culture of the Proletariat," noted that "It is Mr. Abraham's opinion that when the history of American literature is written, the name of Jack Conroy, the outstanding proletarian writer of America, will be placed far above that of Sinclair Lewis and other popular contemporaries."

But this was the extent of his political discussion with the students in Alpine. He told a campus reporter that his novel was to deal with "the working-class in Southeastern Illinois," a sign that he was keeping the purpose of his stay in Alpine secret. He may have enjoyed duping those who thought he was a prominent writer when he knew he was nothing of the sort ("I think I told them I was Theodore Dreiser's nephew or something," he joked later); but there was also that part of him he'd discovered in Urbana, the part that wanted to live inside his head, isolated from people. Keeping things to himself was one way to do this. He did not connect to the world by allowing people to know him intimately; he connected through his writing. And though there were people there, the Alpine of Nelson's memory is unpeopled. The students, attending college in the midst of the Depression, came from the upper middle class of the community; and Nelson's residency among the outcasts created a gulf between him and the students that was almost impossible to bridge. But it is more likely that his memoirs of Alpine seem desolate for the same reason those from the gas station do: though in fiction he could make himself a lone hero, pitted against an unnatural environment, in actuality there were very few times when he was not emotionally alone.

Since part of the novel would be set in Chicago, he thought of heading north in January. His money was almost gone. He decided to leave town on Saturday, January 27, and planned to stop in Moberly, Missouri, to have Jack Conroy make suggestions on the manuscript. This way he would reach Chicago by February 1, and would have six weeks to complete and revise the book. In the meantime, by leaving on Saturday he could get in a full week of typing at Sul Ross.

But the prospect of returning to a place where he had no typewriter nagged at him. He was not going to ask Joffe again, and buying one was out of the question. Moreover, he had developed "almost a compulsive attachment, a sort of possessiveness, about typewriters," especially the upright Royal he'd been using. With all those machines sitting up at Sul Ross and no one using them, liberating one was not hard to imagine—it was hard not to. If he went that evening before the college closed but when most people had gone home, no one would realize that it was missing until Monday. By that time he'd be well out of the state. It was a beautiful, foolproof plan.

The next morning his freight left at ten-fifteen, so he said goodbye to Mrs. Nettleton and, according to one memoir, to the Widow James too, and took the newly stolen typewriter, now crated, down to the freight depot shortly before his train was due in. There he addressed it to 4834 North Troy, Chicago, Illinois, and got on the Southern Pacific freight that was heading toward Sanderson.

But Nelson Algren Abraham was, for all his traveling, a city man, and there was one aspect to the whole affair that he hadn't considered, as he congratulated himself on the perfect crime all the way to Sanderson: in a small town like Alpine, people talk.

At Sanderson, "the train slowed up and I got out. It was sort of sunny and I'd been in the boxcar and I put my back up against the wall there and started rolling a cigarette with one hand. Everybody had to do that in the South. You had to roll a cigarette one-handed . . . and the string—the yellow string had to hang down from your pocket. This was ritual. I noticed the sheriff coming along. He looked like he was looking for somebody. I said, 'Good morning,' and he asked me who I was and I told him. Well, then I was on my way back to Alpine."

Theft of personal property over fifty dollars was punishable by two years on the state pea farm at Huntsville. But before the sentence good old Texas justice called for a trial. Before the trial he had to wait in jail for the circuit-riding judge, who was now about a month away from Alpine. The horror and finality of his situation came to him. He was scared.

That night he wrote or wired to his mother. "Dear Ma, I'm not leaving after all. Don't send money to Moberly. Nobody will arrive. I'm here at least a month longer. Letter will follow." Deciding what to tell Henle was more difficult. Crossing out every few lines, for it had to sound just right, he wrote: "Dear Mr. Henle . . . I will be here in Alpine for a month at least, perhaps even longer. I seem oddly irresolute at this time and please bear with me. A letter will follow." It must have sounded too vague, for he apparently gave up this draft and wrote that he was going to a mining camp farther south to gather material.

Incredibly, a month and perhaps two years of his life were going to be taken to pay for a crime that had hurt no one. Nelson was bitterly aware that his stay in jail was not for rehabilitation, but merely the result of daring to defy the unshakable American laws of private property. But by throwing him in jail they also told him he was a bum, and not of their class. A mocking notebook entry, in poem form, reads: "Lumpenproletariat, me / trespassed private property / wondering always how it comes / there's just no rest for such poor bums."

The Brewster County Jail was little more than a cage. There was one cellblock of iron bars whose cell doors, always unlocked, opened onto a hallway where a communal toilet was flushed with a bucket. Adjoining the cellblock was the runaround, a locked outside hall from which the trustees doled out food on trays known as "troughs." The floors and walls were cement, and an unidentified "wet filth" sometimes sopped parts of the floor and occasionally froze. In the winter, when Nelson was there, it was cold.

On his first morning, Nelson learned an unwritten jailhouse law. The jailer and his family lived on the floor below, and on Sunday mornings they liked to sleep late. The communal "thundermug" roared like Niagara when flushed and for an hour after made strange seeping noises. Therefore the men waited, uneasily restraining themselves until the family got up. The toilet was also off limits at night. For flushing at the wrong time, Nelson would make the hero of his novel, Cass McKay, go without food; one can only hope that Nelson was luckier.

Later in the day he was brought downstairs to make a statement. The theft was so obvious there was no point denying it: when the freightmaster called the sheriff, it hadn't taken much ingenuity to realize that this was the same machine reported missing that morning from Sul Ross. Undoubtedly he was told that things would go easier if he made a statement. All he could do was tell the story that showed him in the best possible light:

THE STATE OF TEXAS,

COUNTY OF..BREWSTER............................ Date........January 27, 1934..........

TO WHOM THIS MAY CONCERN:

After I have been duly warned by....C. E. Patterson...............................:................to whom this
statement is made that I do not have to make any statement at all, and that such statement I make
may be used in evidence against me on my trial for the offense concerning which this statement is made,
I wish to make the following voluntary statement:

My name is.....Nelson Abraham....................................and I am..24........years of age;

I was born in.......Detroit, Michigan...................................and at present I consider the

following address my home:..;

The names and addresses of some of nearest relatives are:...

Mr & Mrs. G. Abraham, Chicago, Illinois

....

and I wish to further say:

I went up to the College between 5;30, and 6;00 in the evening or afternoon on 25th of January this year, I walked in the south door and it was

in my mind to do some typing, I had permission of Dr. Morelock to use
the typewriters, and the door to the typewriting room was locked, but the
door to the office was open and there was a typewriter there, I assumed
that this typewriter was property of the school, the same as the other
typewriters as in the room that was locked, I typed on it for about 15 minutes in t his office, I don't know where I went up there
just to type or to take a typewriter, this is not clear in my mind.

I wanted a typewriter very bad because I am a writer by profession, I've
never owned a typewriter of my own, I was eager to finish a manuscript
on which I've been working in Alpine since October 3, 1933, since it was
necessary for me to return to Chicago, since it was also necessary that
I have a typewriter to finish my book, I decided to take the typewriter.

A typewriter is the only means I had to complete a book which means either
a few dollars or utter destitution.   There is nothing that is more vital
to my mere existence as a typewriter, it is the only means I have to earn
a living.   If I can write I can earn my own living.

I am not certain of the make of the typewriter.   I was nervous, I had
idea in my head, and I put cover on the typewriter, I opened the drawer
to put in the desk where it belonged, but instead of this I put it under
my arm, and walked out of the door.   I came out the front door and took
the typewriter to the Nettleton House to my room, when I got to my room
I put it into a wooden box, the box was taken to the depot the next morning, and at that time I arranged for the shipment of this box, and I knew
that the typewriter was in the box, the box was billed to my parents'
address in Chicago.   I left town on a freight about 10;15, after I had
mailed receipt of this box to my parents' address, and I was going to
Chicago, at Sanderson, Texas, I was arrested.   I didn't have the feeling
that I was stealing from an individual, I felt like I was takin g it from
the school

Witnesses:

1. Pete Crawford

2. John E. Smith

Nelson Abraham

C. E. Patterson didn't know where a sentence ended, but Nelson, in no position to correct the grammar, signed it.

There was nothing to do in the jail. Every day one of the three or four prisoners was allowed into the runaround to sweep it clean, catch a patch of life through the window, and be that much closer to the outside. The other prisoners watched him jealously, for they too wanted to be doing something, even just sweeping. They stood around listlessly and argued, listening to the chimes from a nearby clock tower ticking off the hours. There was nothing to do in the jail, nothing to read.

Boredom and frustration created a pecking order within the tank, a "play-pretend of the underdogs aping the wolves on top," as Nelson described it, by which the men sought to raise their self-esteem. Blacks and Mexicans were the lowest of the low. "They made Piedmonts and Camels to keep niggers from smoking Chesterfields"; someone might call out laughing, and whores too were always the subject of cruel mockery by this crew of thieves, vagrants, and murderers. "Charlotte the harlot / queen of the whores / scanned the eastside / covered with sores" was a favorite saying, and Jews were also ridiculed.

There were beatings by the prisoners among themselves. Belt buckles were the favored instrument, and Algren remembered one particularly perverse jailhouse game that was used to pass the time. One of the men was blindfolded. Then he bent over so that the others could, in turn, whip him on the buttocks with their belts. If he guessed which man had hit him, then that prisoner would take his place. This cruel inanity could go on all afternoon, because fear of a fight on the jailhouse floor, fear of random violence on cement and iron with no one to stop it, kept men playing.

Cellblock justice, ruled by a kangaroo court, flourished in such an atmosphere. When a new man came in, court would convene, and as the official looked the other way, the prisoner, depending on his color, crime, or other status, might be searched, robbed, beaten, or simply told to behave according to the Rules of Court:

> Man found guilty of breaking and entering this jail will be fined $2.00 a day or 40 days on the floor at the rate of 5 cents a day. Every man entering tank must keep cleaned and properly dressed. Each day of the week is washday except Sunday. Every man must wash his hands and face before handling food. Any man found

guilty of marking on the wall will be given 20 licks on rectum west. If the man breaks these rules he will be punished according to the justice of the court. On entering this tank each and every man must be searched by the sheriff, he will search everywhere.

Each and every man must turn his spoon into the court as he goes out. Each and every man must make his bed when he gets up in the morning and he must also sweep out his cell. Each and every man using the toilet must flush it with bucket. Throw all paper in the ash tub. Do not spit in the coal tub or through the windows. When using dishrag keep it clean. Any man caught stealing from any of the inmates of the tank gets five hundred licks. Any man upon entering this tank with venereal disease, lice or crabs, must report same to the court.

The "judge" of this court seems to have been Nelson's cellmate Jack, a vagrant who had lost one of his hands. He had developed the remaining nub into a callused piece of flesh that could bend tobacco tins or be used as a hammer. A small man with a large ego, he claimed to be the brother of silent movie star Art Acord. In *Somebody in Boots* he appears as "Judge" Nubby O'Neill, whose "highly feigned hatred of anything not white and American was the high point of [his] honor."

Another prisoner was a homicidal rodeo rider named Jess, reincarnated by Algren in "El Presidente de Mejico." Jess had fled to Mexico after killing a Mexican in Texas. But there he'd killed another Mexican, so as a choice between being tried for killing a Mexican in Mexico and being tried for killing one in the U.S., he'd taken his chances on the American side. An Alpine resident, Jess would no doubt have friends on the jury. And killing a Mexican in Texas, Algren wrote in his fiction, was not much worse than stealing a horse, "a legal hangover from a time when stealing a horse meant leaving its rider helpless in the desert."

The value of a Mexican life was very low, to judge from Nelson's notebook: "They hit the Mex's head against the spoonholder and then with the boot knocked him out." The notebook reveals that more vicious acts were also officially sanctioned. One was the death of a Mexican prisoner whom Nelson called P. in his notebook. A religious man with a romantic nature, Sunday mornings he would call out to his pregnant wife on her way to church, then pace back and forth on the cement floor, praying. He was mysteriously released; but shortly afterward was carried back to the jail, in agony from a gunshot wound. He had been shot resisting arrest, the officials said, and instead of being taken to a hospital, he was brought up to the cellblock. The officials didn't want to risk operating on him without his permission, Nelson recalled, and he was in too much shock to give it. "His face was grayer than I had ever seen a living face, and the eyes were dilating with shock," Nelson wrote later. "They stared fixedly and without understanding, at the monstrous and ragged navel of his wound. . . . The fingers . . . wandered, aimlessly as a mad-man's, about the wound's gray edge, tracing the torn tissue." The jailers just left the man there, and the prisoners were forced to watch him die.

Along with the callous violence came hunger and weakness. The jail was often cold, the cement-confined air close and thick. The food, just coffee, oatmeal, cornbread, and beans, with an occasional turnip or tomato, was never sufficient. "It was a very sparse diet because I think the warden was allowed sixty cents a day for each prisoner, but his own take came largely off of how much he could save on that, so there were two very thin meals a day," Nelson recalled. "Hunger our enemy, how can we quell it?" he asked in his notebook. And answered himself by drinking warm water. Once he caught the traveling hives: huge itchy lumps from head to foot, trans-ferred at a touch like poison ivy. No doctor was brought in to examine him, but one of the jailers "brought me up a can of insecticide, something like that," Algren remembered dryly. "But I thought I was better off with the hives."

He appealed to no one in the outside world. He must have felt homesick at times, but he had withheld his parents' address on his confession: he did not consider their house his home. To them he would be a "bum" and a "thief," and if they did grudgingly lend him bail money, he'd only have to pay for it psychologically later on. And even if he made bail, how could he write while waiting for a trial that might send him to Huntsville? Nor could he jeopardize the novel by telling Henle about the theft.

Instead he sat in a cell and listened to his nutty one-armed cell-mate's prattling about his conquests, punctuated by an anti-Semitism it was hard not to find belittling. But any evidence of frailty was taboo here. He was never a man to bare his soul, but in an unguarded moment he recorded in his notebook: "One terror: being alone. One word: home. I do not know what it is that strangers mean by this word 'home.' I know what they do not mean: being alone. Two ways of cursing one unlike yourself: call him 'Jew'; call him 'fool.' I am alone, I am a Jew, in all the world I have no home."

"Very few people went to see him," said Nelson's friend from the college Paul Forchheimer. "When the crime was committed, we were all shocked . . . in those days maybe you just didn't go to jail. But I felt compassionate and I must say I was a little curious because I'd never been in a jail before. I went by myself and brought him candy and cigarettes." Nelson seemed depressed, shamefaced, and Paul sensed that there was no point in talking about the crime.

"How're they treating you?"

"OK."

"Are you getting enough to eat?"

"Yeah."

"Would you like some cigarettes?"

"Well, OK."

"Can I get you anything?"

"No."

"The amazing thing," Paul recalled, "was that he never, at any time, asked for anything. He could have asked any number of people, myself included, sure, if you want to borrow my typewriter, go ahead, take it and send it back when you're finished with it. This is, and was then, a small, trusting community, and it's not unusual for a friend in need to ask." But Nelson never said that he needed a typewriter, just as he now told Paul Forchheimer that he needed nothing, in spite of his hunger and boredom. "A P.R. guy he wasn't," Paul realized.

Each day grew closer to the March 15 deadline for the novel. Despite his earlier resolve not to tell Henle of his predicament, in the middle of February he drafted a letter in his notebook:

Dear Mr. Henle,
    This may come to you as a mild shock, to say the least. My letter of January [27] was wholly a fabrication, deliberately calculated to mislead you. I have not been for the past three weeks in a mining camp south of here—I've been in jail.
    Although I could crawl out of this myself, if I was to have a telegram addressed to the sheriff, this might result in having my case tried. . . . [My crime] is not political, and more it is a first offense, thus good reason to hope for a suspended sentence. Such a telegram need only say the date of publication of the book on

which I am working is dependent on the length of time I [stay] here. Whatever experience you—

But apparently he thought the better of it. On Friday, February 16, a grand jury convened to review his case, and trial was set for Wednesday, February 21. The sheriff's office began to subpoena witnesses.

The trial, held in the ornate and imposing Brewster County Court-house, took up most of the day. Paul Forchheimer and his entire English class attended. Surprisingly, Nelson had been given a public defender, a white haired old man with the improbable name of Wig-fall Van Sickle who, like many lawyers in the West, was commonly known as "Judge." Rumor had it that he drank, but he was polite and articulate and instructed Nelson to enter a plea of not guilty. Various witnesses were called: the sheriff, the railroad clerk, the justice of the peace, the typewriter's owner. The signed confession was produced. The district attorney, addressing the white, all-male jury, described Nelson as a "militant, defiant man," and the state rested. Things looked bleak, indeed.

But then old Judge Van Sickle rose to speak. Calling Nelson "the youth with the mysterious brain," he asked the jury, in a surprisingly literary plea, to consider the ancient English common law that held that a mechanic is entitled to the tools of his trade. According to one account, he likened Nelson to the hero of Victor Hugo's *Les Misérables:* "What is a carpenter without his tools? What is a writer without the use of a typewriter? This man was not stealing because of any criminal intent. In these troubled times of economic depression this man was stealing for the same reason that Jean Valjean stole a loaf of bread, to survive. You would not be hard on a carpenter or craftsman if he stole the means of work to earn his daily bread." Was there not some justice, he continued, in Nelson's claim that the law and society owed him the tools, the means by which he can make his living? Besides, he added shrewdly, if novelist Nelson Algren Abraham became famous, the jury would disgrace Alpine and Brewster County by making it known as the place that had put him behind bars.

"Then I got on the witness stand," Algren recalled. "I was on the stand to hear the verdict and the verdict was guilty and the sentence was two years at Huntsville. . . . But then . . . one of the jurors recommended mercy and then the judge—I had to stand in front of the judge—he said we are recommending mercy. He impressed on me that I was going to serve the time but it wasn't necessary for me to serve it in Texas. He said I could go home and serve it. They don't want to keep you in Texas. There were too many, you know . . . the understanding was that if I got out of the state within twenty-four hours and went back home . . . that if at the end of two years I would come back to this court and swear that I had not been in any more trouble, then it would be considered that I had served the two years."

He was freed, only to go back to the evening session of the Brewster County Court to see the fates of Jess and Jack. The newspapers thought this very strange. He was a "glutton for punishment," as if, now that he was free, jail were something he should just shut out of his mind, when in fact it was something he could never shut out: a man was in jail in every novel he wrote. Years later, he would invariably remember having been in the Alpine jail for four or five months rather than the three and a half weeks he was really there: his perception of time apparently became confused, and it was not so much because he tended to portray himself as the tough guy, although there was some of that, but that the experience so stirred his imagination and assumed such proportions in his mind that he probably felt he had been there longer.

The next morning he drafted a letter to Henle saying that despite being jailed on a housebreaking charge, he planned, though he needed more time, to continue with the novel. Then he climbed on top of an eastbound freight. By coincidence Paul Forchheimer happened to be downtown and they waved to each other, Nelson's body outlined against the Texas sky. Algren was glad to be going. It had been scary, a near-miss, but a farce. As he said later, "Had I been black, of course, I would have gone to Huntsville."

6.
The Near North Side

SUDDENLY ALGREN KNEW a great deal about refrigerator box-cars, and he probably learned it on the long journey north. "Reefers" had a thick overhead door with a traplock that had to be closed very, very gently. To let it click from inside was to be sealed into a cold, tiny compartment walled by wire screening, with little air and almost no light. A man caught inside could only hope someone had seen him go in and would let him out the next day: in three weeks a patrolling brakeman would find only a well-preserved corpse. Reefer cars would figure in Algren's novel, and in "Lest the Traplock Click," an apparently autobiographical first-person narrative published in June 1934, Algren described a radical college graduate and veteran boxcar transient named Jonathan Harris who is trapped in one of the cold, dark tombs. Famished and sickened by the car's every jolt, his head taking "little cloudy-yellow swimming spells," Harris hallucinates until the morning sun sifts ever so slightly into the car: his frozen fingers move, and he sees mountains of oranges, though he cannot get a one through the screening. And "all the time . . . I thought I was going to die! . . . As though a man could die in broad daylight! In this day and age! As though a man might freeze when the sun was shining! As though a man could starve in the midst of plenty or die a dozen feet from thousands of oranges!"

Arriving in Chicago, thin, exhausted, Algren had to act as if nothing had happened: his family didn't even know he'd been in jail. And there was no time to recuperate. The relief of freedom, tempered by the train trip, was lost to the problems of locating an accessible typewriter, being way behind deadline, and returning immediately to work. Henle thought the first sections of the novel showed "tremendous promise," and the prestigious *American Mercury* had taken a chapter about Cass's stay in a mission for its April issue, so Algren had reason for optimism about the writing. Jack Conroy, whom he told about being in jail, accepted two Texas stories for *The Anvil,* and while rejecting a third, had interested four other magazines in excerpts from the novel. Moreover, the time in stir hadn't been a total waste: he could use the Brewster County Jail almost exactly as he had experienced it, only Cass would have to be arrested on a more run-of-the-mill charge, like loitering with a Negro.

He returned to the John Reed Club. More than ever, it was the natural place to find people who appreciated and encouraged his work. Dick Wright, whose career was also just taking off with a poem in *The Anvil* and another in the national leftist journal *New Masses,* was now club secretary. Aspiring novelist Sam Ross was there, along with Sam Gaspar, an Armenian who apparently introduced Nelson to his gambling friend William Saroyan, then passing through Chicago. Another poet, Howard Nutt, later became an editor of *Direction,* which published Ezra Pound, E. E. Cummings, Kay Boyle, and William Carlos Williams. Nelson also met Jan Wittenber, a painter with a Christ-like air whose work exalted the unity of the proletariat and appeared regularly in *Left Front.* The goal-oriented optimism surrounding the club—the idea that justice could be achieved and the system responsible for the Depression overthrown—was attractively contagious, and that spring Algren joined the Chicago John Reed Club.

The club seemed more political than before, perhaps because Wright had joined the Communist Party several months earlier. Though organized by the Communist Party, the John Reed Clubs did not require members to join the Party and was overtly a cultural club. But Wright later wrote that a small faction of the club included secret members of the Party and met outside to decide club policies; in meetings, their carefully thought-out arguments usually convinced non-Party members to support them. By now Algren completely embraced the idea of revolution. In a later deleted section of the novel, published in Canadian *Masses,* he warned the smug and comfortable rich, "Oppressed man will rise up! . . . All shall rise up as one . . . pouring fast out of the mines and the fields, off of the streets and out of the factories, from great dim mills and dark, dank prisons, driving you then as vermin are driven off the face of the earth we will drive you." Violent overthrow seemed imminent—the Depression was no aberration but capitalism's death throes. His first novel "was originally intended as a trumpet-call to arms," Algren recalled almost forty years later. "The author was dead serious. Survival was the story and revolution was the theme. . . . I even put in quotes from Marx and Lenin to show I was one of the good guys," he said with an amused cynicism that he lacked completely in 1935.

For many people like Algren, Wright, and the feminist writer Meridel Le Sueur, the hope and support offered by the movement were succor to be found nowhere else. "I don't think any of us would have survived without the Reed Clubs and our bond with each other," Le Sueur recalled. Though these writers were surrounded by chaos and unable to make a living, the Party encouraged them to see themselves not as destitute people, but as fighters for human dignity. Still, it was not easy. "It was a very hard time to live to be a writer," she wrote. "The left was very severe on you. It had its own orthodoxy. . . . But it also summoned us forth. . . . We wouldn't have tried without them . . . the Communists gave us light and even love."

And yet, said Meridel, who occasionally saw Nelson at Party functions, "Going to a meeting seemed to be painful for him. He would be hanging around in back as if about to disappear. I never understood how he went into the underworld. . . . I think the underworld saw him as an innocent and therefore safe."

On Wednesdays the poet Larry Lipton held literary evenings at his rambling Rush Street house on Chicago's Near North Side, and poets and writers were invited to read their work. Nelson, Dick Wright, and Sam Ross were usually there, and another reader was the novelist Stuart Engstrand, who would drown himself in the 1950s by walking into a lake. It was a committed, serious group, but in a much more bohemian, emotive atmosphere than at the John Reed Club. Lipton, though a likely Party recruit, was more interested in beauty and art and culture. "Those who came to the house were brought under the influence of this more tender, artistic kind of love attitude which [my girlfriend] and I had," Lipton remembered, "and some of them were influenced in that direction, although they felt guilty. It was against the Party line." There were deep discussions about literature, and Nelson undoubtedly felt a certain similarity in aims and views with the poetic, nonconformist Lipton. He liked the

Rush Street house: the group respected him, and he was a big shot there with his novel under contract.

That was important. At home, respect for his work was surely not forthcoming: 4834 North Troy was in turmoil. Gerson's dwindling income couldn't pay the bills, and in May court proceedings were held for mortgage foreclosure. Though the judgment granted the Abrahams fifteen months to redeem the house, there were no real prospects for more money. Nelson was certainly no help: he'd been out of work for three years and showed no inclination to take responsibility for them. Though he later faithfully helped support the aging Goldie, Algren did not believe he should give up what he wanted to support others: he felt there was something morally wrong with being at someone else's behest. It was *his* life, and he would live it as he wanted. Even in jail, he had never considered their house his home; and he was not an available body to make money for people with no conception of his talents or who he was. Giving up the only thing he found meaningful, the only thing that gave him an ounce of control over his fate, would have been unthinkable. If he could help them with his writing, fine. But his writing came first.

Not surprisingly, he spent much of his time away from the house, working in the apartment of a woman who apparently became his girlfriend. She had a job during the day, so he used her typewriter while she was out. Evenings he went to Lipton's or the club. As June approached, he became fascinated with the second season of the Century of Progress World's Fair and later said he took a job on South State Street selling hot dogs. In addition to earning him a little money, it allowed him to watch the people who thronged the sidewalks near the entrance to the extravaganza.

The World's Fair, built at a cost of thirty-eight million, covered twenty-six city blocks along the lake. Twenty-two million admissions had been sold the first year, and once inside, visitors entered what Algren called "a zigzag riot of fakery": they could take a Venetian boat ride, tour Hollywood, Old Heidelberg, a Moroccan bazaar, Turkish mosques, Belgian and Oriental villages, an Egyptian museum, the Café de la Paix, and a chaos of over seven hundred other concessions, exhibits, and entertainments. There were alligator wrestlers, fire-eaters, Lincoln's cabin, Dante's Inferno, and Byrd's South Pole ship; Algren described "college-trained men pulling jinrikshas . . . hundreds of Negroes scraping for tips . . . cane-sellers, peep-show houses, prostitutes, trinket-vendors, dinosaurs": he saw it all as a Big Business showpiece, an absurd attempt to provide escape from the city's hideous poverty.

And surely there were times when he stayed downtown late, prowling around the night people in burlesque shows and rented rooms. There was much to the fair that do-gooders and visitors tried not to understand as they headed for their houses or hotels; Algren described the nocturnal emergence of old men rummaging through garbage cans like dogs, of children begging from darkened doorways, of prostitutes walking the streets near the fairground, fearing disease and the police. Some of these women could become waitresses at the fair, or peep-show dancers, "But these were only the few and the highly fortunate. Others spent their days in Grant Park lying about among old men and boys . . . like men sleeping in louse-ridden charity flops when a night was cold or rainy." He described a transient jungle right next to the fair that city officials were powerless to remove: the jails were already overcrowded, and "when a few were driven off or jailed the ranks were shortly replenished with new hordes of incoming transients; there was little to do but let them stay and pretend in the papers that they were not there."

This was just the kind of scene where Algren's protagonist Cass McKay could be found. Having come to Chicago with his one-armed cellmate O'Neill, Cass was making a living as a stickup man. He would cut loose from O'Neill and briefly enjoy steady money and love—with the mulatto hooker Val—for the first time in his life. But Algren knew Cass's armed-robbery path led directly to the Cook County Jail, and to dramatize the stretch used his old college story "Sweat," forcing Cass to listen to the Irish Costigan mentally torture his tubercular cellmate Moore, waking the man as he slept and hastening his demise in every way possible. Cass's only respite from violence had been with Val, and when he was through serving his time, he set out in the city to find her. But in the whirling commercialism of the Century of Progress, between the peep shows and the prostitutes, the jam-packed sidewalks and the hunger, she was lost.

By early July Algren sent the last section of the novel to Henle and then headed to the central Illinois mining towns of Nokomis and Hillsboro, where five hundred jobless miners had demonstrated against an unconstitutional ban on public assembly and for the right to refuse work on a forced-labor relief plan. Three days after a bloody battle between protesters and a militia of Ku Klux Klansmen, businessmen, and American Legionnaires was averted, vigilantes arrested ten organizers on charges of plotting to overthrow the government. According to the *Daily World,* Nelson's friend Jan Wittenber was beaten amid cries of "Tar and feather 'em" in full view of city officials.

Always ready to see another jail, Algren headed a Chicago contingent to gather information, protest the beating, and make sure Wittenber received fair treatment while awaiting his secret trial. Algren was preparing an article on events in southern Illinois for *Left Front.* But for lack of money, the planned issue never appeared, and " 'Politics' in Southern Illinois" was published in *The New Republic* in early August. Its factual straightforward style has no recognizable connection to Algren's fiction, but the final sentiment, aglow with faith in the rising power of the working class, was certainly his.

Although *The New Republic* brought desperately needed money, there was no real question of continuing with this kind of writing. He was already gaining a reputation for his fiction. Since returning from Alpine he had finished a novel, had had a story printed every month, and was furthering his career through literary connections in the radical movement, though Party directives sometimes interfered. When he returned to Chicago, the John Reed Club organized a Midwest conference of left-wing writers to discuss political commitment. Many of the writers were experiencing a conflict between the time demands of writing and the Party's demands for political work, and were especially eager to hear the Party's latest position on this issue. It was, however, unequivocal: they were expected to spend a few hours a day writing and the rest demonstrating or picketing. Though Richard Wright argued passionately that a man either wrote or organized, Party leaders were adamant. And even *Left Front* apparently took more time from political work than it warranted: with no further help from the Party, the magazine that had launched Wright's career was voted out of existence.

Moreover, the John Reed Club no longer served the Party's new agenda, which had shifted from revolution to the anti-Fascist cause. When Hitler refused to sign a nonaggression pact with Stalin, the Russian leader realized that Soviet safety lay in alliance with the capitalist West. The new People's Front Against Fascism presupposed a nationally coordinated, nonsectarian effort, but the John Reed Clubs lacked national leadership, and most members were not well enough known to be used for propaganda purposes in the fight against Hitler. The clubs would be dissolved. Instead, an American Writers' Congress, open only to established writers, would be held in New York the following spring.

If Richard Wright feared his meager publications would exclude him from the Writers' Congress and further Communist literary work, Algren did not. The novel would more or less guarantee his inclusion in the Congress—where he would meet bigger, more important writers from outside the Party. Besides, the clubs would not be closing for almost another year, and even then he could still go to Larry Lipton's and see many of the same people. His novel and his writing career were uppermost in his mind.

The flip side to the disillusionment with society that had led Algren to the Communist Party was an unbridled optimism concerning his work. The faith in human nature that made him think the working classes would change the world also convinced him that society was going to sit up, take notice of what he had to say, and demand an end to the daily waste of human life in America. His chosen literary path had to be vindicated: he was an artist, special, able to speak for the downtrodden and portray their experiences to society. His book would prove that—and get his family off his back if it made some money. Saroyan's success with *The Daring Young Man on the Flying Trapeze* had perhaps made him think a successful book was possible in 1934–35, but the Depression had been disastrous for the trade, and book sales had dropped dramatically: people losing their homes had neither the money nor the leisure for new novels. "He expected [the book] to have huge sales," James T. Farrell recalled later, "and I told him, at the time, he might as well forget such expectations."

But Algren *needed* a sensation. Since the foreclosure on the Abrahams' house, the mood at home must have been gloomy indeed. Gerson and Goldie had dedicated their lives to owning property, and they were undoubtedly devastated by their impending eviction. The failure of Gerson's tire and battery shop had left him with no other way to make a living, nothing to show after a lifetime of six- and seven-day weeks. Nelson's unwillingness to help must have bewildered and infuriated Goldie, but he could not be depended upon. So they took some of the equity out of their house to live on but made no effort to redeem the building itself: they hadn't enough income to keep up the payments. Hopeless, they waited out their fifteen months.

In New York, Henle had asked James T. Farrell to read Algren's manuscript, which arrived, as Farrell described it, in "very bad shape."

On the surface, Farrell seemed a natural choice for a reader, but he and Algren had many different views. Though a revolutionary, Farrell was unpopular in the Chicago John Reed Club because of his Trotskyist position and disenchantment with pro-Stalin Party dogma. He was critical of Party cultural policy, opposed Party efforts to oversee the development of its writers, and had an active aversion to proletarian literature, having attacked *The Disinherited* as dull, lacking technical skill and depth of characterization. Thus, approaching the first novel of a John Reed Club member and Conroy's protégé, he was significantly less impressed than Henle had anticipated.

Though Farrell himself was hardly a stylist, on July 2 he wrote Henle that "Algren has little concern with, or else feeling for, or else knowledge of, literary style . . . he has all kinds of bad writing." Henle seems to have been put off by Farrell's harsh words: he was now sorry he hadn't read the manuscript before writing the jacket copy—for though he'd liked immensely what he'd first seen, he now found the early parts muddled and the novel on the whole "almost incredibly bad," despite Farrell's assurances that there were "damn good things in it." Then Farrell sent Henle a more detailed, sixteen-page report, correcting specifics about Chicago and suggesting almost fifty pages of changes.

In July, when Algren received the reader's report on "Native Son," he was furious. He'd had no idea that Trotskyist Farrell was reading the manuscript. "Algren resented the hell out of Farrell's criticism of his book," said Sam Ross. "He had put a tremendous amount of work into the book, and a lot of himself," and now Farrell—who didn't even see the value of *The Disinherited*—wanted enormous changes. Probably expecting his first novel to go as smoothly as the publication of his stories, Algren was completely unprepared for the difficulties he encountered in getting it into print. It was the first time his writing had ever been severely, actively criticized, and he did not take it well.

Farrell saw many inconsistencies in the book. For a start, he found the relationship between Cass and the mulatto woman, Val, totally unbelievable: a white man and a black woman could not live together "as if it were not an extraordinary union which would have effects different from the mating of two people from the same race." As far as Farrell was concerned, Algren was "putting in the party line." Farrell did not object to including a black woman who is raped—a victim—but could not accept one as the love object of a white man. No matter that the character of Val was at least partially based on a mulatto burlesque dancer Algren almost certainly knew, or that interracial love existed in Chicago in the 1930s and was perhaps more likely among the lowest, jobless classes than among the working-class Catholic families from which Studs Lonigan came. Cass McKay, scarred, illiterate, nothing but a criminal, was already a member, like Val, of a despised class. And Cass was not a racist—he feared white supremacists. They had thrown him in jail, where an equally racist kangaroo court wanted to beat the hell out of him for "nigger-loving." Over and over, Cass was made to mouth racist attitudes under threat of violence, while his deeper feelings were incapable of approaching that level of hatred. Farrell's emphatic rejection even of the *idea* of such a love affair seems, despite his revolutionary stance, more an indication of his inability to perceive such a love, perhaps of his own bias. Yet these views, not unusual for the day, prevailed, and a relationship rarely seen in literature was suppressed.

Henle agreed with Farrell that it was a mistake to make Val a black woman. Val should be transformed into the blond, high-school-educated Norah Egan, a vulnerable-at-heart gun moll who, physically at least, was the stereotypic American version of womanly beauty. The title "Native Son" would also have to go, Algren remembered, because somebody named McAdoo from California was running for President on a "native son" candidacy, and people might think the book was about politics. The new title, "Somebody in Boots," was taken from a line in the book alluding to those who had power, but it was far less compelling than the original title, and Nelson was not happy with it.

Algren was stung by the criticism and angry but, apparently lacking the self-confidence and experience to contest Henle's judgment, he went along with most of the Vanguard president's demands, saving his rancor for Farrell, though not all of Farrell's criticisms were unjustified. Algren took many of his suggestions, and seems even to have thanked him: the rancher Boone Terry's scenes were deleted; an invective published earlier in Canadian *Masses,* wildly out of tone with the rest of the narrative, was also taken out. Looking back, Algren would realize how much he had to learn about writing, but at the time he probably angrily acceded because the book's publication and ensuing sales meant the difference between life and death—indeed, between money and nothing at all, between being a writer with a respected identity and being a bum, between being accepted by his family and being seen as a failure.

But by mid-November 1934, five months after its submission, "Somebody in Boots" was still not in type. "We are having a great deal of trouble with it," Henle wrote to Farrell. "I think he has improved it a lot, but I lean to the opinion that it is grossly overwritten." Algren continued trying to place sections in magazines such as *Esquire,* but he did not have much further success, and to read his cover letters, written on cheap yellow paper and full of typographical errors, is to appreciate his desperation and how much he had to learn. Publication was set for March.

Whatever Henle or Farrell thought, *Somebody in Boots* stands as one of the few American novels of the 1930s to convey the chaos and devastation of vagrant life, and later Depression anthologists used excerpts from it in recognition of this. Exceptionally few writers, especially of Algren's talent, were willing to write about the most unfortunate, and of the fifteen proletarian novels appearing in 1935, Nelson's was the only one, strictly speaking, to deal with this lowest of classes. Perhaps only Tom Kromer's *Waiting for Nothing* more vividly depicted jungle life, while Edward Anderson's *Hungry Men,* which treated similar themes, now seems excessively gentle. Algren spared nothing in describing the myriad ways in which a profit could be turned on the backs of the homeless, from the railroad bulls paid by the head to the soup kitchens that made sure transients left the shelters hungry by making them chop wood or clean beans for hours after supper. This material, and in fact the whole existence of the underclass, was unknown to the majority of Americans, and it was exactly the kind of material Algren would choose to expose again and again in later novels.

The inevitability of jail for those forced to make a living outside the system was a familiar Algren theme that first appeared in *Somebody in Boots*. Algren's characters move toward jail, literary historian Maxwell Geismar noted, "just as surely as the young executives of middle-class American life aspire to join the country club." The El Paso County Jail scenes show a society within a society, with its own kangaroo rules, at the mercy of harder, more powerful men. Algren's understanding of the pain of incarceration made the jail scenes exceptionally vivid—from the belt whippings to the starvation diet to the sexual brutality and hierarchy of violence maintained by cruel, cold Nubby O'Neill, one of the most disturbing characters in the book.

Another Algren trademark was the theme of frustrated love. Until he reaches Chicago, Cass's only relationships are the warped intimacies of his family life and road friendships born of necessity. Love is a complete revelation to him. "He shrugged off self-consciousness like an unclean hood. . . . He realized that heretofore he had been ill. He had been ill and had not known." The only constructive and motivating force in an otherwise useless life, Norah allows Cass to see that there can be more to life than just pain. But love, like everything else that makes life worth living, requires the right material circumstances, a stability nearly impossible for the lumpenproletariat. When Cass is jailed after a bungled robbery, Norah must return to prostitution, not telling him where she is. A year after his release he finally meets her by chance on the street, but she is hardened by her trade and unable to trust men. Dimly, she remembers their love but knows that returning to it is hopeless: she has contracted venereal disease, then very difficult to cure. Left by her, Cass returns to the road with Nubby O'Neill. What he had with Norah was nothing more than a dream, a momentary aberration in an empty and desperate life. In the end, he sets his sights on a tattoo, his old, attainable goal, and returns to the road, knowing that love and security are impossible for him. There is no hope for redemption for either Cass or Norah. As early as 1934 Algren knew that more tragic than death was no escape from a living nightmare; that worse yet was the spiritual death that comes before the real end.

But parts of the book were indeed vastly overwritten, especially the violent scenes. In the first sixty pages, Cass witnesses atrocity after atrocity: decapitation, severed arms, hunger, cold, savage beatings, knifings, and vile exploitation. He endures a sadistic father, a war-crazed brother, and a homicidal pimp; when he wanders the streets begging for water after being dumped for dead, he is physically thrown out of a gas station and only finally allowed to drink warm rusty water from a radiator hose. To show the violence of Cass's life, this was certainly more than enough.

The West Texas accents, rendered through Algren's urban, sophisticated ear, seem hokey and heavy-handed, almost caricature. "What good's it do fo' us to know folks or fo' folks to know we?" Cass's sister asks clumsily. "All folks us know is plum harder up 'an we." The insistence on dialect, despite his lack of intimacy with the nuances of southern speech, hindered the very realism he sought to create. And there were images so strained they were ludicrous. "After dark they met on the corner of Chihuahua St. under a lamp that looked, in the windy cold, like a bright teardrop from a nose hanging by one dark curved hair." "A woman with furred shoulders went by on high heels, her head in the air and her nose sniffing elegantly, as though about to spew green phlegm sunward."

It had also been a mistake to indulge in direct political statements. The novel was divided into four parts, three of these prefaced with quotations from the Communist Manifesto. "The red day will come for your kind, be assured," Nelson warned, hopelessly dating the narrative. Though he had enough literary instinct to want to transcend the politics of his audience, he had too much anger to accomplish this. "In the latter portions of the novel he sometimes indulges in direct invectives which seem merely hortatory and add little to the texture of the narrative," Jack Conroy had to admit in *New Masses*.

But more central to the book's problems was the character of Cass McKay himself. At times Cass seems a strange blend of dimwit and sophisticate. Cass has the ability to question life—"Could no one else know . . . what went on in *his* head? . . . Was there no way to learn how someone else felt?"—and wonders why all poor people do is eat, fight, and die: he feels there should be something more in being a man. At the same time, he is uneducated and naive, the lowest common social denominator, and this diminishes his vitality. He is a victim as much of his personality as of society. He would be a failure in almost any class; his plight is simply illustrated more vividly in his own. Ignorant, ugly, he has no dream except to be tattooed, no goal except a place to lie down; it takes years of being bullied before he acquires the courage to become a stickup man. His ambitions have been atrophied by constant deprivation and humiliation, but his lack of aspiration renders him a social type who can evoke only limited sympathy. Future Algren heroes Bruno Bicek and Frankie Machine at least have dreams on which to hang a tragedy.

Somebody in Boots finally appeared on March 27, 1935. In later years Algren would imply that it had not received good reviews: it did, but they were not the rave notices he wanted, and it was not reviewed nationwide. The conservative *Chicago Tribune* naturally found it full of "social criticism so violent it loses its force," but most critics treated it seriously and found it the work of a talented writer. In *New Masses,* Jack Conroy called it "a violent and brutal book . . . mirroring an aspect of American existence that few writers have dealt with, and doing this in a passionate and convincing way," finding its flaws minor ones in a "moving and tremendous canvas, brilliantly and solidly executed." The New York *Sun* called it a "powerful and disturbing book," noting that the homeless "have figured before in contemporary fiction but seldom with such terrible vividness." H. W. Boynton of *The New York Times,* in the most influential review, negated Algren's thesis by saying the characters "cannot be accepted as fair representatives of those innumerable thousands to whom the book is inscribed," but also saw "a creative impulse which declines to be subdued to the uses of mere realism and propaganda," using "brilliant pictures of prison and sweatshop and dive" and passages "to haunt the memory like music."

But the mixed reviews and lack of attention were not the shock, outrage, and recognition from the bourgeois press that Algren had expected. He knew his material was horrific, appalling; but he saw now that the presentation was faulty. He had not lived up to the subject. He had not made an impact, not helped the homeless, not even helped himself. The reviewer Boynton noted perceptively that the book had the "bitterness not of revolutionary fervor, but of disillusioned youth," and the book's reception was yet another step in this process of disillusionment.

The failure of the book he hoped would launch his career, after four solid years of unemployment, was an enormous blow. Most great writers had proven themselves by age thirty, he believed, while he had not: he knew he had talent, but he had blown his chance to prove it. "If I can write I can earn my own living," he'd testified in Texas, but the novel's sales were so sluggish as to be almost non-existent—after a full year, it had sold only 762 copies. Writing would not earn him a living—and what else was there? He did not need to imagine the worst that could happen without money: he had already lived it and relived it in his writing. And now, if the future held nothing but the same rootless existence he had known, he began to pay the price for sticking himself, as Meridel Le Sueur described it, "like a thermometer into that burning hell" of the lower depths. It was a high price. The Depression's long-term unemployment had of course resulted in psychological distress among the population at large, but Algren's experiences had been excessively violent and traumatic, especially for an educated, self-conscious person with professional aspirations. Because of his exalted expectations, his deep disappointment, and his intense, highly sensitive nature, he became deeply depressed; then he attempted suicide.

He was still staying with his girlfriend, but the relationship did not seem to be providing him with much security. Despite friendship and intimacy, the affair seems hardly to have been primarily important in their lives; while he was working on the novel, she was apparently still involved in another relationship. She knew him only as Nelson Algren and had no idea of his real name or his Jewish origins. But she had provided meaningful support for his work, and he may have seen her as the only force that could keep him from being once more adrift. He had no home—and he did not want to be lost again. His needs were now more significant than just a typewriter and a place to write. But the relationship was breaking up. It was not just one more rejection but more proof of the lifelong Algren theme that love, the only possible redemption, was generally unsuccessful.

Sometimes his girlfriend went out at night, and one night he waited up for her, alone in the apartment. He had read Daniel Fuchs's *Summer in Williamsburg,* published by Vanguard in 1934. Farrell thought Fuchs more talented than Algren. . . . But in this book an old man named Mr. Sussman had taken a basketball and cut off half to form a mask. Then he fitted the stovepipe to it and gassed himself to death. Gas, widely available, was a common method of suicide attempts in those years. Even if Algren was aware that it was a slow, often unsuccessful means, or that the hour he had chosen carried the risk of discovery, he was so wounded and disturbed that he began breathing from the gas line in the apartment.

When his friend came in he was barely conscious, lying on the floor with the gas pipe in his mouth. She brought him around and he was able to speak: he wasn't going to a hospital and he didn't want anyone over. But he finally said he'd talk to Larry Lipton.

"Put him in a cab," Lipton said when she called him. "I'll pay."

So Algren spent the rest of the night restlessly pacing the floor and talking to Larry, who had liked his book a great deal. He told

Lipton that he had been a fool to write a book that not only was getting bad reviews but was not even being dignified with reviews in the places where he'd like to see them. He had written himself out for that book, had even suffered jail for it, and he had nothing to show. He'd received no recognition and he was broke. He even owed the publisher money: the sales had not recouped the advance and did not look likely to. He had nothing to show for more than a year and a half of solid work, and it was all his fault. His love life had gone sour, and he had no place to go. He was always alone. "He was broke and dispirited, despondent and self-hating," Lipton recalled.

Lipton had lost a girlfriend to suicide, and he did not take all this lightly. He devoted himself to Nelson's care. He was familiar with psychoanalysis and had read extensively on it, and as best he could tried to apply what he knew. So Nelson settled in at the Rush Street house. He felt sociable enough to attend the Wednesday-night gatherings, but his depression remained. He had to be watched constantly, and Lipton feared he might harm himself at any moment. He knew he had to find Nelson's parents.

"I don't have any parents," Algren said.

So completely had he separated his two lives that even Lipton, the son of a German-Jewish mechanic, had never known his real name was Abraham. In his soul, as a writer, his name was Algren, and neither his lover nor his friends at the John Reed Club—except Abe Aaron, who had left Chicago—knew him by any other name. Lipton was later unable to recall the complicated trail he followed tracking down the Abrahams, but when he found them he saw, disappointedly, that they wouldn't be able to help him at all. They would never be able to understand. Lipton remembered, "They said, 'It just shows that when a boy goes on the road all by himself too early in life, doesn't listen to his parents . . .' [and] all the rest of this nice middle-class bit . . . I had to listen to this, all this crap. . . . I thought to myself, No wonder he didn't want me to know." So Nelson stayed on at 737 Rush Street.

Algren had been named a delegate to the First American Writers' Congress, sponsored by the League of American Writers and held in New York beginning April 26. He was also scheduled to speak on proletarian fiction. A change of scene, the community of writers— the trip might do him good, and most of his John Reed Club friends were also going. Some, like Richard Wright, knew his state of mind and were looking out for him. He was in New York for about two weeks, though how he got there and where he stayed is not clear. It's obvious, however, that he was in no condition to appreciate the congress he had once eagerly anticipated.

Held in New York's Mecca Temple, the Congress attracted four thousand spectators and 216 writers and critics including Theodore Dreiser, John Dos Passos, Kenneth Burke, Malcolm Cowley, Langston Hughes, and Louis Aragon. Three days of speeches and panel discussions were led off by Communist leader Earl Browder's reassuring assertion that the Party was more interested in fostering good writers than in making writers into bad strike organizers.

Nelson Algren was a new name to be bandied about in discussions of the proletarian novel. Meridel Le Sueur, speaking of the literary scene in the Midwest, included Nelson's work alongside that of Conroy and Farrell. In a speech on the short story, defending art against political tyranny and propaganda, Farrell himself praised Algren's "So Help Me" as "assessing the costs of capitalist society, bringing before our eyes some of the lineaments, as it were, of contemporary American life, and recreating a sense of the meaning of life, the feel, the atmosphere of it amongst the lower strata of our dollar casualties." But "So Help Me," to judge from the handwritten drafts that survive, was probably authored in a frenzied burst of creativity, while *Somebody in Boots,* the cause of Nelson's anguish, had been hard, hard work, and a failure. A fresh wave of depression came over him, which his election to the National Council of the newly formed League of American Writers did little to dissipate.

At the May Day parade Conroy noticed that Nelson, hypersensitive to criticism, was unusually grim to a friend who found his stories gloomy and pessimistic. The following day, Conroy, Le Sueur, Algren, and Mike Gold spoke at a New School forum on proletarian fiction. "It was the first time any of us had spoken in New York or for the great intellectual machinery of the *New Masses,* for which we had great respect," Meridel recalled. "We were naturally timid." The audience of radical Jewish garment workers looked sophisticated and aggressive. "The three of us were sitting there, tortured." Nelson looked pale, fragile, and really so ill that when Mike Gold called upon him to speak first, Meridel wondered how he'd even be able to stand. Legs shaking, he managed it, but Meridel had to run up and assist him. Mike Gold came to the other side, held him, and prompted Nelson with questions about his writing, how he came to write about the underdog—and Nelson mumbled something at first inaudible, then inarticulate. "Nelson was always shy, diffident, modest in outward expression," Sam Ross said. "He just stood there silent for several minutes. It was almost embarrassing. . . . Then he talked about how his book had failed—haltingly, quietly"—as if he were pleading with the audience to buy it.

In the days that followed, friends from Chicago realized he was becoming increasingly disturbed. They were worried he might try suicide again, and some remember walking around and around the city blocks trying to calm him. "Frankly, he was in terrible shape," Farrell wrote later, "and his friends appealed to me." Farrell was one of the first writers to stay at the fledgling artists' colony Yaddo and was friendly with the director, for whom his wife, Dorothy, worked as an assistant. Both Algren and his comrades thought the country would be a salvation for him, and, by telegram, Farrell arranged for Algren to rest at Yaddo for a couple of weeks, securing money from Vanguard to pay for his meals. In his diary entry for May 5 Farrell wrote that Algren was "almost insane" but that he had managed for him to visit Yaddo, "if he will go." Though now apparently unsure about it, Nelson agreed to go; and the next day Farrell walked around with him for hours until his train left, "never stopping talking to keep him from doing anything berserk."

Dorothy Farrell and the writer Nathan Asch picked him up at the Saratoga station, and then they headed out to Yaddo. A long driveway through the grounds and an imposing mansion met them: and it must have seemed incredibly decadent. The giant spruce trees and meadows, the rose garden and sundial—the colony was the epitome of tranquillity, built on the grounds of a large, luxuriant estate, a huge symbol of the capitalist wealth Nelson loathed. It was a strange, schizophrenic transition from the revolutionary atmosphere of the Writers' Congress to the moneyed, untroubled elegance of Yaddo. He didn't feel like talking to novelists Josephine Herbst and Evelyn Scott, or to Thornton Wilder's sister Charlotte, who were also staying at the farmhouse. Dorothy he liked a great deal, but even as she showed him to his room he knew he didn't belong there, and told her as much. She begged him to stay. "Nelson wasn't doing anything," Dorothy recalled. "He was just alive. He didn't want to talk, and you had to pull at him to make him eat. I pulled at him." But it was impossible to relax in such an environment. In the morning he didn't come down to breakfast, and there was a note for Dorothy in his room: he had hitchhiked to Albany and caught a bus to Chicago.

What happened next is unclear, though the penniless writer seems to have redeposited himself at 737 Rush Street. The stress of the New York trip had not helped him. Lipton must have heard about his stay there and renewed his close watch. But as the weeks went on, he sensed Nelson's feelings toward him changing as the depression lingered and deepened. "His condition got worse. He more and more looked upon me as a kind of jailer rather than a healer, and I could see the resentment building up. He had not been able to make anything of his sex life, and the signs were all bad." Lipton knew Karen Horney and a number of influential psychiatrists at the University of Chicago Psychiatric Clinic and began arranging for Nelson to go there. Though Lipton never really describes Algren's behavior in detail, it is clear from his somewhat jumbled recollection that something was desperately wrong:

> I sought out the parents and I said, "you must commit . . . him," and they did, and they came and got him, they took him out there to the hospital.
> I remember it was not quite so simple as that. In fact he got rather bad one night, and I had to have him admitted to a private, small private hospital where there were bars on the windows. I vaguely remember leaving him there in a padded cell . . . and I said, "Only until I can swing this thing with the University of Chicago, which takes time."
> You see, I had been taken rather suddenly with this thing. It'd come upon me suddenly, because I didn't realize he was getting so much worse, and so he had to stay there a few days, and he wouldn't even look at me. He was terribly resentful, and then we did manage to transfer him to the University of Chicago.

In the more than fifty years that have passed, the records of Nelson's hospital stay have been lost or destroyed, but Lipton's account suggests that his treatment probably consisted of some form of psychoanalysis, a practice which he later, perhaps revealingly, completely scorned. Certainly it's impossible to imagine him exposing ̴self to a psychiatrist—for he was not at all self-analytical and ̴rote about people vastly different from himself, touching ̴ast only much later, when it became nostalgic. Un- ̴hed the hospital—as Lipton observed—and one can imagine the frustration he must have felt at finding himself, once again, incarcerated. Only this time the jail was far different from the one in Alpine. Here, learning the ropes required understanding something that was not economic in nature—something sinister, unfamiliar. His rebellious survival instinct reasserted itself. Apparently he was not in the hospital long—friends remembered it as a short period of time. However he felt, he acted well enough or cooperated with his doctors to the point that he was allowed to leave. Though he may have been there for a number of weeks, it was probably a short stay: Gerson and Goldie were broke; and Bernice and Morris Joffe were paying the bills.

And so he was free again, to face his defeated father and the overbearing, increasingly distraught Goldie, waiting to be dispossessed. Whoever his petite, dark-haired girlfriend was, she may have brought him home, for Nelson later said that when she came with him to the house, the shrill, hysterical Goldie, looking for a scapegoat and incapable of comprehending what was happening to her son or even to her world, shrieked at her words like "Whore! Get out, get out of here, you filthy whore!" while the utterly exhausted Nelson listened to her raving, knowing he would have to leave again soon.

But he had decided to survive, and to do so everything connected with the breakdown would have to be covered up. "What I tried to do," he told Sam Ross not long after, "I don't want it known." The love affair, ending anyway, was now cut off, and none of his friends, in later years, would ever remember the name of the girl. References to the book would be shunted aside as if it had been a big mistake, a faux pas rarely mentioned unless necessary. "That old book?" he'd say, and in time it would be almost forgotten, out of print and hard to obtain; later he charitably called it "an uneven novel written by an uneven writer in the most uneven of times"—though it is much, much better than that. The loss of his parents' house would be mentioned only in the most cursory, passing remark; and after this time, except officially, Nelson Abraham virtually ceased to exist. The Jewish son who couldn't earn a living and had written a book that failed was almost completely buried. After a difficult beginning, Nelson Algren had come into being: a strong, confident writer who worked to achieve success and avoid literary failure as if his life depended on it. In a sense it did.

*

He had not fully recovered when the John Reed Club, under Wright's direction, held a publication party for *Somebody in Boots*. To entertain the forty or so guests in the club's bare second-floor hall, there was probably a speech extolling workers' literature, and then people could buy copies of *Somebody in Boots* and have them autographed by the author. Algren himself was distant, laconic. He stood against a wall, apart from his friends, quiet and sad and lost-looking. In his distraction he left behind a copy of his book, which a young woman named Amanda Kontowicz, who had seen the forlorn, detached look in his eyes, found as she and her boyfriend, a young poet, were leaving. Picking it up, she decided to call him about it later in the week.

When Nelson came by for the book, the poet was out of town, and he and the petite, dark, sensual Amanda were immediately attracted to each other. She was soothing, quiet, nonjudgmental; they talked about books. She was sensitive to his loneliness because most of her own life had been spent alone. Her widowed mother had always worked, her brother had had his own friends, and she had spent much of her childhood in Milwaukee inside the house, reading. After her mother remarried a difficult man, Amanda finished high school and then moved on her own to a small furnished room. At the time she met Nelson, she was twenty-two and eager to leave her boyfriend.

Amanda's quiet ways made her seem mysterious, and her madonna-like serenity had already captured the imaginations of some of Nelson's friends who had seen her at salons like Larry Lipton's. Her desirability and the triumph of wooing her away from another man undoubtedly helped Nelson's shattered ego, but he was also drawn by her appreciation of literature and her Polish background, so similar to those of the North Side people he'd described in his college stories. She in turn was drawn to his lost look. It was a shy courtship, with long walks and handholding on double-decker buses. Amanda couldn't have men up to her room, but sometimes they stayed out all night to watch the sun come up over the rocks of Lake Michigan. It was not a lustful, tempestuous affair. They looked to each other for comfort, and soon her boyfriend was gone.

She was gentle; she accepted him; he told her about the hospital, carefully downplaying the suicide attempt. He had taken a bunch of pills, he said, because all he wanted to do was sleep: he had been tired and had wanted to sleep. He never spoke of his feelings toward his work; and his efforts at emotional intimacy were guarded. After Nelson and Amanda had seen each other a few times, he asked her if she knew he was Jewish. He *assumed* this would make a difference, though to Amanda it made none whatsoever. In those moments he was Nelson Abraham again; it was as if he had internalized all the dreadful anti-Semitism he'd heard on the road. "Somehow his Jewish origin bothered him," Larry Lipton recalled. "He resented the fact that I had gotten in touch with his parents, and that I knew who they were. I know he resented it because he said so. He didn't want it known." He had a public image now, of a writer—and being Jewish didn't fit into it.

At other times he was happily arrogant and self-assured. He rushed to Amanda's and gave her the breathless news that he'd been in a big street demonstration, followed by mass arrests. Proudly, he boasted that they'd rounded him up along with the others, but once downtown he'd talked his way out, claiming he hadn't been there to protest—he was a writer, preparing a piece on the demonstration. The fact that he'd published a novel convinced them, and he walked.

And where was he that summer when not with Amanda? On June 26 there was a telegram from Harry Hansen of the New York *World-Telegram:* Would he grant permission to reprint "The Brothers' House" in the O. Henry Prize Story volume for 1935? Absolutely, of course. It was an old story he'd always thought too sentimental, but maybe there was hope for his career in spite of the novel. *The Daily Worker* reported that he and Conroy were heading a contingent south to bring radical magazines into counties that banned them, but at the last minute he told Conroy he wasn't going. He may have spent time on the Indiana dunes; and he also probably wandered around Chicago, still drawn to the cheap furnished rooms above South State, for he wrote a few sketches of Chicago life there.

But none was more than two pages. "A Lumpen," about a down-and-outer selling political newspapers, oblivious to their content, appeared in a special short-story section of *New Masses* on July 2, along with Alan Calmer's comment: "Nelson Algren . . . is equipped with a sensibility that is unique in American literature, and it freshens the material he touches." "Dear Alan Calmer," Algren wrote in a fragment now at Ohio State University, "Just read your essay on the proletarian short story and I was left amazed at it—" Amazed at Calmer's praise, or at the essay? For on July 17, a review of *Some-*

body in Boots in *The New Republic* said flat out what he was perhaps already thinking: "that it would make a fair book only if its author had thrown it out and used what he has apparently learned to write another." Surrounded alternately by damnation and praise, the two-page sketches seem all he had the heart for. "Within the City," which Jack Conroy took for the October–November issue of *The Anvil,* was a simple description, red with revolutionary fever, of a quiet mulatto girl from a dime burlesque on South State Street; and there is a photograph of Algren, taken that August, with a mulatto woman by the beach—she is gay and laughing, he has downcast eyes and a small smile. "An American Obituary," which appeared in the October 1935 *Partisan Review* alongside Gide, Malraux, Le Sueur, and Ehrenbourg, gives some idea of what he was feeling that summer:

> The highways of America are white with summer now, and through the dust go the homeless. Till one thinks of America as a long dust road leading to nowhere. The road curves by the wharves of New Orleans, where merchant ships wait high in dry-dock; past the freight yards in Council Bluffs, where the box-cars rot on the sidings. This is America, the vast heart of her, with grey boy-faces pressed to the cold blue bars.
>
> On Madison street in Chicago the boys stand on corners, waiting.
>
> Down at the morgue I saw Frank Mears, address unknown, lying on his back with his eyes still wide and his belly still blue from the water. The ticket on the box said, Frank J. Mears, no address, cause unknown. This is the American thing, the unknown death in the heat of midday, and the country boy in the long ice-box.
>
> Say this is how it happened; say this is how it was.
>
> Frank Mears turned south on Dearborn Street, and no face turned to follow. He went into a tavern where music was, and he'd been drinking four straight days. He banged on a table till they threw him out, and he walked back south down Dearborn. On Harrison street he stood and swayed; a dollar bill was all he possessed, and he waved it like a flag. Two lean men saw him doing that, and when he walked on they followed. Frank Mears turned into a dime burlesque, and he watched till they threw him out.
>
> Frank Mears, no address, slugged for ninety cents.
>
> The lean one said, "Let me help you, friend," and Frank Mears leaned on his arm. The other one said, "This way, kid," and Frank Mears followed, swaying.
>
> American youth, as a boy you sat on a barrel in front of the general store in Sangamon county, watching the farm-carts coming

into town. Dust rose uneasily from betwen their wheels, and the country dogs lay in the sun. Between Hurricane Creek and the slow-winding Sangamon there was a kind of tumultuous, rough-and-tumble wildness about the Illinois prairie that all the railroads had not yet tamed. It was still a vast and sprawling country of shaggy hills and undammed creeks and half-cleared forests. In the moment before the dark came down, Frank Mears, you remembered these farm-carts coming into town. You saw the slow dust rising from between their wheels.

You didn't know, that morning when you caught a slow freight through Sangamon county, Frank Mears. When you got into Springfield you gaped at Lincoln's tomb a while, and then you got on toward Chicago.

Frank Mears, unemployed by civilization, age 22 perhaps. Perhaps 25. And whether you came from Council Bluffs, from Sangamon county or from East St. Louis, you still wouldn't have gotten drunk one day if you'd had a day's work to do.

So cover up the box. Beside the low siloes on prairie farms, below the tipples of mines long abandoned or above zinc smelters silent now in the valleys, red cedar and black tamarack wait, creeping to claim back their own. Though Sangamon county has been laced with long steel rails the prairie still plunges, like a wild horse with outstruck hooves, across the planned ties and over the planned Sears Roebuck fences, past the low siloes, through the Indian corn, across the fields and the farms and the mines and the factories between Hurricane Creek and the slow Sangamon. America is a long dust-road. And Frank Mears sways in the sun.

Though his novel appeared that September of 1935 to more receptive reviews in Britain, it was hard to get started again as a writer. Except for a review of Conroy's new book, an article about the Federal Writers' Project in an obscure art magazine, and caustic, disparaging appraisals of Farrell's *Collected Stories* and *Judgment Day,* he published no creative work until 1939.

7.

The Literary Left

NELSON AND AMANDA moved in together. She found a shabby but genteel one-room basement apartment in a brownstone on the Near North Side for six dollars a week, with linens and housecleaning. Neither of them had jobs. For a few months they lived off a hundred dollars of Amanda's; with the banks short on cash, she could withdraw only twenty-five dollars a month. For food Nelson rose at five-thirty to follow the milk wagons, proudly returning home with stolen milk and tomato juice. Occasionally he went to see his parents, now living on relief in a small basement apartment, and came back with a salami or other food. Or Amanda's mother would say she had too many potatoes and onions—and for days on end they'd have potato and onion soup.

But the refined basement wasn't Algren's style, and when Amanda blew her last money on a fifteen-dollar pair of suede oxfords, Nelson, flabbergasted, decided the rent was too high and found them a place in a rooming house where the common bathroom was down the hall. It was respectable, but roach-infested. And after Conroy's protégé Howard Rushmore and his girlfriend visited for a few days and used their bed, Nelson and Amanda were attacked by bedbugs, and moved again.

Their next home, also on the Near North Side, was only five dollars a week and closer to the impoverished life Algren wanted to see. A tiny room on the third floor of a skinny building, it had a chair, a bed, and a closet with a gas burner for cooking. There was barely enough room to walk, and the only saving grace was a window overlooking the street. The landlady's idea of clean sheets, included in the rent, was only one—a used sheet stayed on the bed. The room next door housed a hopeless alcoholic who almost burned himself to death in his vomit-and-cigarette-littered squalor, and the two men on the other side were also strange—they washed long gloves in the bathroom and then stretched them to dry on hand forms, which they carried, bobbing, back down the hall to display in the window. Dressed in kimonos, they smoked cigarettes on long, flamboyant holders and leaned out the front window, soliciting.

Though Nelson usually tried to avoid Morris, he introduced Amanda to the Joffes over dinner, paving the way to off-season escapes to Bernice's cabin on the Indiana dunes. Sometimes they went up for a week at a time, hitchhiking to save money, and Nelson would complain about Joffe along the way. As an artist, Nelson felt he had much more to offer the world than his well-off, culturally deficient brother-in-law; his dislike of Joffe was so intense that Amanda found it somehow anti-Semitic. But the dunes on Lake Michigan's shore were worth having to deal with Joffe. Nelson loved it there. The vast lake, the sky: he never minded the rustic cabin, the beetles, and the outdoor privy. It was a break from the stress of Chicago.

For Nelson and Amanda lived in poverty. She did occasional housecleaning, and he found part-time work at an exclusive men's health club, where he hosed down naked businessmen after they worked out, strongly suspecting that the elite, all-gentile club had hired him because he was Jewish. It must not have paid enough to live on, for by November 1935, Algren wrote later, he "accepted a job with a small local freight house" and "felt obliged to abandon literature." He seemed to feel he had no alternative, but he was probably also practicing a withholding of self after rejection that he would repeat again and again.

It was not long before his exalted ambitions returned. Within two or three months, by his own account, an urge to observe and take notes about Chicago life reasserted itself. When the urge became a compulsion, he returned to creating street-corner dialogues and clipping newspaper stories about the unfortunate. By the summer of 1936, he began writing and made plans for a tetralogy of novels, hoping to complete one volume of about 90,000 words every year for four years. "Volume One was to deal with the Poles of the Triangle [on the Northwest Side]," he wrote later in a grant application, "Volume Two with the Italian areas centering around Taylor and Halstead Streets, Volume Three with the Negro Belt between 47th and 35th Streets, and a final volume with the Mexican sections of East Chicago and Gary, Indiana."

His literary connections were somewhat at a standstill. The John

Reed Clubs were gone. Though many of his friends went to Lipton's, he avoided Larry. Along with Dick Wright, Erskine Caldwell, Jack Balch, and Alfred Hayes, he was listed as an associate editor of *Partisan Review and Anvil,* a short-lived, ill-advised merger of the two magazines; it was, however, an honorary position, as Philip Rahv and William Phillips did most of the work in New York. He probably attended the Middle West Writers' Congress in June, but it was Dick Wright, whom he accompanied to a speaking engagement in Urbana, whose friendship was important. Since November, Wright had been working for the Illinois Writers' Project, a branch of Roosevelt's newly formed Work Projects Administration, at an enviable, well-paying job that left enough time to write. Other writers Algren knew were already working for the WPA, and since the only requirement was a minimum of publications, he knew he was eligible.

Probably at Wright's suggestion, he tried some of the local project's directors, but he was unable to stir enough interest to get an interview. Having either lost or resigned his trucking job, he tried speeding up his appointment by registering on the relief rolls. This too failed. In June he wrote to Orrick Johns, the playwright and director of the New York Writers' Project, whom he had probably met at the Congress, and asked for help. Johns contacted the assistant director of the Federal Writers' Project in Washington, and finally, around September 1936, Algren was hired at a salary of about $84 a month.

"Had it not been for [the Writers' Project] the suicide rate would have been much higher. It gave new life to people who had thought their lives were over," Algren said thirty years later; and he connected the idea of suicide with the projects on several occasions as if he could not possibly have been talking about himself. "It served to humanize people who . . . had . . . lost their self-respect by being out of work and then living by themselves began to feel the world was against them. To such people the WPA provided a place where they began to communicate with people again. They got a little self-respect back."

For the first time, the federal government supported art with an open wallet. The Writers' Project was only a small part of Roosevelt's efforts to employ people and stimulate the economy. There were mural projects, theater projects, writers' projects, and more, organized on a state-by-state basis. The Federal Writers' Project claimed an astonishing number of writers who went on to successful careers; and the Illinois Project to which Algren came was surpassed in talent perhaps only by the New York Project. Arna Bontemps, Saul Bellow, Gwendolyn Brooks, Frank Yerby, Margaret Walker, Richard Wright, Sam Ross, Stuart Engstrand, George Murray, and George Victor Martin were some of the writers he met in the downtown offices; Louis "Studs" Terkel often wandered in from the radio project in the same building.

The Project's main goal was the creation of high-quality state and local guidebooks containing essays on the art, literature, history, commerce, and folk backgrounds of the regions, and by his own account three years later Algren was first employed as a field worker. As sources for the guides, large numbers of interviews, neighborhood and immigrant studies, and case and life histories were gathered by field workers such as Algren. Folklorist Benjamin Botkin noted that the Federal Writers' Project "trained writers to record what they heard as well as what they saw with an ear for the characteristic phrase and rhythm of the vernacular." This was very close to Algren's own work, and in fact sociological observation was undoubtedly encouraged on the Illinois Project by its first director, sociologist Louis Wirth, who helped Wright and also recommended Algren for a Guggenheim grant. Thus, Algren noted that his job offered him an opportunity, though limited, to work on the tetralogy. He described his work as sporadic but said he managed to write some 160 pages during his first year on the Project.

Though he would never have admitted it later, he was surely thankful for his job, and the effects of decent work and a salary were immediate. Before long he and Amanda moved out of the tawdry rooming house with its gay prostitutes. Their new home, at 35th Street and Cottage Grove Avenue on Chicago's South Side, was one of a number of storefronts in an arcade built for the 1893 World's Columbian Exposition. Off the main thoroughfare, the storefronts faced each other across an alley and were rented out as "apartments" to artists who enjoyed the huge front windows and mewslike setting. "Rat Alley," as Algren and Conroy would name it after its unpaying inhabitants, was a kind of artists' colony. Nelson and Amanda's neighbors included the artist Gilbert Rocke from the John Reed Club, the composer Ernest Brooks, and a sculptor who made a living turning out busts of Abraham Lincoln. Around the corner a huge

Louis Sullivan house, run as a cooperative, was home to a collective of actors, painters, literati, mavericks, and radicals, many of whom worked for the WPA. Richard Wright was also living on the South Side, but not among the white bohemians.

Nelson would have been content to continue living with Amanda, but he also liked her Polish Catholic mother, and Amanda wanted to make the relationship legal. They had an apartment and financial security and were happy together, so there seemed no reason not to marry. In March 1937, Algren took a half-day off and they went to City Hall for a small civil ceremony. But there was no celebration afterward. Instead, Amanda went over to her mother's and later saw an old girlfriend who lived nearby. As she and her friend sat talking, Amanda said simply that she had been married that morning. Nelson had already gone back to work.

Marriage meant more to Amanda than to Algren, but there was no question that he cared a great deal for her. Like him, she was low-key and quiet. He took pleasure in the way she talked in stories, and they were both avid readers, exchanging books and articles and discussing what they had read. They enjoyed each other. And for Nelson, there was something compelling about having a family— never to be alone again, never to be lost—he loved that idea. In a macho way he was proud of being married: he wanted Amanda to use the name Algren, which she didn't, and he wanted to have a baby. Amanda, who wanted a more traditional life and encouraged Algren to buy nice new clothes from expensive department stores, did not want to raise a child in poverty, and she wanted to be able to stay home with her baby. But for Nelson that would lead straight to bourgeois convention—and if he had to provide for others, he could not devote himself to literature. In those years, when Algren was caught between his desire for a personal life and his artistic ambitions, there was never any doubt which won out. He did not want to support anybody. In fact, he wanted to split all the expenses and keep the upper hand: he paid the rent and she paid for food, so he would feel that the apartment was more *his* place.

Shortly after their wedding, they went to a Communist-sponsored St. Patrick's Day party, where he met Frank Sandiford, a thief and future novelist whose brother would die fighting for Republican Spain. When Sandiford told Nelson how impressed he had been with *Somebody in Boots,* Nelson began pumping him for information about incarceration, violence, stealing, and racketeering, in the process cultivating a friendship with the articulate burglar. Sandiford, who later did time with the celebrated genius-murderer Nathan Leopold, had known Roger Touhey, an outlaw criminal framed for kidnapping by Chicago mobsters. Thieves saw Touhey as a lone hero, but they regarded a man like Capone as a capitalist exploiter. Thus, Algren enriched his knowledge of youthful offenders, burglary, and the penitentiary system.

He continued to be close to Dick Wright, and the two of them urged Abe Aaron to come back to Illinois and get put on the WPA. One friend remembered that Algren seemed especially good and kindly with Wright, who was talented, confused, and sometimes fearful of people. Wright came to Cottage Grove occasionally, once bringing along the young black poet Margaret Walker, with whom Algren continued to be friends after Wright left for New York in the spring of 1937. She was working on a poem called "For My People," and with Wright, her usual critic, gone, she took the unfinished poem to Algren. He helped her resolve it, and after their conversation she went home to write the last stanza in the title poem of a group that later won the Yale Younger Poets Award.

Algren continued to be active in the League of American Writers. In June 1937 he attended the Second American Writers' Congress in New York with Conroy and Lawrence "Bud" Fallon, an aspiring writer from East St. Louis. The civil war in Spain caught his attention, and with it came greater warmth toward the Party, though, to Algren's and Conroy's displeasure, Popular Front rhetoric was now in ascendance. Scenes from *The Spanish Earth,* a film whose script was written by Lillian Hellman, Archibald MacLeish, and Ernest Hemingway, was shown, and Hemingway himself spoke on the writer's responsibility to oppose war and Fascism. Algren again saw Dick Wright, who, having reconciled himself to the New York Party as he had been unable to do with the Chicago faction, was once again zealously working for Communism. After a visit to a Harlem nightclub and an evening in Greenwich Village, the charged atmosphere of New York, the Congress, and the proximity of CP faithfuls seem to have inspired Algren to political work.

He had no doubt that the Communist Party was right in its position on Spain, as it had been right in its position on the invasion of Ethiopia. "Spain . . . was a war in which a demand for recognition of human dignity was being pitted against an entrenched sense of property," he said later. He admired revolutionaries who had laid down their lives against Fascism, but though he said he was asked and that it was assumed that he would go to Spain, he didn't want to be killed. And he knew that his political contribution, despite its fervency, was actually quite small: "I don't think I've ever been either militant or profound as an anti-Fascist."

If there was any time at which he might have joined the Communist Party, this was it. His self-esteem and sense of belonging had been bolstered by his job; he believed in the Party's work and was undoubtedly anxious to connect his name with those of Van Wyck Brooks, Erskine Caldwell, Malcolm Cowley, Paul de Kruif, Langston Hughes, Meridel Le Sueur, and Upton Sinclair, all of whom served as vice-presidents of the League of American Writers. Within six months, Algren was secretary of the Chicago chapter of the League. Certainly Party membership would have been preferred for this post, and at one point Abe Aaron could have sworn Nelson was a member, but then couldn't be sure. One friend believes he definitely was, and Algren wrote to Howard Rushmore about his involvement in the Party in language plain enough to have convinced the FBI that he was a Communist—though that, of course, didn't take much. Whatever his official status, Algren worked actively and openly for the Communist movement, and he definitely considered himself a Communist, indicating as much in letters to Dick Wright. Whether he actually signed a card is of secondary importance to that belief.

An important source for his work in the League was the Writers' Project, where many young people were sympathetic to Communism. Algren recruited for the League among them, but their radicalism was factionalized. Stalinists, who followed the Party line, and Trotskyists, who didn't, sometimes wouldn't talk to each other. The Stalinists read only Party-approved books, were hard-line and critical. On the other side were the more intellectual types like Saul Bellow; they read books off the approved list. Though years later he would mock himself for his unabashed adherence to the Party line, Algren sided with the Stalinists, was enthralled by Baudelaire, but was vehement in his distaste for "decadent" writers such as T. S. Eliot.

Algren was also active in the Project's union, which, receiving support from the LAW, sought to improve working conditions for creative writers and lobby Congress for WPA funding. "We move in a world of petitions, pleas, bulletins, protests, indignation meetings and partisan sharpshooting," he wrote to a friend. Management made the union's life difficult by forbidding bulletin board space on the grounds that posted material might offend those who didn't choose to have a union. There were protests and nondisruptive demands made in the office, and one Project member recalled that a strike was planned over hours and work pressure, but the Stalinists and Trotskyists could not agree on strategy.

Despite tensions with the new director, John T. Fredericks, that probably stemmed from his political stance, Algren did well at his job and in September 1937 was appointed supervisor. But he rebelled against his promotion because it meant being in the office as often as five days a week. In later years, Algren, noting that Fredericks used to fire him regularly, liked to give the impression that he was irresponsible, but most likely he was just trying to save his time for writing.

Ultimately, however, he felt obliged to accept the position, perhaps grateful that a program like the WPA existed to keep artists from living in poverty and despair. Algren was well aware that throughout history the makers of literature had been primarily well-heeled men—those free from the degradation of economic fear. Though France, Germany, Scandinavia, and the Soviet Union had programs supportive of artists, he noted in the only article he published around this time, until the WPA, the American government had not taken an active role in supporting creative people. He had been especially struck by the fact that Melville had spent twenty years as a customshouse clerk without putting pen to paper: "The loss to American literature was not only immeasurable," he wrote, "it was typical." So now, though he supported the Project, he was still frustrated at the way his new job, which his superiors knew he didn't want, thwarted his plans for the tetralogy, which he quite consciously, and perhaps petulantly, put aside.

His new job involved more writing and editing. Algren was largely responsible for the high-quality guide to Galena, a historic mining town a few hours from Chicago. The chapters on Galena's history, written by Algren, were peopled with renegades and hustlers, and he brought energy to historical writing. In an unpublished piece he told the story of a Polish-Jewish financial wizard who made possible the cash flow necessary to wage the Revolutionary War, in a narrative approaching fiction in tone and detail. He tried to get a feeling for a time period, rather than rely on standard texts. In an unused section for the Illinois guidebook called "Commerce in Illinois," his sources included Chamber of Commerce material, folksongs, ballads, Carl Sandburg's poems, and International Publishers' *Proletarian Literature in the United States,* though to be acceptable to Uncle Sam, writing from the Project had to be as free from political bias as possible.

He found he could use the job to advantage. Since the failure of *Partisan Review and Anvil,* talk had been going around Chicago of a literary magazine, and Algren wrote to Conroy suggesting they revive *The Anvil* as the *The New Anvil,* either as the League organ or as an enterprise supported by the League. Conroy, who had been fired from the Missouri Project for participating in a strike against an ineffective management, welcomed the idea, especially when it looked as if Algren might be able to swing him a job on the Illinois Project. So, on a raw March day in 1938, armed with little more than a bus ticket, Conroy, leaving his family in Missouri, arrived to live with Nelson and Amanda for six to eight months. Treating him royally, Nelson offered Conroy the bedroom. He and Amanda slept on two different couches in the living room, marking the beginning of the end of their marriage.

It was a time when many people who had long been nursing their private traumas felt solvent and whole again, for the WPA was now providing employment in many sectors. Steady income brought an unabashed desire for celebration. Among liberal cultural circles in Chicago, the Spanish Civil War, now at its height, gained ready support from people still reeling from the Depression. Into this atmosphere *The New Anvil* was launched.

With no money forthcoming from the League, Conroy and Algren realized they'd have to fund the venture themselves, a difficult task, as Conroy was broke and Algren, hardly a saver, never had any cash on hand. They quickly planned a series of fund-raisers for *The New Anvil,* staging "The Drunkard's Warning," a tear-jerking melodrama about one James T. Barrelhouse, who, reminiscent of James T. Farrell, was "a minor trilogist" whose alcoholism caused domestic strain with his wife, Phyllis, and small daughter. Presented in several Chicago locations, the play was a success in terms of entertainment, if not in actual receipts. Conroy recalled the show nostalgically: "Algren grew impatient of the temperamental antics of the actress cast as Phyllis and took over the role. The long gray wig he had borrowed from the Chicago Repertory Company gave him a woebegone air of injured innocence that was both pathetic and appealing." Conroy played Frittertitter, a temperance crank with an unrequited love for Phyllis, and the play was produced music-hall style: drinks were served, and enthusiastic audiences cheerfully threw beer-bottle tops at the actors.

At one performance following a nearby event to aid Republican Spain, the atmosphere became rowdier than usual. The show was being staged in the loft apartment of Jack's friend Theodora Pikowski from the Writers' Project, and Nelson and Jack were quite drunk. As Conroy remembered it, someone in the hall stairway fired a shot Chaos ensued. At the landlord's urging, cops came through and arrested Theodora, Jack, and Nelson. They spent the night in jail, and as Conroy recalled, Nelson loved this stint, which amounted to little more than being thrown in the drunk tank. Theodora, released in the morning, convinced Jack Scher, a lawyer from the Project, to defend the others. Before the judge, Scher stated that Conroy was a stranger to the city who had just been singing Irish songs. Both were let off with a warning.

But a few days later Algren received a letter from the head of the League of American Writers, who had heard disturbing reports of drunkenness and disorderly conduct, and urged a meeting with district leaders to discuss their behavior. "This went against me," Algren said. "My reaction to this was simply to tell him that my conduct was no concern of his. . . . I put it in a way that would offend him because . . . what kind of operation is it when somebody will write to New York and say somebody else was drunk? . . . There wasn't anybody I knew that wasn't friendly. Obviously, I was with people who had a higher obligation than the personal one; that is, the personal obligation to inform, to keep the other people thinking the same as they did, which I thought was what we were fighting the war against." Not long after, Algren and Conroy were "called onto the carpet," rebuked for bohemian ways that reflected badly on the radical movement, and told to take it easy.

Despite signing a rather reckless, hard-line, and jargon-filled statement defending the Moscow show trials and purges, Algren began more often to challenge the Party line. At a League of American Writers meeting, a friend recalled that Nelson made a fool of himself and was greatly criticized for defending Ben Reitman, the whorehouse physician, lover of Emma Goldman, and former hobo who also sometimes deviated from Party orthodoxy. The dogmatic Party seemed to have no room for individual variation, and Algren had never liked being told what to do. A coworker on *The New Anvil* remembered that the moment he was given an order he became belligerent.

Yet he remained loyal to Party work. Much of the manpower for *The New Anvil* came from local League members. Working on the magazine was a devoted group of not more than a dozen who originally contributed five dollars apiece and helped stage "The Drunkard's Warning." When those revenues weren't enough to start publishing, they planned a series of receptions featuring prominent writers.

One of the first speakers was Max Bodenheim, a twenties poet who had converted to Communism during the Depression. He was a name, a character, and a shameless drunk, and his high-spirited reading degenerated into a drunken brawl. Max smoked his pipe and chatted up everybody's girlfriend before the beer and bourbon began to hit him. By the time he was set to go on he was plastered, and Nelson and Jack had to walk him around to try to get him sober. A reception for A. B. Magil, an editor at *New Masses,* followed, and another one for Ben Appel was also more respectable. Precariously held in a rented hall without a liquor license, there were a dozen or so of these well-attended and enjoyable receptions from late 1938 to early 1940, staged "whenever we could get someone" and hosting Langston Hughes, Shaemas O'Sheel, Richard Wright, and Kenneth Fearing, whose work Nelson especially admired.

By now, Conroy had been hired at the WPA, and he and Algren were big shots on the Project. Recalled Saul Bellow: "We had little to do with each other. I rather looked up to them; they rather looked down on me." Another, more bitter Algren acquaintance recalled Algren as incredibly conceited. Others remembered the Algren-Conroy penchant for practical jokes. One Project worker had a brand-new car which was the jewel of his life: he kept it polished, locked, and parked safely, and it was his constant topic of conversation. One day he received a phone call from someone identifying himself as an official, telling him the car had just been destroyed by thugs. Everyone else knew who was behind the prank.

Though there had been some trouble about appointing Conroy to a supervisory post because of his radical politics, he was soon promoted by Curtis McDougall, who had succeeded Fredericks as director of the Project. By December 1938, a folklore project, with Algren in charge, had come into being. With an oral history emphasis, the folklore unit "investigated the lore of the packing house, auto plant, post office, and steel mill," and it seemed tailor-made for Algren and Conroy. They did fieldwork in a bar, listening to people telling tall tales. Algren claimed special interest in the industrial tall tale, in which the heroes were the biggest and best on the job. He and Conroy, whose small-town Missouri background came in handy, put together a never-published historical collection called "A Tall Chance to Work." But the origin of these tales, Conroy warned, may be somewhat in doubt: he, for one, sometimes found it easier to dash off a piece himself than to trudge all over town gathering material. Nelson's "Hank, the Free Wheeler," gives a good idea of the genre. Modeled on Henry Ford, the dead hero awakes to admonish his pallbearers: "You call this efficiency? Put the thing on wheels! Lay five of these birds off, and cut the other one's wages 'cause the work is easy and the hours ain't long and the pace is slow." Both "Hank, the Free Wheeler" and several of Conroy's stories were later anthologized in Benjamin Botkin's *Treasury of American Folk-Lore.*

They hung out in a bar named King's Palace a little too often, but the sociable and easygoing Project practically invited slacking off. The nearby Arena bowling alley, where Algren bowled with Studs Terkel, Howard Rushmore, or Chris and Neal Rowland from the co-op, provided another opportunity for socializing. Algren was popular on the Project, especially with women. "We thought he was gorgeous," said one friend, and Arna Bontemps remembered him occasionally flirting with women in the office—"dames," Algren called some of them, "who didn't know the day of the week." "Oh, yeah," Theodora Pikowski wistfully remembered almost fifty years later, "he had a feeling." But his new popularity came at a time of increasing estrangement from Amanda, who during these years worked at a variety of nine-to-five jobs which took her outside the clique of Nelson's world on the Project and in Rat Alley.

Soon after Conroy arrived, Bud Fallon and his East St. Louis Fallonites came to Chicago to meet some "serious arthurs." Fallon was a handsome young fallen Catholic with a Missouri twang and a magnetic personality. A natural wit who sometimes wrote poetry, he charmed Dorothy Farrell on one of his first trips to Chicago; she was now separated and had recently returned from New York. Though a hard drinker, he was ordinarily a jolly one, and at a party once ended up on the front lawn with twelve melted ice cream cones in his arms. He only occasionally got into a fight, and he was a natural leader. His Fallonites were a self-styled gang, rougher than the high-spirited arty types who frequented the Writers' Project. Most of Algren's friends remembered them as "working-class people" who weren't as tough as they claimed; yet some remembered Fallon, who later tried the University of Chicago and wound up a pari-mutuel clerk, as somewhat immoral.

Though Algren's friends saw them as harmless, spirited, petty thieves, the Fallonites were surrounded by unsubstantiated rumors of rape, thrived on bravado, drank too much, broke up parties, insulted their hosts. They fascinated Algren. He saw in their nihilistic risk-taking a dark side that immediately compelled him. "The Fallonites were a gold mine for him," Jack said, "because a lot of them were literary material. Most of the episodes he described were not about Chicago at all, but East St. Louis." For Algren, a door to the underworld had once again been opened.

Over the next years, Algren and Conroy would make many trips to East St. Louis, to go out drinking or to the whorehouses Algren was always eager to see. If the women there were sometimes grasping or attempted to rob him, he saw this as a result of the whole profit-making system of which they were a part. Once, in East St. Louis to give a fund-raising speech for *The New Anvil,* Algren headed off for the Valley, the local vice district where the girls came outside in their underwear in broad daylight. Conroy recalled that Algren fell in with a Negro prostitute who somehow got his *New Anvil* funds and then pulled a knife on him. Never willing to be treated as a mark, he went out and found a policeman. The cop retrieved his money, then slapped the girl around. This made Algren furious— he had his money and there was no reason to treat the girl that way. "He always believed in the legend of the golden-hearted whore," Conroy said later, somewhat oversimplifying. "He thought all whores wonderful people. It was a romantic attachment, and it was deep-seated."

Back in Chicago, his impressions of East St. Louis's Valley materialized in a large, lap-sized artist's notebook where he scribbled in a dreamlike stream of consciousness, his almost illegible handwriting spreading hugely across the pages without stopping.

And the slender brunette girl who queened it all over the place and called herself Val de Val jumped down the well of a Walton St. bawdy house, and she still looked snooty, the way she draped herself half over the bannister and half over the wall, as though disdaining to touch the uncarpeted floor . . .

. . . and Frieda the German girl who got two of her cousins and her sister into the house before it closed in 1930 . . . and the quiet little Bohemian named Mary who went to work a year or two too soon, and she wasn't built for "the life" as they call it among themselves, and she did everything everyone asked her all the time, because something had frightened her in the year she was fifteen and went to work too soon, and now she has peace and quiet at last, and no one to frighten her, or make her run an elevator for $6 a week, or make her drunken, or beat her, for she has a room of her own that she keeps clean herself and . . . she sits on the dusted chair in a freshly laundered smock and begins spitting, and she spits all day, all day, and . . . it goes dark, and the lights go on and she spits, in sleep, when the little unshaded light overhead is out at midnight . . .

WPA manuscripts reveal that he spent time interviewing Chicago prostitutes for the urban folklore project, and he also began to observe those who fought and were beaten for a living, frequenting the boxing ring at White City on 63rd Street in Chicago, often betting on the outcome. He went alone or with Conroy, then came back to his notebook and in the same breathless scrawl graphically recorded the grisly choreography of the fights. Other times he was drawn to the dance marathons, where couples sometimes danced themselves to death trying to win cash prizes and food and shelter along the way. He remembered staying at one for a couple of days; a friend recalled his total absorption as he tried to figure out which drooping, exhausted couple would next join the ranks of the losers. Going around Chicago with Conroy, he frequented places like the True American Business and Social Club and private social clubs and hangouts for gangs. He stayed out late playing "twenty-six," a common barroom gambling game.

Perhaps under Conroy's influence, he had begun sending out poems, some of which were printed in *The New Anvil*. Soon came the articulation of himself as a Chicago artist:

> I belong to this city irretrievably
> like a cross-town transfer . . .

> There is no one speaking who can speak of it as knowingly,
> [who's] been where I've been and come back whole—
> . . . I can speak for you better
> than you can for yourself,
> and better than the Negro middleweight
> who lost my bet . . . in a TKO at White City,
> or the Irishman in the death house.

This confidence in his artistic powers went along with the strongly held belief that he was a loser in a nation of winners.

> Being a loser I speak only for losers,
> Only for those who "leaped or fell" through the skylight of the Capitol building thereby imperiling pedestrians, "leaped or fell" down the well of the Monadnock Building after calling the police, "leaped or fell" from the roof of the Hotel Atlantic after sitting on a ledge twenty-five minutes apparently trying to make up her mind, "leaped or fell" from the eleventh floor of St. Luke's Hospital . . .
> Cry "He shoulda stood in bed" for the Pole in the death-house at 26th and California . . .
> Being a loser I speak only for those who leaped or fell, losers being the only ones left with something to say and no one to say it.
> All the time, day in and day out, in a city where everyone has to win every round just to stay alive.

He identified with those whose destructive elements overcame them. Frank Sandiford remembered his special interest in violent criminals: the suicide and the murderer were linked in his mind, as if he saw a tremendous similarity between the force of self-destruction and the impulse to destroy others. He seems also to have tied the idea of risk closely with that of a death wish, a willingness to approach a pervasive sense of imminent death. "This sense of imminent death reverberates through all of Algren's works," wrote the critic George Bluestone, who Algren said "cut in" closest to his work. Bluestone noted that Cass McKay was never free of a sense of imminent death, that madness and violence were already linked in his consciousness with it. Critic Blanche Gelfant would later observe that Algren's people are not defeated only by poverty or urban dispossession: "Rather it is some inexplicable, irrational destructive force loosed in the world, which drives people on to frenzied and unrelenting acts of self-destruction."

Algren had seen the impulse to blind destruction, however

masked, among the Fallonites. They stole a slot machine from a South Side whorehouse when they first came to Chicago, then learned it was owned by gangsters and thought they were lost. This robbery, which later materialized in a tightened, condensed form in *Never Come Morning,* obsessed him, and he began writing it in the form of a violent story. In one early, sixty-page version called "Barefoot with Shoes On," or "No Shoes for Novak," Algren began the tale with the boys' kidnapping a former member of the gang, now a married WPA worker, to assist them in the heist. Then follows a hellish flight down U.S. 61 to East St. Louis, during which, drinking away their fear in the '33 Chevy, they knock off so many gas stations, beating the attendants, that they can hardly count them. As the spree of violence progresses, the pecking order within the group becomes clear: it is the loveless, alone men who are violent, and the trusting married man is seen by them as weak. Completely victimized by participation in their crimes, this man represents a hope that must be destroyed. As did "So Help Me," the story ends with a weak, trusting man murdered, his head literally kicked off like a football.

As Bluestone suggests, that irrational force in Algren's characters is the impulse to destroy love, which is tantamount to death. This impulse, often culminating in rape, murder, or suicide, comes, Bluestone observes, after the destruction of an important love object. In many stories, characters are rejected by their families or lack any at all; the prolonged absence of love stunts their emotional capacities. For, as Bluestone notes, "in a world where social relations are based on parasitic oppression and brute survival, love is the only way in which human beings may meaningfully relate." And if love cannot be had, by either poverty or circumstance, or because through its repeated denial it is no longer trusted, life becomes a living death. For some, this can trigger the impulse toward suicide, for others the outward aggression to murder.

Algren's fictional preoccupation with death was compounded by outside events. In early February 1939, Bernice, recently promoted in her teaching job, was diagnosed to have cancer of the rectum that had already spread; surgery to remove the tumor was not even attempted. Thirty-six years old and the mother of two small children, Bernice, who had encouraged him to read, sent him to college, made sure he got psychiatric help, and allowed him vacations on the dunes, had seen something worthy in him, despite his inability to succeed financially. She was the only member of the family with whom he had anything approaching a normal relationship, and she was going to die.

But as always, he presented to the world the face of a tough guy. "Nelson always gave the impression he wanted to run with the guys and get into a lot of trouble," said Frank Sandiford, and others also sensed an act. Another friend, recalling him as a middle-class person pretending to be lower-class, thought his punching bag and pugilistic attitude an affectation, and observed that, though his attraction to the defeated was constant, he seemed unsympathetic to other people's troubles. Another friend recalled that he was never at a party where Nelson wasn't drunk, that Nelson could be nasty and Amanda used to sober him up. But sometimes he'd get smashed and lean up against a wall and sing "The Three Little Fishes," an old song from his childhood, and some friends became aware of a Nelson they never knew. "He was always behind a screen," Sandiford said. "You never knew who he really was." Conroy concurred: "He kept a large part of himself isolated. He was gregarious, he'd go around and all that, but he was always apart."

As if paralleling the destruction of love in his characters' lives, the reawakening of his artistic identity led him increasingly away from Amanda. Though Conroy had moved out when his wife and children joined him from Missouri, Nelson's relationship with Amanda had not improved. Jack's wife, Gladys, heard Amanda chiding Nelson for drinking and carousing with Jack and the Fallonites when he should have been writing, a charge he would have found irksome, since the Fallonites seemed to directly fuel his work. And he was often hard on her. She was taking an art class on Saturday mornings, and when she showed him one of her paintings, he judged it by his own ambitions: "It's very nice, but what does it *mean*?" he asked, dogmatically dismissing anything that was not social realism. Once he hung one of her paintings in the apartment, but he wasn't especially interested in her dreams or her friends.

As always, he separated his personal life from his writing. Amanda was not even allowed to be present at League of American Writers meetings in their apartment: she had to stay hidden in the back room, though she often typed his League correspondence. Perhaps he could not see her as part of the public persona he was increasingly developing. They didn't go out together, and if he was invited to a party, Nelson could not be depended upon to bring her, claiming instead that she didn't want to come. Amanda became lonely and isolated.

Dorothy Farrell felt instinctively that Algren was more interested in writing than a relationship, but at the same time Jack described him as "omnivorous—a tom cat." He was frequently unfaithful. He had already been seeing prostitutes, and he flirted at the office. Now he began an affair with a trim, healthy girl, a would-be writer from the Sullivan house co-op who had been pursuing him. Amanda was terribly hurt and disappointed. But she was not the type to make a scene. This girl was very different from Amanda, very possessive and forthright. To Amanda she seemed like his aggressive mother and Nelson acted passive, like his father. She was so forthright that one weekend when Nelson and Amanda were going to Cairo, the Ohio river town he knew from his hitchhiking days, she insinuated herself into the trip. Amanda didn't want her, and Nelson didn't really either, but he was unable to tell her no. She came along, even attempting to sleep in their room to make sure they couldn't make love. But amid this female rivalry, Nelson seemed to hold himself aloof. What emerged from that weekend was a poem about his past, describing "pale Americans stricken with pale blue sleep / on rented pillows" in an early-morning bus stalled on the highway: "above, a rented neon moon, / Tethered all night to an all night restroom: Bathing Americans in a blue and rented sleep."

"Nelson never spoke of his work," said Abe Aaron of the time when Nelson began to publish poetry, "except to say that he wasn't able to produce. He was plagued by the fear that he would never be able to do what he wanted to do and was always talking about the men of note who had made their mark in their early years. This was constantly on his mind and I can't remember how many times he said this."

By spring 1939, three of Algren's poems had appeared in *The New Anvil.* Though one had been published under a pseudonym, the other two, while hardly establishing him as a poet, kept his name in good company. *The New Anvil,* appearing in March 1939, was of high quality. William Carlos Williams, Jesse Stuart, Karl Shapiro, Margaret Walker, and Frank Yerby were early contributors; Tom Tracy's "Homecoming" won an O. Henry award in 1940 after appearing in the magazine. Before it ceased publishing, anthologist Edward O'Brien would rank it fifth among American magazines for percentage of distinctive stories. Conroy and Algren rented an office from the Institute for Mortuary Research for $10 a month and worked on the magazine there, sending out rejection slips on their landlord's ghastly blue stationery. *The New Anvil* was probably the subject of favorable discussion which reflected on its editors at the Third American Writers' Congress in New York in June 1939.

Held in the last summer of peace, the Congress was dominated by discussion of Hitler; the optimism of earlier congresses was gone. But Algren made literary connections. He met the psychological novelist Millen Brand, with whom he established a long-standing, cordial correspondence. At an elegant penthouse party, he met Erskine Caldwell and Margaret Bourke-White, all the while enjoying a high-spirited pretense that another woman at the party was his wife. Despite his lack of production, his name, through *The New Anvil,* the League, and the numerous signings of radical petitions, was well enough known that he could mingle with the luminaries, and he used it. While in New York, Algren also went to Montefiore Hospital to visit the twenty-six-year-old tubercular poet Alexander Bergman, whose work appeared regularly in *The New Anvil*. Bergman encouraged Nelson in his work, and they corresponded, the way Algren would later conduct many close friendships.

That summer, Nelson and Amanda probably went up to the Indiana dunes, where the Joffes, because of Bernice's illness, would soon give up their house. Bernice's son Robert remembered that Nelson would write—and then inexplicably get up to slug at a boxer's punching bag whenever the impulse seized him. He was doing what he felt like doing, and he was consolidating his energies to describe the violence and hopelessness of the underworld. But he had not yet found a narrative style that would allow him to avoid the problems of *Somebody in Boots*. Almost all the stories he wrote that year show an insistence on the first person—the tone used in "So Help Me"—rather than the third-person narrative that he thought had failed him so miserably in *Somebody in Boots*. "No Shoes for Novak" even had the same monologue form as "So Help Me," with a gang member relating the story to a judge. "You Got to Be Careful" was narrated by a hooker; "The Lightless Arena," about a boxer killed in the ring, was told in four different voices: the mother, the girlfriend, the manager, and the boxer. Whether the insistence on the first person showed a lack of self-confidence or nothing more than the desire to use a successful though cumbersome formula, he continued to avoid the third person until the early fall of 1939, when he realized that, beginning a story in an East St. Louis whorehouse and ending with "No Shoes for Novak," he was writing another novel.

He had high ambitions for it. Stating that his "ultimate purpose would be an accurate description of Chicago in his time," he described the novel for one foundation as a "presentation of economic and political factors making toward juvenile criminality among some 300,000 Poles . . . on Chicago's Near Northwest side . . . through the methods of naturalism. . . . Data would be gathered . . . in schoolyards, public playgrounds, churches, poolrooms, taverns, hookies, amusement parks, street carnivals, the Boys' and Women's Court at 11th and State, the Juvenile Detention home at Ogden and Roosevelt, the Juvenile Court and the Institute for Juvenile Research, in private homes and at police showups, at the Illinois State Training School and in meeting places of gangs functioning as 'Social and Athletic' clubs; and through correspondence with two inmates of the Illinois State Penitentiary at Joliet and with one inmate of the Wisconsin State Penitentiary at Waupun. . . . Authorities to whom the applicant possesses access include social workers, precinct captains, police lieutenants and Mr. Frank Konkowski, an indicted alderman." But despite such direct sources, the project was not funded.

Writing again, he knew satisfaction and independence; and he was once again moving into his own, away from all the important relationships that had sustained him. He continued to be unfaithful to Amanda, distancing himself from a life-style he no longer found comfortable. And she too was beginning to look for other relationships. Perhaps already anticipating their fate, he consoled Millen on the Brands' separation: "Sometimes, though, a sharp break works out better, in the long run, than a slow one." His political commitment had also changed: the political struggle was now completely different. The dream of an American revolution was gone; Republican Spain was dead; World War II had just begun. The Hitler-Stalin pact, defended so vociferously by the CP and coming almost as soon as he had signed a declaration reiterating the differences between Nazism and Communism, had deeply damaged his support for the Party, though he would remain anticapitalist all his life. And his relationship with his family was also altered. His father, defeated and old and fragile, had been unable even to keep up a basement apartment, and he and Goldie had moved in with the Joffes. Bernice was dying. The cancer had spread to her abdominal cavity and lungs, but her spirits remained high: no longer able to work, she volunteered to type books into Braille for the blind. Though Nelson never, anywhere, discussed his feelings about her illness, her approaching death must surely have added intensity and urgency to his work. He moved gratefully toward writing, and the novel, which he first luridly titled *Harlots and Hunted,* would be dedicated to Bernice.

The need and the ability to write were so strong that, in spite of his sister's illness and the continuing disintegration of his marriage, his letters from that fall of 1939 took on a much happier tone. Not only was he writing but also he was convinced that somewhere, somehow, he was going to be able to get money for his work. With two pieces appearing in *Poetry* in November 1939, he sent poems to the lucrative *New Yorker,* he said, "without an inkling of self-doubt," and *Esquire* paid him fifty-eight dollars for fifty-eight lines of verse. Perhaps most important, he had interested a New York literary agency, McIntosh and Otis, in the beginning of his novel. He asked George Dillon, Millen Brand, and James Henle to sponsor him for a Guggenheim and easily convinced critic Granville Hicks to recommend him for the $1,200 Alfred A. Knopf award for an unfinished novel. He also applied for funds from the Authors' Club at the Carnegie Fund. *This* time he was trying to make sure he had enough money.

In mid-December, he and Jack were both laid off from the WPA because they had been working there more than eighteen months, but despite being reinstated early in 1940, Algren kept reiterating the need for money in letters to Dick Wright and Millen Brand. As he neglected to mention his gambling losses, they must have assumed he wanted to write full-time. "He was a compulsive gambler," Jack remembered. "On the Project, he used to mail his rent money home. He'd put it in an envelope and address it to himself so he'd have enough money to pay the rent. Then he'd go out and gamble the rest away." Once he challenged Chris Rowland to a Ping-Pong game. As she slid down the banister to the basement she hurt her arm, but Nelson waited, tossing the ball; afterward she found out the arm was broken. He took games seriously, and when he played cards, he couldn't leave the game a loser. He played the horses and "twenty-six"; he also claimed to have worked as a bookie in the mornings and as a card dealer over weekends. Maybe he hoped for a win big enough so that he could work full-time on his novel and quit his job, the way he'd been able to get out of Gerson's tire repair business so many years before.

On all fronts the desire was for escape; and the opportunity for domestic flight came in early 1940, when Nelson, Amanda, Jack, Fallon's friend Russell Lynch, and others went out to a club for the evening. John Barrymore was on hand, and as usual there was lots of drinking. Algren, who didn't dance, watched Amanda and Lynch, an attractive and attentive man, glide together across the floor. When they all walked home through the park, he stayed ahead with Conroy. Amanda, walking far behind with Lynch in the pitch dark, had had too much to drink. When she started getting sick, she went with Lynch to his nearby apartment and slept it off. In the morning, after a chaste night, Amanda nonetheless felt apprehensive and asked Lynch to accompany her to Cottage Grove.

When they came in Nelson was sitting in a chair, grim-faced and unwilling even to look up. As far as he was concerned, they had slept together; and when he spoke there was real hostility in his voice. Lynch, seeing he could do nothing, left. Alone with Nelson, Amanda began explaining that nothing had happened, that she had gotten sick. Though he had suspected her before of infidelity and had not been upset, this was a public matter of honor, his standing with the Fallonites, so necessary to his writing and to believing he could really be a part of the underworld. He would not be humiliated: he was leaving.

Amanda said that she would leave instead. She felt she was more capable of taking care of herself than he was; he should have the apartment. Moreover, she had debased herself pleading with him, and she had too much pride to stay. That day she moved in with Theodora Pikowski.

"Amanda's gone with Lynch," was all he would tell Conroy.

Amanda later felt sure that he had blown the whole thing with Lynch out of proportion so that he could justify severing the relationship. If he was going to start writing seriously, he had to do it now, and it wasn't just a matter of cutting out the drinking and parties. A married man couldn't carry out the kind of investigations he'd set for himself; moreover, he needed to be alone, to begin his research and lose himself in his work. And he had obviously sensed that he and Amanda weren't right for each other. Amanda had been attracted to him at his most fragile and vulnerable; even her offer to leave him the apartment, as if he weren't capable, suggests that she still regarded him as weak. Much later he would complain mightily about women who made their men feel inadequate in order to mask their own insecurities, and he did not want a woman like that. He was not inadequate. He was strong, sure of himself; and the relationship had changed.

It's possible, of course, that Amanda's actions disturbed him deeply, that they called up memories of the girlfriend before the suicide attempt, and that his responses were instinctive rather than deliberately planned. "Nelson was not an easy person, he was temperamental, he'd be upset at little things, but he was loyal and it seemed to me very much in love with Amanda," said Theodora Pikowski. "He had been untrue to her many times, but this was a trauma for him, a real trauma." Sexist and unfair as it was, part of him must surely have expected Amanda to wait always for him. Still, he knew too that she was loyal, if not physically, then in her heart, and he seemed somehow aware that he had precipitated it all: after this time, heroes of his fiction were not betrayed so much as they betrayed the trust of someone who loved them. He would carry feelings of guilt toward Amanda for decades, for pushing aside someone who loved him to pursue his own happiness.

An important part of his life was coming to an end. In the tumult of feelings and his desire to keep up with the Fallonites, he attempted to justify his behavior according to a code of honor not his own. When Bud Fallon suggested they go with Conroy to Theodora's, where Lynch was visiting Amanda, the three of them got liquored up and went. At Theodora's he made a complete fool of himself, getting down on all fours, meowing like a cat, and then provoking Lynch into a fistfight in front of the living room's plate-glass window two stories above the street. Amanda recalled that somebody had a knife—perhaps Nelson—and that Lynch finally wanted to take the dispute outside. They went out, Conroy remembered, but Nelson was too drunk to actually fight.

In spite of his macho posturing, the belligerent bad-boy act, there must have been a sense of relief at living alone—even if it was tinged with guilt. He could take the two hundred pages of manuscript he had and move up to the "Triangle," where the Poles lived. In March 1940, he received Richard Wright's new novel, *Native Son,* the title of which Nelson had lent Dick after it had been discarded for *Somebody in Boots*. The encouragement from the inscription was all he needed:

> To—
> My old friend
> Nelson
> Who I believe is still
> the best writer of good
> prose in the U.S.A.
> —Dick

The effect upon him was tremendous. "Dear Dick," he wrote in response, "Native Son arrived this morning. I haven't begun it yet because I can't get past the autograph. I hope you meant it all the way, because it did something to me: I had a luncheon engagement with a man from Houghton-Mifflin and I guess before he was through he figured he was talking either to Emile Zola or Lipton. In short, I'm now hoping I can do something—just a little—toward earning that inscription." He felt that he was glory-bound.

II

I feel I am of them—
I belong to those convicts and prostitutes myself—
And henceforth I will not deny them—
For how can I deny myself?

—WALT WHITMAN

8.
White Hope

NATIVE SON hit Algren so hard he felt he'd been clubbed over the head. "When I come to," he wrote Richard Wright, "if I really am a communist in any real sense of the word at all, I'll be grateful for being slugged out of a coma." Algren saw that the story of Bigger Thomas, a black Chicago youth who murders a white girl from fear of being found alone with her, had literally scared whites into thinking about Negro life while attacking the whole idea of capital punishment. Algren himself was made aware of his own racism, his own "surface look" toward blacks that Wright had described so masterfully. "It was the thing to write," he told Dick; the Party's criticism was just foolish and narrow-minded. "There are 'books,' and then there are books. I think NS is a book."

Algren had at first dismissed Sterling North's comparison of *Native Son* to *Crime and Punishment* as reviewer's excess, but after reading Wright's book he felt that if Dostoevsky's triumph had been psychological motivation, he'd never read anything more psychologically convincing than *Native Son*. And he could no longer say which was the more important book. This was a book that moved men's minds; and he promoted it in local literary circles. Though he was disconcerted when readers dismissed Bigger by saying he was just no good, dumbfounded by the way they continually dropped him out of his social background, and had to defend Wright against the reader who "always asked with something like a leer—'Does Mr. Wright *really* hate whites that much?'—hoping that he does, of course," the important thing was that people—even racists—had been affected by *Native Son,* were talking about it, and were buying it.

The success of Wright's book, soon a Book-of-the-Month Club selection, undoubtedly encouraged Algren. He too hoped to prove the need for change by showing the stunting effects of poverty on the young. Bigger Thomas's plentiful sales were a sign that brutal urban reality could find public acceptance, fill a public hunger so intense it could accept a black author. To Algren, it now seemed that the public wanted to *know,* to hear the truth; perhaps his work, like Wright's, could make a difference. This optimism, deeply threatened by the reception of *Somebody in Boots,* was crucial to his writing.

In a letter, Wright noted that Algren reacted to *Native Son* more honestly than anybody he knew, and extended his encouragement by praising him to Edward G. Aswell, his editor at Harper and Brothers. By spring Aswell had already written Algren twice asking for material. But Nelson demurred: he wanted to be careful this time. The novel had to be ready before he showed it around, and that might take another year.

By May 1940, Algren had moved to the Polish "Triangle" near Milwaukee and Division, an old-time proving ground for Chicago hoodlums. Only two streetcars from the frenzied bohemians of the South Side, it seemed like another country. In tavern jukeboxes, crooning love songs lived next to Polish accordion tunes and polkas, drugstores were still called "aptekas," and women wrapped their heads in old-world babushkas, heading once or twice or several times a week to a nearby Roman Catholic church. Algren's ambivalent yet passionate emotions pictured the beautiful Amanda Kontowicz in this foreign world, but when he went to reconcile with her, she asked if he had filed for divorce. So he lived alone in Little Polonia; and it was better for his work. Now he saw Chicago as he had always seen it in his mind's eye—not the arty colony of Cottage Grove or the quiet humdrum of North Troy, but a teeming mass of humanity like "the Petersburg of Dostoevsky—a place of extremes of heat, a sort of sprawling chaos of men and women, taverns, els, trolleys, markets, brothels, poolrooms, with no two persons going in the same direction and no meaning to the whole insane business of milling and elbowing and clutching until you stop to look at just one person, any one, going just one way all by himself."

His apartment in a two-story brick building on the side street Evergreen was quiet and cheap, and he lived without a phone. This and the long trip from the South Side discouraged visitors, but when friends from the WPA dropped by on occasion, they found a Nelson they had never seen before. He was much happier. He was more housewifely and very proud of being a good host and providing food. He had a big pot of stew that was never emptied and never cleaned, into which he tossed meat, potatoes, and vegetables. On Evergreen, he seemed friendlier: he had his own place, he was writing, and he had survived.

But such visits were rare. Aside from working on the Writers' Project and writing a novel, he was trying to finish a long story about a woman in a hotel, probably a precursor to Sophie in *The Man with the Golden Arm,* and (or it may have been the same piece) a sixty-page story unfortunately titled "They Wish to Be Wept for." His leisure time was spent gathering material. Alone, he visited the psychiatric institution at Lincoln and trekked again to the transient hotels on South State. Occasionally the Fallonites might visit the apartment, but more often his guests were local people, "twenty-six" players or boys without jobs whom he invited in for beer so he could listen to them talk. He presumably met them as he went about finding his way to dark hideouts beneath the el, where the afternoon light fell down in slats, to back-room poker games that went on till all hours, to the shop of a crooked barber who lured young men into bike stealing and racketeering. He went to the fights, intrigued by the possibility of describing professional fight hexers like "Evil Eye" Finkel. He opened his ears to colloquial speech, alert to dramatic possibility. From boys who'd been in jail he learned the sounds heard from the Triangle's precinct-house holding cells: St. John's bells, the Chicago Avenue trolley, squad cars filling up with gas and pulling out, conversation. He recorded dialogue and anecdotes, calling it "data" in his notebooks, once again noting the treatment of Jews among the lowest classes.

> "Hey, you wanta go'n drink dime beers all night?"
> "You make me feel so unconscious."
> The boys rolled a Jew on Division Street for $6 and his topcoat. A few days later, they were picked up on suspicion. After they were in the cell awhile the same Jew was thrown in with them, drunk. So they rolled him again.

At an all-night hamburger joint he found the opening lines to his story "Is Your Name Joe?" when he heard a girl say to the counterman what sounded to him like poetry:

> "I hate t' see the Spring 'n Summer come so bad," she was telling him, "I just don't seem so good as other people any more. Sometimes I'm that disgusted of myself I think: 'Just one more dope,

that's you.' I won't set up there in that room another Spring alone,
thinkin' stuff like that. It just starts goin' through my head as soon
as I come in that door. Like someone who lives there I can't see,
somebody who knows better, tellin' me: 'Just one more dope, that's
you.' I hate t' see the Spring 'n Summer come. So bad."

And he visited brothels, memorizing the parlors, probably paying
the women for their time, and meeting a quack doctor who dispensed
sulfanilamide pills, used to treat gonorrhea, rather freely. Like the
area he lived in, his literary influences, outside of Baudelaire and
Crane, some of whose work he knew almost by heart, were Slavic:
Dostoevsky's murderer Raskolnikov and the prostitute Sonia in
Crime and Punishment; more important, the Russian writer Alexander Kuprin, whose novel *Yama,* or *The Pit,* Algren reread throughout his life. Set in a Kiev whorehouse, *Yama* is the tragic tale of
several women trapped by fate into "the life." Kuprin had made a
sociological study of prostitution and its laws, and, it was said, had
lived platonically among the women in a brothel to observe them.
For Kuprin, prostitution was a scourge as evil as war: the material
he found in the brothel was "tremendous, downright crushing, terrible. . . . And not at all terrible are the loud phrases about the
traffic in women's flesh, about the white slaves, about prostitution
being a corroding fester of large cities . . . an old hurdy-gurdy of
which all have tired! No, horrible are the . . . business-like, daily,
commercial reckonings . . . [in which] are completely dissolved such
feelings of resentment, humiliation, shame. There remains a dry
profession, a contract, an agreement, a well-nigh honest petty trade,
no better, no worse than, say, the trade in groceries," Kuprin fumed,
providing Algren with the quotation that opens *The Man with the
Golden Arm.* "Do you understand, gentlemen, that all the horror is
in just this, that there is no horror!"

For Algren, exposing that horror was crucial. He set the novel in
the East St. Louis "Valley"; his characters were poor white crackers
and foreign immigrants. The first section, highly reminiscent of Kuprin, began in a brothel, where the heroine Minnie Mae lands after
being gang-raped. Though numbed into depression and apathy by
the long hours, she refuses to sleep with a drug-crazed customer and
is forced to leave the house. Penniless, clutching the address of a
Chicago brothel, she hitchhikes north.

The scene then shifts to the Triangle, where Stash Paycheck, a
would-be boxer anxious to prove himself to the racketeering barber,

graduates from petty crime to an arson-and-theft job and a reform school stretch at St. Charles. Upon his release he meets Minnie Mae, now working in the barber's "house," and they become lovers. But she too is sent to reform school, and Stash loses his big debut in the ring. Disgusted, his manager walks out, and the battered fighter is finally mugged on the deserted night street.

Algren concentrated much more on characterization and description than he had ever done before. He preferred to write without haste, disregarding the critics and "all set ways of conduct and thought." He wanted to let the story grow within him—to "feel" his way into it. Dick Wright, who saw the work that summer, dubbed him the "Proust of the Proletariat"; flattered, Nelson replied that he preferred "the poor man's Dostoevsky," having never read Proust. Dick encouraged him to show the work to Aswell, who was also impressed and asked for a synopsis of the last two hundred pages. But Algren's laborious observation and characterization had been, somewhat, at the expense of plot. With his only extra copy in Dick's hands in New York, he seemed unable to summarize the last sections of the book—a sign that he didn't know how it was going to end.

Plotting the book would have required calculating intellectual decisions, whereas his working method so far had been through *feeling,* in the poetic expression of his unique vision of the lost. To re-create the emotions and actions of his characters was emotionally satisfying for Algren, even cathartic. Farther up on the North Side, Bernice was dying; and writing could transcend death. That was the "use of the printed word: to stand up against time when our tongues are stopped; to represent those aspects of the human spirit which stand up, since those are the only things that do stand up." And so he worked furiously as Bernice drew closer to death. The tumor in her abdomen was so enlarged that she joked, valiantly and pathetically, about being pregnant. Living on the North Side, Nelson could have visited her frequently, but it is not at all clear how often he did: Joffe, Goldie, Gerson, and the children were there, and the pall of illness hung over the house.

After Bernice died on August 9, 1940, he attended the funeral but confided his feelings to no one. There were, as he would later say, some things that should be kept private, and Bernice's dying was one such deeply personal event. He didn't talk about her death with Jack or Amanda. His only surviving mention of it is an aside, couched in stoic Marxist terms, to Dick Wright, who was safely at a distance in New York. "Trouble and tribulation. Economics and death. My sister, age 37, died last week, leaving two little kids, 10 and 6. Trouble, trouble"—the children, of whom he was fond because they were Bernice's, would be living with Joffe now, lost to Algren.

Bernice's tragedy moved him deeply, and his mute reaction shows, in an odd way, just how much. In memoirs written much later, he would never even mention the loss of Bernice; however, forty years later one friend remembered hearing Nelson say that Bernice's death couldn't have been worse if he himself had died. But at the time he buried deep inside all things that mattered and that might belie the tough stance which, like the hero of his novel, he felt compelled to maintain. And withdrew into his work.

Aswell liked Algren's writing a great deal, but he expressed concern to Wright that the book seemed almost plotless. Wright agreed: the writing was excellent, but after 263 pages he couldn't tell where the story was moving. He conveyed this to Nelson with a touching awareness of his friend's deep sensitivity to criticism, first assuring him that he had never seen such descriptions of men and women except in Russian literature. "You have a sure sense of depicting the utter hopelessness, childishness, and fumbling of people's lives," he wrote, especially praising the dialogue. But, he added gently, "I think some plot would not hurt at all, Nelson . . . a definite sense of *progression* should be built under the story and if you do it, I see no reason for not feeling that you will have a first rate book, utterly different from anything anybody is now writing, something new."

Algren, gratified by Dick's approval, heeded the advice to hang on to Aswell by assuring him he could get the plot under control. Aswell thought locating all the action in Chicago was a solution, and Wright suggested combining several characters to help focus the development. Incorporating these ideas, in late September 1940 Algren, aware that he needed an "integrated, center of the stage struggle," signed with Harper and Brothers for a five-hundred-dollar advance. He was somewhat innocent about dealing with his editors on a professional level, as a flurry of letters, with admonishments from Wright, indicates. Immediately after signing the contract, Algren wanted to change the book's title from "White Hope" to the hopelessly sentimental "The Lost and the Lowly," whose alliteration caught his now soaring confidence. He apparently bombarded Aswell with new ideas, appearing changeable and flighty, and making Aswell feel untrusted. Wright had to smooth Aswell's ruffled feathers and then tell Nelson—oblivious to the trouble—to play it cool.

With the novel due the following May, that fall he began working seriously, banning as many outside activities as possible, especially parties. Now he saw Jack only at work; *The New Anvil* was losing readership because of the war and had been temporarily halted from a lack of funds. In June his name had appeared alongside those of three hundred fifty writers protesting U.S. entry into World War II as a foreign adventure that would restrict civil liberties, prolong hostilities, and rekindle economic depression, but he cut down on League activities, having seen from the reaction to *Native Son* that Party approval meant little. He hoped his contract would allow him to attract funding for the novel so he could escape the increasingly annoying Writers' Project. Changes in the Project's direction, perhaps war-related, now meant that, as supervisors, he and Conroy had to really work for their money; and he was no longer popular in the office—Conroy and Abe Aaron were practically the only people with whom he was still on speaking terms. He felt his departure would be a relief to all concerned, yet poker games and the horses kept him bound there. Aggressively seeking literary funding, he again applied for a Guggenheim, with Wright, Kenneth Fearing, Louis Adamic, and Edward Aswell as sponsors. To sell more stories to high-paying magazines like *Esquire,* he changed agents from McIntosh and Otis to Ingersoll and Brennan, who soon obtained a generous check from the prestigious *Southern Review* for an excerpt from the novel about a young boxer's confession to a murder.

An exchange of letters concerning this story gives an interesting glimpse into Algren's daily life. He had to change the title of the story from "Paycheck" to "Biceps" after its acceptance, because the original title, he told the editors, "is only a very slight variation of 'Paycek,' and the latter is the name of an actual person . . . in the neighborhood in which I write. His real name is Pacek, and he changed it to 'Paycek' while fighting professionally. You may recall his defeat, at the hands of Joe Louis, some months ago. . . . I could get my neck broken, figuratively speaking, if someone he knows can read and happens to get wind of the story. I'm not too certain he can read himself. Although I don't know him personally, we have many mutual friends."

This intimacy with Chicago and the old Polish neighborhood grew deeper as the novel became more entrenched in the Triangle. He soon began visiting, as he had done in college, the weekly police lineups, where a nonstop parade of the poor passed before him. He wrote completely on location in a dense city of neighborhoods and rivalries that was now building a subway, a "pavement-colored" city, often sad and monstrous: "Chicago gets bigger and greyer and sootier and more clamorous every day," he wrote to Dick Wright. "There's a steam hammer half a mile from where I live, which pounds steel rivets all night, putting buttons on the subway. Every so often it makes a sound as though ripping up all the steel it's been sewing down, and all the neighborhood dogs howl for half an hour after, as if something had torn inside them."

Like his earlier work, the new novel was suffused with a sense of imminent death, and if the published version seems gloomier than his later work, perhaps this is because death upon death followed Bernice's that year. "Edith Lloyd is dead. Sam Gaspar told me. Cancer," he wrote to Dick. And the high-spirited poet Alexander Bergman, who liked Nelson "all the way through," was in the last stages of tuberculosis at Montefiore Hospital in the Bronx. "It's all up with me, Nelson," Bergman wrote shortly before the shreds of his lungs ceased to function. "I swore never to take oxygen but I'm taking it." Drugged with morphine, he wondered how much sickness his poor body could tolerate; he finally died on May 17, 1941. Twenty-four years later Algren would use Bergman's poem "They Look Like Men" in his preface to the 1965 edition of *Somebody in Boots*.

In early June, Algren traveled alone to New York to attend the fourth and last American Writers' Congress, a gathering dominated by opposition to American intervention in the war in Europe. Algren met with Aswell, sought Wright's comments on the novel, and apparently saw Orson Welles's production of *Native Son*. And he was again confronted with Alec Bergman's death when the Poets, Song Writers, and Folk Singers Session of the Congress turned into a messy tribute to the man. His poems were read and his movement work remembered. Bergman's close friend Celia and brother Nat were there, and Algren knew them both, but he stood alone, withdrawing into himself.

He returned to Chicago to find that Gerson was ill. In recent years, he had come to a new appreciation of his father, having long overcome his adolescent contempt for him. At Amanda's urging, they had gone fishing together; and, away from Goldie and the household,

had enjoyed a long, satisfying talk. Father and son were united in
their feeling for Bernice, who resembled Gerson and had been his
favorite daughter. Gerson had been badly shaken by her death. He
was old, feeling useless, broken by his failure to support himself,
and his daughter's illness and death had all but destroyed his will to
live. As Goldie had made herself useful cooking, cleaning, and mind-
ing the children, they continued living with Morris Joffe; but Gerson
seemed only a ghost of himself. In the evening he would retire to a
rocking chair in the basement, swaying for hours and pulling on a
bottle of liquor. If he was in the way upstairs, Nelson's nephew
remembered, Goldie would chase him back down with threats and
insults, the way Stash would later be treated in *The Man with the
Golden Arm*.

That June, Gerson, now past seventy, underwent surgery to remove a tumor in his urinary tract. Afterward, he tried to recuperate
with Goldie and the Joffes at a summer cottage Morris had rented
on the Indiana dunes after selling the old place. Nelson came out to
see them for a few days, bringing his work and spreading it out on
a big table. But the rest wasn't enough for Gerson. In August he
contracted pneumonia and died in a Chicago hospital, a victim, as
Bernice's daughter remembered it, of a broken heart. For Nelson,
it was not his father's death that was so tragic, but his life. Undoubtedly embroidering, he recalled his father's deathbed many
years later:

> They saw his right had taken the fingers of his left as though
> something had gone wrong with the fingers; and saw he was trying
> to fix the machinery of his left hand with the machinery of his
> right.
> They saw him pass from life into death still trying to fix ma-
> chinery.
> His old woman saw him go; yet she did not weep.
> So the son knew that, for all his fixing, the old man hadn't fixed
> anything that mattered.

In New York, Aswell had agreed to a six-month extension for
White Hope. Although Algren was again worried about losing his
Project nest if it became known he had a book coming out, the
reasons for the delay were artistic. Before his death, Alec Bergman
had pronounced *White Hope* "an American classic," but Algren had
not received Wright's latest comments before he saw Aswell, and

was unsure how well he had incorporated Wright's suggestion for a "conceptual structure." More important, he felt the longer he worked on the book, the more convincing a job he could make it. He soon had reason to feel extremely optimistic. In July he learned that "Biceps" would appear in the 1941 O. Henry collection under the title "A Bottle of Milk for Mother"—taken from a line in the story—and he and Studs Terkel were adapting a radio version of the story that would air on NBC's *Authors' Playhouse* in the fall.

Aswell was pleased with Algren's work despite the delay, for each successive revision represented a significant improvement. And he probably sensed that Algren was not a fast writer. Algren agonized over each sentence, over whether to use a semicolon or a period; each word had to fall perfectly on the page. He was, perhaps fortunately, again laid off from the Project, along with twenty other supervisors and a hundred field workers who were feeling the effects of the Red-baiting Dies Committee investigations and the war. Unemployment gave him valuable time, because he did not yet consider the manuscript in readable shape. A new typewriter, inherited from Bergman, was on its way and would help him through the long, tedious job of retyping.

In a 1962 introduction to the novel, Algren mentioned having used newspaper accounts of the trial of Bernard Sawicki, a nineteen-year-old reform school parolee who had coolly confessed to murdering four people, one a police officer, during a summer crime spree. He was a classic case of juvenile delinquence. A three-day-old doorstep foundling, he had been taken in by the Polish Sawicki family. His stepfather, a heavy drinker, had beaten him excessively, and from a young age Bernie began running away for extended periods. He had played with guns in the fifth grade and also acquired the nickname "Knifey" as a child. Seemingly completely remorseless, Sawicki held it a point of honor to maintain outward composure at all times while in custody, breaking down only once, after a warden sat down to talk with him like a human being. Described by a doctor as sane but a "moral imbecile," Sawicki was nevertheless of above-average intelligence. "I'm nuts, I'm nuts, but I think they'll roast me," he breathed in a stage whisper during the trial's final arguments. He had bet the bailiff who thought he'd get life a pack of cigarettes that he'd "burn" in the electric chair. When the judge sentenced him to death, Sawicki sneered, "The hell with you, I can take it." He had sensed all along the inevitability of his deepest fear: the day of his arrest he'd said that he "never expected to be twenty-one anyway."

Algren may have incorporated "data" from the case into the novel in much the same way Wright had used a black teenage murderer executed in Illinois as material for *Native Son,* but chances are that Algren used news accounts of Sawicki's June 30 confession, rather than of the trial, which occurred a week before Aswell's deadline. At any rate, Sawicki had far less moral conscience than the already developed character of Bruno Bicek, and his troubles were used not for plot but for details to strengthen the book as it already was. Before the crimes that precipitate his downfall, hero Bruno Bicek knows that that a couple of neighborhood boys like himself have "burned" for shooting a cop; and this foreshadows Bicek's own fate. Bicek's efforts not to let investigating cops know how much they get to him is much like Sawicki's behavior. But most important, Sawicki's speech, revealing so much about his self-conception and his profound ignorance, must have been a tremendous boon. Certainly the crude expressions "roast" and "burn," reflecting the barbarism of capital punishment, were useful, but it was the clipped self-preserving haughtiness, the stubborn pride even in the face of a death that renders it pathetic, that was of most use to Algren.

The novel, which finally appeared as *Never Come Morning,* concerns seventeen-year-old Bruno "Lefty" Bicek, a poor Chicago Pole who dreams of becoming a prizefighter or major-league pitcher while living with his widowed mother behind their milk store. Jobless, Bruno is scornful of hanging around "a crumby relief station, with a mob of crumby greenhorns, for a fifty-five a month pick-and-shovel job" when he can get by shooting pool, pitching softball, or pulling off petty crimes. Ambitious but frustrated, he graduates to hoodlumhood by stealing a slot machine and taking over the local social and athletic club for the racketeering barber who'll promote his fight career. But as president of the gang, Bruno must be "regular" with the guys; and he doesn't want to share Steffi Rostenkowski, the girl he loves and has known since childhood. A coward at heart despite his size, Bruno hasn't enough courage to defend Steffi when, after they spend the evening at an amusement park, the gang materializes to take turns raping her. Threatened with a knife, Bruno sneaks off, only to hear her awful cries of "Next! Next!" as a dozen more men line up. Frustrated with rage, "disgust coming up in his throat like a forkful of contaminated meat," he breaks the neck of a Greek trying to join in. Later, however, he feels no guilt for the murder of the Greek. All his guilt is for Steffi R., who after the rape is manipulated into a house of prostitution run by the barber and Mama Tomek.

Bruno becomes a mugger, spending six months in jail in a rite of passage that renders him useless for anything except working for the barber. As a pimp and bouncer in Mama Tomek's parlor, he succumbs to drunkenness and depression, admitting to Steffi his remorse for all that has happened. Despite her treatment at his hands, she still intuitively trusts him, and her only hope for freedom lies in his finding enough money to pay off the barber. Once they admit their love for each other, they find the strength to plan their escape.

Bicek returns to his career in the ring, determined to make a new life for himself and Steffi. He cuts the barber out of his winnings when he fights "Honeyboy" Tucker, and the wrath of the barber, who resents Steffi's love for Bruno, is brutal. As Bruno wins the fight against Tucker, at last freeing himself and Steffi, Tenczara the cop walks quietly into the dressing room where the trainer, Finger, is cleaning Bruno's wounds; and Bruno knows that the barber has turned him in for the murder of the Greek.

Through this story of crime and retribution, Algren explored the psychological nature of the criminal and the exploited. Bruno, growing up in the streets because he was in the way in the rooms rented by his immigrant parents, is morally lacking and highly self-centered. He hopes without malice for the downfall of his pitching rival, "as he hoped for any possibility which would clear a pathway to being known throughout the ward as 'Iron-Man.' " His life is a "series of lusts"—for women, tobacco, whiskey, meat—a blind search for gratification. Inarticulately dissatisfied, prone to sudden bursts of violence, Bicek longs only to be a man among men—but he has no trust in himself and is too insecure to believe in Steffi's love. In fact, he dimly resents her trust of him, since it implies a moral responsibility he is ill equipped to handle. Instinctively loving to her, he can neither admit this to his friends nor act honestly on his own feelings: "The thought broke over him like another man's idea: 'Get some liquor in her. That's what dames are for.' " In the true test of his manhood—his defense of her—he fails utterly.

Steffi's personality has also been blunted by poverty. "At seventeen Steffi Rostenkowski was one of those women of the very poor who feign helplessness to camouflage indolence. . . . Her indolence was that of one who fears that, if she fulfills one duty well and swiftly, she will be called upon immediately for a less pleasant one." She has the natural selfishness of children who have been denied "possession of one thing, no matter how small, all to themselves." When Bruno wins a doll for her at a carnival, "Steffi's fingers reached for it, like a baby's fingers reaching: it would be something of her own." But her selfishness is innocent and her will easily vanquished: passive in the face of Bruno's seduction, she hopes "uselessly for the sound of her mother's foot on the stairs." She resigns herself to go with Bruno to the shed, later the scene of the rape, though she feels they are acting like "animals" and cries on the inside.

With so little inner strength between them, they are no match for the hideous barber, who, "too old to understand any need that was not the need for money," is the epitome of manipulation and exploitation. His favorite saying, "When the thunder kills a devil, then a devil kills a Jew," shows he accepts and believes in the inevitability of the scapegoat. In Algren's view, he is depraved, for he enjoys seeing people made fearful and is attracted to Steffi at her most helpless, aroused completely after he has beaten her. The barber trusts no one: though he gets a percentage off cards, baseball, boxing matches, and Mama Tomek's women, he worries constantly that someone is trying to cheat him.

For they all live in a world of "hunters" and "hunted," a poverty-stricken world where everyone cheats and exploitation reigns: "Ever'thin's crooked, Widow," Bruno assures Mrs. Rostenkowski easily. Even the Heat expects to be paid off. "Always pay off for rape if you can," Bruno counsels his jail buddy; ten dollars will do it, and as little as a quarter will keep someone who doesn't want to go out of jail, where the inmates shake down new arrivals for money—and pay a percentage to the guards, of course. Police captain Tenczara has been promoted since a teenage murderer's electrocution, and his coworker Scully got his job through patronage. It isn't surprising that Bruno Bicek's final downfall occurs when he dares to defy this world by excluding the barber and believing he and Steffi can live straight. For, as whore-turned-madam Mama Tomek could have told them, it does no good to fight the law of averages—which is always too heavily weighted against people like Bruno and Steffi.

Such a world, where love and trust, if they exist at all, are the target of scorn and suspicion, is a joyless place, as Algren draws it; and from this springs the dark, oppressive atmosphere of the Triangle, a neighborhood so insular that the world outside can be gleaned only from Hollywood movies or the world's foremost boxing magazines. The same oppression pervades the rest of Chicago too, a city "murmurous with poverty," covered "with a low slow pall of locomotive smoke," where "men watch the weather . . . in the hope of a snow-shoveling job before night." They hope for so little because the world rarely offers them more. Here, in the city's weekly lineup, a con man might turn himself in for nothing, preferring prison to a life of being hunted, knowing he is but a "stumblin' block" for all who might have loved him. Here, Bruno evinces no shock when his cellmate threatens to kill himself. "Go it, guy," Bruno tells him, "you're a done man, anyhow." Even the ambitious Bicek considers suicide, though only when faced with the prospect of spending more than six months in the workhouse.

For death is clearly an alternative, especially for a woman like Steffi R.; as it was for the prostitute Jennka in *Yama;* as it had seemed, once, to Algren himself. Amid the sad little distractions of the brothel jukebox, the endless stories of Tookie, Chickadee, and Helen, Steffi can see ahead, knowing that the pride in the women's eyes "hardened to a burnished dime-store stare . . . and the only pride left was in lack of shame, and the greatest respect went to the most shameless, the most drunken, the most foolish, the most cruel, the most treacherous: the women with death in their eyes were envied by those still half-alive." For Steffi, it is too much to live in a world where everyone is trying to cheat her, where decent women, sensing who she is, move away from her on the bus. Deep down, she is aware of the monstrousness of her position and is helpless before it. "The enormity of being accessible to any man in the whole endless city came to her like a familiar nightmare. It was true. It was really true . . . it was to her that this had happened and to none other. It was true." As in a fevered dream, she moves almost instinctively to the gas jet. But it isn't working.

In these poetic sections, seen through Steffi's eyes, Algren intensified the same vision of the world he held seven years before. Each man went alone. "Everyone went through the streets of the world alone, averting the eyes and disdaining other faces, disdaining other hands." Each person is forever "making the same endless plans for escape, repeating the same light songs to pass the time and inventing the same false gossip; like convicts living in the same cell for years together." When the outside world no longer exists for her, Steffi expresses an idea Algren had earlier set down in a unpublished poem about Chicago:

> She ceased to go down to the pavement at all except for early Sunday Mass at St. John Cantius. The world was a street one never went down to. The world was a wall, like a sealed-up room. The world was a room like the barber's room. Like an inside room in some exclusive madhouse.
>
> The city itself was a sealed-up room; the city itself was a madhouse.
>
> The world was a madhouse where everyone was refined.

"A book, a true book, is the writer's confessional," Algren would write two months after the book's publication. "For, whether he would have it so or not, he is betrayed, directly or indirectly, by his characters, into presenting, publicly, his innermost feelings." And while it is true that *Never Come Morning,* inspired by compassion, concerned external circumstances completely different from his own, on deeper psychological levels Algren had much in common with his characters. Like Bruno, he was moody, subject to bursts of anger that could culminate, as in the suicide attempt, in violence. Then too, Algren's delinquents, both in this novel and in other published and unpublished stories, are usually the victims not only of adverse social conditions but of thwarted childhood love. Bruno and Steffi, like the heroes of every Algren novel, are both missing a parent, and Bruno's mother has taken no interest in him since his adolescent brush with the law. Algren too felt alienated from his mother's love: he once told Geraldine Page that, growing up, he felt like an orphan. Bruno and Steffi are, more obviously, akin to two completely distinct aspects of his psyche—the stoic repressed male who cannot express his innermost feelings and the poetic soul so sensitive to the atrocities of life that it seeks to destroy itself. One can only wonder whether, in this optimistic phase of his life, he saw his own yearning for death as he saw Steffi's—part of the strange machinations of a soul greedy for life.

One other character also seems similar to Algren himself: the Jewish whorehouse doctor, Shapiro. Having lost his professional standing through blunder, he now works among the brothel women, "where his clumsiness had room enough to be redeemed by compassion." Like a writer, Shapiro steps in and out of the women's lives briefly, observing their health and testing their blood. Like

Algren, Shapiro sees them not merely as prostitutes, but as oft-times damaged, stunted beings. Watching Chickadee's rapt absorption in a comic book, he leaves "feeling troubled to learn that Miss La Rue wasn't a woman after all, but a child whose pain was a child's pain, as sharp as it was bewildered. That, to M. Shapiro, was infinitely the greater outrage." Like the Russian Kuprin, the doctor sees that the whores live "without developing, without being enriched by experience . . . altogether like children." He blames himself that the girls must be examined for disease as if they were cattle, because "he had other sins on his soul. And found expiation by assuming, silently, a burden of guilt not his own." Was Algren, like the doctor, finding expiation among the wretched? For what? Was his guilt, like that of Bruno for Steffi, all for Amanda? Or something deeper? Whatever it was, he kept it, characteristically, to himself.

By September the book was in its final form. He had no doubts at all about the quality of the writing. He was, however, concerned that Dick Wright wouldn't like changes he'd made affecting the book's overall statement. But he needn't have worried. Dick was tremendously enthusiastic about the book, as a letter to Aswell shows: "I was constantly reminded of the work of Faulkner; not because Nelson derives from Faulkner, but it seems to me that Nelson does for the Polish folk of Chicago what Faulkner does for the poor white folk of Mississippi. Algren's ability to get into the maze-like minds of these twisted people and make them think and talk and reveal themselves is something that holds me spellbound." To Nelson, along with his praise, Dick confidentially pointed out a few rough spots: one character seemed to dangle, and overblown rhetoric occasionally intruded into the narrative. "I know," Nelson wrote back, scurrying to cut the offending lines, "I overdo this copper wires against the moon shadows within shadows moving boats on the moving river stuff. It's a hangover from a rhetoric class I have difficulty in curbing."

All that remained were small corrections and agreement on a title, as neither Algren nor Aswell was completely satisfied with "White Hope." Nelson favored "He Shoulda Stood in Bed," but Aswell strongly suggested he consider "Never Come Morning," taken from a passage where Steffi, dreaming, imagines that "morning would never come again." For Nelson, "Never Come Morning" was too literary, but it did cover the story of both Bruno and Steffi better than other suggestions, and he agreed to it, brushing aside the last obstacle to the book's long-awaited publication.

The crowning touch was an introduction by Dick Wright, for which Nelson had been hoping ever since signing the contract with Harper and Brothers. *"Never Come Morning,"* Wright said,

> depicts the intensity of feeling, the tawdry but potent dreams, the crude but forceful poetry, and the frustrated longing for human dignity residing in the lives of the Poles of Chicago's Northwest Side, and this revelation informs us all that there lies an ocean of life at our doorstep—an unharnessed, unchanneled and unknown ocean. . . .
>
> Most of us 20th century Americans are reluctant to admit the tragically low quality of experience of the broad American masses; feverish radio programs, super advertisements, streamlined sky-scrapers, million-dollar movies, and mass production have some-how created the illusion in us that we are "rich" in our emotional lives. To the greater understanding of our time, *Never Come Morning* portrays what actually exists in the nerve, brain, and blood of our boys on the street, be they black, white, native, foreign-born.

Aswell and his staff were also unanimous in their enthusiasm. "It's a book of great integrity and power," Aswell wrote Algren. "I myself am amazed at the skill you have shown in revising it. There was always power in it, but you will remember that I thought the first version lacked integration as a story. No one can say that now. You have thought the whole thing through and have built it up into one solid piece that hits the reader with the force of a blunt instrument. My heartiest congratulations to you. I simply can't tell you how pleased I am, both with the book and with you. Unless I badly miss my guess, it is going to make a stir."

9.

The Great City's Nighttime Streets

*N*EVER *COME* *MORNING* was a "brilliant book and an unusual book," *The New York Times* announced; *Saturday Review of Literature* declared it a "knockout" that towered "head and shoulders above most novels," with "powerful achievements on almost every page of character, of color, of poetry, of understanding"; Philip Rahv praised its "utter sincerity and psychological truth" and compared Algren's brothel scenes to those in Faulkner's *Sanctuary*. Though some reviewers thought the writing stylized, the plot too swift, or the ending pat, almost all had to admit its power: "I, for one, found myself believing his hellish descriptions of police lineups, jail inmates, street murders, and life as lived in a cheap brothel. An ugly, effective slice of low life, carrying plenty of concealed, and, one hopes, salutary propaganda," Clifton Fadiman allowed in *The New Yorker*. Amid the inevitable comparisons with Wright, critics were taken by Algren's fresh, authentic language. Malcolm Cowley, enthusiastically placing Algren in the esteemed tradition of Chicago realism, went further: "The girls sitting around the juke-box in Mama Tomek's, the boys playing under the El, the look of Chicago streets in the rain . . . It is this poetry of familiar things that is missing in the other Chicago novels and that shows the direction of Algren's talent. . . . He is not by instinct a novelist. He is a poet of the Chicago slums, and he might well be Sandburg's successor."

Congratulations poured in, especially from those who remembered *Somebody in Boots*. "It is the most solid kind of novel and very clearly establishes your reputation as one of the most honest and clearest sighted of American realists," Granville Hicks wrote Algren. "I know what a hard time you have had, and I think your persistence has been damn near heroic. It's swell to see you getting the recognition you deserve." Farrell was also moved to write, both to Algren and Aswell, though, predictably, only the letter to Aswell survived: "*Never Come Morning* is not merely one of the finest works of American literature that I have read in recent years: it is also a challenge, a true, and a telling social indictment." Larry Lipton, who admired *Never Come Morning,* thought "it would do a good deal to set Nelson right side up again (in more ways than the financial) if his book has a really good sale."

Important writers now discovered him. Novelist Martha Gellhorn, at that time married to Hemingway, was tremendously impressed by *Never Come Morning:* she told him that it was "first rate," that it revealed an unknown world, and made it so real that it stuck in the mind, as if one had been there. Hemingway himself was praising *Never Come Morning* around Cuba and told Maxwell Perkins later that summer, "I think it very, very good. It is as fine and good stuff to come out of Chicago as James W. [*sic*] Farrell is flat, repetitious, and worthless. The first Farrell book about Studs Lonigan had some marvelous parts in it and gave a fine picture of the utter horror of that district of the South Side. But this man Algren can write the pants off Farrell, and the North Side of Chicago that he writes about was always about twenty times the place that Farrell's bailiwick was anyway." Elsewhere, Hemingway pronounced that it was "about the best book to come out of Chicago."

All this adulation naturally left Algren brimming with enthusiasm, at last certain he could have a life as a serious writer. Now he felt that a true book would always be accepted, even welcomed. "Great rewards do, at last, come to the boldest; to those who permit neither avarice nor shame to modify what they truly feel and know," he was soon proclaiming in *The Writer.* "The happy truth of the matter is that there isn't a solid publisher going who won't take a book dealing with any strata of society so long as it is a true book." His optimism, in keeping with his politics, also extended to Americans at large: "The average American reader is a knowing sort of cuss, and he knows when a book is false or true," he bubbled on easily.

He was completely convinced that art grew from close observation and intense emotional connection. It was the writer's job to feel rather than think, he wrote to Martha Gellhorn, who saw him in Chicago later that summer. She agreed, as did Hemingway, that the novelist's work was to understand, an altogether different process.

She believed that Mark Twain had *felt* deeply, and correctly, but his judgment had to have been faulty since he was always in financial straits.

That spring Algren used his eyes and ears to further explore the Triangle, not completely unhappy that the book had indeed cost him his job on the Project: life was "a lead-pipe cinch" when he didn't have to work, and he hoped the good reviews would bring good sales. Now he shopped for a camera so he could wander the streets taking pictures, as he and Wright had apparently done on the South Side after the publication of *Native Son*. As a realist, Algren had a long-standing interest in visual representation, having earlier fixed New Orleans and the Alpine jail in his mind through crude crayon and pencil drawings. Now too, the photography seemed meant to serve the writing, as he flirted with the idea of a sequel to *Never Come Morning* and thought of writing a biography of old-time boxer Stanley Ketchel, the legendary Polish White Hope who had become a flashy, big-spending star, frequenting saloons and brothels before being shot to death at age twenty-four by a jealous husband. But neither of these plans seems to have gone anywhere. If he was unsure about his next big writing project, he had no intention of going to New York, the way writers so often did after their first successes. He had no desire to risk his realism to the "veil of sophistication common to N.Y. writers." And anyway, Babylon moved too fast to live in. He liked Chicago—it was all there for the taking, and he didn't want to leave it as long as he had writing plans, which he definitely did.

In mid-May, angry, outraged articles calling for *Never Come Morning*'s removal from the public library began appearing in Chicago's Polish newspapers, especially *Zgoda*. Polish community leaders were deeply threatened by the book. Perhaps unable to come to terms with a social message that indirectly attacked their own hand in local Polish life, they chose to see it as Nazi propaganda. Thus, through "the furious logic of illiteracy," as Algren later described it, one writer claimed the book could not have been written "without the assistance of enemy Germans and traitorous Polishmen," and another patriot suggested that "Herr Goebbels' devilishly cunning mind could not have published a more rotten propaganda volume to discredit and degrade the Polish people. If Mr. Algren is not on Goebbels' staff—he should be, and on the payroll, too." Members of the

Polish Arts Club, the Polish American Council, and the Polish Roman Catholic Union saw the story of Bruno and Steffi as "strictly an insulting falsehood calculated to discredit Polish American life in Chicago, where it flourishes with freedom in exemplary fashion." About the same time, an onslaught of lengthy, single-spaced letters from the Polish Roman Catholic Union began arriving at Harper and Brothers, excoriating the firm's publication of such a "Polish-baiting, church-hating, and filth-dealing book."

In a letter, Aswell tried graciously to appease the irate Poles: "If the book was written against anybody or anything, it was intended as an indictment of all of us for being indifferent to the plight of unfortunate people, many of them of foreign birth or ancestry, who have been herded together in large cities with no adequate provision made for giving them a decent way of life." Algren, mistakenly thinking the Poles could be convinced with words, wrote some four pages answering the accusations of a man named Czech, one of the most vociferous critics. Czech was "all wrong, strictly wrong, wrong as a man can be," if he found no good characters in it. The characters spoke for themselves, Algren pointed out, trying to make Czech see them as human. But Czech was not moved: in his view, the author spoke through his characters. Algren then explained that Bruno and Steffi were not bad characters, and that he had in fact started the manuscript before the war, but after more heated exchanges Algren impatiently suggested that perhaps they could iron everything out at a forum the library was sponsoring to discuss the issue. By now he probably wanted to quell the protest. He didn't want the antagonism, and he preferred to have the book available at the library.

But by this time, Chicago mayor Kelly had assured Czech that the book was being removed from public circulation. The library forum about *Never Come Morning,* where Algren reiterated that the conditions he described had nothing to do with nationality but everything to do with poverty and neglect, apparently had no bearing on whether the book remained on the shelves. Martha Gellhorn protested to the Chicago Public Library about the banning, but the decision on what Chicagoans should read, Algren said later, was a collusion between "the crocodilism of minds (transfixed around 1903) . . . of the Chicago Public Library," and offended community patriarchs who saw no contradiction between suppressing freedom of speech at home and fighting Hitler abroad. And who could make a dent in such self-serving indifference? A typical complainant examined Algren's "filth" with the complacent, dismissive view of the lost Algren had tried to counteract: "Any sane man knows that inmates of brothels or pimps are not bothered with civil, let alone religious duties," the Polish man concluded, as if a woman like Steffi could not entertain religious beliefs like anybody else. The people of *Zgoda* failed completely to identify with the outcast; for Algren, "anything less than such identification [was] contempt."

As late as 1962, Algren found *Never Come Morning* unavailable at the Chicago Public Library, but the furor over the book did damage to more than Chicago's public library patrons. In its vehemence, the Polish American Council had sent a copy of a resolution condemning *Never Come Morning* to the FBI, which had just reopened its internal security case on that erstwhile threat to the American government, Nelson Algren.

Algren had been in the FBI files as an internal security risk since at least October 26, 1940, but because so much material released under the Freedom of Information Act has been blacked out, it is unclear why he first came to the FBI's attention. It was not, as he may have thought, because of the Marxist rhetoric in *Somebody in Boots*. More likely it was the result of his signature on the June 1940 League of American Writers petition against entrance into the war. J. Edgar Hoover himself kicked off the investigation, asking the New York office to ascertain Algren's occupation and whereabouts. The slow wheels of the FBI's machinery began to turn. The New York office planned to interview Communist Party affiliates about Algren, but almost a year later, on August 30, 1941, Hoover hadn't received any information. Nevertheless, Hoover was preparing a custodial detention card on Algren, part of "a comprehensive list of potentially perfidious individuals who would be immediately detained in time of national emergency." He again petitioned the New York office, which now shifted into high gear, checking telephone directories and records at the Department of Motor Vehicles and Immigration. They checked their lists of signed election petitions and registered Communist voters.

The files state clearly that "a search was made of a list of 38,000 individuals maintained in the New York Office who voted as Communists in the State of New York in the 1940 primary." Though it seems straightforward, it is possible, of course, that the notation was poorly worded as a result of FBI incompetence; if not, however, the suggestion that the FBI interfered with American democracy at its most fundamental level—the ballot box—is chilling: the secrecy of primary elections is constitutionally guaranteed.

The New York office could find nothing on Algren and by late November suggested closing the case. Six months later, in April 1942, Hoover agreed. Algren, who didn't live in New York, could not be found. Coincidentally, however, the assistant director of the New York office read about *Never Come Morning* in the May 10, 1942, *New York Times Book Review,* and on May 29, the Polish American Council's resolution condemning the book reached Hoover's desk. The investigation was resumed, though by this time Algren's political work seems to have dwindled to signing petitions. Once begun, the FBI's investigation moved inexorably forward; but it took the agency more than a year to discover Algren's address.

By the summer of 1942, despite Algren's hopes for large sales, money became a problem. Although the book had gone into a second and apparently a third printing, Nelson was disappointed with his earnings. So when he was offered the opportunity to go to East St. Louis, live with Bud Fallon, and become a union man as a boiler-maker's assistant, he accepted: where the Fallonites were, literary material seemed to follow. But the unmechanical Nelson didn't re-alize how much the ribald Fallonites would enjoy seeing him wield an acetylene torch. They constantly played jokes on him on the job. Knowing he had vertigo, they made him climb tall poles and walk out on high crossbeams, experiences he later used in *A Walk on the Wild Side.* Still, he loved it, Dorothy Farrell recalled: it paid good money, and in the evenings he played poker and went out drinking. One day, he introduced himself to bookseller Lillian Friedman, a friend of Jack's, looking, she recalled, like a "timid bookkeeper." Soon she was going out with Nelson and his friends, whom she saw as *Studs Lonigan* characters. "Once when we were out and I got up to dance and left my purse on the table, they took money from it," Lillian recalled, but the incident seemed to leave no bad feelings.

After coasting in East St. Louis all summer, by September Algren was back in Chicago as a field worker for the Venereal Disease Control Project, a wartime scheme to eradicate syphilis and gon-orrhea at home and on the battlefront. Algren quickly enlisted Con-roy, languishing on yet another project, on what they jointly called the "Syph Patrol." They scoured the streets of Chicago for infected people and urged them to come in for treatment, often with a summons. Because the diseased people most likely to be contagious were those who could not afford medical care, Algren saw many poor, uneducated people, and he paid close attention to their speech, recording it in his field notes. He was stockpiling colloquial Chicago expressions. "I may get drunk, but I don't stagger," one woman who would find her way into an Algren story boasted to the investigators; "I fall down alright, but I don't stagger." Touring the bars with Conroy, he also met Lorraine Kimion, a singer and dice-thrower for the gambling game "twenty-six" who worked, according to various recollections, in the King's Palace, Queen's Palace, Shamrock, or Pink Poodle, and was always claiming she was higher than the highest peak in the Himalayas while flying on narcotics. Algren's friend for over a decade, Kimion kept company with many artists and musicians, read Proust, and was described, Conroy recalled, in Josephine Herbst's novel *Somewhere the Tempest Fell.*

But for the most part, the Syph Patrol involved a constant, depressing exposure to the extremely unfortunate. There was no penicillin in those days, and treatment for syphilis usually consisted of a series of dreaded arsenical shots, sometimes given spinally. When confronted by investigators, some people said they felt fine, some denied knowing about the disease, some refused to tell their spouses, some begged to be let off; some claimed the government tried to experiment on their bodies. Others, upon hearing it would take two hundred shots to cure them, quit going to the clinic altogether, headaches and numb limbs notwithstanding.

Said one woman: "Those shots give me a chill. They make my leg so bad I can't walk. When I tell her she say take a bath in hot water but that don't do no good. Seems like it don't get no better. But she com*pel* me. She say if I don't come up once a week she gonna put me in an institution. It cost me a dollar'n a half'n I just don't have that kind of [money on] me."

Said another: "I was born that way. My mother told me about it when I was ten, that I shouldn't have children. So I had an operation, that I shouldn't have no children. Then I got spinals. It keeps coming back. I'm afraid of those spinals. They give me malaria for two months, 'n there was so many bugs in there they said it would kill that germ. But it came back. It just ain't any use. I don't even have fare to go there. They say it'll make you crazy some day. It keep comin' back."

"It involved some detective work on our part," Conroy recalled, "because very often the diseased person would say, 'Oh, a girl named Peggy—she hangs out at a bar on so and so street.' . . . We'd go into places, sometimes we were kindly received, sometimes the bartender would give us information or sometimes he wouldn't be forthcoming at all . . . sometimes we couldn't deliver a summons because there'd be a pimp or a husband there and we'd have to beat a hasty retreat and send a policeman instead. . . . Once in a while we'd ask a soldier, 'Who have you had relations with?' and [he'd] say, 'Nobody but my wife.' So the next thing you know we'd have to take a summons out to a little cottage where a lady was busy with her housework and say in effect, 'Madame, I have to inform you that you have gonorrhea. Come in for treatment.' Sometimes they'd get very indignant and come after us with a broom.

"I didn't like it," Jack continued, "I was dismayed. You had to go down and harass these prostitutes, get them to come in. . . . [They lived in] miserable places. You'd go up two or three flights of dark stairs and find them huddled under a blanket with rain coming in from the roof. They were always scared." Algren was sympathetic to the whores, who could often talk him out of giving them a summons; it was in these cheap rented rooms, he wrote later, that "one feels life more deeply," referring as much to himself as to the room dwellers. If, as Conroy recalled, "he liked the whole atmosphere," it was probably because of the intensity of feeling it aroused in him. "The gates of his soul," Conroy liked to say, "opened on the hell side."

Not surprisingly, Algren began a series of Chicago sketches and stories that grew organically from his observations, making plans for a short-story collection which ultimately became *The Neon Wilderness*. Some stories, like "Kingdom City to Cairo" and "The Children," were originally sections of the novel that he later reworked, but many represented new material. One of the most significant was eventually titled "Design for Departure." As Algren recalled it,

> I had a very ambitious hope of writing a really great story, and I went about that in a very determined way. I slept in bum hotels and talked to prostitutes, and I knocked around State and Harrison Streets, trying to hear conversations going on in the next room. . . . I worked very hard on that. I worked on it off and on for years. That was to be such a great story.

In "Design for Departure" a young girl named Mary lives with her stewbum father and his ginmill woman in a littered basement off

North Clark Street. Life is chaotic; and as a child Mary imagines death as a place where there is "no noise, no fighting, no shouting, no arguing; no cursing and no blows." A depressed girl, she leaves home at fifteen for a bacon-wrapping job and a room in a cheap hotel, living in a "twilit land between sleep and waking." Here she is seduced by deaf Christiano, a con man who loves her fiercely and loyally, even showing her how she can sleep, on sleepless nights, with the help of the needle. She slips into complete dependence on Christy and, when he is jailed for three years, loses the ability to fend for herself: "She drifted without effort into the fluorescent jungle of the fourth-rate cabarets." After two years as a common whore, she becomes incurably diseased, floating into insanity with "Veronal. Allonal. Luminal. Veronal." When Christy finally returns, he immediately senses her condition. They both know that "he had spent the first half of his life in institutions; . . . he would help her, because he loved her a little, to keep what remained of hers out of them." And he goes, on her request, to buy a needle large enough to make her sleep forever.

"Design for Departure" deepens the theme of death as an alternative already touched upon in *Never Come Morning,* but the characterization of Mary makes the story more tragic. Mary grows up with no dreams at all except to fulfill an incessant desire for quiet and sleep. She toils mindlessly at her job: "Her fingers learned to work without her mind's attention. But her mind, once freed, wandered to no green hills or wooded places: it returned always to the doorless room." Unlike Steffi R., Mary is weak and has no deep greed for life; it is this psychological unpreparedness that makes Mary seem designed for departure. Though Mary lives in the same world as Steffi, where each person goes alone, Steffi's suicide attempt, the product of an intense yet fleeting depression, seems mild in comparison to Mary's final judgment that death is the best thing for a woman like herself. For Mary, the depression and insanity have become permanent. If earlier Algren characters could have blossomed in better circumstances, here it is the *combination* of poverty and psychology that renders Mary so useless. Algren seems to say that if society makes no allowances for the emotionally weak, who are always among us and part of humanity, then their dissipation may be the result. Moreover, society needed to know this: "I felt that if we did not understand what was happening to men and women who shared all the horrors and none of the privileges of our civilization, then we did not know what was happening to ourselves," he said later.

In writing such a long story, spanning ten years in a woman's life, Algren was quite consciously striving to create a literary masterpiece. Critics have drawn parallels to Crane's *Maggie: A Girl of the Streets* and have noted the Christian allegory in Mary's hope for final deliverance from evil through a benevolent mortal Christ. The story's importance to Algren is evident not only thematically, but also in the fact that he originally titled his short-story collection "Design for Departure." But though it has been recognized by some as on of the strongest in the collection, at the time no one wanted to publish it.

More spontaneous and commercially popular was the widely anthologized and translated "How the Devil Came Down Division Street," which Algren claimed to have written one afternoon before going to the track and revised only once. "How the Devil" combines elements of the ghost story, the tall tale, and the folktale in a significant departure from his usual realism. The Orlov family, crammed into a Noble Street tenement with only two beds, has no room at night for Papa O., who, traveling the taverns with his accordion, no longer sleeps with Mama O. All goes well until the ghost of a young suicide haunts the superstitious family's apartment, and Papa O. abandons the accordion for his wife. With the bed configurations altered, the son, Roman, is left with no place to sleep—and turns to the taverns, becoming the biggest drunk on Division Street. The story shows Algren's first successful use of humor, which came easily to him—perhaps explaining why this was often the genre he turned to after he stopped writing serious fiction in the late 1950s. But in 1942 he had more respect for the serious, labored story. "How the Devil" was published in *Harper's Bazaar*—it was the first time he had ever appeared in such a magazine—and Nelson couldn't believe the success of such a light piece when nobody was at all interested in publishing "Design for Departure." "He had an idea that he had to slave over a piece, that he had to be like Dostoevsky," Chris Rowland recalled. "That story, 'How the Devil Came Down Division Street,' he'd say, 'oh, that was nothing, I wrote it in a half an hour, and it should be the one who gets me started. . . . Well, I just can't get over it.' "

A less successful piece from this time was "A Lot You Got to Holler," another study of juvenile delinquence. In keeping with Al-

gren's usual pattern of the parentless child, a motherless boy is continually beaten by his father, until, aware of his damaged state, he
declares war on the old man and turns to a life as a runaway thug.
The intelligent and articulate narrator-hero's name is Augie, a nickname the Rowlands used for Algren, and the ice-cream sprees and
newsboy routines found here were later recycled into Algren's childhood memoirs, leaving in doubt whether this story was originally
from the Triangle or his own past. Along with "The Children,"
however, recycled from *Never Come Morning,* this story seems to
mark the end of Algren's preoccupation with adolescence, juvenile
delinquence, and the forming of personality. Although he would
keep on with boxing and gambling stories, he was now branching
out into police lineups and narcotics—yet other areas of the sprawling
and uncharted underworld.

He continued to write reviews for *Poetry* magazine and in September 1942 began to review books for the *Chicago Sun-Times,*
though the pay was minimal. These reviews reveal, for the first time,
a great respect for Hemingway. But, more important, they intruded
on his Chicago-bound existence by exposing him to new fiction by
Finnish authors, U.S. naval officers, and others writing firsthand
accounts of World War II. For by late 1942, the ever-expanding war
that overshadowed everything else was the only threat to his work.
Throughout 1941, many Americans had opposed entry into the war,
but isolationism had died with the twenty-four hundred Americans
killed at Pearl Harbor. From that time on, the country was united
in purpose, and since Hitler had already invaded the Soviet Union,
even the previously antiwar League of American Writers supported
his total defeat. Many of Algren's friends, including some of the
Fallonites, had already gone off to war; Abe Aaron, who had been
totally disgusted by the Hitler-Stalin pact, had enlisted as early as
March 1941. Even the formerly intransigent Richard Wright would
change his mind about the war. But though Algren naturally opposed
Hitler, he wasn't sure he wanted to fight for a "freedom and democracy" he knew included only some Americans. More likely he
didn't want to fight at all. He had been fortunate in receiving high
numbers since registering with the draft board in 1940, but even at
thirty-three, he could still be called. He did not want to go.

However, life in Chicago was not perfect. Despite fleeting love
affairs, he was lonely, and he remained ambivalent about his personal

life. Algren thought the artistic impulse related very deeply to the sexual one, and while part of him wanted a shared life, another large part preferred sacrificing a personal relationship for a kind of universal love. The writer, he told an interviewer years later, "wants to use this particular ability he has. Everybody he knows, anybody can get married and have children. He wants to be the one who does it differently . . . not many people can get love the way Dickens had, where people, an ordinary housewife, would follow him down the street and thank him for the people that he had given her. So this is a very rare opportunity and if you see this, and . . . even if you begin to get through letters from people you've never seen a kind of a love and a kind of a recognition that you're helping them, this is something more from the plain artistic viewpoint. This is something that can seem . . . to make it worth while giving up the stable situation."

This exalted view of art's rewards was probably encouraged by a difficulty, except when writing, in expressing love, a continual repression of feeling that art did much to liberate. His inability to communicate his unresolved feelings toward Amanda had been obvious since their breakup in 1940. That first summer, Amanda had, after all, moved in with Lynch, and Nelson told Chris Rowland he couldn't believe she'd gone off with another man. "You thought nothing of taking her away from someone else," Chris reminded him, and he looked shocked. *He* was different. Thinking once again to get her back or have it out with Lynch, he had one day gone looking for them. The front door of their apartment building had a small, eye-level window, and, finding the door locked, Nelson started pounding to be let in. Lynch had no desire for another nasty, unpleasant scene and wouldn't open the door. There was little discussion, however, before Nelson suddenly drove his fist through the glass, then left as abruptly as he had come: perhaps, like Bruno Bicek, he was enraged that his woman belonged to another, even though he had driven her there. Later that summer he continued to initiate meetings with Amanda, at least once hoping to reconcile with her. In the fall of 1940, when Lynch left for the war and Amanda moved to her own apartment, they began, like Steffi and Bruno, to talk for a few moments or to take a cautious walk in the park, with little being discussed. Amanda recalled that Nelson expected her to be the nice girl who always accepted his behavior, making clear his sexist, idealized view of her.

By 1942, however, their relationship was more cordial. He would drop by occasionally, and once in late May rapped excitedly on her door at one A.M. He had been rolled and his watch and overcoat had been taken. He had hardly even felt fear when one of the muggers had brandished a knife: it was an *experience,* and now, as a crime victim, he would have regular access to police lineups—no more having to borrow a pass from a newspaperman. Amanda went with him once or twice to the lineups, where his eye was so good he didn't even take notes, and soon they were seeing each other again. They were still married and had never legally separated, and Neal Rowland now played matchmaker, hinting to Nelson that living together as a married couple might keep him out of the draft. Sometime in the late autumn or winter of 1942–1943, Amanda moved into the apartment on Evergreen.

Nelson was in good spirits when she returned. In the mornings, he fixed her coffee, oatmeal, and poached eggs so she could have a good breakfast before she went off to her lucrative position on a labor arbitration case between the railroads and nonoperating brotherhoods, and he insisted on doing the dishes because she was working. For a while, life functioned smoothly, even when Amanda found someone else's brassiere in the dresser drawer. Nelson sent the laundry out and hired Bernice's cleaning woman to straighten the house, giving him an opportunity to reminisce about his sister. He fed stray cats on the back porch and wrote, reporting to the Syph Patrol only a few times a week.

Unfortunately, money was a source of friction. Nelson didn't come close to earning on the Syph Patrol what Amanda was bringing in. Once again, he refused to pay for anything except rent and utilities and wanted to do what he pleased with his money—gamble with it. Yet he seemed unhappy that Amanda always had money and he didn't. Resentment about the job also flared, Amanda recalled, because she had many friends there and often worked late. Once Amanda invited him to a coworker's wedding reception in the Bismarck Hotel. He felt excluded at the wedding, Amanda remembered. The people were liberal and represented labor organizations, and Amanda was happy among them: Nelson was the outsider—though he didn't really want to be involved.

The tables were completely turned from Cottage Grove, for Amanda sometimes worked overtime till early in the morning, and he was alone. But as before, he wanted everything on his terms. The place was his, and he was infuriated when she and a coworker came home drunk one night, and the woman had to stay over. He didn't want Amanda bringing anyone there. Perhaps he was jealous of her staying out late, but more likely he was ambivalent, guilty, and irritable about the whole relationship: it interfered with his work, and he seems to have sensed that she wasn't the right woman for him. Something he wrote to her later suggests this in his usual un-analytical way: "When we lived on Evergreen you stayed downtown until all hours because you didn't want to bother me in the eve-nings. . . . If you were honest you'd realize that when it's like that it isn't a marriage and say the hell with it."

He seemed to have an idea in his mind about how Amanda should be. She should understand and help in the life-style necessary to his writing, but at the same time it was too rough for her—she should be with someone who made more money and could buy her the kind of expensive clothes she liked. Once, apparently after winning at cards or the track, he called her at work: "I've got some dough today," he said shamefacedly, "let's go out for lunch." Apparently trying to be this person who would make her happy as much as his personality could allow, he put her on a pedestal, which in effect excluded her. "Watch your language when Amanda's in the house," he would warn the Fallonites and neighborhood friends until, with the easy old atmosphere gone, they stopped coming around; and, dismayed at this potential threat to his work, he began looking for another apartment where they could hang out unself-consciously. But he couldn't find one. "You'll have to find another place," he told Amanda too bluntly in his first mention of the issue. "The guys don't want to come around any more."

Naturally assuming that by asking her to move out he was ending the relationship, Amanda was devastated; and she immediately made arrangements to leave. She had been planning a vacation in San Francisco, where her boss had his main office; now she asked him for a job and decided to move permanently. She and Nelson never even discussed why he had asked her to leave; and yet, typically, he was very sad at her departure. He wanted to take her to the train station, but she refused to let him. Instead they said goodbye in the apartment, Nelson handing her a book by Woody Guthrie inscribed "To Mrs. A with love all the way from Mr. 1A, April, 1943."

That spring he wrote book reviews, attended a writers' group called the Authors' Round Table, and, according to FBI files, worked for the Abraham Lincoln School in Chicago, a progressive center where Josephine Herbst taught. Amanda's departure certainly put an end to any faint hopes he might have had of avoiding the draft, and perhaps he was ready to go when he was finally called early that summer. But "he was a reluctant conscript," Conroy recalled. He put his furniture into Amanda's mother's garage, passed his physical, gave up the apartment, and went into the army in August.

10.

Private Algren

H E HAD NO ALTERNATIVE: conscientious objection demanded proof of long-standing pacifism. Later he could poke fun at his attitude toward conscription—"They never had any right to send me overseas in the first place, as I had contributed to democracy by writing book reviews for liberal periodicals"—but at the time he was antagonistic. He'd been snatched away from his work and was not at all sure he wanted to fight for a racist, imperialist U.S. Army in a war to maintain the status quo he'd been protesting for ten years. He knew Hitler had to be defeated, but he wasn't convinced that the American side was so anti-Fascist, and he thought the segregated Negro troops felt this much more keenly. The real anti-Fascists, members of the Abraham Lincoln Brigade who had fought in Spain against Hitler-backed Franco, were not even wanted in the service.

Though many other writers in the armed forces were put to work on service newspapers like *Stars & Stripes* or *Yank,* or secured assignments in propaganda work or entertainment, Nelson Algren was sent to the infantry. This may have been the result of antileft military policy: the FBI was in contact with the army about Algren; his induction form was strangely stamped *Special Assignment,* and his incoming and outgoing mail was routinely opened. He listed his occupation as literary writer, but he was shipped out a dog soldier.

His attitude from the beginning was that they could make him shoot a howitzer, but they couldn't make him do it competently. They could make him wear a uniform, but they couldn't make him wear it well. Sent to Fort Bragg for field artillery training, he joined an outfit made up mostly of kids just out of high school who called him Grandpa and talked endlessly about the guns. When Nelson tried desperately to interest them in Chicago boxing tales, their talk always returned to weapons, especially to the grand finale of basic training, the actual firing of a howitzer. "They couldn't wait," he wrote later. "They were afraid they might get sick, or transferred, before the great day came." Private Abraham hoped for KP. He loathed the guns, especially the formidable howitzers. "Somehow those dumb and eyeless mammoths troubled me more than the machine guns that crouched, like some low-built carnivore, morning, noon, and night, beside the barracks door. . . . I could have seen every weapon, weapons-carrier, weapon-pusher, weapon-cleaner, weapons-polisher and garage in one vast pit, the size of the camp, and never felt the smallest sense of loss: I had a dream where I stood peering over the edge of such a pit with a pair of field glasses: miles below, doomed to rust into volcanic dust for keeps, lay all of the machinery of warfare."

The realization that he'd be heading overseas to bloody carnage, that he might end up dead or irrevocably damaged, like Carlisle Ansorg and the shell-shocked veterans from his novels, became very real. He had finally made a life for himself, and he could not allow the army to kill him. And he seems to have known that he was not mentally stable enough to endure the battlefield. The aversion to guns that had first surfaced in college ROTC now became an outright hatred. He had to find a way out of the infantry, and this became even more crucial in early 1944, when his unit was shipped to Camp Maxey, near Paris, Texas, a large training camp from which troops were shipped overseas. There, however, amid the army tedium and endless hand salutes, he thought he recognized a contributor to *New Masses* in the lieutenant who delivered the weekly current events lecture.

And he had. As historian Herbert Aptheker recalled, "I was an officer in a field artillery battalion . . . when an enlisted man carrying himself and uniform clumsily approached me and saluted—poorly. . . . He said he was Nelson Algren. Of course I knew his name and had read some of his writings. I expressed my pleasure and invited him into my quarters. . . . We were seated. He began rather quickly indicating that he had to get out of the artillery, that it was most urgent if he was to maintain sanity and that he knew nothing about guns and did not think he could learn or wanted to learn. It was clear that he was in deep distress." Algren, who kept repeating he simply could not go on with the guns, seemed so distraught that Aptheker felt it urgent to do whatever possible. He took the tale to his commanding officer, who listened seriously and promised to do what he could. Aptheker is still astonished at having been able to help: miraculously, Algren was transferred to a medical corps.

Now a litter-bearer, he spent six months with a good company. Part of his training consisted of nighttime attempts to gather men playing wounded on a mock battlefield. He felt so much better that he was even able to joke about the work in letters to Jack, and he had enough free time to write book reviews for the *Chicago Sun-Times* and *Poetry* magazine. But he was unable to concentrate on his own stories, set so long ago and far away in Chicago. He thought he'd rather do a novel, but there was no way to do it in the army. And now that he was in a unit of no strategic importance, his feelings toward going overseas were changing. Remaining in Texas had been an insurance policy when he was on the guns, but now he began to want not only the adventure but to share, as a writer, "in the big stuff of our times."

By early summer of 1944, when it looked as if his unit might indeed be sent abroad, he wrote to Amanda, asking her to visit him before he left. They were still legally married, and Nelson's monthly soldier's pay, half of which was earmarked for Goldie, was being sent to her. Relations between them remained surprisingly cordial. Despite his erratic behavior toward her, Nelson felt their relationship would continue for a long time: he wrote Martha Gellhorn that they broke up periodically, as if this were how their understanding worked. Their friendship did remain intact, but their love relationship was repeatedly damaging to Amanda. Still, she took a train to Texas that summer: it was wartime, and he was going overseas.

Their first night in the camp's visitors' quarters, Nelson wanted to make love, but when Amanda got up to get contraceptives, he immediately became upset: there was absolutely no question, Amanda recalls now, that he wanted to make her pregnant. And it was not, she believes, because he feared death overseas—he knew he would be safe. Rather, it was egotism: he wanted to pass part of himself on to a child. He didn't want to raise his child, but he did want to have one. Amanda had no interest in realizing his fantasies, so Nelson stalked around and sulked. For Amanda, hurt to think this was why he had asked her there, it was the same old story: he wanted what he wanted and she would have to suffer for it. He wanted only to *act* on his emotions, not to analyze them or weigh their consequences.

Since Amanda didn't force a discussion of the matter, they were able to have a friendly visit, eating out in Paris and enjoying themselves as much as was possible on an army base. Nelson, ever eager to outsmart the authorities, finagled six days of visitation instead of three by booking additional housing on the other side of the camp. He seemed to enjoy having passed his detail to someone else, and he was especially delighted when he and Amanda walked right by his CO without being recognized. The rest of the visit was without incident, and he continued to write to her throughout the war.

He had been Class A all along, so he was furious when his company received orders for shipment to Europe in late September and he was left behind. He had a hunch that someone higher up had written "subversive" on his Form 20—not an unreasonable assumption—and he also suspected anti-Semitism. Though he had legally changed his name to Algren in early 1944, he was still going by Abraham, as it wasn't until that fall that the army recognized him as Algren. He was undoubtedly uneasy about being forced to live openly with his true name, and he brooded mightily over his separation from the company. "I didn't know there were so many ways of getting screwed," he wrote Dick Wright. "Needless to say, the Army does all the screwing."

Now he was sent to a field hospital unit where it seemed to him that privates and noncoms alike were trying to outdo each other in pulling rank on misfits like himself who didn't play the game. He took one look at the bunch of them and asked to be transferred. "Transfers are froze," the first sergeant told him, "the only way you get out of here is to get throwed out." They could start throwing anytime, was Algren's view. Any place would be an improvement.

Whatever incentive he'd had for good conduct was lost. After more than a year of soldiering, he felt he had the right to go overseas—otherwise there was no point to the army at all. His disgust was obvious. Various sergeants remember Nelson Algren as an unreliable, uncooperative soldier with an I-don't-care attitude, an enigma to his superiors because he was obviously educated. They naturally assumed he would want to advance in the army hierarchy, but he showed not the slightest inclination to rise above his lowly station of litter-bearer. Algren wanted nothing more than to bring up the rear and be left alone. He did the minimum work and made the most of his time. When alone, he wrote—whether letters home or something else, his buddies never knew. He seemed to play cards constantly, and whenever he could, got a pass to town—invariably coming back late and, if possible, drunk. If we are to believe him, he tried to wrangle a two-day pass to Dallas by feigning a religious calling to attend Rosh Hashanah services. Some of the sergeants dubbed him "The Shame of the Nation" because he never volunteered for anything. Shortly before the unit was shipped overseas in December, endless military forms required typing, and Algren was asked to help out. He refused, though everybody knew he was the best typist. From that time on, whenever there was a dirty job to be done, it was always "Get Algren to do it."

One sergeant, whom Nelson described as an obnoxious redneck Ku Klux Klansman, took great pleasure in testing the limits of Nelson's frustration at being incarcerated by the army. The sergeant used him as an example to enforce discipline, once sending him to the mess hall staff and telling them to have him do anything and everything they wanted. Nelson hated him so much he "would wake up every morning thinking how to make this man now alive be dead forever. I wanted to kill him. I couldn't." Once the sergeant invited Nelson outside so they could have it out man to man, and to his everlasting regret, Algren refused. Seven years later he still dreamed of killing this man, of getting him on the ground in the dark and putting his knee in his neck. He wrote that the only thing stopping him was the fear of lifelong remorse and of being caught, cynically noting his passivity in the face of authority.

Being forced to endure discipline and abuse by officers he found corrupt and stupid brought out a sulky rebelliousness. Algren hated to be ordered around and often talked back to his superiors because he just didn't see them as superiors—especially when they verbally abused him. So he was often put on KP, and within two weeks he had been "put on the ball"—restricted to barracks—four times, repeatedly admonished, and told he needed discipline. "I told him it wasn't dis-SIP-line," Algren responded after one such incident, mocking the sergeant's pronunciation, "it was protective custody and why didn't he call an MP and make it official?" Then he put on his khakis and went to town.

Another sergeant recalled that Algren would have nothing to do with anyone of rank or intellectual ability, instead choosing to hang out with the far less educated cardplayers, who understood his unwillingness to vie for promotion. He was also drawn to them—and possibly Paris boxing matches and cheap Texarkana hotels—at least partially because they seemed the most likely source of literary material. Aside from memoirs of his own army unit in *Neon Wilderness,* the characters Algren drew from the war were never officers but enlisted men and women made poor by the war. Isaac Newton Bailey in "He Couldn't Boogie-Woogie Worth a Damn" was an AWOL private from Memphis, and the pathetic Wilma in "Depend on Aunt Elly" was a laid-off Texarkana defense worker turned prostitute. Algren played cards with a dealer who was reincarnated as Frankie Machine in *The Man with the Golden Arm.*

With the cardplayers he could gamble—an increasingly important activity that didn't even interfere with his salary, which was sent directly to Amanda. Whatever his luck, he spent more and more time betting and drinking, habits that were significantly curtailed when writing—or allowed to write, as he must have thought of it. Poker and dice were good ways to lose himself for hours at a time, to forget he was a prisoner, that his life was not his own.

Finally, in early December 1944, his company received orders for shipment to Europe—but again Algren almost didn't make it. He found out his bag wasn't being stenciled, and he had to assure one of the more reasonable sergeants that he really wanted to go and that he'd been goofing off only because Texas was "goof-off country." In the same orderlies' room there was a young guy who was begging not to go, and, surprisingly, the army made the switch.

After a long train trip to New Jersey and a few days on passes in New York, they set out to sea in the *Dominion Monarch,* formerly a luxury liner on the Australian ocean lanes. After twelve days at sea under blackout conditions, the enlisted men sleeping in hammocks or mattresses thrown over tabletops, their convoy reached Southampton. During the two days before personnel disembarked, the men on deck watched huge electric cranes ferry cargo from ship to shore, witnessing a large case slip from its ropes and crush the skull of an enlisted man.

Algren couldn't stomach the shameless disregard with which the officers treated the enlisted men. At Camp Penally, Wales, the privates' beds were sacks of straw over board bunks, and the toilet facilities—no hot water—were outside in a damp fog where the wind drove in bitterly from the sea. Although Amanda is very sure that Algren met Dylan Thomas while in Wales, there is no other evidence for this, and in his ostensibly fictional but surprisingly accurate army reminiscence, "That's the Way It's Always Been," Algren describes a much more mundane existence:

> The days, like the sky, passed in a pleasant decadence; they were conducted for us by mildly demented quacks and a few specially selected cretins. One day would be about the same as the next: chow, inspection, and then, like a call to arms, all men not on detail would be summoned to a stoveless, chairless Nissen hut on a hill to listen to The Man without Any Brains beat his gums till noon. . . .

As Algren saw it, officers took whatever privileges they could grab. "Officers were using the enlisted men's mess to entertain their Welsh girlfriends. Our breakfast had been reduced to tea and Pep. . . . They never used their own rations to bargain for the girl's favors; it was cheaper to use ours." In his view, the officers, headed by a "strutting stage prop" he called Colonel "Bull," didn't know what the war was about and didn't want to learn. They cared only for rank, booze, women, and food. "The most comical aspect of the colonel's attitude," Algren wrote, "was that he sincerely felt we had confidence in him and his staff," while the men knew that when the going got tough the colonel would be screwing a nurse or pulling on a fifth of Old Quaker without the slightest intention of risking his own neck.

For it became clear, and not just to Algren, that the real reason the unit crossed the English Channel—on verbal orders—to Le Havre on March 12 was that The Man wanted to emerge from the war a full colonel instead of just the lieutenant colonel he now was. So, just seven weeks before the Germans capitulated, the unit was ferried up the Seine to a tent city called "Twenty Grand"—a staging area deep in the woods from which thousands of GIs awaited field orders. Within a week Algren's unit was moved out to Château-Regnault, a French village close to the German border that had been plundered by Nazis and left without manpower, machines, food, or running water. For the first time the men had contact with the French, and Nelson liked them: "The people were lively and gracious, though destitute," he wrote home in a letter. Although an American GI, he wrote later, he felt he was on the side of the victimized French.

But the unit was quickly moved into the now liberated lands of

France, Belgium, and the Netherlands into Krefeld, Germany, near the Rhine. Unfortunately, it seems that The Man without Any Brains had led them forty miles ahead of the fighting unit they were serving, ordering the hospital to set up on a bombed-out racetrack. "They were looking for us to their rear," Algren described it. "We were supposed to be ten miles behind them, to evacuate their wounded." Instead, the 94th Battalion bumped the wounded on rutted roads trying to find the hospital, which was sandwiched, one sergeant remembered, between combat units and which, according to the official army history, came under fire when someone built a fire under the grandstands to make coffee. After over a week of the nightly artillery barrage, orders were received to move to nearby München-Gladbach.

There Algren's unit spent a month in the field before moving into the buildings of the local St. Francis Hospital, which, untouched by the war, had excellent mess facilities, even refrigerators. For the first time in months, the men slept on mattresses and clean sheets. Seventy Catholic sisters remained on hand to do housekeeping and run a laundry and a bakery. "Nobody wanted to leave that place," Algren recalled. "We lived in complete comfort. They had German girls waiting on us, everything. A big mess hall, fresh eggs, everything."

Though glad to be in Europe, Algren was trying to make the best of things in the army. Thirsty for liquor, he and a buddy might leave the camp without a pass, and if they did manage to liberate a wine cellar, coming back from such an outing could be tricky, because as far as Algren was concerned, the real risk of getting shot came from the American side: "This wasn't an infantry outfit and legally we weren't permitted to bear arms, being medics. But our guards, who never had any experience with small arms, were allowed to have them or had picked them up from the Germans. On duty some of them wanted to get into the war. They wanted to shoot somebody; it didn't particularly matter [whom], so that . . . when you went out to get wine . . . you had to watch out sneaking back." To Algren, one of the most absurd things about the army was that they always seemed to hire the wrong man. They'd tried to put a writer in the infantry and had put Murphy, a slow-witted southerner who liked to fight, in the medics.

Algren continued to find escape at the card table and also with women, though he feared getting venereal disease: one sergeant remembered that he had himself tested at the hospital. While at

München-Gladbach he became friendly with some Polish women, probably displaced people, and there is a rumor, begun by Algren himself, that he fathered a child in Germany. When he remarried Amanda after the war, she asked him to see a doctor when she didn't conceive. "There's nothing wrong with me," he said, "I had a child in Germany." Friends in New York from the early 1960s seemed to think the child was a girl, and another rumor has it that the child was somehow not normal. If you wanted to get him to shut up, recalled writer H. E. F. Donohue, who interviewed Algren in the early sixties, one way to do it was to mention that child. But Nelson may well have been engaging in wish fulfillment. After the war he sent shoes to civilians he'd met in France and Poland, but among their letters and Algren's papers there is nothing, nothing at all about a child.

For a few weeks close to Germany's surrender, business was brisk at the hospital. The enlisted men worked twelve-hour shifts. In addition to his duties as a litter-bearer, Algren also administered first aid, bandaged wounds, applied leg splints, took temperatures, treated patients for shock, and fed them. The hospital had to be kept clean and beds made. Perhaps the improved living conditions made him less unwilling to work, for army records indicate that he did ultimately earn a good-conduct medal—despite his later claims to the contrary—as well as his more or less automatic overseas bars, campaign medals, and battle stars.

By early May 1945, the war in Europe was almost over, and while the hospital surgery treated some battle casualties, like hand, arm, leg, and foot wounds, the majority of cases were medical ones— pneumonia, diphtheria, hepatitis, and respiratory infections. The hospital never saw large numbers of battle injuries or concentration camp victims but it did treat displaced persons, however, including one who miraculously responded to intravenous feedings and transfusions and was soon able to take nourishment by mouth. "Saw a ghost last night," Algren wrote in a letter home, describing a sixteen-year-old Russian boy who had been captured two years before for slave labor. A couple of doctors had found him in a barn. Somehow his feet had frozen and been amputated, and then the Nazis quit feeding him because he was useless. He weighed thirty-five pounds and could be picked up in one hand; what the doctors had thought was a bedsore was his protruding spinal column. "The terrible part of looking at him," Algren felt, "is that his breath still comes and goes—and you still have to reckon with the eyes—which are still living—and look out with a gaze of unrelieved horror from the skull. Even if you wanted to believe in such an atrocity, you couldn't believe it without the evidence of your eyes and hands."

He disliked the Germans. He had been homesick for France almost as soon as he arrived in Germany, and though he knew the language somewhat, fraternization was forbidden—"and who wants to anyway?" He felt uncomfortable with the Germans' relative prosperity, and they seemed to act as if they were without any responsibility for the war. "You people have a bill to pay before you can be friends with anybody," he told a German woman who suggested, after the Nazi capitulation, that now the countries could be friends again. "Maybe in a hundred years we can be friends. If we let you be friends now, in another ten years you'll have yourself another Hitler."

But though Algren must have known of the concentration camps, in his surviving letters home he never mentioned the plight of the Jews, nor would he ever really address it in his work. He rarely spoke about the Holocaust; it seems that as a Jew, Algren thought it would not be protest for him to make a statement. To him, protest was altruistic: it meant speaking up for those whose interests differed from one's own. Witness his remark in response to reminders of Irwin Shaw's anxiety about the plight of the Jews: "But this wasn't protest; he's Jewish."

"[The] arrival of VE day was unmarked, here, by any holiday spirit or sense of celebration," Algren wrote to a friend. "We expected the end for so long, and the news came so uncertainly, that the actual difference between war and peace was a qualitative one. Besides, the prospects of getting home remain so remote that we don't actually feel the war is over." Peace brought more liquor rations and softball games and time to dip into the excellent swimming hole at Bad Kreuznach, Germany, where the unit moved next. But orders soon arrived for redeployment to the Pacific theater, and the unit was shipped to chalky, barren Camp Philadelphia in Reims, France, for processing. On furloughs to Paris and the Riviera, the men lived in fear of being sent to the Pacific, so when word came of the Japanese surrender, spirits were high: everyone was going home. Though orders still read for shipment to the Pacific, and the unit entrained for Marseilles, the homesick men were convinced that the evacuation hospital was homeward bound. So in mid-September, when new orders came through for occupation in Passau, Germany, the general feeling was one of solemn gloom.

But Private Algren got separated, because everyone over thirty-five with more than one year in the service was sent home.

The army was trying to get him on a boat, and Algren found himself suddenly free of his outfit's discipline, suddenly on his own after so long with men. The three months he spent in Marseilles, he said later, were the most isolated and least despairing he'd ever known. In the morning he would crawl out of his tent and with or without a pass hop the truck into town, there he threaded his way through the city's poor streets as he had roamed the Polish slums in Chicago. In the war's aftermath canned speeches and "La Marseillaise" rang daily from the loudspeakers of Vieux Marseilles, and the place was flooded with Allied troops waiting to go home. On the city's age-old French and North African faces Algren saw a thousand years of war and defeat of which the current occupation was only the most recent. Far-off sea bells tolled; great morning sea fogs burned off to announce afternoons of white Mediterranean light: the stone streets and narrow passages had the sun-dried look of North Africa. And "always the children who had never been children, the ancient, in-nocent wiseacres with the light of old Egypt in their eyes and Amer-ican slang on their tongues." It was a "Wild West town" where there were never enough military police to cover the troops, who were often trying to unload guns they'd picked up from the Germans, a city of corruption and vice where Senegalese and Moroccan traders, eager for black market goods, lurked in shadowed doorways.

Nelson spent his evenings gambling for high stakes. If he had a bad night he made it good by peddling cigarettes, razor blades, contraband jackets, shoes, and other luxuries on the black market. He may have been able to buy the stuff from the PX or cheaply from other soldiers, but it wouldn't be surprising if he stole it from the supply depot, like the AWOL soldier he would later describe in "He Couldn't Boogie-Woogie Worth a Damn." He made a lot of deals with the Senegalese, who would try to lure him into an off-limits bar, have him spread his wares on the table, and start shouting, "Hey, Joe! MP! MP! MP! Run, Joe! Run!" so he'd flee, thinking it was a raid. Or they'd try to get him in a hallway, drop the money on the floor and then grab the jacket while he was bending over to get the cash. He knew all these tricks, but he could hardly have

blamed the traders: hadn't the Americans started it by selling cigarette cartons full of wadded newspapers? It was safer to sit in a little
pizzeria with a warm oven in the back, eating pizza, drinking Chianti,
and making deals with the traders, than to risk the out-of-bounds
bars. But he didn't want to drink too much. All around him were
soldiers accustomed to killing: if they saw a drunk GI and could use
his shoes, it was "very easy to push him in the river."

Prostitution flourished to accommodate the soldiers. Algren remembered one house where "the guys would be just running up the
stairs, thousands of guys. They must have had twenty-five or thirty
women up there, available all the time." The MPs would often raid
the houses, so the women also waited in the streets. Perhaps Algren's
reactions were similar to those of his fictional character Katz, a
middle-aged American private who fell in love when he saw four
GIs baiting a little French whore. "Combien?" they asked, and,
outraged at her price "for such a cheap item," gestured her back.
"They called her once again, and again she went curiously forward,
and again she was driven back, until Katz touched her elbow. . . ."
Later, in her room, he saw that "she was so thin he could feel her
rib beneath her slip. Somehow it was in part the touch of her poor
thin body, that and what it meant, that did it. . . . It made him want
to give her something, he didn't know what—he offered her a cigarette case, a chocolate, then suddenly took her to bed instead . . . in
the night he felt her hands touching his face: they traced the line of
cheekbone and jaw, then rested like a child's in the hollow of his
throat."

But Algren's plan was to have Katz find he was in love only with
an image: her need was of money. Marseilles was so hard-pressed
that twelve-year-old children sold themselves.

And so the months passed, in a Mediterranean sea of wine and
old-world faces, Algren trying to strike it rich. No longer attached
to an outfit, he was a private citizen in uniform, with just a tent and
his belongings. He had few friends in the tent city; he came and went
responsible to no one, his only ID very likely somebody else's ration
card. When he crept back into his tent with only half a bottle of
cheap red wine to show for a long day's toil selling contraband, it
felt wonderful. "I was the anonymous man," he wrote later. "I was
finally myself."

He was shipped out in mid-November of 1945, arriving in the States
November 27, then traveling to Camp Grant, Illinois, to spend an-

other five days being processed for separation. With $160.60 in hand, officially ranked as a private first class, he headed for Chicago. When he reached the city, his mother wasn't home. After years among men he wanted to see women, and he called Dorothy Farrell, who was staying at her mother's with her sister Virginia. "He came out to the house and he had a great big bunch of red roses," recalled Dorothy. "We welcomed him as though he were our own son—he was so pleased by that . . . so happy." The black marketeer was a war hero. He stayed the whole day.

11.
The Neon Wilderness

H E ARRIVED to that Chicago winter with the simple longing to stay in one place for a long, long time. After so many years of rootless wandering, he no longer wanted to do anything but write. Once again he found a place deep in the Polish slums where nothing could distract him: two back rooms on Wabansia and Bosworth, overlooking an Ashland Avenue alley, for ten dollars a month. If his new home was almost Siberian in its austerity, it was perfect for writing, containing only a bed, a table, a stove, a typewriter, lots of books, and a sink with one faucet. He showered at the Y. It was the bare minimum, but after two and a half years in the army, privacy and the right to do as he pleased seemed luxuries.

Though each month he gave money to Goldie, who was now living in a small West Side apartment, he didn't need a job. He had his veteran's benefits, and shortly after his arrival Doubleday editor Ken McCormick, tremendously impressed by *Never Come Morning,* had offered him a contract. Nelson, dismayed to find the novel out of print and a steady advance from Harper and Brothers unlikely, was lured by the Doubleday offer and rather oblivious to the literary prestige of being edited by Aswell. He asked McCormick for fifty dollars a week, and McCormick raised it to sixty. Algren would complete his collection of short stories and start on the new war novel he had planned.

He prepared for writing like a boxer training for a fight, worrying about his weight and limiting himself to two meals a day. He pedaled a bicycle to the YMCA in all weather, presenting one of several forged cards which he bought for $2.00 apiece—a saving of $18.00 over the membership fee—so he could jump rope and work out on a punching bag before his shower. Though he occasionally went to the racetrack or spent an entire day reading by the oil stove, he worked furiously, and in eight months wrote and resurrected at least twelve stories. He wrote two angry, evocative army memoirs somewhat reminiscent of Céline, whom he was just discovering; he used Marseilles's black market for the story of an AWOL black GI's decision not to return to the racist United States. From his Camp Maxey forays to cheap Texarkana hotels and Paris boxing matches came "Depend on Aunt Elly," about the calculated exploitation of a small-town hustling girl. Two stories emerged from as far back as his hitchhiking days and his jail stint; and he grafted an old Stash Paycheck scene to the tale of a crazy man in love with his cat. He recycled material freely.

When he ran out of stock he turned to the streets. At first he sought to return to the world that had been interrupted by the war, the "life-size drama" he had built "using the neighborhood people for all people." He had so longed to step back into that world that he was crestfallen when Jack Conroy told him the Syph Patrol had been discontinued. So he turned to the taverns, the only home for the walking wreckage of a city that seemed somehow changed after the war. "The last of Chicago's gaslamps had gone out," he wrote later. "Fluorescent neon lit brands of beer never named before. Some of the drinkers had been to the war and some had sat it out; yet all seemed equally survivors." And they wandered in a "neon wilderness" through a life they knew had long ago been lost; in frustration they beat each other in the uneasy comfort of the bars. "They fought—not because the liquor was in them, but because it did not fill them enough. Because there wasn't enough whisky on South State to fill the emptiness of a single lost man of them all. The twisted, bitter taste of defeat parched their throats, and they blamed it on [the] pretzels," he wrote in one story.

Other nights, Algren frequented the police lineups. Sometimes he went three evenings a week for several hours at a stretch, returning for sessions at the typewriter to record the hunted explaining their arrests:

"Somebody died in my room—manslaughter."

"Missed-a-lane-us. Like speedin' 'n' domestic relations."

"Possessing and passing," said one man.

"What kind of bills were they?" the captain wanted to know.

"Pretty good—oops, I mean twenties," said the counterfeiter.

Algren was still fascinated by the captain, who, watching the parade night after night, year after year, was forever passing judgment on these losers. "You're a sick-lookin' cannibal—stay out of our parks," he'd warn a molester; "You look too lazy to steal," he'd accuse a thief. In Algren's fiction, the captain, growing infinitely weary of the endless parade, advised suicide some nights, and Algren knew how he felt. He would continue at the police lineups for years, but he wrote a friend that sometimes even he felt like throwing up his hands at their hopelessness. One thing was clear: "Neither God, war, nor the ward super [could] work any deep change on West Division Street."

Except for minor changes, the stories were finished in September. McCormick was pleased; he even liked the army piece Nelson worried he would find offensive. Algren, never happy with the names of his first two books, wanted a good title. When he suggested *The Neon Wilderness,* McCormick thought it was absolutely marvelous and brought the stories together thematically. "And the minute I liked it, he hated it," McCormick recalled. "So then I had to get a third party to convince him that he had a good title because he was . . . suspicious and contrary. . . . If I liked it, there must be an angle, and what was it?" But despite Nelson's suspicions about the creative judgment of the publishing trade, *The Neon Wilderness* it would be.

While awaiting the book's publication, he read extensively, especially French literature. While in the army, he loved Jean Malaquais's *War Diary* and was tremendously impressed by Céline's *Journey to the End of the Night.* When asked who, of his day, was trying to break out of the middle-class world and show the underworld legions of the city, Algren answered in one word, "Céline"; and indeed critics have drawn parallels between the blackness in Céline's and Algren's work. Proust, however, failed to stir him: he hadn't been able to get beyond page thirty-four of "Let's Research Around Sometime or whatever it is." In the spring he reviewed books, many of them mediocre, for the *Chicago Daily News,* and truly admired Jean Giono's *Blue Boy* and *The Good Soldier Schweik* by Jaroslav Hašek. As for American writers, he joked that he knew Stephen Crane so well that sometimes he thought he'd written him himself; he found the "bad" but compassionate writing of Theodore Dreiser—"most representative of American naturalists"—important, even if Dreiser's heroes were sometimes "characterless and remote." By fall, he began dropping in at the Seven Stairs, a tiny literary bookstore on the Near North Side with a woodstove, a barrel of apples, a hanging salami, and a knowledgeable owner named Stuart Brent.

He was also trying to get started on the novel, though he had no clear sense of direction. Early longhand drafts reveal the autobiographical GI, Katz, from his army sketches, but Marseilles, where he had planned to set the book, drifted further and further away. He was instead taken with writing about an army pal, an Italian-American card dealer and crapshooter who was always telling his buddies he had a golden arm. Algren changed him into a Polish GI named Frankie Machine, just returned from the war, a card-dealing man of no other skill living above a bar in a poor Chicago neighborhood. He would live with a wife he no longer desired, who chained him with guilt because he had crippled her in an auto accident while driving drunk. She would end up, as many Algren characters had and would, in an insane asylum. Perhaps revealingly, her name would be Sophie, the same as that of a Polish woman he'd known in München-Gladbach. And indeed, babies seemed to figure in various ways in early drafts of *The Man with the Golden Arm:* Sophie blames Frankie for her inability to bear children; an abusive drunk and his wife and baby live in wretchedness next door. Algren may also have been thinking about including a child killing in the plot, for he combed Chicago criminal records to review the inquest of an infanticide.

Certainly he toyed with the idea of a suicide, and from early on planned to include a murder in the plot. From inquest records, he had also noted an eyewitness account of an alley slaying: "I heard a dead sound." Here, Algren made his second attempt at putting a "high-yellow" mulatto woman in a novel, this time as Frankie's lover, and when a dope pusher threatens to reveal their affair to Sophie, Frankie breaks his neck in an impulsive, infuriated moment. The murder, like Bruno Bicek's crime, arises from an unrelated rage— Frankie's self-loathing for having crippled Sophie. Like Bicek, he cannot feel guilt for the murder because it fails to alleviate the underlying trauma causing it.

Though Algren—afraid of what he might find—claimed opposition to psychoanalysis, his characters always seem to act as if their behavior were subconsciously directed in the manner described by Freud. Mulling over his own dreams, Algren constructed important dream sequences in his writing; and his working method was emotional rather than planned. "I just had an over-all *feeling,* I didn't have any particular theory about what I ought to do," said Algren, who could not write a whole book in one draft. "I've always figured the only way I could finish a book and get a plot was just to keep making it longer and longer until something happens—you know, until it finds its own plot—because you can't outline and then fit the thing into it." Still, describing dreams and psychological states didn't seem to make the novel fall into place, and he sometimes felt he was writing *Never Come Morning* all over again.

The Neon Wilderness, thematically coherent as few collections are and boasting three award-winning stories, was published in January 1947 to favorable, though not extensive, reviews, most noting his extreme compassion for the underdog and his intense social vision: "He is determined that we . . . should see, as he sees, the personal delinquency of the characters dissolve within the greater, more terrible delinquency of our synthetic society," wrote *The New York Times.* If most critics, including Algren himself, found the collection uneven in quality, a decade later critic Maxwell Geismar would call it "an excellent collection of short stories, perhaps one of the best we had in the 1940s." But though Geismar noticed correctly that the stories were in a softer vein than his earlier work, two separate reviewers drew parallels between his work and the growing philosophy of Existentialism in France. "There is enough horror, ugliness, and ghoulishness to satisfy Sartre," wrote *Saturday Review,* and *The New York Times* declared that "Algren's world is an Existentialist world, a sunless place of whispering, tangible shadows, where nightmare becomes reality, and the future is slain by the intolerable present." It seems incredible that after such comparisons Algren would not read up on Existentialism; yet he would have us think that he did not.

Despite some unexplained "unfortunate sales confusion" on Doubleday's part, *The Neon Wilderness* did well in Chicago. Its opening reception was held at the Seven Stairs, where Stuart Brent had become an important Algren fan. Brent, hoping to propel the store into a literary hotspot, enthusiastically placed the book in his customers' hands, selling hundreds of copies and holding periodic parties to keep sales alive. Algren was already known about the city as a novelist and reviewer, but now he was clearly recognized as a Chicago writer. Jack Conroy interviewed him on the brand-new medium of television; for this pleasing event, "like being up in a stratoliner," he brought his beaming mother and had his picture snapped for the newspapers. Algren spoke at library forums on the Chicago literary scene and became a trendy guest to groups like the Friends of Literature—when he could get along with them. Before one appearance, he was warned that *Neon* wouldn't be on sale because the other speaker's book wasn't available. When Nelson told the event's organizer he didn't intend to come downtown for a pat on the head, the woman warned him against being presumptuous, hinting at the group's annual $500 writing award. He told her he felt the presumptuousness was entirely on her part and said goodbye. And he felt wonderful to be able to turn her down again when she called the next morning to apologize.

He had not allowed himself to be either exploited or bought: yet he didn't refuse money when it came his way. He joked about being published in a high-class magazine like *Harper's Bazaar:* "Far from being ashamed of being published in 'that rag,' I've been waiting so long simply to be had, at the usual fee, in my little barren room above the traffic's roar, that I often wonder whether my agent is still procuring in earnest below: I still fear that she's a little choosy and doesn't solicit everyone with a buck to spend and an hour to kill. I keep hollering down, '*Anybody,* honey, *anybody*'; but she doesn't seem to hear."

More important than money was gathering material. "My idea of money is the stuff you use to get around to pick up things for books," he later told an interviewer. "For instance, I remember a morning, about four in the morning, when I was with . . . a six-and-a-half-foot drummer from Arkansas. He's an addict. I wanted to go home. It was getting late. . . . He wanted to make a stop somewhere. He wanted to go into some little restaurant and just wait. I was tired of it and he said, 'Well, you don't know what it's like to have a monkey on your back.' This is pretty stale stuff, by now, this phrase. It's been used in a hundred dozen paperbacks. It's common language now. But at that time . . . I don't believe this phrase had come into the language of articulate people. It was something that musicians, that drug addicts said. I happened to be there and I repeated it. . . . If I found something like that, I'd go home. That's what you make books out of."

*

In those years Algren was a tall, lanky, attractive man with mussed blond hair, steel-rimmed glasses, and a sensitive face. He dressed casually and at formal gatherings was able to mock convention yet maintain a conservative profile by wearing a pinstripe suit, a loud shirt, a ridiculous tie, or sometimes even a bow tie that lit up. He knew how to put others at ease and gave people his undivided attention in conversation. Yet even when greeting someone warmly he could manage to maintain distance through body language.

Certainly there was detachment in his relationships with women. He ignored a letter from the Polish Sophie he'd known in the war, and though Amanda again visited him on her vacation to help him retrieve the things he'd stored at her mother's house, in mid-1946 he filed for divorce, ostensibly because a lawyer told him it would be cheap. "If you get anything in the mail, just ignore it," he told the amenable Amanda, and divorce was granted on the grounds that she'd deserted him. Probably as much because of their genuine fondness for each other as because of his guilt, they remained friendly, but a lag in their letters ensued. "I wrote you a letter which you didn't answer," he wrote her the following year, "you send me a card asking why don't I write for a long time."

The relationships he did maintain were casual. He squired different women to Brent's *Neon Wilderness* parties, attractive friends or people he was using for characters. "He had a lot of one-night stands," recalled Ted Liss, an actor who, though remembered as Nelson's sidekick, insists they were only acquaintances. "Nelson liked one-night stands—there was no commitment. Nelson went through people—they used him, he used them, and that was all right. . . . He used people to develop other parts of himself. This doesn't produce contentment, but it did bring a focus to his life . . . it was a process of survival—saving energy from friendships that you want for your art. What he had to say in his writing was so insightful there wasn't anything left."

One such mild romance was with Mary Guggenheim, whom he'd met before the war at parties with Chris and Neal Rowland. Raised in France and the United States, Mary was making her way in New York by working at *Partisan Review* and translating French stories, among them work by Nelson's adored Jean Malaquais. She had received friendly letters from Nelson during the war and looked him up on a September 1946 trip to Chicago. They spent three days together, going to baseball games, movies, the races.

The twenty-three-year-old Mary found Algren "very sweet. He put her on a train back to New York, and on that train it hit her, all of a sudden, that she was wildly in love with him.

He didn't encourage her feelings, Mary recalled. She went back in November of 1946 and they had a love affair. She was in Chicago for a week and he was very gallant; he took her to meet his mother. Mary felt that he was proud of her, that this was an occasion. It probably meant only that she was a nice girl Goldie couldn't complain about, but Mary left Chicago even more in love and determined to return with or without his consent. In the meantime, her letters regaled him with stories of New York literary life, including details of a party where the French philosopher and novelist Simone de Beauvoir, then touring America, was the guest of honor.

By 1947, both de Beauvoir and her intellectual companion, Jean-Paul Sartre, were well known. De Beauvoir, dubbed "the hope of French literature," had published three well-received novels: *She Came to Stay, The Blood of Others,* and *All Men Are Mortal.* Sartre, whose plays included *The Flies* and *No Exit,* had received high acclaim for his prewar novel *Nausea.* They were both politically left-wing and known for repudiating bourgeois convention. In addition, each had written important philosophical essays for which the press had dubbed them "Existentialists." This new philosophy of Existentialism which swept France after the war held that man is born for no discernible purpose and can rely only on himself to justify his existence and give his life meaning. In spite of his material circumstances, each person must create himself and he cannot expect intervention from heaven or elsewhere. Confronting this realization provokes anxiety, but a person must take responsibility for his life in order to be free. His accomplished acts define him. Always confronting new choices, man is in a perpetual state of becoming.

Algren, whose *Never Come Morning* was the kind of novel de Beauvoir praised as placing "the whole human being opposite the world" and who exactly fitted her prescription of the writer as one who "must commit himself, make a choice, and feel responsible because he is free," knew little about Existentialism and did not much care for philosophy. Theory made him uncomfortable; he much preferred to concentrate on reality. So when Mary wrote to him of de Beauvoir, he didn't think much of it and mocked her in a hick-macho mode: "That Simone de Budoir sounds real chi-chi and I'm sure J-P Sartre, whoever he may be, is real lucky. I bet she says,

J-P honey, bite my little titties. And J-P, the hog, chews her tits clean off." If later he could have bitten his tongue, surely Mary Guggenheim must have regretted giving de Beauvoir Algren's phone number. At any rate, the phone rang one February night while Algren was cooking dinner in his little Wabansia Avenue flat. "Often when it rang it'd be somebody with a . . . very strong Polish accent who had never used a telephone before and they would holler into the phone," Algren said, "and so this time . . . somebody hollered into the phone, screeched something, and I hung up. . . . I got back to the stove, the phone rang again and I got that same hoarse screech and I did this three times. . . . About half an hour later the phone rang and a very clear voice said, 'Would you mind holding the phone for a minute, don't hang up for just a minute, there's a party here would like to speak to you.' So then I listened and next a heavily accented French voice was saying that her name was, ah, ah, something, I didn't quite catch it. I said, 'Where are you at, I'll come down.' "

Upon arriving at the elegant Palmer House, he saw a very attractive woman. Approaching forty, Simone de Beauvoir looked energetic and youthful: her chestnut hair was piled high to show off her smooth skin and aristocratic face; her petite body had been kept firm by long walks in the European countryside. Algren bought her a drink and told her about the war—all about the war. "Where I thought *she'd* been while I was fighting it I didn't stop to think," he remembered, unconsciously admitting his excitement. "Simone de Beauvoir's eyes were lit by a light-blue intelligence," he would describe her later, "she was possessed by something like total apprehension." Simone wrote later that their mutual affinity had been immediate. She liked local bars, had heard a good band only in Harlem, and had no more interest in going to a bland middle-class nightclub than Algren. So when he proposed a tour of Chicago's lowlife, she immediately accepted.

He took her to Chicago's Bowery on West Madison, where wasted-looking men loitered in shadowed doorways, Simone reported later in *America Day by Day*. They entered a seedy bar where a little band was playing and watched wretched men and women, old, ugly, drunk, and lame, dance in a fleeting ecstasy of joy and escape. Simone, bewildered, stared and said, " 'It's beautiful.' N.A. was astounded; it seemed to him very French. 'With us,' he said, 'ugliness and beauty, the grotesque and the tragic, and even good and evil, go their separate ways: Americans do not like to think that such extremes can mingle.' "

Intrigued, he steered her to a combination bar/homeless shelter where dirty, useless old men sat amid a foul smell of squalor. A woman who could only have been Lorraine Kimion tended the cash desk. "Everything I know of modern French literature I owe to her," Algren said. When she began questioning Simone about Existentialism and Malraux's latest novel, the Frenchwoman was dumbfounded. Later Simone and Nelson walked the cold streets. For Simone, this strange evening, on the arm of an unprepossessing man who wanted her to see the pillar of poverty on which American society was based, had been, according to her biographer Deirdre Bair, upsetting and emotionally draining. Algren brought her to his apartment to relax, and there they made love. "I think he initially wanted to comfort me," de Beauvoir said later, "but then it became passion." It was Algren's first encounter with a woman whose reactions and opinions went beyond the cultural restrictions of most Americans to see the tragic beauty of wretched people that he too saw. Most of the women he had known had come from either the respectable world or the completely unrespectable one; Simone, like himself, could look at both. In all this, there was possibility.

The next day they continued their Chicago sightseeing. "I showed her the electric chair, the psychiatric wards, neighborhood bars where I told her everyone sitting around was a sinister character," Nelson described it. "She looked around a while and then told me, 'I think you are the only sinister thing around here.' Then I took her to a midnight mission. I thought it was time to SAVE HER SOUL. I took her to cheap burlesques, Maxwell Street, a police line-up, and the zoo. I explained American literature, the Loeb-Leopold case, the Heirens case, the Haymarket riots, and why I was the only serious writer in Chicago since Dick Wright left in the 1930s." Because of other commitments, dinner together was impossible. Nelson, asking her to come back, gave her one of his books. From the train station she called to say goodbye once more; and her friends had to take the phone away, Simone recalled later, by force.

After she left, Algren maintained, he picked up a copy of *The New Yorker,* which carried a long article on de Beauvoir and Existentialism, and discovered who she was. Then came a letter saying how much she had enjoyed the book and Chicago and him: "I was happy, being with you—I did not like to say goodbye, perhaps not to see you again in my whole life." She did not know if she would be able to pass through Chicago again; and if this parting was difficult, would not the next one be more so? Impatient with prudence, he told her it was just too bad if another separation proved difficult.

Within a week of this momentous meeting, however, the unfortunate Mary Guggenheim, having given up her job and apartment to move to Chicago uninvited, arrived at Nelson's Wabansia Avenue flat. Unaware of her sacrifice, he was not overjoyed to see her, yet not unpleasant. Mary, at the time unaware that he must surely have been comparing her reactions to Simone's, recalled that they toured fire sales, rough dives, and other sights on Clark Street near West Madison with Ted Liss. After some days in his cramped apartment, they visited the Rowlands in Gary, Indiana. By now the whole thing seemed to be getting on his nerves; he seemed to feel suffocated and put upon by a love he did not feel. Unlike his easy natural feeling with Simone, who was close to his age, his relationship with Mary had no basis in common values. Mary felt he was ill at ease to have the Rowlands know they were lovers, and when they returned to Chicago his marked indifference soon drove her away. He later told Simone that Mary had "disobeyed" him, and though it was unclear how, Algren became angry whenever her name was mentioned, inventing an argument over a borrowed typewriter that ended with him crassly telling her to get her douche-bag—not that she had one—out of his house. "Nelson constantly got angry with women," said Ted Liss, echoing Jack Conroy's feelings about Nelson's blunt, inexplicable behavior toward them. "He was a bit of a misogynist."

Once free, he sent Simone more books and again entreated her to return to Chicago. She still didn't know if she'd be able to, and while she was traveling out west, he fell back into his usual austere routine. "Haven't seen the Rowlands for weeks," he wrote to Amanda a short while later, "except Neal dropped in for an hour last Saturday afternoon. I see Jack now and again, and he's staying sober, but from week to week I seldom see anybody and I like it that way." His main diversion was a local poker or bingo game on Saturday night.

Then he received the startling news that he had been awarded a thousand dollars from the American Academy and Institute of Arts and Letters. He hadn't even known he was being considered: he had given up on the Guggenheim and other fellowships so zealously pursued in the late thirties, his constant rejections convincing him they were given only to New Yorkers. During the war, a special Guggenheim for writers serving the armed forces in a war zone had seemed made to order for him, so he'd applied, sponsored by Carl Sandburg and Ernest Hemingway, to write a war novel, but was again turned down. The Academy's award marked the first time he had ever received any outside help, and he was so encouraged that he approached the Guggenheim Foundation yet again. Then he settled down to shaping the two hundred or so pages he had already written.

Although he felt better about the novel, he still couldn't see it all the way through. Like the surviving drafts of *Never Come Morning,* almost all early drafts of Algren's third novel lack endings, though a poem called "Epitaph: The Man with the Golden Arm," published in the September 1947 issue of *Poetry,* presaged a tragic ending for Frankie Machine. Increasingly, however, the novel relied on neighborhood atmosphere, as Algren peopled Frankie's life with a host of minor characters who were regulars at a tavern called the Tug and Maul. The most important was Sparrow, Frankie's loyal sidekick and an extension of the department-store thief in the story "Poor Man's Pennies" from *Neon Wilderness.* An ugly, bespectacled runt with a boundless admiration for the dealer, Sparrow makes his living steering marks to the card game at Schwiefka's, regularly dealt by Frankie. A goofy punk who'd try to talk his way out of anything, in early drafts Sparrow appears as a sex offender who follows women around department stores with a hand mirror to look up their skirts, an idea Algren found in a newspaper clipping. Sparrow provides comic relief while demonstrating Algren's observation that many lawbreakers are harmless, unskilled people who end up in jail through stupidity, misfortune, or lack of fear.

For the first time Algren's characters were visited not by a consistent, relentless sense of loss but by occasional moments of humor and laughter, reflecting Algren's personal happiness with his work, perhaps, even, his enthusiasm about Simone. But his basic vision had not changed. For those like Frankie and Sparrow, there was still the inevitable trip to the Cook County Jail, which Algren now toured, visiting the laundry room, the bakery, and the electric chair where North Clark Street denizen Dolly Weisberg was going to sit the following day. He listened while the guard in charge of the chair explained the whole process. The condemned prisoner waited in a special cell, changing into a pair of black tights and a white shirt with two buttons. Then he or she was escorted about ten feet to a door, took four steps to the left and was seated in the chair, which was painted entirely black. A black hood was put over the head. One contact was secured to the nape of the neck and another to the right ankle: the whole operation, with six doctors watching, took a minute and a half. Algren listened as the guard told him quite seriously that they used less voltage for Negro criminals because they were so frightened that they died more easily than whites. Thus was the state of capital punishment in 1947.

In late April, Simone wrote and asked Nelson if he might be able to join her in New York, and despite his vertigo, he took a plane there, then moved into her room at the Brevoort Hotel in Greenwich Village. They went to parties with New York writers and intellectuals but spent most of their time in bed, and Simone began to fuss over Nelson "just like all the American women I had ridiculed for the way they catered to men's needs. I was surprised at how much I enjoyed it." They confided their pasts to each other and their passion became even stronger—Simone said later that she experienced her first true orgasm with Nelson. It seemed natural for Algren to express his feelings in physical passion, as even his writing, which he saw as a physical thing, came from the gut. He was so sure of his feelings that during those days in New York he was the first to admit his love, though Simone too admitted a love stronger than any she'd ever known.

They had much in common. They shared compatible political views and reactions to the world; Algren, who was himself so open to experience, liked de Beauvoir's "furious curiosity," her eagerness to see and understand the truth rather than façade. They were both incredibly ambitious and intelligent. According to biographer Bair, Algren took de Beauvoir's work seriously, suggesting she look at Gunnar Myrdal's study of black Americans to find ideas for organizing her own study of women; he also suggested she might find a link between women's oppression and that of the disinherited characters of *The Grapes of Wrath* and other American novels of the thirties. Algren had never had a relationship that was so passionately intellectual and physical. Nor had de Beauvoir, whose letters constantly expressed amazement at having found a love of mind, soul, and body. That Algren went for women who, like de Beauvoir, were petite brunettes, was merely icing on the cake.

The fact that Simone was French also appealed to Algren. His perspective on America had always been that of an outsider, only partly because of his personal isolation. His heritage was German and Swedish, he had married a Polish woman and chosen to live in a Polish section of Chicago, his idiosyncratic literary tastes led him to the Slavs and French: a European sensibility in his artistic vision was as evident in Steffi Rostenkowski's old-world face as in the fact that he saw his own city as "the Petersburg of Dostoevsky." Simone's curiosity and exuberance confirmed his feelings that the French generally were more capable of enjoying their daily lives than Americans, just as his own nonmaterialistic life—he lacked a refrigerator and picked up his daily pork chops and custard pies on the little blue bike—reflected a joy in simple pleasures that most Americans do not cherish.

"Algren totally bowled me over, turned my life upside down," Simone said later. His obvious feeling for her, passionately erotic, brought a new level of excitement to a life dominated by intellect. Though as a young woman she had been romantically, irrepressibly, jealously in love with Sartre, their sexual relationship had ended years before, and she had repressed her sexual and sensual side to focus on philosophy and ideas. In Algren's love for her, in his tenderness, intuition, sensitivity, and innate artistic imagination, she found something completely lacking in her intellectual relationship with Sartre.

Nelson, in love, stimulated by New York, and a thousand dollars richer after picking up his award money, was exuberant. Their love was a rare human connection which Algren thought incredibly lucky. Simone de Beauvoir's happy disposition harked back to his sister Bernice, and she offered Algren the complete and unconditional love his characters were always seeking. And Algren, who had never made his mother or Amanda happy, who had caused everyone concern as a young man, brought Simone tremendous joy simply by being himself. She loved him even with his moods, and he liked that way of loving, he told her; he could feel how strong it was. In the face of Simone's unreserved acceptance and loyalty, Algren was able, for the first time, to express the same. On Broadway, he put her in a cab that would take her to a flight to Paris, and the cabdriver, seeing them say goodbye, asked Simone if Algren were her husband. In fact she had already told Nelson she was his wife: he had placed a ring on her finger that would astonish her friends in Paris.

*

In Chicago, he wrote Simone that he could still feel her presence, and twice a week long, loving letters to "My beloved husband" from "Your own Simone" arrived in his mailbox: he must come to Paris as soon as he could afford the airfare; she would support him, her money was his; she wanted to travel with him; she had given *Neon Wilderness* to her publisher. Her warm, chatty letters related minute details of her daily life in Paris in an attempt to minimize the vast distances between them. She assured him that she was in her Chicago home with him as well as he was in France with her: they had not parted and would never part; she was his wife forever. Could he not feel her love all around him, following him through the Chicago streets?

Perhaps he did. But Algren, the loner who lived in a country that de Beauvoir knew created isolation, whose characters longed for love and who seems to have felt he was impossible to live with, was deeply, painfully aware of their separation—the distance between them was more important for him, and he could not help but be aware of it. "I did not think that I could ever miss anyone so badly," he wrote her that summer. "If I were to hold you now I should cry with pain and happiness." In his solitude, even her letters, filled though they were with deep love, sometimes made him enormously sad, for they were a continual reminder of what he couldn't have. As if she could will it, Simone desired deeply that their love should bring him only happiness and felt terrible that her letters caused him pain. She told him she had a great hope that they would spend a long time together and that the happiness and love they would feel then would be worth the wait. After such reassurances, he would become optimistic again: "Do you think we have gotten closer?" he asked her in a letter; she replied that she felt they were nearer than ever; their love was not a trick of flesh and blood, and she repeated her conviction that their meeting would be joyful beyond words.

Too distracted by their affair to resume writing the book on women she had started earlier, Simone began work on a book about her trip to America that she assured Algren would not mention their relationship. But the writing could not settle her, and she missed him terribly. In late July she decided that in September she would again visit Algren, from whom, on the very day she returned from buying her ticket, she received a letter asking her to come back. Before leaving him in New York, she had told him that her life was permanently fixed in Paris. He had believed her, she wrote later, but hadn't really seemed to comprehend what she was saying. Now she sought once more to clarify her position to him, unsure of whether she even deserved his love. "I tried to explain to you I cannot give my life to you. Do you understand it? Are you not resentful about it? . . . Will you always believe yet it is really love I am giving to you?" The letter did not make clear that she would never even consider living with him in America, and it is hard to believe a writer of de Beauvoir's caliber was unaware of this. Yet his response told her he had understood completely. Just because one could not give up one's life, he wrote back, did not mean that one did not love much; besides, they would share and love much more than many married people. He did not yet know that it was not just work but Sartre—even if he wasn't her lover—that kept her so irrevocably tied to Paris.

Their reunion in the Wabansia flat was a happy one. Though they toured more prisons and slaughterhouses and visited Algren's friends in radio and television who were feeling the first stirrings of the cold-war witch-hunts, for the most part they passed the two and a half weeks in domestic harmony, trying, in Simone's words, to develop a "deep intimacy." In the tiny book-laden apartment the gramophone played "Lili Marlene"; Simone, who had acquired the taste, sipped scotch while Nelson straightened up the kitchen in his bathrobe. She read a draft of his novel "High-Yellow and the Dealer" on yellow paper covered with crossouts; then dipped into Lindsay, Sandburg, Masters, and Benét. She had decided to try to have *Never Come Morning* published in France, possibly translated by Jean Malaquais. Amid literature and lovemaking, Simone found the visit "the fulfillment of love." She sometimes cried with joy or at the sadness of having only two short weeks with him, and her letters reveal that Nelson also admitted crying a little inside. Their tranquillity was occasionally marred by Algren's ill temper, but she accepted these dark moments, accepted his moods: she believed that he possessed a deep inner goodness and a rare love for people. And she liked being the only one who understood him.

If Nelson called her a funny wife because she would not sacrifice herself to love, in a way he understood that she couldn't live for love any more than he could, and though he once again asked her to stay, their parting was not entirely sad. In the spring they would travel together to New Orleans, Mexico, and Guatemala. There was a tender moment as Simone prepared to leave: he showed her a book about a "fine lover," and the moment was so sweet that in the months that followed she wrote that she could hardly think about it for the pain of missing him. Alone in the airport she sat dazed, carrying the whiskey and books he had given her; then a messenger appeared with a bunch of white flowers he had sent. She rushed to the phone to hear his voice, and upon hanging up, she wrote him later, "something broke up in my heart, something which will remain silent and cold, dead, until the beloved day when you kiss me again."

In the months of waiting that followed, he lived like a monk. He no longer wore the suspenders she hated, he did not gamble, he sent her long letters, often twice a week. Despite his loneliness, he suggested to Simone that he feared to spoil a perfect love by being unfaithful. He was tempted by other women, but did not give in, and since they had sworn, on his insistence, never to lie to each other, he recounted the episodes in little stories to Simone. At first, she wrote, she felt jealousy, then relief that he had been so careful of their love. But though she herself had no desire for anyone else when she longed for Nelson so deeply, she was soon remorseful: he shouldn't deny himself pleasure on her account, she told him; the next time he should just sleep with the woman if he wanted to. He seems to have found her insistence on not depriving him of his freedom amusing—how could it really be true?—and teased her about it. Still, perhaps reading her relief, he apparently made love to no one until they met again. Since he still believed that it was work that kept her in Paris, he suggested in a letter that during the months apart they should work furiously and make their writing excellent: the only way to believe that all the endless months alone were not a waste.

Until this time, Algren's knowledge of drugs had been, in his view, limited; but that autumn he fell in with a group of junkies. Patty, Karl, and Jack lived together. Patty, about forty, was a habitual user; her pallid ex-husband, Karl, was also a hard-core addict, playing drums at night and by day driving a taxi around the city looking for fixes. Jack, Patty's lover, was a Polish ex-con Nelson had known from way back.

At first he wasn't aware of the junk. After drinking beer one night until the bars closed, he and Jack had climbed the stairs to the trio's walk-up apartment. There, Jack disappeared behind a curtain, and from the other side Algren was bothered to see him swinging his arm up and down. "Jack is having trouble," he heard someone say, but he was so full of beer that he didn't realize what was going on. Later, he noticed they never ate real food, only sweets, and when they began visiting his apartment, he saw things more clearly. "They would come in and out with cigar-boxes under their arms," Algren remembered, "and a guy would say to me, 'We're just having breakfast. Would you like some breakfast?' I'd say, 'No, I guess I already had breakfast.' So he said, 'You want to see how it's done?' I said, 'Hell, no, I don't want to see how it's done.' " He'd had an aversion to needles even in the army, but if they wanted to shoot up it was their business. Jack said he did it only occasionally and could kick whenever he wanted, and Nelson thought him lucky to know what he was doing.

But one night Jack got sick. A couple of his friends came by in a cab to get Nelson, and they scored the stuff in a cloak-and-dagger deal in a North Side hotel. When they finally got back with the stuff, Jack was just bawling, crying and sweating and looking as if he'd lost fifteen pounds. "He came out with a sheepish look, like, 'Well, you know, it happens to everybody,' " Algren recalled. "So I felt a little contemptuous of him." The junkies always needed money, were constantly trying to borrow a few bucks, and sometimes Algren got mad: he thought they were trying to con him, and he hated to be conned more than anything.

But he met other addicts there for whom he felt compassion. One seems to have been Margo, a hooker from Ohio in her early twenties who was against the stuff and never should have been on it at all. And there was a guy with a pushed-in mug named Acker, who was also very troubled by using the stuff. These were Nelson's friends; he felt comfortable with them. "These were people you just went to hear a band with," he said later. "It was only now and then that it'd come to you—like it might occur to you that one of your friends is crippled or something—that the guy is on the stuff. But it didn't stay with you very much."

It took him a long time to make any connection between the addicts and his novel. Sometimes he felt he was goofing off and taking time away from the book if he went to see them; but he liked listening to music with them, and they didn't always go for the needle, because they didn't always have it. Very dimly he began to realize it all might be workable material. He worried it might be too sensational, but his agent, Elizabeth Ingersoll, told him to use it. She liked the writing in the novel, but the story didn't seem to be hung on anything; the plot needed a peg. The narcotics angle might provide exactly what was needed.

Outside of the underworld, America was changing. If in 1947 de Beauvoir saw Algren as a "striking example of the intellectual solitude in which writers of America live today," this was not only a result of his self-enforced isolation. The community spirit which had supported the 1930s struggle for better social conditions and the wartime fight against Hitler had all but disappeared. The atomic bomb brought not a feeling of safety, but the insecurity of all those who rule by force. And as the Soviet Union began to dominate Eastern Europe in the aftermath of the war, loyalty became the watchword in the United States.

The "Communism in government" fear finally scored with voters, as heavily financed Republicans, equating all liberalism with the Red Menace, won the 1946 elections and established the most conservative Congress in twenty years. The Democratic President Truman, hoping to escape the dreaded label of "soft on Communism," chose to try to outdo the opposition in the witch-hunt. In March 1947, he ordered a screening program for over two million government employees, each of whom was made to swear—under threat of suspension or possible dismissal—that he had never directly or indirectly associated with "subversive" organizations, including publications. In June, the Taft-Hartley Act, which included labor union and strike restraints, compelled all union officers to sign oaths that they were not Communists. In New York, the loyalty campaign targeted educators; in Hollywood, certain writers and directors—known as the "Hollywood Ten"—were cited for contempt after deciding to test the First Amendment. The print media, especially the Hearst press, whipped up a war fever by daily warning that conflict to stop Russian aggression was inevitable; *Life* declared that the world was already at war. As the American Civil Liberties Union described it, "The national climate of opinion in which freedom of public debate and minority dissent functioned with few restraints during the war years and after has undergone a sharply unfavorable change."

With the suppression of ideas came spiritual malaise. For a special poetry issue of *Chicago Sun-Times Book Week,* Algren noted a distinct difference since the time when Carl Sandburg had described Chicago as a place of vibrant, healthy laughter. "We no longer laugh well out of our own spiritual good health. . . . Here the poor man, to laugh, feels he must go to a fourth-rate cabaret or listen to Bob Hope, to be wheedled and prodded into laughter. . . . Whole audiences wait tensely for the placard bearing the sponsored command: 'Laughter. Applause. More Laughter.' " He linked this nervous dispiritedness with the lack of connection Americans felt among themselves: "When a man dies on the street of such a city as Marseilles, he does not seem to die alone: his death, like his life, is shared. But when he dies on W. Division or N. Clark, he dies lost and disgraced"—he has failed to make money in a society that, in the midst of postwar economic growth, increasingly revolved around financial success. In the article he included a quote from his lover: "The cult of money which one encounters here does not spring from avarice or meanness. Making money is the only aim one can set oneself in a world in which all aims have been reduced to this common denominator."

In the fall and winter of 1947–1948 Algren spoke often at Chicago forums on literary, cultural, and political affairs. *The Neon Wilderness,* now into a second printing, had gained him a solid local reputation, and he appeared at public-library events and on several local and national radio shows, sometimes partially sponsored by Doubleday. He was a guest at the Midland Authors' Society, and under the auspices of the Midwestern Writers' Conference debated Louis Bromfield about Existentialism—not surprisingly, one of Nelson's new interests. If anyone found his attack to defend Existentialism excessive, he thought himself quite successful.

In February 1948, he began campaigning for Henry A. Wallace, Roosevelt's former Vice-President and Secretary of Agriculture, then making a heroic bid for President. A progressive capitalist, Wallace was anathema to the Red Scare: he advocated compromise with the Soviet Union to ensure a lasting peace, would not sleep in segregated hotels, and conducted a campaign that was, in effect, the last liberal stand before the onslaught of the McCarthy era. On May Day, 1948, along with Alvah Bessie, Herbert Aptheker, Marc Blitzstein, Howard Fast, Meridel Le Sueur, and twenty-some left-leaning writers, Algren signed an open letter to Soviet artists repudiating, in the timeworn rhetoric of the hard-line left, "the tide of war which our ruling class has set in motion . . . the exploiters who hope to convert America into a Fourth Reich." The signers described Stalin's Russia as a country that "surrounds [artists] with the love of millions of people and provides them with the means to carry out their social responsibility." To Algren, who lent his name freely to petitions, such documents seemed mere statements of faith. It's hard to imagine that he still took such rhetoric to heart—he ridiculed the Party in letters to Amanda and told Simone that the CP had failed him. After raising a brief excitement in the bourgeois press, the letter ended up, of course, in the FBI files.

To Algren, writing, speaking, and in general feeling hopeful, the winter of 1947–1948 was, despite the increasing political insanity, far better than the one before, all because of Simone. In letters he called her his "frog wife"; she called him her "crocodile." Though he wrote her that sporadic, uneasy feelings of entrapment sometimes came over him, he surrendered to an overall happiness at being truly loved. And every few days Simone reassured him of her feelings. He seemed to love the contained intimacy of their relationship, which existed independently of everything else. He confided that before loving her, he had consciously tried to keep people away from him; he told her how he felt about being Jewish; he described his dreams. He was so confident of their relationship that in December he light-heartedly sent her a list of good "frog commandments": to have no other crocodiles before him, never to make light of him, to be a faithful frog and covet nothing but him. They didn't seem to bother one of the foremost feminists of the twentieth century—she loved them. In February he said he felt he had fallen in love with her all over again, and in March he wrote that he felt their love was growing.

So was his novel. In January 1948, the Newberry Library, heeding Carl Sandburg's advice, awarded him a $750 fellowship, which he successfully parlayed into the more standard-sized $1,600 package spread out over eight months. The novel, alternating between the maudlin titles of "The Dead, the Drunk, and the Dying," "The Weaker Sheep;" and "Hustlers' Hearts," now constituted a complete draft; but the plot was far from tight. Sophie was now a user, "shooting the main" and remembering old times, and Frankie, like Bruno Bicek, had served time for a crime unrelated to the murder. It remained a story in which Frankie Machine's guilt ultimately brought no change in his life: he would end up wandering the streets, no longer sought for the murder but unable to make any kind of life, given the burden of his culpability for Sophie's decline. Despite problems in plot, which Algren knew from experience he could overcome, he had wonderfully developed the characters of Sophie, Sparrow, and Frankie; Ken McCormick told him he had "mastered [the] language" of query captain, prison inmate, and tenement denizen. He would need, most likely, six months to pull the book together.

But beginning in May, he was planning to spend three or four months with Simone—though they had originally discussed as long as six months together. The itinerary for the New Orleans–Mexico–Guatemala trip seemed a bit overwhelming to Algren, who had never traveled as a tourist and had serious doubts that one could really *see* a country from spending a few days in a hotel room; yet he looked forward to traveling with Simone and had arranged his work so that the time off would coincide with the end of the finished draft. Work and love seemed nicely balanced.

As May approached, Simone, too distracted by thoughts of the Wabansia nest to concentrate on her own work, assured him that he could not have a more faithful or loving wife. "The frog would give everything belonging to her to her crocodile (including life if it was *really* necessary) and she knows he knows it—and he would give everything for her, and she knows it too," she wrote. Simone had not yet reached the later height of wisdom that would allow her to explain such proclamations not as untruths but as the simple result of ardor: "Love's promises express the passion of a moment only." And certainly Algren had no reason to suspect that she did not mean exactly what she said. Later he would see things more clearly, but for now he made plans for their honeymoon down the Mississippi in the kind of riverboat Mark Twain had piloted.

12.

The Man with the Golden Arm

T HE MORNING AFTER SIMONE ARRIVED Nelson felt she simply *had* to meet the junkies, so they rode the streetcar through the rain to the West Side walk-up, where Patty tried to appear decent while Karl rushed into the bathroom to shoot up. But de Beauvoir, far more interested in Algren than in his friends, wanted only to be alone with him. After they "found each other" in bed that night, Simone spent the entire next day reading *Hustlers' Hearts* while Nelson wrote letters and looked at photographs of abandoned girlfriends—"that is, women I had personally abandoned. Just to be sure I knew what I was doing this time." Two days later they were off.

Alongside Simone's brief, routine entries in the joint diary they kept of their trip, Nelson dashed off spontaneous, illuminating descriptions, even in Cincinnati, the boat's point of departure and in his view an exceedingly boring city. Over dinner, he noted the elitism of his tourist status as he watched himself and Simone having dinner. "While we gorged ourselves in the diner, in limped a little bearded cripple with an aristocratic face, a humble manner, and wearing hillbilly clothes. He studied the menu, asked the price of one egg, then a cup of coffee. The porter finally gave him a glass of cold water and we ordered dessert."

The side-wheeling boat began its gentle voyage down the Ohio to the Mississippi, docking each day to allow them a few hours on shore. Louisville was sad, rainy; Algren still didn't feel they were traveling. But Paducah was suddenly better: a poorer, rougher little Kentucky town where after a few beers in a hillbilly bar he felt the quickening excitement of entering another world. There was a certain joy in traveling as a tourist after all: changing camera film by a little Negro store where two parrots cursed each other, eating chicken dinners in Memphis, playing bingo all night on the boat. And it was wonderful to be with Simone. Days, they read, chatted, and sipped cocktails on the sundeck while Simone translated Nelson's "The Face on the Barroom Floor." Evenings, the Mississippi slipped by, and the fires and lights from shore glimmered in the distance. The water's gentle slapping and the light, suspended moon were soothing, romantic; Lewis Brogan, Algren's fictional counterpart in *The Mandarins,* de Beauvoir's novel that recounted their love affair, was awed that he had never believed in loving or being loved.

As they drifted south, he assured Simone that they would soon indeed see cottonfields. They wandered through the Negro quarter in Natchez, then took a cab to see old slave plantations, driven by a white racist who later took them to an unfinished slave labyrinth, inhabited by a man living alone. By the time they reached New Orleans Algren wrote that he was really traveling. But the city had changed. Now it was a respectable tourist town living off its flamboyant past: more prosperous but much duller than in 1932. When he sought out the Southern Pacific tracks where he had so long before left for Texas, he saw that the old cheap wooden bungalows had been either boarded up or bulldozed for housing projects. The Depression was gone; at a friend's house he and Simone ate a southern feast he could once only have imagined: a myriad of vegetables, gumbos, seafood, salad, cakes, and pies. If there was anything left of the pathos he remembered from the thirties, it was in the haunting jazz at a Negro place called the Slave's Bar; or at the fights, in the face of "a punchdrunk fighter staring at the moon after the ring lights had gone out."

On Mexico's Yucatán peninsula, they fled annoying hordes of American tourists to a sparse jungle hotel lit by candles, where a Mexican strummed a guitar in the courtyard amid croaking frogs and the scrabble of pigs and chickens; they slept beneath mosquito netting. But the nearby Mayan-Toltec ruins at Chichén Itzá, which Simone was eager to see, brought the false tourist world back to Algren. At first he felt like a discoverer among the giant stone edifices and temples, but he was quickly sickened by the knowledge that he viewed not the supreme accomplishments of a great civilization but monuments to slavery: he saw thousands of peasants turned into animals by powerful priests, endlessly hauling boulders under a merciless sun, their routine relieved only by tortillas. And this in a climate where corn flourished and the Indians had to work no more than a few weeks a year to feed themselves. Sullenly, he "sat in the lost sunny Yucatán on the walls built so long ago, feeling the same sun and nothing so much changed in 1000 years." Simone was probably also offended by a legacy that served only tourists and archaeologists, but did not share his anger: the injustice was so long gone, and she had never had to sweat to eat. But despite his feelings, they had to trudge on to Uxmal on a four A.M. bus with no place open for coffee. When he wrote that they "finally saw the wonderful ruins of Uxmal," he could only have been sarcastic: Simone's entry reports "Nelson *very bad,*" and in her memoirs she recalled that Algren was brought to despair by the stones and refused to even glance at them.

In Guatemala City, beyond the thick sweet smells and the long yellow streets and smoky Arabian colors, Algren was struck by the "phony Broadway: The NY bars, the slot machines for American nickels—like a modern paint job over the country—so lost and far-away and forgotten." And so poor. Although the markets teemed with bright fruits, woven baskets, old women and young children selling belts, sandals, and colorful shawls, the malnourished peasants lived in mud huts, only twelve years out of indentured servitude. Later, Algren and Simone went swimming in a lake made by a volcano, where they seemed "the only two people left alive in the world." In their mountain hotel he told a long tale as Simone listened, getting tight on whiskey, naked by the fire. Later they saw churches with "carpets of candles"; were led to a hilltop altar by a shepherdess in Chichichastenango. Everywhere the cool heavy air of the mountain jungle: Guatemala was a place where they were most in love.

Not every moment was blissful, however. If Algren could suddenly become sullen, the willful de Beauvoir at times dragged him through her rigidly planned agenda like a suitcase; the ruins had been only the first instance of this. "We didn't even have time for coffee in order to see the vanishing magician," Algren complained in the diary, "and then you made me sit for hours through some horrible melo-drama. You were very bad." Urban Mexico City was a welcome change, but after two days Algren's diary entries suddenly became distinctly shorter. The nearby Toltec ruins may have clammed him up, and then they were caught by one of those horrible, fake, ex-ploitive "native dancing" nightclub shows for tourists: after a half-hour, Algren gladly sought refuge in the slums of Corregidora Street.

But more unsettling was the likelihood that Algren had again asked

Simone to live with him. For each day brought closer the inevitable discussion of their future, an anxiety-provoking subject for Simone, and not only because she could not consider living with him. Before leaving Paris she had agreed to accommodate Sartre's love life by interfering with her own: Sartre's girlfriend was leaving Paris in mid-July; he had asked Simone to return then, six weeks earlier than Algren expected. Simone had put off telling Algren but finally broke the news clumsily on a bus to Morelia. Then she fabricated a lie about a film script she and Sartre were writing, but Algren seems to have realized that she was returning to Paris because of Sartre—and that he, the man she loved so deeply, could not keep her from going.

He pretended indifference, but once in Morelia he had no interest in sightseeing. Simone, meanwhile, strolled contentedly through the streets and bought embroidered blouses. Upon rejoining him, she began making the next day's plans, but Algren stopped her: he'd had enough of traveling and markets. He hurried ahead, and though at the hotel his silence reduced her to tears, he left without speaking. Realizing that her time with him was dictated not by love but by Sartre's schedule was a tremendous disappointment; now he knew that her life belonged to Paris and Sartre and could never be his. How could he not have felt betrayed? All her letters had led him to believe that he was the most important man in her life, as she was the most important woman in his; he must have resented the fact that he was expected to interrupt his work and devote himself to love completely while she was, in a way, unwilling to do the same. They reconciled without words and returned to the States early. If they were to have a schedule, it would be his.

In New York's stifling heat he tried to regain himself by focusing on business. He met with his publishers and his agent and had lunch with Martha Foley. He and Simone had two weeks until she left for Paris, so after he looked up a thief from Chicago, they saw movies, plays, the wax museum, Chinatown, baseball, fights, races at Aqueduct and more at Monmouth. Gambling was always an attempted escape from tension, and sightseeing allowed them a respite from Simone's guilt and Nelson's disappointment. Evenings were harder. "Real bad night," Simone noted in the diary where Nelson now wrote little of interest, "another bad night." They disagreed over movies; he was loath to dress in a jacket and tie for the air-conditioned East Side French restaurants where Simone sought refuge from the heat. He didn't speak to her in the same way as before and sometimes she felt hostility from him. When she asked if he still loved her as much, he said it wasn't the same. "You can't love someone who isn't all yours the same way as someone who is," Lewis Brogan says in *The Mandarins;* and he was, in a sense, right. She could demand all his love only if she was willing to give all of hers. But unfortunately for him, his deepest feelings had not really been altered. In a heated exhange after an evening when he had been especially sullen, Algren suddenly blurted that he was ready to marry her that instant. From that moment Simone would never be able to remain angry with him: all the wrongs were on her side.

Algren's disappointment, his realization that the terms of their affair were decided in Paris, revealed to him, de Beauvoir wrote later, a state of affairs he could never have tolerated for long. But even so, they had both already established their lives and could not have moved them elsewhere: as writers they were each rooted in the country of their native language. De Beauvoir's work was bound to Paris intellectual life, and by her own admission she could not have lived in exile. For Algren, who had chosen as his literary territory the city of Chicago, with its distinctly American vernacular and culture, moving to Paris would have severed an intimacy with the city cultivated over decades. Still, de Beauvoir remembered, they both bitterly regretted that they would never come to live with each other.

If it was unfair—some might say sexist—for Algren to think that de Beauvoir should give up everything to live with him, it was equally unfair for her to assume he could either do the same or remain so deeply involved with a woman who would see him only a few weeks a year. Algren was in turmoil: they had talked everything out, but the state of affairs was, basically, unacceptable. At age forty he had begun to feel that he *did* want a life with someone—someone who was his. He still loved Simone and assured her that she was still his wife. They parted without bitterness, though without plans to meet again.

Algren sent Simone a long warm letter as soon as she left, but when, upon finding that Sartre's girlfriend hadn't left and that he didn't need her so badly after all, Simone asked if she could come back to Chicago, Algren cabled that he had too much work. Throughout the fall and spring, they continued to write each other, but Algren was redirecting his emotions into his fiction, for he put aside everything to return to the novel. That August he wrote or revised two hundred pages, resuming his spartan routine of rising early, working many hours, exercising at the Y, and allowing no distractions. He wrote slowly and carefully, line by line. McCormick's suggestions entailed many changes in the plot, the most important making Frankie, not Sophie, the morphine addict. Entirely new scenes had to be invented. "It comes in lumps," he wrote later, "and each lump has to be smoothed and grained down and then, when it's just so shining and smooth and you read it aloud to yourself and love the sound of every perfect word, you find you can't use it, it doesn't tie in, it's fine in itself but it diverts the whole story. So you gulp and put it away, assuring yourself you'll make use of it another day." But his only self-doubts were concerned "with whether it would *say* anything, and say it well, as nobody could ever have said it." At night, he read and reread classic writers such as Dostoevsky and Chekhov, for he didn't think it could be done without them.

In those days he developed what he termed a "kind of innocence" that came not from escaping reality, but through making contact with it: an unworldliness achieved by recognizing and seeing beyond social and moral trappings. This brought a spiritual dignity instantly recognized by friends. "No matter what you hear, he was a very kind man. He was a very beautiful man, spiritually," said photographer Robert McCullough, who came out to Wabansia to photograph him. "I thought he had—and I think this is a very simplified version—I thought he had a Christ complex," McCullough remembered. "He wrote that story about the captain being impaled ["The Captain Has Bad Dreams"], and I felt all through this that Nelson was—well, it was an enigma—glorifying these people and at the same time crying to them. I felt Nelson was the captain. Anyway, when I shot the picture, the windows made a cross behind him in the background, and when I took the picture I don't think I thought that. It must have been intuitive." Arthur Shay, a *Life* photographer Nelson met in 1949, later recalled a similar feeling when sitting with Nelson over a morning newspaper. A hitchhiker with "HARD LUCK" tattooed across his knuckles had murdered a whole family after they had picked him up. "Nelson looked at the picture," Shay recalled, "and said, 'That poor sonofabitch.' My wife wanted to throw him out." Later, when a writer in the Chicago papers had questioned Nelson's humanity, Shay thought, "Nelson's humanity. He could see what could drive a man to something like that. Only Jesus Christ himself could have that kind of attitude."

Though the monklike existence necessary to reach this state seemed poetic to Simone, Algren found it not just lonely but self-centered and sterile, and he wasn't happy about it.

> I'm stuck here . . . because my job is to write about this city, and I can only do it here. It's pointless to go over all that again. But it leaves me with almost no one to talk to. . . . Without consciously wanting to, I've chosen for myself the life best suited to the sort of writing I'm able to do. Politicians and intellectuals bore me; they seem to be unreal; the people I see a lot of these days are the ones who do seem real to me: whores, junkies, etc. However, my personal life was sacrificed in all this.

Still, art was the only work that could bring real happiness. With literature there was no limit to what he could do—he could reach people long after he was dead. Yet that human love constituted the driving force behind his artistic vision is beyond dispute: within him raged a tremendous conflict between ambition and inner need. Simone, experiencing the same conflict, could put art first, secure in the intellectual love of Sartre; Algren had no such emotional support. Yet until the early 1950s, art always won out over his personal life, no matter how lonely it made him.

So he sat in the Wabansia nest compulsively polishing each word until it was just right, believing in a care in craft that took no notice of publishers or delivery dates: the writing had to be perfect, word for word. His obsession with greatness and the desire to say something new meant that projects were never really finished but abandoned: "I judge that I rewrote 'Golden Arm' a dozen times in some places, and more in others," Algren wrote seventeen years later of the novel McCormick already felt had "the poetry of Faulkner and the doom of Gogol." "I suppose there were, for some sections, forty rewritings that still aren't right," Algren continued. "If Mr. Doubleday hadn't come and wrenched the thing away from me by brute strength, I'd still be up there on Wabansia Avenue, rewriting away." Perhaps frustrated by Algren's breezy assumptions that yet a few more days past deadline wouldn't hurt, McCormick mistakenly found something self-destructive about Algren's rewriting, which was finally checked only by the threat of having to pay for changes in the galleys. For though McCormick wanted a fine book, he wanted it on time; and Algren wanted a great book.

It was, of course, not easy to pick a title, for Algren sensed that the Doubleday favorite, *The Man with the Golden Arm,* was not quite right. He favored "Night Without Mercy," which, though remarkably close to the bland *Never Come Morning,* he thought gained meaning after reading. "It does so because it is a subjective title, carrying emotional overtones," he wrote to Ken McCormick, "whereas all that 'The Man' is is a flat statement of objective fact, a description of a novel's central character and that is all. Thus I suspect that even though 'The Man' is unique, it will not stand up as well, once the novelty of the title has worn off, as will 'Night Without Mercy.' " The title did stand up, though not the way Algren hoped. As a result of Otto Preminger's movie, or what happened to Algren himself, it brings to mind a cheap detective thriller or sensational narcotics paperback, instead of the first-rate novel it is.

Friends found a sharp difference between his down-to-earth ways and his stunning literary ability, yet it is in his work that the most important expression of his personality, his talent, and his profound understanding of human nature emerges; and in the tragic, poetic, and deeply sensitive *Man with the Golden Arm* that expression reached maturity. Algren began the story in the query room of Captain Bednar, a veteran cop utterly weary of condemning a never-ending lineup of criminals and losers. Frankie and Sparrow have been picked up because their boss, Schwiefka, is late paying the cops to keep his poker game going. They have been here before. In fact, their innocence hardly matters, since, like every other inmate, the card dealer and the punk have been irrevocably touched by "the great, secret and special American guilt of owning nothing, nothing at all, in the one land where ownership and virtue are one." They are strangely doomed:

> These were the luckless living soon to become the luckless dead. The ones who were fished out of river or lake, found crumpled under crumpled papers in the parks, picked up in the horse-and-wagon alleys or slugged, for half a bottle of homemade wine, in the rutted tunnels that run between the advertising agencies and the banks.

The pair is released, but Frankie's freedom is only a cheap room in the tenement of Schwabatski the Jailer. There his nagging, half-crazy wife, Sophie—nicknamed Zosh—waits in a wheelchair. Their marriage, long postponed by Frankie's indifference, had finally been forged out of Sophie's false pregnancy; and the doctors insist that her paralysis, which occurred when Frankie drunkenly crashed their secondhand car into a light pole, is also psychosomatic. Still, her crippled state binds him. Saddled with a guilt he can never shake off, he is caught on a treadmill of trying halfheartedly to satisfy her endless demands—for a dog, for beer, for attention, for a love he does not feel.

The only place to escape Zosh is in the Tug and Maul, where a Dickensian host of luckless losers forget their failures while drinking cheap whiskey and beer. Here are Antek the Owner, a high school dropout; blind Piggy-O, betrayed by his eyes; the "mouth at the end of a whisky glass" named Drunkie John; and Sparrow, tortured by his ugliness. Only "Nifty" Louie Fomorowski, the slick, smartly dressed ex-junkie turned pusher, has made his ugly peace with life: "Anything that pays ain't nothing to be ashamed of. . . . The only thing a man got a right to be ashamed of these days is bein' broke," Louie justifies himself easily.

Beyond the grim poverty of Frankie's life, it is the guilt for Sophie's accident—far more than the aching, icy pain of the shrapnel in his liver from a war wound—that leads him back to the morphine that helped so much in that windy field-hospital on the Meuse. Even the goggle-eyed Sparrow doesn't know he's using, and as Sophie continues to stone him, breaking all their dishes so she can humiliate him as he picks them up, the morphine, cheaper than drinking in taverns, becomes an increasingly tempting escape. Frankie knows that he keeps the "monkey on his back" to expiate his guilt for Sophie, knows too that he is destroying himself. And yet, as the drug obliterates his sincere yet pathetic dreams of becoming a drummer—that too is all in the wrist—Frankie wants to live, to escape this life with Molly-O, a hustling girl with "a heart-shaped face and the wonder gone out of her eyes" with whom he finds brief happiness and understanding. With Molly's love behind him he manages for a time to stay off the M; but the guilt of crippling his wife and then cheating on her drives him back on the needle: he feels that he hurts everything he touches. It is all he can do to hang on to his job as a card dealer; then, in a single moment of fury, he breaks Fomorowski's neck in the alley after a brief dispute at the poker table.

He is eventually sent to jail—ironically, not for murder but for shoplifting—and here he works his habit down "from monkey to zero." But upon his release nine months later, Sophie has stepped even closer to madness, and without Frankie's love, Molly-O has degenerated into a cheap cabaret stripper. Nobody mourns Louie's passing; and were it not that it is an election year and Louie owes money to powerful Chicago officials, his would be just one more unsolved murder. The pressured Captain Bednar finds a way to pin the murder on Frankie by threatening Sparrow with other charges until he talks. The rest of the novel reveals the inevitable tragedy in which Frankie, trapped by his drug habit and hunted by the law, finally hangs himself.

But in *The Man with the Golden Arm* Algren did much more than expose a few of the legions of hunted, forlorn lives, as he had already done through Bruno Bicek. The crisis of Captain Bednar, a hunter for the law, lifts the novel's social perspective beyond that of the oppressed to society as a whole. Nicknamed Record Head because of "the retentiveness of his memory for forgotten misdemeanors," the captain has justified his life's work in the corrupt Chicago justice system by telling himself he is only doing his "honest copper's duty," yet he uneasily begins to feel that he is guilty, envying each condemned man for "the sentence hanging over his head like . . . salvation." When a human wreck under the interrogation lights advises him that "we are all members of one another," Bednar cannot at first understand what is happening to him; but in a Dostoevskian moral crisis, he comes to understand that in condemning those without chances, he has tragically condemned his own humanity. Bednar thus becomes a symbol for all those who sustain themselves by oppression of the less fortunate.

But Bednar continues to bludgeon his own humanity by relentlessly pursuing Frankie for the murder of the well-connected Louie. Bednar has, therefore, some of the same irrational self-destructive urges shared by Frankie and Molly and Zosh—but because he has choices, his are somehow harder to figure. With this understanding of both the oppressed and the oppressor, Algren demonstrated that he was as much a psychological writer as a social one. "I don't say my characters are always the victims of society," he told an interviewer; "psychological make-up is also important." This theme of self-destruction reverberates through all of Algren's major work.

As noted by critic George Bluestone, the force to self-destruction comes only after the love of another is sacrificed. Characters responsible for the annihilation of love are doomed. Frankie is indeed responsible for such destruction, first of Sophie's love, then of Molly-

O's. He leaves Molly-O waiting alone for him night after night; when she visits him in prison he inadvertently yet almost instinctively hurts her by asking about the bar where she hustles drinks, immediately realizing that now she will never visit him again. He therefore makes no attempt to find her after his release, sinking back into the morphine he'd worked so hard to kick. His later attempt to reconcile with her is thus doomed to failure. It is not simply, as Bluestone suggests, that "Frankie's destruction of Zosh has made Molly's love impossible." It is also that Frankie has not faced up to the responsibility of the completely shared life that love implies. The consequence is death. The price for the destruction of love is so terrible, because in a world of survival and oppression "love is the only way in which human beings may meaningfully relate. Nothing else is finally reliable."

In Algren's fictional and psychological world the past assumes enormous significance; actions have irrevocable consequences that influence the outcome of future events. Fresh chances are thus never really possible: "there was no escape from the dead end of lost chance. No escape from the cold steel blue bars of guilt." Algren's whole life had prepared him to describe the emotional climate of guilt that came to dominate the story of Frankie Machine. "From early manhood to 40 he was pursued in dreams almost nightly, always the fugitive, filled with guilt," he wrote in an unpublished fragment that can only be autobiographical, "sometimes pursued to the peak of a skyscraper, and he had always feared high places in the cold and wind and the rain and far below the flashlights climbing slowly up toward him. Other times he would be walking down a dim-lit hospital corridor late at night. The smell of ether from secret illegal operations being performed for the sheer pleasure of certain surgeons, a place, perhaps, where madmen were hired to tend the mad. And here, again, he must not be found, though he was, of course, guilty, guilty of everything."

For though Algren is not like Frankie, or Simone like Molly, or Amanda (whom he called Mashya) like Sophie, the dramatic configuration of *The Man with the Golden Arm* corresponded closely to Algren's own personal drama. If on the surface he seemed to have moved beyond his relationship with Amanda, he nonetheless continued to write to her even as he did to Simone, and he had kept her picture on his dresser since their first breakup in 1940. His inscription on her copy of the book, "For Amanda—who helped write this book a long, long time ago," is especially revealing. Clearly this old relationship troubled him, as the past always did, for hadn't he known that giving up love for anything else was unforgivable? Yet his admission to Simone that he had chosen his life "without consciously wanting to" curiously indicates how much his actions were dictated not by reason but by feeling, so that he was moved and pushed and manipulated by subconscious desires that could and often did control his life. Writing was the only way to master them, and even then, he was not always aware of what he was doing. Of Captain Bednar's crisis, he wrote to Ken McCormick after the book was in its final form, "What occurs to me now is that the point of the scene . . ." as if he became aware of the rational significance of things only after the fact, not in the midst of creation. He believed in the novelist as an emotional writer, always criticizing books that lacked feeling. His views on Hemingway and Faulkner reflected this: "The only things that last are the things that are done when the writer doesn't know what he's doing—that kind of innocence. Faulkner didn't really know what he was doing . . . because he was working out of a compulsion. He didn't know and he certainly would have defended himself against having it broken down. He knew that much about it. He had a drive. Certainly, Hemingway, in this sense, never knew what he was doing."

Writing seemed a talisman against the very guilt, regret, destruction of love, and self-destruction that developed into the decisive themes of Algren's life. It was like a pressure valve for those emotions that threatened to engulf him, and after finishing *The Man with the Golden Arm*, he was, quite naturally, elated. There was also his usual innocent, almost wistful optimism—always to be shot down— that this book would really dent the thick armor with which the middle classes shielded themselves from seeing the "civilization" they supported. Creating the book had brought him to new heights of understanding; a new softness came into him. He was relaxed, generous; he nicknamed himself Uncle Awg and Uncle Nels as if he had reached some height of sagacity, come through a rite of passage.

Finishing his book had given him a sense of empowerment, and he now determined to resolve his relationship with Simone on his own terms. Life was too lonely to remain faithful to her if he could see her only a few weeks a year, and in the fall of 1948 a brief affair with a divorcée from the Wallace campaign represented the home and wife he really wanted. When he wrote to Simone of his need for a wife who would live with him, perhaps a subtle threat to force her to a decision, she seemed to miss the point entirely, saying she would still be his friend even if he was married. But *she* was the woman he wanted, and, vowing to see Sartre and the life that kept her in Paris, he wrote her that he was coming to France as soon as he could. She told him she was mad with happiness: he should come in spring, so her book would be finished; they could travel to Marseilles and other places in Europe and Africa. After a bon-voyage party in Chicago, meetings with Doubleday's lawyers in New York, and a cocktail party at his agent's, in May 1949 he embarked on a boat to Le Havre, knowing that whatever else happened, he had written a great book.

Arriving in Paris loaded with chocolates, whiskey, books, and gifts, Nelson radiated happiness; and everything about the old-world city delighted him: the buckets positioned to collect the rain in Simone's fifth-floor tenement, Arabian jazz drifting up from the café below, the polite give-and-take of conversations in the shops. Almost as soon as he arrived, he and Simone went to meet Sartre. Algren expected that they would confront each other like jealous adversaries, but his small and rather unattractive rival—who reminded him of a cheap shoe merchant—greeted him with a warm handshake and guided him into a café as if they were longtime friends. Later he often met Sartre and was always struck by the philosopher's complete lack of jealousy and his obvious pleasure at seeing him. Later, Sartre would help take the inadequate translation of *Never Come Morning* and along with Simone turn it into a good French novel.

That spring everything seemed fresh, just beginning, for the French as well as for Nelson. The Germans were gone, the war was done, and though the country prospered only to the extent that the French ate something every day and could afford a daily paper, artistic rebirth was in the air. Through Simone, Algren entered the very center of French literary and artistic life, where he was accepted as an artist and felt himself among a community of creative people, a feeling he had not had since he had left Cottage Grove almost ten years earlier. He met twenty-year-old Juliette Greco, a concentration camp survivor who was just beginning to sing and act. She smiled, Algren remembered, "and the lights in the room came up a little." He also met the young Arab Mouloudji, who would later succeed as a novelist, painter, and café singer. He met novelist Jean Cau, who would become his French agent and win the Prix Goncourt; Boris Vian, author of *I'll Spit on Your Grave;* and Jacques-Laurent Bost, who wrote *The Last Profession* and was Sartre's closest friend. Others, such as Raymond Queneau, Camus, Giacometti, and Merleau-Ponty, were also just beginning to gain the world's attention. But it was Simone herself who became the big star when the publication of the first volume of her study of women, *The Second Sex,* provoked furor in the French press. The book sold more than twenty thousand copies in one week. De Beauvoir received letters calling her frigid and a lesbian, was ridiculed in cartoons and articles and snickered at on the streets of Paris. Algren was impressed by the imperturbable self-assurance with which she faced the wild publicity, but according to her biographer, Deirdre Bair, it was his presence that helped her to do so.

As a writer, Algren felt no competition with Simone. He simply considered himself better. About the only de Beauvoir works available in English at the time were a play, *Les Bouches Inutiles,* which Algren diplomatically implied was poorly translated, and the philosophical tome *The Ethics of Ambiguity,* which he found less than enthralling. "It's like eating cardboard," he joked to a friend. "If she didn't think I was so great in the sack and had such a great mind, I'd send her back to Jean-Paul Sartre." Later he was more to the point: "She couldn't write a scene in a restaurant without telling you everything on the menu," he told journalist Carolyn Gaiser. Imaginative and a strong believer in the importance of style, Algren looked for poetry and emotional connection from writing, and judging from these criteria felt himself superior to Simone. Curiously, and fortunately, the size of both their egos kept them from clashing. "I never really thought you were my equal," she told him lightheartedly in 1950. "I just said that to try to be polite." Later she would size him up imperiously. "He was not an intellectual. He had no interest in abstract thinking, only in the concrete. . . . He often said he was the better writer. . . . *I* am the better writer." Since each was merely being generous by acknowledging the other's talent, both remained comfortably convinced of their own superiority.

That summer in Paris, he and Simone enjoyed themselves at parties, holiday street dances, museums, races, boxing matches, and nightclubs; it was a time in his life Algren later said he would most like to go back to. Only his visit to Richard Wright provided an exception to the feeling that everything was beginning. Their meeting, which Algren remembered as their last, sadly underscored the differences that Wright's self-exile had brought between the two defenders of the inarticulate. Algren considered it inconceivable to live in Paris, because he believed the writer had a responsibility not to desert those he had chosen to defend: Wright's life in Paris therefore seemed a betrayal of the belief that had inspired *Native Son*. Wright had left the States hoping to find a less racist society in France, but Algren felt Wright's departure was a loss, both to Wright himself and to literature. Wright "somehow assumed that I had left Chicago for keeps and was setting up in Paris," he later wrote to Wright's biographer, "and I told him I'd be afraid to do that for fear of losing contact with my roots. He really blew up at that—'Don't you realize that some of the greatest novels have been written in exile?' he asked me. 'Look at Dostoevsky.' I answered that whether a man was exiled from his country, or had exiled himself, made a great difference. We didn't have anything more to say to one another after that." Nelson's seemingly callous reaction harks back to his memory of refusing to open his father's store and the break it caused between them; one suspects that Algren later regretted his dogmatic judgment of a man for whom he felt tremendous, unqualified respect: within six years Algren would also wish to exile himself.

In late June, typewriter in tow, Nelson and Simone flew to Italy. In Rome, they met Ignazio Silone and listened to *Aida* in the Baths of Caracalla. But the city was quiet, and there were too many ruins. On to Naples, which Algren adored, praising the bay and taking photographs of the crowded slums as friendly children scrambled for the hot bulbs from his camera. They lounged on the beaches at Ischia, were happy and relaxed at Sorrento and Amalfi, and Algren even found himself enjoying the ruins at Pompeii. Then they flew to Tunis.

Algren loved the strange North African sunlight; the earthen walls; the stately, robed Arabs slowly riding by on camels; the secretive, veiled women; the dust. On the island of Djerba, they witnessed the activities of the last days of Ramadan. Every night the Muslims waited for the moon, and the frenzied music and chanting of the dancing crowds filled the dusty streets. Algren was astonished by the beautiful Jewish women draped in black shawls like women he'd seen in Chicago; he and Simone visited a synagogue to which Jews from all over the world came on pilgrimage. Later they relaxed in a grotto bar, and Algren got a little buzz from smoking kef.

Driving them back to Tunis by way of Médenine, their chauffeur, Hassine, tried to impress them with his travels to France, his ability to communicate by telephone, his two suits, his garage. Was there oil for cooking in Chicago, he demanded of Algren, and eggs and flour? Then he could make his fortune selling fritters at Chicago crossroads! But Hassine was disappointed in his travelers. It may have been amusing to watch a nervous Algren ride high upon a camel, but Algren—an American!—absurdly claimed to have neither a car nor interest in a fritter business; worse, he and Simone caused Hassine to lose his dignity by demanding to see "women who were not serious" in the Rue Sidi Yahya, a street of prostitution where black and Jewish whores serviced the common soldiery. "I knew we were in the wrong neighborhood as soon as we passed the guards," Algren recalled: Simone, a white European woman, looked completely out of place among these darker outcasts, and the whores knew the group hadn't come to spend money. One girl wrangled a look at Algren's camera and demanded a thousand francs to return it, while Simone, in Algren's undoubtedly embellished account, fled a crowd of jeering women who chased her to the gates and pulled up her skirts, shouting, "See, she has one too!" Simone, of course, was the first to observe that their treatment had been perfectly justified—once they were safely back in the Citroën and on the road.

Free from Hassine, they traveled across the desert to Algiers, Fez, Marrakesh, then to Marseilles, where Algren found that all the Wild West feeling was gone. At the Bosts' house on the Riviera, overlooking terraces of olive trees and the sea, Algren was in wonderful spirits. One night he consumed almost a whole bottle of whiskey while Juliette Greco perched on his lap; he then danced with a chair. Later, he and Simone lost a little money in Monte Carlo before heading back to Paris.

During these four months, Simone and Nelson had never gotten along better. He asked her to come to Chicago the following September and spend at least four months with him; and if, in the enthusiasm of the literary success coming to both of them, Simone felt that her "contingent" love for Algren—love that existed outside her lifelong pact with Sartre—could not have been working out better, Algren seems to have made his peace with a relationship that allowed them to create great works and then to have wonderful months together each year. After a season with her, he was no longer lonely; he had told Simone that he wanted to have a new novel started before she came to Chicago. It was good to be going home. During the plane's refueling stop at Gander, Newfoundland, he read an excellent review of *The Man with the Golden Arm* in *Time* magazine, and landing in the United States seemed like one more beginning—this time of a round of cocktail parties, checks, interviews, and good reviews. He rode back to Chicago with a friend, and he wrote Simone that it thrilled him to see American trees once more, the wide rivers and plains, the huge open sky. The U.S. wasn't as colorful as France or as awesome as Marrakesh, but it was home. "It's just huge, warm, and friendly, confident and sleepy and taking its time," he wrote. He was happy he belonged to it, and was relieved to think that no matter where he went, America was the country he could always come home to.

13.

"You Are Going to Be
a Champion"

TIME'S declaration that *The Man with the Golden Arm* was "a true novelist's triumph" was the beginning of a host of good reviews for Frankie Machine. "Algren [is] an artist whose sympathy is as large as Victor Hugo's . . . an artist who ranks with this new novel, as Hemingway predicted he would, among our best American authors," said the *Chicago Sun-Times*. In the *Tribune* Algren was compared to Dostoevsky; elsewhere he was compared to Gorky and Dickens. *The New York Times Book Review* found "virtually nothing more that one could ask" in "his grasp of his material and his attitude toward it," and even *The New Yorker* applauded Algren's "broad compassion, his charged, metaphoric style," and his "unforgettable" characters, finding the novel's occasional lapses into sentimentality "overwhelmed by its virtues." The praise continued nationwide.

Algren was soon a celebrity. Three hundred people lined up around the block to see the famous author at an autographing party at the Seven Stairs bookstore, and for three hours the book sold a copy a minute; Brent alone may have sold a thousand copies in the first two weeks of publication. "Now add the name Nelson Algren to the honor roll of Chicago authors: Ernest Hemingway, Carl Sandburg, Sherwood Anderson, Theodore Dreiser, Floyd Dell, Ben Hecht, Edna Ferber, and James T. Farrell," proclaimed full-page ads in *The New York Times Book Review,* curiously omitting Wright. The prestigious Book Find Club chose the novel as its December selection, and the story of Frankie Machine was soon the best-selling book in Chicago; it would stay among the city's top sixteen best-sellers until the following April.

Algren's longtime supporters, including Simone and Carl Sandburg, were as enthusiastic as the press. Malcolm Cowley found that Algren's defense of the individual brought a new dimension to naturalism, and Ernest Hemingway, who sent a letter of congratulations to Algren (which he taped to his refrigerator), later provided a promotional quote that thrilled Nelson but made Doubleday leery of reprisals from the publishers of Wolfe and Faulkner:

> Into a world of letters where we have the fading Faulkner and that overgrown Lil Abner Thomas Wolfe casts a shorter shadow every day, Algren comes like a corvette or even a big destroyer when one of those things is what you need and need it badly and at once and for keeps. . . . Truman Capote fans grab your hats, if you have any, and go. This is a man writing and you should not read it if you cannot take a punch. . . . Mr.. Algren can hit with both hands and move around and he will kill you if you are not awfully careful. . . . Mr. Algren, boy, you are good.

Privately, Hemingway told Max Perkins he thought the poetic Algren "probably the best writer under 50, and name your own figure, writing today." Though Hemingway admitted that he disliked the suicidal finish to the novel, there was no doubt that he considered Algren a competitor, noting in his personal copy of *Golden Arm,* "OK, kid, you beat Dostoevsky. I'll never fight you in Chicago. Ever. But I will knock your brains out in the other towns I know and you don't know. But: you are going to be a champion. But: and these are hard buts, you, repeat, you have to knock a champion out to win."

Still, despite all the attention, including a nomination for the Pulitzer Prize, Algren wasn't making any money, and it wasn't because he was gambling. In between radio, television, newspaper, and magazine interviews, he was out autographing books, reporting to McCormick, and making sure copies arrived to important publishing people and critics. But of seventeen thousand copies sold by December, twelve thousand went to pay back Doubleday's advances for the past two years. Algren's standard of living had not changed. "When I get a few bucks I want to put my mother in some place where she doesn't have to sleep and eat and wash the dishes in the same room," he wrote to Amanda. "After that, I'd like to get a place of my own with a bathroom and two faucets, something really swank; for about $14.50, say. I'm getting too old to be dragging up cans of fuel oil all winter." Aside from fifteen hundred dollars from the Book Find Club and eight hundred from French translations, his only real hope for substantial money would have to come from Hollywood.

He didn't have to wait long. By October, West Coast agent Irving Lazar telephoned offering him six hundred a week to spend five weeks writing dialogue for producer John Houseman. But none of the major studios was interested in *Golden Arm,* ostensibly because of the still taboo narcotics angle. The book's social criticism, however, could hardly have helped, since congressional investigations had already been held on Communist subversion in the entertainment industry. Then, suddenly, the rising box-office star John Garfield wanted to play Frankie Machine. The squat, square-faced Garfield seemed perfect for the part, and his previous films, such as the acclaimed *Body and Soul,* which concerned a ghetto kid turned boxing champ, treated themes that interested Algren. Moreover, that an actor of Garfield's caliber wanted to play Frankie truly gratified Algren. Garfield's associate, the producer Bob Roberts, who had worked with Dalton Trumbo, Ring Lardner, Jr., and other writers who didn't like seeing their scripts mauled, came to Chicago in late October for talks with Nelson. Initially skeptical, Algren told Roberts to go ahead. "What stopped me till now," he explained to Ken McCormick, "much as I like Garfield as an actor, is the fact that his outfit doesn't have much money. But the sad fact is that all the major companies have nixed the book and I don't feel like tossing it after 'Never Come Morning.' "

In Chicago, Algren's phone was constantly ringing, and visiting *New Yorker* writer A. J. Liebling went with him to a number of parties. "He was still wearing steel-rimmed spectacles and a turtleneck sweater. He made no attempt to look grim, however, and a diet of turkey, Virginia ham, and cocktail shrimp apparently agreed with him." But Algren soon tired of the fanfare. After a while, when one of the local "bushy-tails" called to invite him to a literary evening, he'd say he'd call back and didn't. Instead he took to prowling the streets with his new friend Art Shay, a "ball of fire . . . idea man and ace with a camera." Shay, an ambitious free-lance photographer and former staff reporter for *Life* magazine, saw in Algren a great artist about to be discovered. He planned to do his first *Life* picture story on Algren and when he arrived at Wabansia he was immediately impressed by Algren's unassuming air, good humor, and the utter lack of vanity which made him the perfect photographer's model.

"We shot on the streets, in Bughouse Square, in skid-row hotels, in all-night restaurants and tough bars, in tattoo parlors," Shay recalled. "We sneaked into the Washem School of Undertaking and into the Cook County Morgue. . . . I photographed a buy being made in a doorway. . . . I followed Algren to Riccardo's restaurant on North Rush Street, where, with Simone back in Paris, he'd dine with Janice Kingslowe, who had played the lead in a Chicago production of 'Anna Lucasta.' "

Soon Shay suggested a picture book from the photos, with an introductory essay by Algren. They planned to produce "an exact and candid representation of life in the backstreets of a great American city in 1950." Doubleday, waiting breathlessly for a follow-up to *Golden Arm,* thought it was a great idea, especially coming on the heels of the imminent *Life* story. Nelson was happy; he was determined to resist Doubleday's pressure and was in no hurry at all to start a new novel. He knew it would take three or four years to work up another book, and he wanted to "just feel around, feel around in the dark" until he found something.

He found out more about narcotics than he had ever known. Frankie Machine had been an isolated junkie, but as Algren met more addicts he became aware of a distinct narcotics underworld. He saw the addicts' fragile junkie identities, their endless shufflings in and out of court and periodic trips to the federal hospital in Lexington, Kentucky. Recidivism was almost predictable; the odds against coming clean were crushing. Yet they clung to the idea of getting off with all kinds of crazy schemes to which Algren usually felt obligated to contribute money.

Algren tried in various ways to help the addicts. He defended them, feeling they deserved a special compassion. Upon her release from Lexington, his old friend Patty found refuge in Algren's Wabansia apartment. She had certainly not recovered; at a party at Stuart Brent's bookstore she began, in a fit, pulling books off the shelves and tearing out pages. Brent, enraged, wanted to throw her out, but Nelson told him savagely that if he did so their friendship was over—and threatened to hit him.

He was becoming increasingly emotionally involved with Margo, the addicted hooker he'd met a year or two earlier through Jack, Karl, and Patty. Margo, raised in a large Ohio farm family, was a classic case of betrayed innocence: seduced by a carnival barker passing through town, she became pregnant, married the man, and bore a daughter. Her husband convinced her they could make their fortunes in a large city, so they left the child with Margo's parents and headed for either Los Angeles or Chicago, where he immediately put Margo on the street and hooked her on narcotics—thus beginning a horrendous battle with drugs which lasted more than a decade. In December 1949, Margo apparently stayed with Algren for a short time; it was probably she whom he referred to when he told Simone— perhaps to make her jealous—that he was living with a woman who was supporting him. To Algren, Margo was "a country girl who'd become street-wise, cynical, comical, and vulnerable," and he became determined to break her habit, believing it to be merely a matter of willpower. In a memoir he recalled cutting off her connection and putting her to bed. But by midnight she was so sick she'd gone blind, and it was obvious she would either die or go insane. Algren had never made a street buy but finally found her connection in an all-night restaurant.

And then there was Acker, who had so obligingly demonstrated giving himself a fix for Shay's camera, and from whom Algren heard nothing but that "he was very, very troubled by using the stuff." Acker was desperate to go the West Coast: out there, where he didn't know anybody, he thought he could really kick drugs. Algren's Hollywood deal had been delayed by both the narcotics angle and Garfield's health, but by early 1950 Roberts and Garfield had discussed the contract with Algren by phone. The money was forthcoming, and in the interest of cash, Algren put aside his gut feeling that Roberts was a con man and a phony. He wanted to have a hand in the film, get a better contract, and perhaps see Amanda, and with Roberts picking up the tab there seemed no reason not to go to California. He arranged with Roberts for Acker to come along as a technical advisor. Immediately seduced by the idea, Acker insisted they buy train tickets for the Super Chief and arrive in style. The night before they left, however, Acker was thrown in jail. When Algren went down to find him, Acker looked terrified—as if he were going to be executed. But when Algren waved the contract naming Acker John Garfield's technical advisor, Acker was released.

A dozen addicts came to see them off at the La Salle Street Station. "Acker looked very sporty," Algren recalled, and the long, luxurious train headed west.

Sunny, leisurely Hollywood, with its glitter and superficial mannerisms, was never going to be Algren's town. "Nelson was like a bull in a china shop in Hollywood," his agent's wife recalled. "He didn't know how to act and he didn't want to know." For Nelson, Los Angeles was a "flying saucer," and the climate was just too balmy: nothing ever seemed real out there. Met at the train by the producer's flunky, Nelson and Acker were whisked to the famous Garden of Allah and the very *apartment* of the great John Garfield, who was staying elsewhere. Instantly, a TV, a radio, and cases of scotch, bourbon, and vodka materialized. Garfield, cheerfully breezing in and out between tennis matches, said he couldn't wait to play Frankie. Roberts appeared fresh from the beaches of Malibu; and they were off to Romanoff's.

Nelson was being given, as he later described it, "The Ten-Day-Hollywood-Hospitality Treatment," predicated on the assumption that five hundred dollars spent wining and dining a writer from the sticks was bound to produce such gratitude that he'd sign for any price the producer named. But Nelson was unwilling to sign the contract he'd okayed over the phone because he realized it wasn't the best he could get. Loyally refusing to place blame on his agent, Madeleine Brennan, he was holding out for 5 percent of the picture's net, which Roberts wouldn't go for. Algren felt he was being cheated. "Roberts was very salty at me because I only let him have 95% of the picture and he knows that, as the producer, he is entitled to 100% and my extra pair of pants," he told Ken McCormick. "He had offered to let me keep the pants, and, very shrewdly, I'd turned it down." Soon relations had so deteriorated that Roberts served Nelson with summonses to prevent his selling *Golden Arm* elsewhere, and, even less hospitably, stopped paying the rent at the Garden. Algren had to pay a hundred and fifty bucks for a week's rent before Acker, starting a career as a sign-painter, found them a down-at-the-heels motel on Sunset Boulevard.

Fed up with Roberts—"his whole manner was insulting. It was one of absolute confidence that he was talking to an idiot"—Algren fired the agents Ingersoll and Brennan had found and hired George Willner of the Willner-Goldstone Agency to negotiate another contract. Much as he didn't want to, he still had to work with Roberts, for, he observed wryly, "we had reached the tacit understanding that neither of us could afford anything less than affection for each other. He needed to make a million dollars and I needed to buy a house in Indiana. So though the very sight of me caused his features to be suffused by a disgust matched by nothing earthly save the revulsion in my own breast, we clung passionately each to each: a friendship based on the solid rock of utter loathing." Willner, soon to be blacklisted, also found Algren work with the King brothers, who apparently worked with the blacklisted Dalton Trumbo. It was natural for Algren to gravitate toward left-wing people, but unlike many others, he completely escaped political trouble with the movie industry.

Hollywood, though jittery from the 1947 congressional investigations into Communists in the film industry, had not yet endured the 1951 hearings that would result in a massive blacklist of those linked, however remotely, with the Communist Party; Algren and Acker had come to a town in an uneasy lull between investigations. To appease the government and atone for their pro-Soviet war films, studios were cranking out anti-Red pictures and would soon shelve a half-finished film on the Indian peacemaker Hiawatha for fear that it "might be regarded as a message for peace and therefore helpful to present Communist designs." However, the decision finding the Hollywood Ten guilty of contempt for refusing to cooperate with the 1947 committee was still pending appeal; and though John Garfield, once connected with the Group Theatre, the Young People's Socialist League, and the left-wing Conference of Studio Unions, was certainly not safe from the gathering storm, he and people who like Algren had campaigned for Wallace or taken a position in support of the Ten could still find work.

Algren in fact had helped head the Chicago Committee for the Hollywood Ten, speaking and generally publicizing the plight of the writers and directors; he had met Dalton Trumbo and Ring Lardner, Jr., in Chicago. In Hollywood he dropped in on Albert Maltz, who wrote, Algren believed, "out of an almost Christlike feeling." Maltz, about to be sentenced to jail for his role in the Hollywood Ten affair, found Algren enormously likable and good-natured, and remembered him fondly. "At a time when everyone was running away," said Maltz, "he was right out in front supporting us."

The FBI kept tabs on him there, but Algren's activities in California were hardly political. While the contract was being negotiated, he and Acker and Tiba Willner went to the local racetrack, where Tiba had access to a box near the finish line. He also took Acker to meet Martha and Adolph Brown, friends from Chicago whose Malibu house had a spectacular ocean view. And he was spending a lot of time with Amanda. Instead of making phone calls from the motel, he used the phone at her apartment during the day and found himself calling her up at her job to say hello: she seemed to have blossomed in California. She was still the same down-to-earth person she had always been, but now she was working for the Screen Writers Guild and was independent and self-assured, conversant in the very aspects of Hollywood life that concerned him most, with firsthand information about the political turmoil. At cocktail parties, she was no longer shy: she wore smart dresses and chatted in a bright and lively way—at ease in a city he would never understand.

Algren saw her as an alternative to Simone, about whom his feelings were confused. He could not understand why Simone insisted on keeping their relationship on a level that made her unhappy and punished him. In December, he had reiterated that she should not come to Chicago before he had the new book started. Throughout 1948 and 1949 their mutual pledge, suggested by Nelson, was that only hard work could justify their long separations; yet now he hadn't started a new book. Simone constantly asked whether he was working and admonished him not to be lazy, but his lack of a project signified a telling change in their relationship that she didn't seem to notice: he was trying to move away from her, and he was seeing other women—Janice Kingslowe, Mari Sabusawa, Margo, another woman named Barbara, and Amanda. Nelson had already offered Simone marriage; for him love, like literary success, had to be all or nothing— yet Simone wanted it somewhere in between. Still, it was difficult to ignore the long, loving, and intelligent letters arriving from Paris every few days; even more difficult to refuse her. In January, a month after he had repeated that he wasn't ready for her, she rather abjectly begged him to let her come to Chicago for the summer. She made it clear that she had to do it for Sartre, as if that would somehow excuse it all in his eyes. "Sartre *has* to go away this summer for three months, no later than June. And he asks me, very demandingly, to go away when he does, not to wait until he is back." Although Algren was unhappy about putting off his own work to accommodate the schedule of the first man in her life, he nevertheless agreed and planned to buy a summer cottage on Lake Michigan's Indiana dunes. Elated at having the best of both worlds, Simone promised to scrub the floors, cook the meals, write both their books, and make love to him twenty times a day.

Perhaps he was just preoccupied with seeing new things in Holly-wood, but he did not write her as frequently as before. It was as if a clear vision of their future, a part-time affair on Sartre's terms with endless separations, had clicked in his head. Simone, panic-stricken at not hearing from him, sent a wire—but he didn't like frantic wires and didn't immediately respond.

Till now most of Algren's emotional energy had been spent making himself a great writer, and with *The Man with the Golden Arm* he had finally gained the recognition and money whose lack had sent him into such a deep depression in 1935. He had always seen his career as a kind of sacrifice completely separate from his personal life. "I had no family, and it was an advantage to me in writing," Algren told an interviewer. "I don't recommend being a bachelor, but it helps if you want to write." Now that he had established himself, he wanted a more fulfilling personal life—and the part-time relationship that Simone envisaged was not what he had in mind. He wanted a home and a woman of his own—a woman for whom he would be the most important person.

And here was Amanda, who had always loved him. Though she was dating a photographer whom Algren encouraged her to marry, Amanda became his steady date at Hollywood events with literary and movie people. Times were certainly better than their lean Depression years, and since Algren thought Amanda deserved a better way of life than he had ever been able to offer, he enjoyed taking her out to dinner and gave her a thousand dollars to replace her 1932 Chevrolet coupe. When he returned from visiting friends in Beverly Hills, he told her, "That's the kind of house you ought to live in."

Any idea of romance between them was necessarily tentative, but Amanda felt he was hinting indirectly at marriage by telling her that many of his girlfriends wanted to marry him—though he did not mention that Simone did not. Nelson had always maintained great feelings of loyalty, guilt, friendship, and goodwill toward Amanda, and he was probably already thinking of trying their marriage a third time. How he could have been so optimistic is a good question—but he nurtured a certain simple, innocent faith that things would work out for the best.

In mid-March 1950, he left Hollywood to fly to New York. *The Man with the Golden Arm* had been awarded the first National Book Award for Fiction, and, ostensibly because he was told to keep the news secret until it was announced to the press, he did not tell

Amanda about it. Feeling that he had indeed written the best novel of 1949, Nelson was delighted, not only because he loved recognition, but also because the award meant literary prestige, increased Doubleday promotion, and a peg for Art Shay's *Life* story, which had been laid out for eight pages. Shay, in New York editing photographs for both the picture book and the magazine story, took Algren to a tuxedo-rental place on Sixth Avenue and photographed him trying on formals. Algren, in his old gray overcoat, stuffed the rope he was wearing for a belt into a pocket. He had never worn a tuxedo before.

That year awards also went to the poet William Carlos Williams for *Paterson,* and to Ralph L. Rusk for his biography of Ralph Waldo Emerson; although there was dissent among the judges for those awards, Algren had clearly been the favorite for fiction. Malcolm Cowley was one of the judges, as was Max Gissen, of *Time*, who had three months earlier given *Golden Arm* the magazine's award for the best novel of 1949. The awards ceremony at the Waldorf-Astoria was a prestigious event, with Clifton Fadiman presiding as master of ceremonies and Eleanor Roosevelt, Senator Paul Douglas of Illinois, and *Harper's* editor Frederick Lewis Allen presenting the awards. Algren's reaction at reaching these heights of literary success seemed a mixture of cynicism and awe. During his acceptance speech he joked that he might one day have to take the award to the pawnshop, but photographs show him looking at home in his tux and docilely accepting the award from Mrs. Roosevelt.

In fact, Shay recalled that Algren seemed bowled over by all the attention from the big boys in New York and Hollywood, and didn't always know how to act. Shay invited him to lunch with some of the Ivy League editors from *Life,* to whom he had been building Algren up as a tough guy from the Chicago slums, an underworld denizen at ease among criminals and junkies. But Nelson couldn't play the part. "I'm telling them he is close to these people and he's coming on as a college professor of English," Shay recalled in exasperation. The *Life* story was further delayed when the magazine's lawyers sent Shay back to Chicago to get signed releases "from every bum, addict, and nonwhore in the story," he remembered. "I wandered around Chicago for a week searching for those characters like a man in a novel, holding up pictures, asking one bum if he knew where I could find another." But he finally got them. The Algren story was about to roll off the presses and Shay was there to watch it. "The presses turned—but out of them came a photo essay on life in a Mexican prison that granted conjugal rights to prisoners. That was *Life*'s sociological story for the time being. They kept the Algren pictures for six months and then returned them with a note about how tough a subject drug addiction was." As Shay said later, "It would have *made* Nelson."

Algren returned to Hollywood to tie up the deal with Roberts, who seemed to take no notice of the award. "He had to protect himself. He could not let any of it have any value," Algren said later. "He couldn't acknowledge the literary world at all." But even though before leaving for New York Algren had been "definitely washed out of the picture" in terms of writing the script, he was suddenly back in. Willner had struck what seemed to Nelson a good deal, apparently getting $5,000 for the option, another $10,000 if Roberts picked it up, and $4,000 for Nelson to write the script: just under $20,000, and—through a clause over which there would be much contention—5 percent of the picture's net if the film were made or 50 percent of the sale price if the rights were sold. It wasn't an enormous amount, but to Algren it was plenty: he was much more interested in seeing a good film made out of his book than in making a lot of money. *The Grapes of Wrath* and *An American Tragedy* had been made into powerful films, and he felt that a good movie of *Golden Arm,* with a fine actor like Garfield playing Frankie, would expose his work to an even wider audience. Now that Willner had put them all on good terms, he assured Roberts and Garfield that he could write the script in six weeks in Chicago—if he had a collaborator who knew about screenplays. Paul Trivers was dispatched to do the job, and Algren returned home.

That spring he returned to a huge stack of fan mail and worked on projects other than his own writing. In three months he and Trivers produced a screenplay that satisfied him. Meanwhile he taught fiction writing at the University of Chicago in jacket and tie, trying to tell well-scrubbed young people how they ought to go about writing: his students' agony, he told McCormick, was matched only by his own. Other times, he wandered around Chicago with Shay, gathering more photos for the picture book. Doubleday had given them each a thousand dollars, but since the demise of the *Life* article, the project had no clear deadline, and Shay felt that Nelson's enthusiasm was dwindling. They did, however, apply for a Guggenheim.

With Chris Rowland's help, Algren was also looking for a house. He had asked Willner to send his $4,000 script payment to Chris Rowland, who was living with Neal and the children in Miller Beach, a small community on the Lake Michigan shores near Gary, Indiana. He knew if he kept the cash himself he might blow it on the horses. He had the script money, the University of Chicago teaching stipend, a lucrative paperback deal with Pocket Books, royalties for *Golden Arm,* and another few thousand of leftover option money—more money than he'd ever had; yet he was frequently gambling at racetracks and poker games. One day, naturally, he asked Chris for his money back, and was astounded when she told him flatly to forget it.

Impulsively, Algren put a down payment on a beach house owned by his friends the Gourfains, sixty feet from the water's edge, like Bernice's old place on the dunes. "What did you buy that house for?" Chris demanded when she heard about it. "You told me to find you a house and I've got the perfect house for you."

The minute he saw the other house he knew he'd been a fool. But he had already paid Gourfain, and he had the gambler's sense that when money was gone, it was gone. Art Shay, who often guided him in financial matters, drove him out to Miller and noticed not only that the beach house was full of sand, but that the kids using the beach would only get noisier in the summer. "What about this sand, Nelson?" Shay asked practically. Nelson said, "Well, there's this other house." The one Chris had found was at the end of a dead-end street; it had a long backyard that sloped down to a lagoon; a little rowboat was tied up there. Gourfain gave him all his money back, less two hundred dollars—prompting Nelson privately to call him a cheap Jew—and Nelson bought the tiny and incredibly modest little cottage that, set back from the road and surrounded by woods, felt luxuriously secluded. Rabbits and squirrels and fieldmice occasionally wandered across the backyard, and on the lagoon's opposite shore there were huge sand dunes speckled with waving grasses. The house was indeed perfect for him, and couldn't help but promise happiness.

In a photograph taken by Art Shay around July 1950, Nelson and Simone seem very much in love: Nelson looks serious, gentle; Simone, in her Guatemalan clothes, radiant and bohemian. But beneath this apparent harmony lurked change. Algren had been brooding over their relationship in the spring, and though he had agreed to her wishes, she could not expect things to be the same. He couldn't have approved of the way Simone was repressing her need for a loving, sexual relationship, and he did not want a futureless affair over which he had little control. Algren had no interest in being an adjunct to the de Beauvoir–Sartre life. So when Simone arrived he began trying to exercise control over his life and emotions. Although he had been sending her happy, loving letters for most of the year, Algren now told Simone he no longer loved her. He refused to become passionate and romantically worked up over the affair. He was perfectly pleasant, but aloof. And to judge from Simone's fictional account in *The Mandarins,* he seemed to feel he had to remain on guard against Simone's amiability: "It seems ridiculous to defend yourself against someone who isn't attacking you," says Lewis Brogan. "So you don't defend yourself. And then when you're alone once more, you find your heart's all upside-down again. No, I don't want any repetition of that."

It was not easy for Simone to adjust to his new attitude, to his body's seeming indifference; she was deeply upset. Finally they left the stifling apartment for the peaceful house in Miller, and though they did not easily adjust to the new state of affairs, life assumed a routine. At first Simone couldn't help attempting to rekindle their love, but she was soon trying with willful optimism to make the best of their dreary lot. Perhaps to reinforce their distance and avoid emotional scenes, Algren made sure they spent time with friends and neighbors at barbecues and fairs. Nelson led Art to believe that privately he and Simone were "quite athletically loving their extraordinary brains out," and Simone played the part of the live-in lover well enough to fool Chris and Neal Rowland, who often dropped by. "I was always afraid, when exposed too long to the searching looks of others, of not being able to play out to the very end my role of a happy woman," says Anne Dubreuilh in *The Mandarins*. Sometimes Algren went to Chicago alone; Simone wrote that she both enjoyed and feared the silence in the house.

Once Simone accepted the arrangement, they were able to comfort each other, to find pleasure in the summer. Though the old passion was gone, and each of them had a separate room for sleep and work, they began to make love again. The weather was beautiful, and

Simone read voraciously in a backyard chaise longue, sipping Courvoisier while Algren's typewriter clicked away inside. Around noon they would row across the lagoon, climb to the top of the mountainous white dunes, and see Lake Michigan rise up like an enormous sea. Light winds passed through the tall dune grasses and long-legged birds pecked at the sand; the beach was usually empty, and they sunned themselves. Later, Neal, who was learning French from Simone, would come by for his lesson. Nights they walked along the beach, saw the moon overhead and Gary's huge steel mills sending flames into the darkness. At times Simone, adoring Nelson and enjoying him, was simply, ineffably happy. Almost all the pictures Nelson took of her that summer show a woman with a smile so complete it can only be called joyous: Simone loved live and hated pain. "I have never met anyone in the whole of my life," Simone once wrote, "who was so well-equipped for happiness as I was, or who labored so stubbornly to achieve it."

Simone never cooked or did housework. "Nelson was always saying, 'She's got me washing the dishes and making dinner,' " Neal Rowland recalled, "but he never seemed to mind." However, this happiness was precarious. Simone remembered that very often, without provocation, Algren would suddenly become silent and withdrawn. Though love fluttered briefly when Algren, no swimmer himself, heroically rescued Simone as she sank in Lake Michigan, he stuck to his determination to distance himself from her. But his resolve was costly: he was gambling more and more. "In 1950, after a break, he left me alone in the house while he went to Chicago to play poker. He often lost," Simone said in an interview the year before her death. "I was astonished." For the first time, she became aware of a self-destructive force within him.

When Simone's close friend Nathalie Sorokine came to visit them in Miller, the two women, who hadn't been together in years, literally fell into each other's arms. Algren took an instant dislike to the extroverted but competitive and challenging Sorokine. One afternoon he apparently watched the two women at a backyard barbecue and saw them gently touching each other, and he told Neal Rowland and his friend Dave Peltz quite seriously that he thought their relationship was more than friendly. Clearly, Nathalie would not be living in *his* house for her two-week stay: he found her a room down the block with a family of annoying Russians. But she was over so often that he threatened to leave for Chicago. Instead, Simone and

Sorokine went to the city. When Simone returned, Algren told her he was considering remarrying Amanda.

By then, Simone wrote later, she was so drained by sadness she could hardly react. The summer was gone—the false peace of Indian summer had taken its place, and they did not discuss the future. When they spent their last afternoon at the races, Nelson lost all his cash. So they could eat, he called a friend, who left them only when they got into a cab to take Simone to the airport.

He acted as if he didn't mind casually wasting perhaps the last day they would ever see each other: he had abandoned his own creed to be true not to his head but to his heart. But after they said goodbye, he sent a messenger back to her with purple flowers and love from Nelson, a poignant reminder of past times, good times. One remembers Lewis Brogan from *The Mandarins:* "I think I'm not made for love," he replied in a slightly hesitant voice. "Before you, no woman had ever meant anything to me . . . if ever there was someone who was made for me, it was you. After you, there can be no one else."

In early October, having been invited in the spring, Amanda arrived in Miller for a two-week vacation. Chris and Neal, surprised at how quickly her visit followed Simone's, remembered that Nelson was very proud to be showing Amanda his place. During those weeks there were lots of parties and people dropped by, and Amanda was happy and extroverted and popular. "We had a party," said Chris, "and Amanda came over with Nelson and she was smoking a Dunhill cigarette in a long holder. She was moving around and holding court. Just holding court. And Nelson sat there wide-eyed. He couldn't get over it."

Old friends by now, Nelson and Amanda, whom he still called Mashya, got along well together. It was a very pleasant, friendly time, Amanda recalled, though not really romantic since they had not discussed being with each other more permanently. But they took walks on the dunes every day, and Amanda was energetic about decorating and fixing things in the house, for which Nelson had acquired a cat. They had such a good time that they decided Amanda should stay a week longer, and Nelson tried to cajole her into acting as his West Coast agent, since George Willner had gone underground with the blacklist. But at the end of their weeks together he was still ambivalent about his feelings. He didn't want to lead Amanda on, and it troubled him, he wrote her, that by seeing her now and then he turned her away from opportunities to marry and lead her own life. He could neither sever their relationship nor commit himself to a real and lasting one. He wasn't sure he wanted children, either, and told her that "living together without baby-raisin' would be pretty meaningless"—unconsciously admitting that any proposed union would be practical rather than passionate. He cared for Amanda a great deal; but he was nothing if not honest.

Meanwhile, Nelson was living the 1950s suburban life in Gary. He planted a lilac bush and narcissus bulbs around the house, bought a Sears vacuum cleaner, and painted his kitchen with some yellowish claylike stuff he found moldering in the basement. He was a complete bumbler at anything mechanical. He was constantly calling the Rowlands for help, and their ten-year-old son, Stevie, had to show him how to put a taillight on his bicycle. When he tried to change the screens to storms he knocked over the rosebushes and became completely confused about which window went where. But his cottage on its little piece of earth was an unmistakable symbol of accomplishment; he loved the place, to him the little rowboat was a yacht.

Oddly, Algren found himself among tens of thousands of white professional and working-class people moving to suburbs. His instincts toward owning property, conditioned by an image of successful writers with houses in the country, were similar to thousands like him who had come home from the war and made it. Returning veterans who married and found jobs and began raising families needed housing; its shortage, combined with prosperity, nurtured the traditional American dream of owning a home. Even Miller Beach, a quasi-resort community a fair distance from downtown Chicago, was not immune to the flight to the suburbs: in the early 1950s many Miller houses were making the switch from summer dwellings to year-round houses. At the war's end the landscape outside a typical city's limits had been rural, with roadside stands offering fresh vegetables and dairy cows grazing within sight of the urban skyline, but a building boom was putting up suburban towns with tremendous speed.

Yet if Algren shared a few subconscious desires with the burgeoning middle class, he found repulsive the anti-Communist ideology that was sweeping the country. The feeling of being at home in America that he had so joyfully described to Simone just a year earlier was gone. Increasingly, he felt alienated. All around him citizens mutely witnessed an increasing erosion of their rights and the rise of the most fascistic trend in American government in the twentieth century. That year the Hollywood Ten went to jail, and the Senate approved bills to exact the death penalty for peacetime spying, then wrapped up more anti-Red legislation in the Internal Security Act, which, supported by Hubert Humphrey and John Kennedy, called for "Communist-action" or "Communist-front" groups to register with a Subversive Activities Control Board; more grossly, it called for "emergency" detention in concentration camps for people with radical ideas. Now that Russia had the bomb, such an emergency meant, of course, an atomic war.

But though it was MacArthur who was pushing so deeply into North Korea that he was about to invade Chinese soil and bring Russia to the defense of the Chinese, Americans so feared random Communist violence that schoolchildren were being taught to hide under their desks in the event of atomic attack. Algren too was infected by this war hysteria: positive that MacArthur's heroics were going to unleash a world war, he invited Simone and Sartre to Miller. But the idea of coming to America, where presumably they would be safe, was, understandably, odious to them.

The growing atmosphere of conformity and distress seemed to change Algren's writing plans. It was not entirely true, as Ken McCormick saw it, that Nelson never knew what to work on next, for Algren's archive attests to a prodigious output. But he did not as yet appear even to be thinking about a novel, though he was further exploring the narcotics subculture through Margo, whom he was once again seeing fairly regularly. Instead he turned to poetry in absence of the novel, sending Simone two politically inspired poems that she proposed to translate: "The Dead in Korea" and "Elegy in Madrid." Roberts had picked up the $10,000 option on *Golden Arm,* and there was neither a financial incentive to start a new novel nor a feeling that he was standing still. The Guyonnet–Bost–de Beauvoir–Sartre translation of *Never Come Morning* appeared to good notices, and *Golden Arm* was also scheduled to appear in France and Italy, Jean Cau having assured French publishers that Faulkner was just an old sock compared to Algren.

In the spring Art Shay had helped land him a story for *Holiday,* a glossy oversized travel magazine, which was planning a special Chicago issue. Algren would be paid $2,000 for an essay he was delighted to be writing: he thought Chicago a great, fascinating, unappreciated city. The project allowed him to use his late 1930s poems and also gave him a forum to discuss what he saw happening in the country. His first major creative work that was not fiction, the piece, which occupied him that fall and winter, represented a new dimension in his writing—the highly personalized essay. It made no attempt to be objective and was basically a prose poem: slangy, down-to-earth, and utterly original.

Algren's essay presented a Chicago whose heart beat in its slums, a city with two faces—one for the haves and one for the have-nots: Chicago had been founded, after all, when the Pottawattomie Indians had been hustled out of town by "the marked-down derelicts with the dollar signs for eyes," and these hustlers had sealed the city's fate as a capital of corruption. Do-gooders like Jane Addams arrived too late to work any significant change, merely keeping the city tied up in a kind of cosmic, endless baseball game where honest folk got only "two outs to the inning while the hustlers are taking four." The 1919 Chicago Black Sox Scandal, when players lost the World Series for a rich gambler's payoff, had been but an instance of this corruption; and as Algren remembered his childhood disappointment at learning that even his heroes were out for money, he wove an essentially nostalgic tale of a "silver-colored yesterday" into a parable of the current persecution of Communists. "The Black Sox were the Reds of that October, and mine was the guilt of association. . . . Choked with guilt and penitence, crawling on all fours like a Hollywood matinee idol, I pleaded to be allowed, with all my grievous faults, to go along with the gang."

For Chicago, "the place built out of Man's ceaseless failure to overcome himself," was the "psychological nerve center where the pang goes deepest when the whole country grinds its teeth in a nightmare sleep"; it had been infected with the suspicion sweeping the country. And yet this had been the city of the great radicals, the freethinkers who "stuck out their stubborn necks in the ceaseless battle between the rights of Owners and the rights of Man, the stiff-necked wonders who could be broken but couldn't be bent: Dreiser, Altgeld, Debs." The town of Big Bill Haywood and the One Big Union, of Jane Addams and Vachel Lindsay, of Dreiser, Anderson, Masters, Sandburg, and Wright. But it was a city now sinking into mediocrity, where Algren, who had intimately experienced the Depression and was uniquely sensitive to the conditions fostering creativity, noted prophetically that there would be no more giants: "You can't make an arsenal of a nation and yet expect its great cities to produce artists. It's in the nature of the overbraided brass to build walls about the minds of men—as it is in the nature of the arts to tear those dark walls down. Today, under the name of 'security,' the dark shades are being drawn.''

And so the essay was suffused with a sense of loss. For if Algren had felt three years earlier that Americans no longer laughed out of their own good health, now he saw them wearing "plastic masks of an icy-cold despair." Behind the masks was isolation, the rarely mentioned terror from which Algren himself suffered and which he would try to articulate in the culturally strangled years to come, like a man desperately trying to keep his head above water, swept down by a tide tolerating no dissent or talk of a disease of the country's spirit. "He was a prey to the harsh loneliness of America," de Beauvoir had astutely noted in the forties; the observation better suited the life he was about to enter in the nightmare decade to follow.

The months went by. The lagoon froze and the little rowboat was locked in ice; the snow piled up outside the cottage, sealing him in. He made occasional forays to Chicago, where he still kept the place on Wabansia, and at Christmas, Karl, Patty, and Margo came out to Miller for a few days. But for the most part he dug into his work, though somehow his burrowing seemed different. For the first time he wrote about his own past, describing his childhood with a nostalgia that would increase with the years. For the first time he was writing history instead of the actual reportage he had cultivated into such an art; and even as he did so, the Chicago of neighborhoods that had inspired his last three books was disappearing. Part of his life seemed closed forever. The house in Gary was a new beginning, but it was not the same as the place on Wabansia, where the whores and the junkies dropping by had lent him a special intimacy with the city's lost. And though Simone wrote that it was completely useless for her to try to change her feelings, that she loved him as before, the innocence that had allowed him to believe he would actually have and enjoy the one great love of his life was completely gone.

Strangely, even as he had noted in the essay, the tradition of great Chicago writers was also receding into the past; and he identified strongly with the social realism and naturalism that, forming the heart of that tradition, had nourished both himself and Wright. Even now he planned an essay on naturalism as an introduction for the picture book, at the same time blaming Wright for deserting the ranks to become a "Café Flore intellectual." He felt Wright should have

stayed in Chicago to "tough it out, Jack, tough it out": he too had
had the chance to live in Paris. But even as he declared his dedication
to American naturalism, which had taken for granted the artist's
right to hold dissenting political or social views, that literary movement was nearing its end. In fact, "the whole great American tradition of social commentary," as Howard Fast described it, "that
produced all our great writers, right up to World War II and for a
few years after World War II," was essentially over. Algren was
unknowingly one of the last of the legacy, which was pushed aside
as the cold war permeated every sector of American intellectual life.
He once remarked that he should have been a pioneer; he felt,
somehow, that he had been born in the wrong century.

III

In a real dark night of the soul it is always three o'clock in the morning, day after day.

——F. SCOTT FITZGERALD

In Algren's central vision, self-destruction becomes operative only after the destruction of some loved object.

—GEORGE BLUESTONE

14.
Rumors of Evening

Though the editors at the up-scale *Holiday* were bound to it by contract and liked its originality, Algren's essay on Chicago wasn't exactly what they'd had in mind. Ken McCormick was much more enthusiastic. Still eager to encourage Algren's production and capitalize on the success of *Golden Arm*, McCormick suggested bringing out the essay as a little book for the Christmas trade, and Nelson loved the idea. "The way I see Chicago, it's a city on the make," Ken was remembered as saying in Shay's Pontiac on the way from Chicago for a visit to the dunes, and *Chicago: City on the Make* was born.

McCormick's enthusiasm offset the inevitable unpleasantness brewing at *Holiday*. In early May, Algren had finally received what he felt was a badly cut-up essay masquerading as edited copy. A week was allowed him to make changes, but as he worked furiously to revive the piece, *Holiday* ran the edited copy without waiting for his revision. Algren saw this as slovenly editing, but more likely it was done to soften Algren's views. "Don't let any of this trouble you," the editor consoled him, "because we are still enormously pleased with your piece . . . and distinctly proud to have it in *Holiday*." Algren's reply was classic:

> I'd be less disappointed were you more honest. . . .
> To restore meaning and order to that piece, more than a week was actually required. . . . And because my concern over the piece was deep, and the limitations of which you advised me were sufficiently sharp, I was pleased to be able to bring it to life again within the promised time. If your taste is really so lacking or your timing so poor that you will publish the hack-and-patch version anyway, all I can say is that you're a sorry sort of operator indeed.

Nor do I feel that being well-paid, which I have been, justifies either the capriciousness of your action or the smugness of the letter with which you cap it. I've been served up with cheap flattery without swooning before this; but have never till now seen so much of it so densely packed.

After a lavish party, laden with liquor and fancy hors d'oeuvres, for *Holiday*'s Chicago issue, he joked to McCormick that he had maintained "complete composure, touched by a kind of cool disdain for all the goodies so near, so free, and so abundant. Nothing was missing but Conroy." But Art Shay remembers that the head of *Ebony* turned to Nelson and drunkenly confessed that, goddammit, he'd known him for twenty years and couldn't believe he was selling out by writing for *Holiday*. Nelson put his drink down hard: "You don't know me twenty years, just five days in the last twenty years." "I've never been afraid of the accusation of selling out," Algren said later. "Nobody makes it but those with nothing left to sell and I'm not accountable to them."

When Doubleday's attractive little volume of *Chicago: City on the Make,* written as Algren intended it and dedicated to Sandburg, was published in October 1951, the *Sun-Times* called it "the finest thing on the city since Sandburg's *Chicago Poems*." The *Chicago Daily News* also thought highly of it, and in *The New York Times,* Budd Schulberg wrote that if by normal standards Algren's book was an unfair portrait of the city, "therein lies its strength. About as unflattering as a Goya portrait of nobility, its degree of distortion is a measure of its creative impact. Intolerance is one of the qualities of art with which Algren is richly endowed." Though disconcerted at Algren's potshots at Truman Capote and Wright, Schulberg found Algren an angry man a bit like Chicago itself, a "Jekyll-and-Hyde sort of burg, a Debs and McCormick town, a Capone and Hutchins town. Muscles and brains. Hustlers and poets." Only the conservative *Tribune,* which Algren had maligned in the essay, was displeased. "A Case for Ra(n)t Control" one reviewer capped his article, and elsewhere the *Trib* called it a caricature, trying to discredit Algren by noting his past connections with the John Reed Club. Thoughtfully, Ken McCormick wired Nelson his congratulations on the *Trib*'s bad review: "Nothing can stop sales now. It's a wonderful book and we're proud of it."

But the book didn't really sell, and its publication coincided with Simone's last visit to Gary. That Nelson invited her again after working so hard to tone down their relationship suggests he still needed her, though Simone felt that he was merely offering a sincere friendship. At any rate, they spent a quiet month in Miller, as if they sensed this might be their last time together. The atmosphere was warm and friendly, Simone recalled—and not loving: just the way Nelson wanted it. Still, their deep, kind harmony made Simone feel, she wrote him later, happier than she had in two years. It was October, and summer came again, and there were walks along the huge white dunes that burned Simone's feet; they went swimming or rowed out onto the lagoon. The weeks were tranquil enough for Simone to finish, ironically, her essay on Sade. Only rarely did they venture into Chicago: for drinks at the Tip Top Tap, for a Renoir movie, for Algren to defend drug addicts and denounce police corruption to an unappreciative Jewish club—Chicago's Jewish community had embraced him in his fame. The weeks passed.

The last few days it seemed cruel to talk about the future. Amanda had visited him shortly before Simone's arrival, and Simone remembered that Nelson said he would remarry her, but there is no other evidence for this, and perhaps it was said to keep Simone from misapprehension. They vowed to keep their goodbyes to a minimum, and under the spell of such finality, the last few hours, Simone recalled, seemed to drag for them both: they refused to talk to each other and their silence was embarrassing. Finally Simone said that she had really enjoyed her stay and that at least they still had a true friendship. " 'It's not friendship,' he replied brutally. 'I can never offer you less than love.' "

Crushed to know love still existed after they had worked so hard to be friends, she boarded her plane and wrote him that he had once again torn down her defenses, reopened her to hurt. From New York she wrote passionately that she had always been miserable at the thought of how she hurt him by being unable to give him her whole life; all the accusations he had hurled at her she had already made to herself. It was fair that he should stop loving her since she could give so little, but his last words had completely thrown her. Now she urged him not to kill their love, but begged him to either keep her or drop her—she had to know where she stood. Her love for him would continue, but she could no longer endure the emotional roller-coaster of their relationship. On All Saints' Day in Paris, when everyone wore black as if in mourning, she had her answer. He wrote that he could still have the same feelings for her but would not allow them to dominate him.

> To love a woman who does not belong to you, who puts other things and other people before you, without there ever being any question of your taking first place, is something that just isn't acceptable. I don't regret a single one of the moments we have had together. But now I want a different kind of life, with a woman and a house of my own. . . . The disappointment I felt three years ago, when I began to realize that your life belonged to Paris and to Sartre, is an old one now, and it's become blunted by time. What I've tried to do since is to take my life back from you. My life means a lot to me, I don't like its belonging to someone so far off, someone I see only a few weeks a year.

It was not a satisfactory solution. He was soon repeating by letter that she bound him all year round. But Simone would have none of the anger he now directed toward her. She replied that for three years she had accepted that he would love another woman, and it was unfair of him to speak of one month against eleven: he had invited her only for a month. If he had agreed to come to Paris sometimes, they could have had three or four months together every year, which would have been very different. On this she was emphatic: *he* had made the choice to kill their love.

They resumed their correspondence as intimate friends; his long letters made Simone want to respond with love and compliments. But he remained thwarted and angry. He admitted that he worked out of emotion; and it was de Beauvoir's repeated and correct assertion that he wrote out of rage. Until now he had channeled that rage outside himself, constructively, into works of art; and this had allowed him to be a better, healthier person, to enjoy immense satisfaction and self-respect—to enjoy life. In the same way, de Beauvoir's love had enriched him. The combination of productivity and love had created the happiest years of his life, when everything felt fresh, new, beginning. But now, that love seemed over: he had been rejected, and, though he had full confidence in his literary powers, fiction no longer presented itself to him as a response to the world. Somehow, with the limbo of his personal life and the depressing changes in society, that emotional outlet was gone.

As 1952 approached, McCormick was trying to pin Nelson down to another project. With no new novel in sight, Doubleday wanted to reissue *Somebody in Boots,* and, needing money, Algren agreed to rewrite it, probably to revise what he didn't like and exorcise the Marxist rhetoric. Doubleday bought the rights from Vanguard, and Nelson signed up for a $1,500 advance in weekly installments. He wasn't enthusiastic about dredging up "that old thing," but it was nice to be getting a salary again, even if it was a kind of gamble with his career for cash. Months later, much of the money spent or lost in poker games, he reread his first novel, decided it was unrewritable, and put the book and the debt out of his mind. It wasn't just that *Somebody in Boots* reeked of failure: the 1930s seemed like ancient history, and he could certainly have had little interest in cleaning up the Marxist pages to suit current political tastes.

For this was 1952, the heyday of American anti-Communism, when Joseph McCarthy, the Wisconsin senator who catapulted himself to fame in 1950 by saying he knew the names of 205 Communist Party members in the State Department, was making a stellar career out of finding radicals in federal agencies. Red spies were believed to be everywhere. In 1951, an obscure Bronx machinist named Julius Rosenberg and his wife, Ethel, had been convicted of conspiracy to commit espionage for passing atomic secrets to the Soviet Union. The evidence was primarily circumstantial and the case had all the elements of a show trial; the Rosenbergs were deemed responsible for the Communist aggression in Korea and were sentenced to death, a clearly excessive penalty since no one had received the death penalty for the far greater crime of treason during World War II.

With each passing year the systematic persecution of Communists, leftists, and liberals was becoming more intense. Their right to assemble had been effectively curtailed, since managers of meeting facilities would not readily rent to them. Localities could also withhold permits to assemble from any of more than seventy-eight groups listed by the attorney general as "subversive." The right to publish was also restricted, by harassment and fear, and the right to work was in jeopardy. The loyalty oaths for federal officials and schoolteachers had cost many people their livelihoods; many actors and performers had been unemployed since the blacklist in radio and TV began in 1950. In Hollywood, Nelson's agent had gone underground; the blacklisted Dalton Trumbo had unsuccessfully asked Nelson to be a front for his work, and John Garfield, threatened with perjury prosecution for saying he didn't know any Communists, died of a heart attack, at age thirty-nine, in May 1952—seemingly burying *Golden Arm's* film prospects.

Though the "police action" in Korea was unpopular, it could not be effectively protested. Since American boys were dying there fighting Communism, any protest against the war was seen as Red sympathy. Political fantasy, going to great lengths to justify the necessity of war, appeared in large-circulation magazines. "Could the Reds Seize Detroit?" asked a 1948 issue of *Look,* depicting a barbarian takeover complete with telephone operators lying dead on the floor after Communists secured the lines of communication. The October 1951 issue of *Collier's,* which Nelson and Simone read, was devoted entirely to a preview of World War III. On the cover a GI pointed his bayonet at a map of Russia, and the text, describing an eventual American triumph, told of the liberation of the Russian people. Sensationalized first-person accounts of life in a Communist cell by professional ex-Communist informers like Nelson's old *Anvil* friend Howard Rushmore were syndicated by the Hearst press. Neither the movies, the radio, nor television could provide relief from the war-crazed anti-Communist onslaught.

What prevailed was a blandness in cultural expression, a dull mediocrity of entertainment sponsored by corporate entities that deliberately avoided anything controversial. Charlie Chaplin, harassed so consistently by the FBI that he moved his family to Geneva and his wife renounced her American citizenship, sensed the American malaise that bothered Algren: "It's so bo-o-o-oring," Chaplin complained to an interviewer a few years later. "America is so terribly grim in spite of all that material prosperity. They no longer know how to weep. Compassion and the old neighborliness have gone, people do nothing when friends and neighbors are attacked, libeled, and ruined. The worst thing is what it has done to the children. They are being taught to admire and emulate stool pigeons, to betray and to hate, and all in a sickening atmosphere of religious hypocrisy."

Algren felt that those still believing in civil liberties simply had to speak out. "The out-loud kind of doubting which rescued American thought, in the twenties, from the files where the McCarthys and McCarrans and Jenners of that decade had locked it, is what is most needful to The States in the fifties," Algren would write shortly, having contributed with William Shirer, Arthur Miller, Louis Adamic (later found dead, gun in hand, after newspaper accounts labeled him a Red spy), and thirteen other intellectuals, to a large ad in *The*

New York Times, asking people to defend the right to individual beliefs and not to be silent in the face of jailings, firings, and loyalty oaths. "Speak up for freedom!" the ad enjoined the public. "It doesn't matter how—it may be done in a letter to your congressman, to a radio network or sponsor, or to your school or college. It may be in conversation in your own home. But speak up!"

Algren was speaking up, though his activities were those of the socially concerned author, not the full-time political activist. Still, the FBI already thought he was a Communist, and now, because the groups he supported, like most progressive groups, had been officially labeled subversive or Communist fronts, he was a potentially active enemy agent. One of Algren's sins, according to the FBI, was to have been active in the National Council of Arts, Sciences, and Professions, an organization of liberal New Deal intellectuals. And since peace was at odds with economic growth through military spending, the Lake County Citizens for Peace, for which Algren spoke and sponsored a meeting, also became a subversive group, along with the Civil Rights Congress and the American Women's Congress, which had honored Algren, Ring Lardner, Jr., and Chicago novelist Willard Motley a year or so earlier. The FBI considered even the Progressive Party of Illinois to be Communist-dominated, and Algren had been part of a group that called on the governor and secretary of state to urge that it be put on the ballot. But Algren's most incriminating action during this time was to become honorary chairman of the Chicago Committee to Secure Justice in the Rosenberg Case.

Until their execution in June 1953, the fate of the Rosenbergs was the focus of international outrage. Rabbis and clergymen from around the globe protested to Eisenhower; the sharply anti-Communist Pope Pius XII pleaded with the President to temper justice with mercy. Albert Einstein, Jean-Paul Sartre, forty Labour MPs, and thousands of clergy and lay people around the globe protested vehemently. Though Algren later complained that the Chicago Committee for the Rosenbergs just wanted to use his name, he took his duties seriously, sending fund-raising letters and organizing and attending clemency dinners. In August, he chaired a large, well-attended Chicago meeting on the case, at which, FBI records indicate, Algren stated that the Rosenbergs had been chosen as traitors because they were Jews, though later Algren said he believed that they were being persecuted because they were Communists and convenient scapegoats. "The whole thing is straight out of Cotton Mather," was his basic view. "A man and woman being put to death for nonconformity. . . . It is medieval."

In this atmosphere Algren began a fifty-page essay about creativity and conformity in American culture called "A Walk on the Wild Side," part of which he delivered as a speech to the University of Missouri Writers' Conference in June 1952. Never published in its entirety, this work, more traditional than the impressionistic Chicago essay, showed that Algren saw himself as a multifaceted writer of the old school—and axiomatically a social critic—rather than simply a novelist. Occupying him for most of the year, the impressively researched essay drew on the words of writers from Chekhov and Dickens to Dostoevsky, Fitzgerald, Walt Whitman and Rimbaud, from politicians including Hitler and McCarthy to Woodrow Wilson, John Quincy Adams, William O. Douglas, and Learned Hand.

In Algren's view it wasn't until now, with democracy weakened as the military-industrial complex stood ready to bully and stifle any dissent from the electorate, that creative people had been so ruthlessly pressured to conform. Algren believed that for the artist the emotional and spiritual burden of the individual was most important, but "whether he's in writing, TV, radio, teaching, or lecturing, [the creative person] sees very well, the way things are going, that the main thing is not problems of the heart, but to keep one's nose clean. Not to trouble oneself about the uneasy hearts of men. But to pass, safe and dry-shod, down the rushing stream of time." Screen stars and writers begging to name names didn't encourage a younger person to hold his ground, and Algren wondered how a creative person could continue in a world that constantly badgered him to please big business. He had reason to be concerned.

Conformity could never produce great writing, the essay continued; and even compassion, pity, and sensitivity were not enough. "A certain ruthlessness and a sense of being alienated from society is as essential to creative writing as it is to armed robbery. . . . If you feel you belong to things as they are, you won't hold up anybody in the alley no matter how hungry you get. And you won't write anything that anyone will read a second time, either."

The lost, of course, could not conform, could never belong to things as they were. Yet so many Americans embraced the status quo, wanted to ignore all the manipulation and suffering in society, to pretend that the republic's permanent legion of lost people had nothing to do with themselves at all. Algren felt that in remaining blind to the true conditions of life, they risked the spiritual illness, the immense irresponsibility that he saw on the faces of too many Americans. Underneath the material prosperity, he wrote,

we live today in a laboratory of human suffering as vast and terrible as that in which Dickens and Dostoevsky wrote. The only real difference being that the England of Dickens and the Russia of Dostoevsky could not afford the soundscreens and the smoke-screens with which we so ingeniously conceal our true condition from ourselves.

So accustomed have we become to the testimony of the photo-weeklies, backed by witnesses from radio and TV establishing us permanently as the happiest, healthiest, sanest, wealthiest, most inventive, tolerant, and fun-loving folk yet to grace the earth of man, that we tend to forget that these are bought-and-paid-for witnesses and all their testimony perjured.

For it is not in the afternoon in Naples nor yet at evening in Marseilles, not in Indian hovels half-sunk in an ancestral civiliza-tion's ruined halls nor within those lion-colored tents pitched down the Sahara's endless edge that we discover those faces most de-bauched by sheer uselessness. Not in the backwash of poverty and war, but in the backwash of prosperity and progress.

On the backstreets and the boulevards of Palm Beach and Miami, on Fifth Avenue in New York and Canal Street in New Orleans, on North Clark Street in Chicago, on West Madison or South State or any street at all in Los Angeles: Faces of the Amer-ican Century, harassed and half-dehumanized, scoffing or de-bauched: so purposeless, unusable and useless faces, yet so smug, so self-satisfied yet so abject—for complacency struggles strangely there with guilt. Faces full of such an immense irresponsibility toward themselves that they tell how high the human cost of our marvelous technological achievements has really been.

Faces to destroy the faith that man's chief duty in the world is to make himself as comfortable as possible in it, stay comfortable as long as possible, and pop off at last, as comfortably as possible.

. . . Do American faces so often look so lost because they are most tragically trapped between a very real dread of coming alive to something more than merely existing, and an equal dread of going down to the grave without having done more than merely to be comfortable?

If so, this is the truly American disease. And would account in part for the fact that we lead the world today in incidence of insanity, criminality, alcoholism, narcoticism, psychoanalysis, cancer, homicide and perversion in sex as well as in perversion just for the pure hell of the thing.

Never on the earth of man has he lived so tidily as here amidst such psychological disorder. . . . Nowhere has any people set itself a moral code so rigid while applying it quite so flexibly. . . . In no other country is such great wealth, acquired so purposively, put to such small purpose. Never has any people driven itself so resolutely toward such diverse goals, to derive so little satisfaction from attainment of any. Never has any people been so outwardly confident that God is on its side while being so inwardly terrified lest he be not.

Never has any people endured its own tragedy with so little sense of the tragic.

That spring Nelson's friend Ellen Borden Stevenson introduced him to the poet Dylan Thomas, then touring America. Algren liked Thomas, though he sensed desperation in everything the Welshman did and was impatient with his "small-boy-got-to-have-his-way-or-he'll-bust" act; later he would realize he'd been with a great man, "perhaps the only great man I had ever known." Algren's thoughts remained on Europe. Less than six months after Simone's visit he was seeking to return to France. The FBI, which read his application, records that he applied for a Fulbright grant to study journalism, proposing to travel to France and review files of the Paris press from 1944 to 1945, his purpose to document a novel about black-market rings operated by GI bands near Paris. Similar to an idea that had struck him before *Golden Arm,* it would have been the story of an AWOL American GI living with a French woman and supporting himself by selling contraband. The GIs who had gone AWOL interested Algren. "In one place in Italy AWOL Americans had their own camp," he recalled. "They set up their own little outlaw army there. It was quite an operation—they had food and guns and trucks and their own women. Outlaws from every army came in." Among Algren's papers are numerous vignettes of army life, some from the late forties and some from 1952; but no sustained passages indicate serious work on this book, and in asking Malcolm Cowley for a Fulbright recommendation he had to admit that he had no ideas for his next novel.

Algren was romantic with women, and in 1952, Mari Sabusawa, the blond Barbara Fitzgerald, and the addicted prostitute Margo came regularly to visit him in Miller. But it was Margo who became most important to him. By the early 1950s, Nelson and Margo had known each other for several years. Margo's husband had abandoned her, and she and Nelson began seeing each other. The feelings between them were intense and emotional. "We were kind to each other before love, and kind to each other after," Algren would recall later in a twenty-five-page poem written to Margo, and she reciprocated these tender feelings. She wrote him that she had never been happier than when she came to Gary: they slept when tired, ate when hungry, talked when they felt like it, and read books and listened to music. He had to work, but he was the only person she didn't fight or lose her temper with.

In her letters, Simone seemed puzzled by the intensity of Algren's feelings for "the little whore"—"Why don't you marry a real *clean* American girl, who will make you a real good American man, with nice cute clean American babies? I don't get it"—but he does not seem to have discussed his desire to marry with Margo. She too had reservations. When he sometimes sent her back to Chicago so he could work, she felt it was because he couldn't take her for very long. He had a lot of girlfriends, and she felt she wasn't special. When he'd call her up for dinner, she knew it meant de Beauvoir had gone, and she felt taken for granted.

Nelson was deeply concerned about the drugs, and would repeat again and again that Margo never should have been on them. Though he had been unsuccessful at helping her break the physical habit, he had been encouraging her to get off since the late 1940s, when he had helped the addicted Acker move to a new life by taking him along to California. A friend of Margo's recalled that becoming close with Nelson was a tremendous impetus to her struggle to quit for good. Algren was goal-oriented, he lived by ideals—he wasn't just another junkie or hustler living in a two-dollar room on State Street. And she was tired of the treadmill. "It's funny, me bein' in 'n' out of jail all the time, just like I committed some crimes 'r something," Nelson remembered her as saying a few years earlier. "I never hurt nobody, never stole things, nothin' like that." With her husband gone and a chance to live for herself, Margo, who had tried the cure at Lexington perhaps as many as four times, wanted more than ever to get off, to live a normal life, perhaps to be reunited with the daughter her husband had forced her to abandon.

A Greek doctor who prescribed a drug to make her withdrawal

easier introduced her to Caesar Tabet, an insurance man who became convinced that something could be done. Putting her up in an apartment building he owned, he told the super to look after her. "When she'd withdraw, she'd vomit, and her arms and legs would just go crazy, up and down, arms and legs, her face twitching uncontrollably," Tabet remembered. "The pain was so, so horrible." One afternoon the super and his wife smelled gas coming from her apartment. The pain had finally gotten so severe that she had put her head in the oven to end it. Tabet resolved to find effective professional help.

He again sought medication from the Greek doctor, this time enrolling Margo in a counseling program at Northwestern and finding her a low-level clerical job in a friend's insurance office. But the drugs had physically weakened her. Nauseated and often late, she couldn't really hold her own, and her coworkers complained. But Tabet's friend owed him a favor, and Tabet assured him he'd be doing God's work by keeping her on. After years of struggle, Margo had finally achieved what most people take for granted: she worked at a job, lived in an apartment instead of a two-dollar room, washed her own dishes, and remained disassociated from the narcotics scene for the rest of her life.

Margo told Caesar about Nelson, and the three became friends. The two men were witnesses when she sued her husband for divorce, and they all went out to dinner fairly often. One night Margo, generally shy but now lively, was talking animatedly about her job and apartment. Nelson must have felt a little sad that he had been so unsuccessful at helping her, while Caesar had done so much. "If you hang onto me you're hanging onto a straw," he said to Margo, "if you stay with Caesar, you're hanging onto a rock." "I got up and kissed him," Tabet recalled, "and I said, 'Nelson, that's not so. You gave her the desire to get off. You've been a rock, Nelson.' "

"Darling poor old ugly rejected you," Simone addressed him in a letter, for Margo was gone, the little house by the lagoon was still lonely, and there seemed no woman at all for him. The Fitzgerald woman was no longer interested, and there was no future either with Mari Sabusawa, who was soon to meet and marry James Michener. The final blow from Simone came on August 3, when she wrote that the young Claude Lanzmann, later to make the epic Holocaust film *Shoah,* wanted to love her; they had spent the night together and would begin a real affair when she returned from Italy in October. If she could not betray the past, she wrote Algren, she could no longer live in it. She seemed to feel that she had finally said goodbye to their affair.

Algren's reaction was more or less immediate. Though Amanda had not been able to visit in June, she suddenly arrived to spend the last three weeks of August with Nelson in Gary. This visit was even better than the year before, and by September he wrote her proposing marriage; she accepted. "I think my affair with Lanzmann had nothing to do with his remarrying Amanda and I do not care to speculate on it," a huffy de Beauvoir said later, but Nelson wrote Simone only once in the next two months, and in his second letter, despite almost no previous mention of Amanda, he wrote that they would remarry. Margo, surprised and hurt when Algren told her of his plans, remembered that he felt guilty toward his ex-wife, as if now that he had a better standard of living he should make up for all their days of poverty; and Nelson's letters to friends bear this out. Jack Conroy repeated over and over again that Nelson remarried Amanda out of spite; but it was not spite toward Amanda. His letters to her that fall were cheerful and optimistic; he hoped very much that she would arrive in December so they could spend Christmas together. They had also spoken of having a child, had picked the name Madeleine for a girl.

Magnanimously, Simone invited them to honeymoon in Paris, an idea Algren had already had in mind, and they both applied for passports. And Amanda prepared to come east, giving up a good job, selling her new car, and breaking many ties forged over the years in Los Angeles.

15.

Entrapment

AMANDA INNOCENTLY WALKED into a nightmare: by the time she arrived in Chicago, Algren had changed his mind about the marriage. He'd hit upon the idea of a novel based on Margo's experiences, and he apparently saw again the folly of trying a third time what had already failed twice. But he didn't have the heart to tell her, and they would both pay dearly for his cowardice. Passively putting off the inevitable, he had not even told their closest friends they were getting married, so when he and Neal Rowland met Amanda at the airport, Neal said brightly, "Hi, Amanda, how long are you staying?" The long, frozen ride to Gary in Neal's heaterless jalopy was bleak indeed.

They would not even be going to Paris; and he was not going to see Simone. In early March 1953, four months after he applied and twelve days before they were to sail on the SS *Liberté,* Algren's passport was denied. "It has been alleged that you were a Communist," the passport office informed him, having asked the FBI for a security clearance. With no time to appeal before the sailing, Algren took two weeks to write a declaration stating he was not a member of the Communist Party, had not recently terminated such membership, and was not formally or informally in support of the Communist movement. But the passport office merely brushed this statement aside, since it was not made under oath and did not answer the all-important question ". . . or have you ever been?" Besides, the FBI was still investigating Algren. In April, two informants of "known reliability" gave evidence that Algren had been a Party member in the late thirties; one claimed to have been present when the CP tried Algren for Trotskyism but dropped the charges on the grounds that he didn't know any better. And in June, Conroy's old protégé Howard Rushmore, now earning money and fame naming names for the Hearst press, later to shoot himself and his estranged wife in a taxi, brought forth a 1937 letter Algren had written him allegedly proving he'd been a Communist.

Algren had little to look forward to. In his remarriage to Amanda there was an element, of course, of self-punishment too obvious to deny; but there seems also to have been the feeling that he could atone for past wrongs—to himself, to Simone, to Amanda—by making Amanda happy. Amanda was a gentle, loyal woman who knew little about Simone, but because he did not tell her about the recent past, he entered the relationship without honest communication. As if fulfilling an obligation, he wed Amanda in a civil ceremony with Caesar and Margo as witnesses. Sadly, he couldn't hide the anger born of forcing himself to go through with what he didn't want. Both Tabet and Margo sensed something strange when they all celebrated the ceremony with a meal: Nelson kept looking at Margo until he finally kissed her. It seems that Amanda gracefully made light of it, but she went back to Indiana alone. Nelson had business in Chicago, most likely gambling.

As Amanda accustomed herself to a sulkiness in Algren she had never seen before, he returned to work in Gary. In addition to writing monthly book reviews for *Saturday Review of Literature,* he was again revising the anti-McCarthy "A Walk on the Wild Side" essay, this time for book publication: an excerpt in the *Sun-Times* had stirred a gratifying outpouring of applause that astonished all concerned. An Episcopalian minister and the chairman of the religion department at a leading Catholic college used it as a sermon text, one reader wanted a hundred copies to use as a Christmas greeting, *The Nation* reprinted part of it, and at Conroy's suggestion, book editor Van Allen Bradley had asked McCormick to release Nelson from his contract so the essay could be published locally as a book. Instead, Doubleday decided to bring it out in book form as "The State of Literature." McCormick advanced Nelson $1,500 and secured a preface from Bradley and an introduction from American literary historian Maxwell Geismar, whose sensitive and flattering critique of Nelson's work had recently appeared in the scholarly review *College English.* Geismar, contributing editor at *The Nation* and author of *Writers in Crisis, The Last of the Provincials,* and the recent *Rebels and Ancestors,* was as depressed as Nelson by the political situation; and he liked the essay immensely: "This will be one of the first books they will burn: congratulations." Always pleased by praise, Nelson took all of Geismar's suggestions for the piece, and Amanda, having retyped it ad nauseam, was happy to see it sent to Doubleday in early June.

As Nelson and Amanda assumed conventional roles, he cast about for projects that would make money. He liked the way Amanda spruced up the house and fixed fancy meals, and to judge from his letters there seemed times when he enjoyed the marriage, though he preferred a simpler life. "I'd like to be raided in some backstreet slum where raids are a matter of course, talk back to the screw, crack wise in court and do time on my ear . . . and not give a hang for anything," he described his conflict, but on Sunday they were having steak with mushrooms, so what could he do? Still, he mocked his efforts to write for money. Working with Art Shay on a collaborative story on the underworld, Algren told Max he had the West Side charted like the Pacific: "For $100 I plummet just below the surface, into a place where nobody ever gets killed. For $250 I dive . . . about halfway down. For $500 I do a real Piccard. Into the Mindanao Deeps where the tiger sharks and the man-eating clams wheel and yawn in the velvet dark. . . . It's a trade, like any other trade." But he added wistfully: "Down there in the deeps below the deeps it's actually more comfortable, and the denizens more amiable, than those above the surface."

For there was much about his new life he found ludicrous. "Do you have pine-scented garbage bags in your house?" he asked Max dryly. "We do." And Amanda liked china and silver and was going to buy herself a brand-new car—too much materialism for a man who often got around by bicycle. No, the conventional marriage was not what he wanted at all. Algren could barely support his writing, let alone other people. He was already sending Goldie a hundred a month, and because he and Amanda had discussed having children, the unspoken but obvious implication that he would support her made him genuinely resent sharing what he had. Though she noticed his new nastiness and possessiveness, Amanda did not seem to recognize the source of this resentment. She remembers six months of living not off Nelson, who sometimes didn't even want to buy groceries, but off her savings. And the way he exploited her typing and chauffeur services, she hardly felt she was a financial drain. Much, though by no means all, of the new financial burden was in his head, but Amanda's penchant for good clothes and quality products from reputable stores undoubtedly increased his anxiety. Before, Amanda had usually found him in good spirits, a healthy, never-had-a-headache type of guy; now he was often sullen and angry.

His study was his sanctuary. Through letters to friends, he tried to ward off an increasing depression. He dashed off multipage, single-spaced letters to Max Geismar, and he was also writing to James Blake, a writer, piano player, and inept burglar he'd met years before at the Pink Poodle tavern and who was now serving time on a Florida chain gang. William Styron once called Blake a "gifted misfit" for whom prison served as a kind of "walled Yaddo"; Blake's fey, sardonic tales of prison life had lured Algren, Conroy, and others to finance a disastrous escape attempt. Algren encouraged Blake's writing, and some of Blake's prison letters were enthusiastically published by Simone de Beauvoir in *Les Temps Modernes* in 1952.

Two weeks after his marriage Algren wrote Simone that he was having bad pangs in his heart about their affair, regretting, it seems, having broken off their love. Now he was suffering: despite his friendly feelings for Amanda, the dependence he had felt on her when she was in California had completely evaporated when she arrived in Gary. It was terrible to be married to a woman he did not love. Simone constantly reassured him that he should have hope, that his life was not over, and that good things would happen to him once again; he was clearly despondent.

It was a strange summer. In June Julius and Ethel Rosenberg were electrocuted, and America seemed headed toward Fascism. He still hadn't heard from Doubleday about the essay; and if they'd liked it, he felt he'd have known. He plowed through an English translation of *The Second Sex,* though Simone said he would never believe she had written it. Perhaps this was an effort to remain close: it was the first time since 1947 he had gone more than a year without seeing her; he also listed his phone number in her name. He became increasingly dependent on their correspondence. Again he felt the terrible pain of missing her, clouded now by remorse. By July it was much worse: in the mornings he felt "a kind of death" sitting in him, caused by being too far away from her, for too long. Mired in the past, he wanted to go to Paris; he wanted magic again.

Magic was gone from Simone's life too, she wrote, but things could not have been more different for her. She was working on an ambitious novel, dedicated to Algren and re-creating their love affair, *The Mandarins,* which would win the Prix Goncourt; she had Sartre, her young lover Lanzmann, and the endless freedom of travel. When Algren asked if she still missed him, she told him not "too much"; but she too was sometimes overcome by the unspeakable loss between them. His letter describing the feeling of death had given her "a real pangish pang" which had made her drink too much at a party, and when the band had played some American tune they'd heard together, the memory was so painful that she'd fainted away for the first time in her life. "So you see, though I fight pangs . . . I am still deeply bound to you," she wrote from across an uncrossable ocean. Perhaps he saw no point in torturing either of them further. It was five months before he wrote to her again and they resumed their letters. Though he told her she seemed like a ghost, he wrote her more frequently than she replied, and he told her too that the weeks between letters were long.

He had told Simone he wanted to write a novel for her, and he now returned to the work based on Margo called "Entrapment." By the summer of 1953, Algren said he had the setting, emotion, and characters for a novel so ambitious he planned to spend four or five years on it, and he did not want the pressure of a publisher's deadline. He wanted to write this book at his own pace, "line by line, day by day, making every sentence count."

His plans involved venturing again into uncharted literary territory. Only secondarily a story of drug addiction, the novel sought to dramatize how a man and a woman could be isolated within a city, chained to their connection's block, and how, within that limitation, they could manage to fashion a human, routine life, with values that to Algren were more real and intense than those of people freer to come and go. In trying to capture the prosaic daily life of people circumscribed by legality, Algren hoped to expose, without the drama of cops and robbers, the quiet, commonplace lives that thousands of bookies, addicts, fences, and hookers lived every day: an underworld society completely segregated from the mainstream. In the mid-fifties, when addiction could not be filmed and TV husbands and wives slept in twin beds, the exposure of this society would have been ground-breaking.

He had been attending the police lineups as early as October of 1952 and now visited the courts with defense attorney Lucius Eccles, and sometimes with Art Shay. He would talk to the accused in the halls, take them out for coffee, hear how tins of aspirin would have to be analyzed for "traces of H" while the accused waited in jail.

He heard how a judge could make a person roll up his or her sleeves to see track marks and then sentence on that, even if the charge were possession; heard the sad, sad tales of being sick behind bars: the blurry vision, the roaring head, the runny eyes and nose, and the endless vomiting. In Algren's view narcotics constituted a medical problem, not a police matter, but in the early 1950s, Chicago had opened up a separate Narcotics Court, the first in the country, to deal with the expanding number of drug cases being handled in the aftermath of World War II.

In seven months Algren wrote a hundred pages of "Entrapment." Many scenes have been lost; the longest surviving section concerns a country woman and her husband who leave their baby in the South and journey to Los Angeles to make a brief fortune—furs and fancy clothes—in prostitution. Luck is with them until Daddy begins using heroin, then shrewdly sees that his wife, Baby, gets hooked too. Run out of town by the law, they head for Chicago with a five-dollar bill and a bottle of Dolophine. There, Daddy is again busted, and Baby learns how to use knockout drops to steal from tricks for his bail, her life an endless cycle of sickness and fixes and jails and tricks. Horrifying yet riveting, the narrative conveys the bleak, relentless violence of the gas-station scene in *Never Come Morning*, written twenty years earlier. For the first time, however, Algren's main character was a woman.

Other characters emerge from the mixed-up fragments—here is Frankie Machine again, and Molly, and Beauty, another girl who fascinates Frankie. Beauty was a new kind of woman in Algren's fiction, a proud, selfish, irresistible woman much stronger than her man. In one scene, she evokes Simone on her 1948 shortened-for-Sartre visit: Beauty comes in to see Frankie after he has been waiting for her for hours and tells him right off that she has only a few minutes and he should get her a cup of coffee. Disappointed, he uncertainly begins making the coffee, then "turns from his fumbling to see the loveliest of smiles: she has her hat and coat off and is obviously ready to stay as long as he wants her to. He realizes only then that she has just been putting him on, and is pleased by a girl who can do that. . . . Beauty's chief characteristic is her practicality, her matter-of-fact-literalness. . . . Every night she plans her schedule for the day to come. Even pleasure has to be planned. . . . Indeed, she goes about pleasure-getting in so business-like a fashion that it becomes more of a duty than a joy."

In fact, much of the novel was emotional autobiography transposed

into the twilight world of the less than legitimate, and in one particular section Algren found an outlet for his deep emotional poetry.
"The Yellow and the Wan," also called "The Man in the Hotel
Mirror," was almost entirely a mood piece, akin to the evocative
dream sequences in *Never Come Morning,* to the poignant passages
of Sophie's descent into madness or Frankie's loneliness in *Golden
Arm.* Strikingly similar in feeling to the circumstances in which Algren now found himself, it was the story of a middle-aged bookie
fighting with a "whirlpool of regret trying to suck him into its vortex":
he had let go the best woman of his life, and now she wrote that she
would marry another man. She was selfish, independent; now called
Baby, this woman, like Simone, did just as she pleased. She was a
woman from another country, the bookie thought wistfully, where
"you didn't have to get lucky on doubles to get by":

> In that land it was always enough just to be whoever you happened
> to be. Here in his own patch between billboard and trolley everyone
> tried, their whole lives long, to be somebody they never were.
> Somebody they'd read about, somebody they'd heard about, some-
> body they never could be. Somebody like George Raft, somebody
> like Frank Costello, someone like Myrna Loy. It was a world full
> of big shots, fake shots that fooled nobody except the big shots
> themselves.

He and Baby, the kind of unanticipated combination that comes
up once in a century, had fallen in love in a familiar story.

> It was fall, but summer came back, a full week, just for them. . . .
> Marriage, he had always felt, was a standing joke. Seeking to mock
> it, he had slipped a ring that he might have found in a box of
> crackerjacks onto her finger. Its stone, as it were, was a red plastic
> dice. He had slipped it onto the finger intending . . . a mock mar-
> riage; instead she had put her lips to it. The mockery failed. The
> very air had married them.

Now all the bookie's hours were clouded by regret. A stranger is
marrying my wife tomorrow, he thought again, completely unable
to reconcile himself. "His legs went suddenly weak and he sat down
on the grey bed's edge again, making a gesture as if a fly had buzzed
him. . . . 'Don't let me go,' she told you, and you let her go all the
same.

> It had been the sort of thing that wouldn't have mattered if it had
> happened when he was nineteen, he decided for the thousandth

time. Even at thirty-five he would have aced it through. But at forty-two it had really started something. Everything . . . had always gone his way right up to the day she left. Then he'd developed a hitch in his swing and everything he did had some sort of reverse english on it. Everything he tried, that had always worked like a charm, kicked back.

It would have made no difference, the bookie thought, if it hadn't worked out in the end, so long as they'd played it out all the way. For something that had been missing all his life had taken just one woman to fill: he'd almost had a commitment that would have made his life, but he had ducked it, and there was no going back. And suddenly the bookie was Algren's very own age, speaking in the first person: and one has only to read his novels to know that it was Algren himself who lived on the bleak side: he was the man in the hotel mirror, and Baby was very much like Simone:

> Baby, I thought all the time you were the one being opened. We all close up, life closes us up whether we would or not by 44. I'd been closed, I closed up early. Over on the bleak side we close up earlier than you do on the bright. We can't afford to stay open. . . . Maybe that was what you had, that was something I needed so. But you were open because you have that kind of heart and always will. . . . And all the while I thought it was myself doing the opening, but I was the one being opened.

"And though I close up for keeps by night, Baby, I'll stay grateful to you as long as I last for making me open for a few weeks at least," Algren wrote. He had pushed away the one person who had opened him to the joy of life, who could have lured him from the deep burdensome sorrow of his own tragic vision. If he had revised sections of *Golden Arm* a dozen times, he rewrote "The Man in the Hotel Mirror" so many dozens of times it was as if he'd gotten stuck there and couldn't get away. Among his papers draft after draft appears— the cataloguer has to give up, the words only slightly changed, the pages out of order—and there is Algren in the corner of the living room that was his study, fitting the paper into the typewriter to write the same story, the same words over and over and over, often on the back of his own work, as if it were scratch paper, never to be used again, never to be fitted together and published. A whole decade's writing would come, upon his death, to be almost completely unsortable, a chaotic, heaped-up mass of emotion, as if he were writing no longer to publish, but to try to make sense of the way he had damaged himself, to try to come to terms with what he had done.

Unwilling to be known as a "Red" publishing house, Doubleday had to be careful with a controversial piece like Algren's "The State of Literature." They still planned to publish it, but they dispatched the young editor Timothy Seldes to Gary to help Nelson "polish" the piece. "Polishing is a polite phrase you may have run on in the trade, and it means polishing a passage until it is polished away," Nelson wrote Max. "Well, we polished here and we polished there, and every time we polished one into oblivion I had a fresh rough-hewn zircon to insert." Seldes, who couldn't help noticing the dish of marijuana casually resting on the living room table, made many helpful suggestions, though Nelson was mildly surprised at the scrutiny. He assumed that a book that small and that limited in appeal would be strictly a minor operation, but Seldes's attention made him think Doubleday might push it.

That was pure optimism. When over a month had passed since his last revision, he began to suspect that Doubleday was wondering how to break the news. And indeed, in September they refused to publish the piece, though what reason they gave is no longer clear. McCormick, who loved Nelson's writing but worked for conservative superiors, did not want to break relations, and forfeited the advance. At the time, Algren was loyal to McCormick and felt he'd always gotten very good treatment at Doubleday; he knew why he wasn't in Paris that very moment and chalked the rejection up to the times. But the enthusiastic Chicago reception of the essay suggested that the book might have made a real impact on the social climate, would have widened his influence, enchanced his prestige. "I put too much work in it not to feel disappointed as hell," he wrote Max. "But I'm still in the land of the living at least, and that's a little something." He would place some of it in *The Nation,* and the left-leaning *California Review,* sending the original to Madeleine Brennan to have her find another publisher for it.

She lost it.

Determined to find enough money to leave his marriage, in late 1953 Nelson realized that *Somebody in Boots,* which he'd avoided for almost three years, could be rewritten into a quick little money-maker for the paperback trade after all. He dropped "Entrapment" and struck a hundred-a-week deal with Doubleday for the rewrite, which would be an entirely new book. Though having the outline of the book made his work easier, he was hardly enthusiastic about the project: "I don't have as much heart for it," he told Max. "The book I had to drop came much harder, but I liked it better because it lent me the feeling of making something new. Something done nearly twenty years ago doesn't feel like your own any more. . . . No, it won't win any national book award. I'm aiming solely at the pocket-book traffic."

For the first time he was writing a novel not out of compassion but for money, and there was a sense of defeat in this. As he exorcised the Marxist rhetoric, he wrote Max that it seemed to him that the writers of the thirties were gone. He could make a list longer than his arm, of writers who had given up as soon as the thirties were done, and were either silent or trying to live in the suburbs as if the spiritual uneasiness of the fifties and the American disease of isolation did not exist. The new standard of living had changed life drastically for the American writer. "Currently I support a wife, a car and two cats and a mother. And believe me, they don't tolerate second-rate fueling," Algren wrote Millen Brand. "You can't be a good writer in the States anymore. . . . Because to be a good one you have to have a country where you can be poor and still eat, and still make your living standards secondary to your writing. Thoreau himself couldn't do that in the States today, I don't believe." He told Max Geismar, "I think that the writers of the twenties were sounder of heart. They took scars but they stayed. Faulkner, Dreiser, Sandburg, Hemingway, Fitzgerald, Anderson, O'Neill, Sinclair Lewis.

"While those of the [thirties] came in on themselves: gave up, quit cold, snitched, begged off, sold out, copped out, denied all, and ran. . . . I think of Millen Brand's *The Outward Room,* Leonard Ehrlich's *God's Angry Man,* Richard Wright's *Native Son* as the best of the bunch. There was a book called *Call It Sleep* by somebody named Roth, too. Ben Appel wrote *The Power-House,* which was worth the doing. . . . But when the thirties were done, they were done. . . . And Fearing, the truest poet, for my money, of the decade, was repeating himself. Now he's hacking, Ben Appel is hacking. I'm hacking too. Nobody stayed."

Stifled by the rewrite, he soldiered on in the hope of getting enough money to go to Paris. The "house-car-cat-money-in-the-bank-or-bust operation" he'd gotten himself into was going nowhere. Like the rewrite, his marriage to Amanda represented merely another frayed flag of his past waving in his face and preventing him from looking ahead: he realized now that all their attempts to live together had failed not because he was a bad person but because they were basically incompatible. There was no need to feel guilty: the only times he'd ever produced were when he'd been away from her. The longtime familiarity they felt around each other was a smokescreen that allowed them to enjoy short visits together without having to see their fundamental differences.

Amanda was the exact opposite of the other women he'd cared for deeply. She was not the strong, self-confident Simone or the valiant, greedy-for-life Margo struggling to bury the nightmare of her past; she said later she had always felt deprived because she'd grown up without a father. Amanda was attractive in a delicate, sensitive way that made men want to protect her. In her desire for the family she'd been denied as a child, she embraced the idea of conventional marriage and did not share Algren's fascination with the outcast.

Amanda's apparent willingness to accept a life that was mutually unsatisfying depressed Algren deeply. He felt he simply could not communicate with her and, unable to tell her he wanted his solitude back, chose the most childish, self-destructive course of action possible. He told Max Geismar later that he began acting so disagreeable that she'd want to get out. He was sulky, he was moody, he would flee to Chicago without saying goodbye. When a Doubleday editor offered her books, Algren told the man, in her presence, not to bother. He would order her to drive him to Chicago and, knowing she had trouble with the nerves in her hands, would refuse to help her brush a heavy snowfall off the car. He was, in short, forcing a divorce.

Escaping all this in the summer of 1954, he flew to southern Texas and New Orleans. He was in trouble with the rewrite and had too much pride not to do a good job. "I thought that by seeing again the places I lived in the early thirties I could swing this dreadful rehash into which I'm trapped into something better than *Augie March*," he wrote Max, who also thought that Saul Bellow's National Book Award winner was overrated. But at the lowest tip of Texas he crossed into Mexico, had a haircut, drank a beer, bought a wood carving, and found no feeling whatsoever to recapture. New Orleans was no better. There was even less of the city he remembered than in 1948, and ironically, though he'd been able to withstand the heat hungry and penniless in 1932, now he became ill, sweating out days in the humidity, "seeing nothing but a back room's broken wall." All he was doing, he wrote Amanda, was "reeling around Louisiana and Texas and Mexican towns lugging a portable I don't use and wondering who I am." The thought of going back to Amanda was probably not in the least appealing, but he hated rootlessness as much as he had twenty years before. He returned to Illinois.

He found six weeks of asylum in an upstairs room at Jack Conroy's, furiously working on the rewrite of *Somebody in Boots,* now called "Finnerty's Ball," later *A Walk on the Wild Side,* tossing crumpled pages out the window if he found he couldn't use them. With Art Shay he made a couple of trips to southern Illinois to gather material for stories they were putting together on the zoot-suiting Pachucos and on stoopers—racetrack scavengers who searched the littered ground for winning tickets. Then he returned to the occupied house in Gary, where he and Amanda passed like strangers, retreating to their rooms. Some nights Dave Peltz, a playwright who'd worked on the Radio Project and who now ran a construction business and lived near the dunes, came over to watch the fights on TV. After Amanda had gone to bed, Algren would work on the book or play records, often the melancholy "House of the Rising Sun" over and over.

The good times were spent in the underworld or with other women. A friend would pick him up and they'd go see Iris van Etten, a middle-class black woman on Chicago's South Side whose husband worked at the relatively good job of sleeping-car porter and came home only once a week. The other six days Iris was a madam for a group of respectable neighborhood ladies, not professional prostitutes but family women who went to church on Sunday and picked up extra money by turning occasional tricks on the side. Discovered through the advice of a friendly cab driver, her place was a find for Nelson, who picked up quite a few stories there, especially for the brothel scenes in "Finnerty's Ball."

During the months he spent waiting for his marriage to collapse, he played poker in Chicago on Friday nights, and on weekends saw a recently divorced friend from the thirties whose passport had also been denied; her wedding to a Frenchman, with whom she was going to live in France, was canceled. She and Nelson became very close.

During the week he'd write her charming letters from Gary, and when he was in the city he sometimes used her apartment to type. He'd always liked her and confided to her his feelings about his dilemma. Sometimes Algren was so morose all she could do was be there with him; nothing she said could help him.

Still hoping to breathe life into the novel, he returned to New Orleans in December. This time he stayed with friends of the Geismars, who were the only saving grace during yet another visit to a hopelessly lost city. He returned home via East St. Louis, staying with hookers, pimps, and ex-cons. The underworld was a comfortable haven from the deceit and hypocrisy of his own legitimate life; for Nelson, the difference between legitimate and illegitimate people was that those off the legit *knew* they were dishonest and the others did not. "Max," he wrote, "I can't tell you how right it seems to me to live—even for an evening—among men and women off the legit. What true, solid people pimps and whores can be—I'm serious. I sat the whole evening opposite five women, ranging in age from 25–38 and in income from a hundred a week to four and five hundred. Of two I know little—but of the other three I can honestly say that they are happily married and I don't know three business-men's wives who are. All three of these women have been with the same men for years—one for twenty-two. Between them and their husbands is honest-to-god love. You may think I'm being wishful and nothing more, but I swear it's so." These people really seemed to be enjoying their lives, and he was especially touched by the story of one woman who had been at the calling twenty-two years. When her man had been in prison, she'd sold his car, taken his money, and run off with someone else. But when he found her dying of tuberculosis upon his release two years later, he'd put her in the best sanatorium available and worked as a steamfitter until she was cured. She still couldn't get over it.

Returning to his own loveless life, neither could he. Simone had won the Prix Goncourt and he was happy for her—"she is the most," he wrote Max—but his own work was in a shambles. Spending time in the underworld always reminded him that he was working on the wrong book, and he wrote Max that he could feel the right book fading out somewhere on the Northwest Side, while he was riding day coaches to nowhere.

Earlier in the spring he'd subtly hinted to Max how demoralized he was about his writing by relating a disturbing dream he'd had. He and Dylan Thomas were seated at a long table full of anonymous writers. They had all gone out together, and now Thomas was dead. He looked alive, but he was dead, and everybody knew it and felt bad. Thomas turned to Algren and asked him, half jokingly but accusingly, what he'd put in the drink: everybody knew Algren had killed him. Algren felt guilty; but he didn't actually believe he'd done it. He told Thomas he didn't really think he was dead. But Thomas was. He was dead because he couldn't write words anymore. He could only drink, saying if he couldn't have beer, he couldn't give the rest of the guests words.

I want a beer, too, Algren said.

And that was all.

Amid the strange, unreal feeling of despair at the all-night poker table, "the cards kept the everlasting darkness off, the cards lent everlasting hope. The cards meant any man in the world might win back his long-lost life, gone somewhere far away," Algren had written in *Golden Arm*. "Frankie would sit back wearily, sick of seeing them come on begging to be hustled, wondering where in the world they all came from and how in the world they all earned it and what in the world they told their wives, and what, especially, they told themselves and why in the world they always, always, always, always came back for more."

About his own gambling, the intelligent and perceptive Algren was bizarrely irrational. After Neal Rowland's card-dealer friend had shown him with a deck how the house couldn't lose at twenty-one, Nelson's response was, "Yeah—but tonight the game owes me." His sensitive face was far too easily read, and he was a terrible poker player. Even as a veteran gambler, he would play for an inside straight: he'd have, say, the seven, eight, ten, jack; he'd need the nine, throw the money in, and bet everything on getting one card, only to be left with nothing. Once when he was asked why he played at an obviously crooked game, Algren laughed: "It's the only game in town." Yet he'd be terrifically insulted if anyone implied he wasn't a winner.

Jack Conroy and Neal Rowland both realized Algren was a compulsive gambler, but, with the exception of Neal, no one wanted to tell him he had a problem. Art Shay found Algren's excessive time at the track vaguely disturbing, but Art was young, and the future stretched endlessly ahead. Simone, whose father had also been a racetrack fan, saw him as "deeply a gambler," and yet, though shocked at his excesses, had not really complained. Amanda too was at a loss; Peltz's attitude was live and let live. Given Algren's disdain of psychoanalysts and social workers, he would never have gone for counseling. Friends had to accept him on his terms, and besides, his attitude about money seemed in keeping with his antimaterialism. "Algren came alive when he gambled," was Peltz's opinion. "He was cleansed when he was busted. The impossible times were when he was a winner—all the swaggering, laughing, drinking, indulging his ego. . . . When he lost he felt terrible but he was able to go home and write. Money was a burden to him." Unfortunately, it was a burden he couldn't live without.

Certainly Algren could have answered yes to at least seven of the twenty questions Gamblers Anonymous asks new members; these seven alone indicate he had a serious problem. Yes, he had lost time at work—writing—because of gambling. He had felt remorse after gambling. He had gambled to get money to pay debts or solve financial difficulties; he had often gambled until his last dollar was gone. He was reluctant to use "gambling money" for normal expenditures; he had borrowed to finance his gambling. His gambling increased with stress; he gambled to escape worry or trouble. He took advances on pay—through Doubleday—and then lost them. He often took dates to the the races and lost track of time playing poker. When he went to congratulate his nephew Bob Joffe and his wife on their new baby, he showed up with a box of diapers and spent almost his entire visit on the phone arranging a poker game. He gambled habitually.

In the mid-sixties, when he was teaching at the University of Iowa, his poker buddies estimated that he lost at least ten thousand of his twelve-thousand-dollar salary; they also remembered him walking miles in a blizzard to get to a game. Friends tossed off the fact that he was constantly low on cash as the plight of the writer or the shabby way Algren was treated by the literary establishment; but though he did not earn much and was sending Goldie her monthly check, his house was paid for, he received steady money from Doubleday, modest translation and other royalties, option money for plays of his books, and other residual income. There was no reason, other than gambling, to be writing checks he couldn't cover, to have his local bank account closed on him, and always, always, always to be living on the edge of bankruptcy.

On Wabansia, the poker games behind the tavern or barbershop could be passed off good-naturedly as "gathering material" or relaxation, for the relatively low stakes set by the clientele kept the damage within reason. But in the early fifties Algren's gambling became more destructive. For the better part of two years, he ran a poker game in the basement of a North Michigan Avenue mansion owned by Ellen Borden Stevenson, the ex-wife of Adlai and heir to the Borden dairy fortune, whom he'd met through *Poetry* magazine. The other players were businessmen, the stakes higher than Algren could afford. What, for instance, happened to the three thousand in advance money he'd received in the summer of '53 and no longer had by December? Algren claimed that in 1954 he made a thousand dollars from gambling, but one can only wonder how much he had to lose to do it. One morning around five A.M. Amanda woke up and met Nelson, just in from playing poker, in the kitchen. His face was green and he had a crooked smile he was trying to make light-hearted. Amanda asked him how much he'd lost. "How much do you think I lost?" he asked. When she guessed five hundred dollars, he said, "No, more." As she named higher figures, he kept saying, "More, more": he'd lost a thousand dollars in one game. And it was apparently the last thousand dollars he'd had.

When Algren had money he was extremely generous, but when he didn't some people saw him as hostile—especially when he'd refrain from picking up a tab or wait for other people to pay in restaurants. He was always having to hold up checks, refuse Amanda a dollar for a movie, wonder where the next money was coming from, or use slugs in pay phones. Once he persuaded a friend to charge jewelry and a typewriter on a department store credit card and then report the card stolen. Later, pacing the room and running his hand back and forth across his hair, he'd curse himself for having been so stupid, but when he needed money everything overrode common sense.

He saw the world and described it in terms of betting and sports language, good luck or bad. Since the 1930s he'd seen a world made up of winners and losers, hunters and hunted; a "rigged ball game." The man in the hotel mirror, who'd developed a hitch in his swing and used up all his daily doubles, thought constantly in those terms, and Algren had written Simone that he saw their love as an incredible stroke of luck. On what would ultimately happen to *The Man with the Golden Arm* in Hollywood Algren later said, "Either you win or you lose. You come to bat in the last of the ninth with one out and two men on and you're two runs behind, and you hit a drive over the third baseman's head—a direct smash into the left-field seats. Both runners start moving home. But the ball ricochets off the flagpole into the outfielder's glove. He throws it to [third], doubling off the man there and catches you coming into second. The game's over. You didn't win four to three. You hit into a double-play, that's all. You hit a flagpole, that's all. . . . It [was] not important what was in the book, because this is what was done to it. . . . Both of these books I did turned out on film to be flagpole shots."

In January 1955, an article called "How Writers Live," disclosing the twice-a-month poker game Algren ran in a mansion basement, appeared in *Time* magazine; and though her name wasn't mentioned, Ellen Stevenson cordially but firmly put an end to the games. Naturally, Algren felt an important source of income had been lost, and he told his agent he was looking for money. Though he had a reputation for being standoffish and above Hollywood, Brennan mentioned his need for cash to Robert Goldfarb, a representative of the West Coast Jaffe Agency who was in New York on business. Goldfarb provided an interesting insight into Nelson's second brush with Tinsel Town. "Asking producers for work for my clients in the normal course of business, I visited Otto Preminger," Goldfarb recalled. "He said, 'I need a hard-hitting writer to do a rewrite,' and I suggested a few people, and he said, 'No, he's not right, this has got to be very special, it's a secret.' I said, 'Well, I was told in New York that Nelson Algren might consider a screenplay assignment.' He was bowled over, because what he was talking about was *The Man with the Golden Arm.*" Goldfarb was surprised that Preminger owned the rights. The Jaffe Agency had a big literary department, he recalled, "so there must have been something strange in that deal or we would have heard about it—they must have had some reason to keep it quiet."

Nelson, in fact, found out about the deal through his agent—six months after the fact. Whatever his thoughts about the dubious legalities of the sale, his immediate concerns were screenplay money and ensuring the success of an off-Broadway production of *The Man with the Golden Arm* that Jack Kirkland of *Tobacco Road* fame was planning to stage. Algren had doubts the movie could even be made under the narcotics ban, but was sure it could hurt the chances of the play, from which both he and Kirkland stood to profit. When Preminger offered him a thousand a week for the four weeks or so it would take to write a screenplay, he accepted, hoping to perhaps slow the movie down a bit until the play was produced. It was dirty money, but he wanted to get to Paris; and in his gambler's mind, money was more of an obstacle than the denial of his passport.

Algren stepped off the train in Los Angeles innocently believing he would have a respected voice in the making of the movie, assuming that since Preminger had liked the story enough to buy it, he would be sympathetic to Frankie Machine and would want to make a good film. Algren was prepared to write a good screenplay. When Bob Goldfarb met him at the station and installed him at the first-class air-conditioned Beverly Carlton Hotel, Algren knew right away he'd have to get another place: sandwiched "between a pretzel-shaped swimming pool and a fountain blowing pink water, in a germ-proof room with a sterilized television set" was no place to write about Frankie Machine. He moved almost immediately to the cheaper downtown Hotel Vermillion, home to theatrical types and a juggler who practiced his craft in the mezzanine. Outside his window a fine red neon sign blinked: GOOD BOOZE.

The picture would be made. "But," he wrote Amanda, "like most things that happen to me, there's reverse english on the event." Preminger had been sitting on the rights, obtained from Roberts, for over a year; and Roberts wasn't coming back from England. Nobody would tell him how much Preminger paid, but Nelson was led to believe he'd picked it up for the purchase price or less, which meant he would get no resale money. That was bad enough; but Preminger also planned to finish the picture two months before the opening of Kirkland's play, dampening Algren's other avenue for potential profits. Still, when Nelson first met Preminger in Malibu, he found him easy to get along with, concerned only with whether Algren could write the script and whether he was "politically clear," though it didn't seem to matter: it was in no one's interest to investigate Algren too carefully.

The honeymoon with Otto, who had a reputation for emotionally torturing artists, didn't last long. First, Preminger changed his mind about the money. The thousand a week was out, Nelson wrote Amanda. Preminger had told Mary Baker of the Jaffe Agency, " 'If he wants $500 okay. Otherwise he can get on the train and go home.' Baker says to me, 'What do you think?' I told her I'd get on the 4:30 like the man said. He upped it to $750 and then stuck there, with no guarantee."

Simply from a class perspective, Algren and Preminger were never going to get along. Otto was a privileged Viennese; his makeup man fixed him up while he and Nelson were in conference. He treated Algren as an employee, told him to be waiting at the hotel curb when his red Caddy with the automatic windows pulled up. Algren stayed in his room until the desk clerk called. He soon realized that Otto couldn't have cared less about Frankie or the narcotics problem. "One of the first questions Preminger asked me was, 'How do you know such people?' " Algren complained. "You know? Such animals, you know. I said, 'I've known them all my life.' " And all the while the agency kept telling him, "Be nice to Otto. Be nice to Otto." Preminger felt he wasn't taking the project seriously, but the problem was that Algren didn't take *Otto* seriously. "If I took *him* seriously, I couldn't take *myself* seriously," Algren said.

Bob Goldfarb liked Algren immensely, but despite his efforts to explain the idiosyncratic Chicago writer to Preminger—why he had moved to a run-down hotel, how he wanted the jukeboxes in the film to have half Polish, half American songs to typify the dilemma of young Polish immigrants—Otto could not be bothered. Algren hadn't been on the job for a week when Preminger didn't so much fire him as excuse him with the insulting comment: "Thank you for letting me meet a very *interesting* person." So Algren, who had been promised a thousand a week for four weeks or longer wound up having to fight, through his agent, just to have his expenses paid. And he suspected that Preminger had never had any idea of including him in the project at all. "I think the idea was that, when two people make a deal about a contract in which three persons are involved, something has to be done about the third party eventually—you have to make some gesture of including him in in the event of legal kickbacks," he wrote Amanda. But he didn't seem to fully understand what was going on—he'd gotten this idea from Art Shay.

The more he thought about the way he'd been chased from the movie as if he were a fly, the more furious he became. Though Preminger was paying Frank Sinatra a hundred thousand dollars and 10 percent of the net profits to appear in the film, he didn't even want to pay for Algren's time on the train, and when things got this petty, Algren felt he simply could not stoop to Preminger's level. "Actually," Nelson explained, "I've never cared a whoop where the gold came from. I've borrowed off a pickpocket and stolen a ten-spot from a whore and never had a pang of conscience. But taking dough off O. Preminger is something the normal stomach can't stand. There just wasn't any question—you can't take money from this kind of man without feeling you've been traded. . . . I've often run into the heroic phrase, where Hollywood characters give up great chances and wealth because 'Well, you have to live with yourself.' I never thought that was quite real until I met Otto. There really is such a thing." And in that spirit he wrote to Preminger, refusing all monies the Jaffe Agency had struggled to secure and concluding that Preminger owed him nothing: "Although I did not find you an interesting person," he wrote Preminger, "I did discover in you an uncanny one. Upon the basis of mutual amusement, therefore, I am the debtor. And since you are decidedly more uncanny than I am interesting, I must, at a rough estimate, owe you close to forty dollars. I will send you this sum confident of your satisfaction in alms from any quarter however modest and remain, faithfully yours, Nelson Algren."

Algren believed that if he took money from Otto he'd have no legal basis for a suit later on, but he also wanted to hurt Preminger, though to a man with a million dollars, his words were hardly adequate weapons. Naturally, he hadn't bothered to consult a lawyer. "Nelson was typical of the obverse of what you would call an honest man," said Goldfarb. "He was a wise guy, a con man, street smart, and by reason of his wife having worked for the Screen Writers Guild, a Philadelphia lawyer, and for this reason he was a patsy. Based on my experiences with him, he not only made it impossible to do our jobs as agents, he frustrated all our attempts to get any more money back by writing that letter."

Determined not to leave town empty-handed, loath to go home, Algren stayed on in Hollywood. If he ever did get to Paris, he wrote Amanda, it would take a war to get him back to the U.S., if a war would even do it. "Nelson felt that everyone from Preminger to the agency had shafted him," recalled novelist Clancy Sigal, at that time a young Herb Jaffe agent escorting Nelson to studios in an attempt to get him work. Nelson seemed quick to take offense if he felt his dignity was in question or if he sensed a bad deal: "If he was conned by people whose intelligence he did not value, he was infuriated." The two became friends after Sigal, knowing nothing of Nelson's love life, confided over drinks that his big ambition was to go to Paris and have an affair with Simone de Beauvoir. Betraying nothing, Nelson told Sigal he'd better watch himself, he might be getting into deep water there. And he remained friends with the younger man for decades.

While waiting for work, he visited friends, seeing the Browns in Malibu and the Millard Kaufmans. One day he and Acker went out with another man and woman and were picked up by the cops in less than an hour. The couple were users, and with the marks on Acker's arms they were off to narcotics detail. Nelson couldn't figure out if Acker was using or not, but on the way to the station he remembered the joint of marijuana in his wallet, which to his great relief the cops failed to discover. In the following days he visited Acker and his wife in their new housing development home, a fifteen-thousand-dollar job with two baths and two TVs, and he was reassured that Acker was staying off narcotics. In the underworld, at least, some things worked out right.

After killing two days in Tijuana, he continued to see people in Hollywood—rats, he labeled them—who might put him to work. But though producers bent over backward to overlook his eccentricities, nothing could be arranged. Algren wanted to sell stories, but only the stories *he* wanted to sell, and he could arouse no interest in the stoopers' story. The fact was that he really didn't have the heart for the kind of assignments the studios wanted to give him. Preminger had made him feel like the biggest bum that had ever come to Hollywood, he wrote Amanda. He'd never felt so lost and fish-out-of-waterish in his life, and he didn't know what he was doing there at all.

He left town broke.

The Preminger affair, which he would parody in writing again and again, marked a turning point in Algren's life. It was a blow to have been treated in Hollywood not as a respected author and unique talent but as a mark to be swindled and dismissed with a wave of the hand. Before Preminger, his business dealings had consisted of pleasant correspondences with Brennan and Aswell and McCormick, and even the deal with Roberts, who had wanted and appreciated his talent, had worked out well until the sale to Otto. He had come to Hollywood in 1955 expecting Preminger to be a decent man and instead found a world with no respect for literature, that stole his property and cared only about getting-the-money-into-the-bank. Before, his focus had been on the outcasts; he'd never had to be personally involved in the business world. He couldn't do two things at once and had never wanted to.

To Dave Peltz it seemed that Algren's belief that the artist was infinitely wiser than the uncreative businessman, who would always seek and need creative talent, had been turned completely upside down: the artist was to be exploited like everybody else. "When Preminger took *The Man with the Golden Arm,* bought it, and had the guts to be the first to cross the Johnston code, Algren knew that Preminger wasn't doing this as a trailblazer, in a moral way, but to make a buck," Peltz said. "And when Preminger invited him out to work on the screenplay, Algren felt that he was the smart one and could be in control. But in Hollywood, they made a horse's ass out of him. Totally and completely. I think that was shocking for him, a rude awakening in terms of his own abilities and strength." Still, Nelson returned to Gary acting like a hero, the truth-seeking poet misused by the insensitive businessman. "I remember him sitting on the beach playing the hero and telling great stories about all his escapades in Hollywood," Peltz recalled, "but he had really been destroyed by it."

He had the presence of mind to put a Chicago lawyer on Otto's case, then gave in to an urge to gamble so great he considered heading for Vegas or Havana but settled for organizing a new poker game on familiar territory. For the cards kept the everlasting darkness at bay, the cards lent everlasting hope: Paris still beckoned. In short order he lost his last three hundred seventy-five dollars, a *Sports Illustrated* advance for the stoopers' article. Not long afterward he left his wildwood nest on the lagoon for a furnished room above an alley and got a date with a girl he used to sleep with, only to have her door slammed in his face later—his marriage, it seems, was an obstacle even to getting laid. In June he filed for divorce.

He was broke and homeless; there was no reason not to teach creative writing at a five-week summer conference at Montana State University. He had only to hold classes four hours a week, though Missoula's perhaps welcome dullness was inevitably disturbed when a long-abused, potentially homicidal wife of a rancher decided Nelson Algren was the answer to all her problems: she interrupted his class, monopolized his office hours, and tried to break down his office door while he hid inside. Another, less stressful though unsettling omen appeared when he cochaired a panel with the critic Leslie Fiedler, whom he secretly dubbed "Lionel Lardass." Fiedler, Algren wrote Max, "suddenly announced that *Augie March* and *Huck Finn* belong snuggled right together on the same shelf. When I came to four professors were dead and the three remaining were trying to pull me off him." Algren and Geismar's shared view of literature, as a product of and response to social forces, inextricable from history, was going out of vogue. Now, with the rise of the cold war, Algren saw a new breed of critic, the safe, Ph.D.-endowed academic who made a comfortable living assessing the failures of better men, such as Hemingway, Faulkner, and Steinbeck. Hoping they would deal around him, he retired to his room and locked himself in, revising the new novel and cursing himself for ever having let Amanda leave California.

For though he found it incomprehensible that she would want to continue a relationship that was for him a farce, Amanda wanted to reconcile. He didn't. He felt he was merely a means through which she hoped to recover the father she had been deprived of. That this meant giving up his life as a writer didn't seem to bother her, he told her in a letter; she clung to him so fiercely he had to keep pushing her away. He told her it dismayed him to realize that the last twenty years had been a long, drawn-out battle not to be married to her, that for the last two and a half he'd been in the absurd position of knocking himself out to maintain a life-style he didn't want. But at least there had been years when he had gotten free, been contented, produced. All he could think about was living that way again. Desperate to have his house back, he begged Amanda to free him. He wanted only to go home, burrow in like a mole, and finish "Entrapment" before it slipped away; and fighting for this he sensed, deep down, that he was fighting for his life.

From Montana he flew to New York and the Hotel Lincoln, from which Simone had once written him such fervent, passionate love letters. The novel was nearly finished, and Margo, who spent a week with him in New York around this time, remembers that it was now, between the heat and the suffocating skyscrapers, that Nelson began to feel unwell. He wrote Simone that the feeling of inner death returned, that he was pained by an endless recurring nightmare. The passage of time frightened him. He felt older all the time and sensed "Entrapment" slipping from his grasp. The new novel still needed revisions, and he was so tired of traveling.

Fortunately, Ingersoll and Brennan invited him to the Ingersolls' summer house in Saranac Lake in the Adirondacks. It was a good, cool, quiet place to work. Each evening the cook brought a wrapped piece of peach pie and a fork to the tiny room where Algren cloistered himself. Undistracted by telephone, TV, or newspaper, he polished page by page the final draft of the novel eventually known as *A Walk on the Wild Side,* keeping in mind Seldes's plea to tone down the bawdier passages. And when the day's work was done, Saranac Lake was a pleasant respite. Despite a case of tuberculosis, Elizabeth Ingersoll was a high-spirited woman, and the occasional visitors were friendly. Herb Alexander of Pocket Books, which had published the successful paperback version of *Golden Arm* and was potentially interested in *Wild Side,* was nearby, and one evening he and Nelson drove forty miles to Westport, New York, for dinner with Max and Anne Geismar at their summer house. It was the first time Nelson had ever met Max, and he was glad to be with literary people who respected his work. Even if the new novel wasn't the right one, he felt good about finishing it. Suddenly all things seemed possible. He figured this book would clear up his debt to Doubleday and allow him to draw a weekly advance on "Entrapment," to which he couldn't wait to return.

By October 1955 he was back in New York with the finished manuscript, which had been completely transformed. In 1954 he had predictably—though mistakenly—found his first novel "deadly . . . such schoolboy poetry." As he started crossing out and rewriting, the book seemed so serious it struck him as funny. "In every chapter some child had had her head cut off, and you know I was really laying it on, and twenty years later it was so silly—and so pompous. So I kept making it funny."

At first he had been willing to work on it only on weekends. Finally he had begun to enjoy the "big silly stud" he'd created out of Cass McKay; and making New Orleans into a "clown-town, thronging with whores with hearts of gold, showboat villains, and eccentric customers in shadowy brothels" was one way to make a distasteful task more entertaining. "It was a goofed-up book and not to be taken seriously," Algren said. More important, it was "a reader's book," so he felt obliged to heap on the slapstick. "You're more inclined to clown, in a reader's book," Nelson explained in an interview right after the book was finished. "You've got one ear to the audience for yaks. It's just an obligation you have to fulfill." In other words, the whole thing was a bit of a joke—if one could look lightheartedly at the long-term effect such writing was to have on his career.

To meet his obligation, he had skillfully worked jail scenes and railroad scenes, numerous sequences from his first book, and a violent episode from "The Face on the Barroom Floor" into a new farcical novel. Geismar wrote perceptively that "Algren [had] found a refuge from the curse of 'normalcy' in his own period through a sort of surrealist comedy of life in the gutter." Algren had created a picaresque tale of the southern underworld during the Depression, a folkloric tall tale of the dispossessed. Like Cass McKay, poor white Dove Linkhorn grows up in a tiny, dusty Texas town. No women enter his life until he reaches sixteen and finds a night of passion in the arms of Teresina Vidivarri, his employer at the town chili parlor. When she refuses to continue their relationship despite his great sexual powers, he rapes her, destroying—it is, after all, an Algren novel—his one love relationship.

Dove takes to the road, beginning a series of adventures that form an ironical parody of the American success story: in 1932 there was no place to go but down. He tries selling coffee door to door and is seduced by his customers, he sells bogus permanent-wave certificates to New Orleans housewives. But in all jobs he is less than successful until he finally takes advantage of his one marketable skill—his sexual prowess. He becomes a peep-show artist and whorehouse stud, only to be beaten blind by his girlfriend's legless lover, and to return home, groping, for the lost love of Teresina Vidivarri.

Despite many colorful and hilarious scenes, however, Algren had violated the one bottom-line criterion by which he judged novels again and again in his reviews: he had created a character who doesn't seem real. Critics who claim that "of all the major works of Algren this book has the most vitality" also admit that Dove is a character of "comic-strip vitality" though "of far greater than comic-strip complexity and significance." But he's a cartoon character nonetheless, complete with a fake southern accent. Tellingly, Algren almost never referred to Dove Linkhorn the way he constantly spoke of Frankie Machine—as if he were a friend he'd known. The critic Alfred Kazin, whose review troubled Algren and whom he would later dislike, put it succinctly: "I don't think his book has anything real about it whatsoever. . . . He does not feel much interest in [his characters] as human beings, and so can only summon up for them, at best, a vague literary pity. . . . That harrowing and grimly honest book *The Man with the Golden Arm* . . . was about something real, the life and death of a man. . . . [and] hurt like a blow, because Mr. Algren saw his lost and damned characters as victims of a system. . . . This new book shows, all too clearly, that Mr. Algren's usual material no longer points an accusing finger at anything or anybody. It is just picturesque." That there are elements in it to please a good number of scholars and critics is a testament to Algren's talent; even in whipping up a book for money, he showed intelligence and wit.

Reading the revised manuscript, Seldes said, he laughed out loud: in place of a salacious scene he'd asked Algren to cut, there was a hilarious story of Dove's employment in a New Orleans condom factory, where brightly colored rubbers hung on the line in a clammy run-down apartment smelling obscenely of rubber. Seldes enjoyed Algren's good-natured disregard for censorship, but he knew his superiors at Doubleday would never go for it. When Algren insouciantly met him for lunch thinking he'd reestablished credit and would soon have financial footing for "Entrapment," the fact that, as Algren recalled, Seldes had to have three martinis before he started to talk should have been a tipoff. The trouble was not just the indecency issue. "[Seldes] told me there was no reason for my having written the book, therefore nobody would want to buy it and over and above that Mr. D didn't want to go into court as had to be done with [Edmund Wilson's] *Hecate County,*" he wrote to Max Geismar. Algren said he'd stand by the book, and when lunch was over, so was his relationship with Doubleday. The last two rejections had convinced him that he was dealing with people who just wouldn't stand up to censorship, and for that Algren felt contempt. But it was another blow to his dignity and self-image following the Preminger disaster.

Several times during the next two weeks, McCormick, Seldes's boss, tried calling him at his hotel, but Algren refused to return the calls. After the rejection he had immediately called his friend Bill Targ at World Publishing and asked him to read *A Walk on the Wild Side:* but all he really wanted was to shake the novel and get back to his own life. He was sick to death of the publishing world, and he left town telling Maddy Brennan to place it. Targ, who read it over the weekend, immediately wanted to make an offer, but on Monday morning Brennan told him that Farrar, Straus and Cudahy had taken it first. Targ was exasperated; but Nelson had just learned that backers for Kirkland's play had pulled out because Preminger's movie would open in the fall, and publishing etiquette was the last thing on his mind.

Desperately needing release from New York's commercialism, Algren turned to the underworld. Still writing to Margo, he traveled to Baltimore in early November to see Jesse Blue, an old friend from East St. Louis. Blue was reputed to be a pimp, stooper, professional horseplayer, and occasional marijuana smuggler. He had only one woman, Totsie, whom he had protected from her abusive father and who now supported him. Blue was a fabulous storyteller who had once been a CP organizer, and Nelson was fascinated by him. Blue and Totsie and another couple were living, in constant fear of a bust, in an old-fashioned brick house on a street still lit by gas lamps. Algren had met the other man, Blackie, once before: Blackie had taken Algren up in his plane and had wanted to land on the racetrack. The man was probably also a pimp. When he expected company he would put his woman against the wall with his hand on her throat: "Don't embarrass me in front of my friends—" and then watch her behavior. He'd hang out on the street corner in pink pants, black shirt, and black hat, having borrowed the most garish, offensive car from the dealership where, at fifty-five, he was working legitimately for the first time.

But soon Nelson and Blue left Blackie for Florida, by way of East St. Louis. They drove west, loaded down like gypsies; navigator Nelson, apparently a little depressed, kept looking at the floor. East St. Louis was hot: a rash of corpses stuffed into car trunks had the police picking up everyone in sight, and the FB "Eye" was looking for Crooked Neck Herman, who walked into a bar where Nelson and Blue were drinking. Nelson's old friend Bud Fallon left his construction job to join them, and the trio cut across the Kentucky-Tennessee cracker belt through Arkansas, then across the prosperous gulf coast of Florida through the Everglades. When they reached the state's east coast, fifty miles of motel, glitter, and conspicuous wealth that had even LA beat, they turned off the ocean trail, and ended up halfway between Fort Lauderdale and Miami at something called the Playland Estates in Hollywood, Florida.

There they rented a house a few steps from a swimming and fishing pond with white sand. It reminded Algren of home in Gary; but he had no plans to return there till spring. It was November, and he missed the snow. In this tourist republic tempers flared if the thermometer dipped below seventy, and the sky was so blue, so blue, the breeze too perfect. But at least he was with people he trusted, people who adhered to a code of loyalty and would not rip him off. He had finally escaped Hollywood, New York, and Amanda, but he had absolutely no idea what to do next.

For the thought of what Preminger and Roberts had done to him made him so angry he couldn't think straight, he wrote his friend Herman Kogan, then literary editor of the *Chicago Sun-Times*. Though his 5 percent of the picture was negated by the resale, it now appeared that Roberts, who had verbally promised the rights to Kirkland, had turned down an offer of thirty-five thousand before selling to Preminger, and Algren and his lawyers figured that Preminger must have paid at least fifty grand, of which Algren should have gotten half the amount over fifteen thousand. In fact, the price seems to have been higher: viewers of Irv Kupcinet's Chicago talk show, on which Preminger appeared in the 1960s, recalled hearing the producer say he'd paid a hundred thousand for it. Roberts's figures, which Algren believed were manipulated, apparently showed that he had made no profit from the sale, making recourse impossible for Algren, who could have comfortably set up Amanda and bought back his life as a writer with the $42,500. A high-powered New York law firm was going over the contract, but it was a little late: by November 1955, Preminger's investment was so large that Algren would have had to put up the cost of the picture to get him into court. Otto, who had also cost Algren the profits from the play and had the audacity to advertise the film as "Otto Preminger's *Man with the Golden Arm*," stood to make at least a million on the film that would launch Frank Sinatra as a screen star.

Algren's life had collapsed around him like a house of cards. "Entrapment" seemed further and further away all the time; Preminger had made him feel like such a victim that it was all but impossible to work, and the severed relationship with Doubleday must have hurt. He had never been able to write seriously without a secure, quiet haven, and the prospects for getting his house back were not good. Despite Nelson's reasonable offer to provide Amanda with a house of her own, renting 6228 to meet payments while he put in a couple years on the West Side for the novel, she had countersued for divorce. If the judgment went her way, she would be entitled to live at 6228 rent-free for a year—while he went homeless. After writing a book for money and having a major Hollywood movie made from his most famous novel, he had nothing to show, and he was $8,200 in debt to Doubleday.

Around Christmas, Algren left the Playland Estates for Miami and took the overnight steamer to Havana, for which he didn't need a passport. Once off the boat he felt he was in Europe, the closest he'd been since 1949. In the old-world colonial capital of Batista's Cuba, vice and poverty flourished with the same apparent timelessness as in Marseilles and Naples. He went to the fights, watched a marimba parade floating up the street, and seemed to feel he'd truly escaped the spiritual poverty of America, where people lived so tidily amid such psychological disorder, where exploitation went by any other name than what it was. All day he wandered the tiny streets of Havana, sniffing the smells, observing life from the cool shaded bars. Then he called on Hemingway.

When Algren arrived at his home, Hemingway was recovering from injuries received in a plane crash, sitting up in bed drinking whiskey, with a white baseball cap over his fringe of white whiskers and rimless glasses. He seemed a sort of professorial Santa Claus, much more intellectual-looking than Nelson had imagined.

They talked fights, sipped whiskey, and then Algren, who had just seen Disney's *African Lion,* began to show the great hunter—blow by blow—how a lioness knocks down an impala deer. Enacting a vivid narration, he was first the intently stalking lioness, then the terrified impala flying in escape, next the lithe, voracious cheetah running down its prey. Watching this performance take place beneath the mounted head of an enormous water buffalo he himself had brought down, Hemingway decided that he liked young Algren and invited him out the next day for Christmas dinner.

Christmas at the Hemingways' was just where he belonged, unencumbered by a wife and knowing he was accepted and respected for his writing, for what he was. The party was significant for Nelson because of the emotional affinity, far deeper than words, stirred by Hemingway. "He sat among [the guests] gravely serious," he would write later. "He carried an air of tranquility. He listened, perceived, and he liked having company. What he brought to a table of many guests was the feeling that everyone understood one another. I remember hearing Spanish spoken, and French, and of understanding not a word of what was said; and of knowing, when I spoke English, that some of the guests didn't understand me. But because of Hemingway's presence everything seemed understood. . . . He was a big man who had a big life; that made those who had known him bigger."

The afternoon ended too quickly. When dinner was over, Nelson was chauffeured to the dock, and after arriving in Miami, he boarded a plane for Chicago.

16.

A Walk on the Wild Side

AMANDA CLAIMS THAT at the last minute Nelson wanted to reconcile, but this may have been a desperate effort to avoid disaster: the judge ruled in Amanda's favor. Algren now owed his divorce lawyer eight hundred dollars and Amanda seven grand; he had been moving around for over a year, was still homeless and had no place to work; he faced another daunting year in limbo. But he was free again; and the contract with Farrar, Straus and Cudahy was the best he'd ever had—a hundred a week for three years and a guaranteed ten thousand in advertising for *Walk*.

But in January he was asked to pay a lawyer five hundred dollars to read the manuscript against the possibility of obscenity charges, and Algren began to feel uneasy about his relationship with Straus. He missed the rapport he'd had with McCormick; Straus struck him as more of an investor than a bookman. "I feel that, in working for Roger, I'm working for film rights, reprint rights, and if a book makes money it's a good one, *per se*," he told a friend. Nevertheless, he was pleased with the upcoming publication. On a February trip to New York, Herb Alexander of Pocket Books, who was eager to buy the paperback reprint rights to *Walk,* put Nelson up at The Players club. Nelson worked patiently with Straus and Sheila Cudahy to edit out the obscenity, and at a cocktail party at Sheila Cudahy's, Anne Geismar remembers, he was absolutely manic: *Wild Side* stood to be a hit. Preminger's movie was involuntarily providing a head start in advertising, and after all the delays Kirkland's play would open at the Cherry Lane Theatre just as the new book was being published. Algren still didn't know whether to go to Paris in the fall or seclude himself in the house in Gary, but he would have money to pay his debts and write "Entrapment." Carey McWilliams of *The Nation* told Algren he might have better luck now if he reapplied for a passport, and Algren did so, trying to ensure he'd get it by signing a statement saying he'd never been a Communist.

Though he'd rather have been in Gary, he spent the spring of 1956 on Chicago's West Side. He rented a single at Miller's Furnished Rooms, a Division Street lodging where the sinks were down the hall, Miller told him, because sleeping in the same room as a wash-basin that attracted roaches wasn't healthy. It was fairly quiet, though a large, disruptive family was crammed into a nearby room. But unlike his marriage, he wrote Max, Miller's Furnished Rooms was *real.*

In April he moved into an apartment in Caesar Tabet's building at 3831 Lexington. Tabet gave him an electric typewriter, and soon Algren was down at the Cook County Jail talking to addicted women in the day room—background material for "Entrapment"—and lecturing in the jail's adult education program. Undoubtedly seeing Margo more frequently, he smoked dime La Palina cigars and played twenty-five-cent stud poker at Lottie Zagorski's low-key, middle-aged bar, watched the fights on television, and wondered how the New York people could have been talking for over a year about the thousands coming his way—stage and screen deals on previous novels, film rights for *Walk,* etc., etc.—when he was being saved every ten days by a check for forty or eighty dollars from an old royalty or book review and often had to ask Tabet for more time on the rent.

If things went his way, among future earnings might be the winnings from a long-awaited lawsuit against Preminger. Harriet Pilpel of Greenbaum Wolf and Ernst—Algren was going first-class in his choice of lawyers—had filed a complaint against United Artists, Bob Roberts, and Preminger in the New York State Supreme Court, asking for $250,000 in damages. The suit charged that the sale to Roberts was not bona fide, that Algren had never transferred any sheet-music rights, and that the exploitation campaign for the picture and the song of the same name, sung by Sammy Davis, Jr., on the Decca label, were destroying his literary property. The suit further charged that, by advertising the movie as a film by Otto Preminger, the producer had arrogated to himself the picture's authorship. Pilpel apparently believed they had a good case. The Screen Writers Guild and the Authors' League of America had already gone on record deploring the way the film was being marketed as "Otto Preminger's

Man with the Golden Arm," and writers and film-trade people awaited the outcome of a suit that might set important precedents.

A Walk on the Wild Side was published in May, and opening festivities were held in Chicago. Roger Straus and the house's publicity director, Lynne Caine, flew in from New York, and after taking them to a downtown burlesque show and a tour of the Central Police Station, Algren appeared at three autographing parties, a press lunch, two television shows, and at Herman Kogan's book-and-author luncheon. But despite Geismar's favorable review in The Nation, the Herald Tribune's praise of the book's "immense vitality and imaginative exuberance," and a now lost telegram congratulating him for having written "an American ballet," the reviews of A Walk on the Wild Side were discouraging. Alfred Kazin panned it in The New York Times Book Review, and Orville Prescott in the daily Times was no less harsh: the characters weren't real, the book was ridiculously overwritten. But in 1956, many critics were outraged simply at Algren's subject matter. In The New Yorker, Norman Podhoretz couldn't fathom why "[he] finds bums so much more interesting and stirring than other people." In Partisan Review and The Reporter, Leslie Fiedler dubbed him "the bard of the stumblebum," and after a long tirade against Wild Side finally dismissed Algren as a "museum piece—the last of the Proletarian Writers." Time, bastion of the status quo, accused him of having approached the edge of nonsense. Naturally, the bad reviews hurt far more than the good ones helped: he'd crumpled the telegram calling it a ballet. Always innocently seeking praise, he had received so few negative reviews in the last two decades he seemed to have forgotten how painful they were. Studs Terkel remembered that Algren seemed terribly hurt. "He never got over the savagery of the attack on Wild Side," said Algren's friend Tom Dardis. "It destroyed him, blighted his reputation." But it still could be a commercial success, and with that hope he headed for New York.

He arrived to a crush of reporters at the airport. Kirkland's Golden Arm had just opened to rave reviews, and with the lawsuit, the movie, and the new novel, Algren was in the news. Suddenly a reporter thrust at him a copy of the English translation of Simone's The Mandarins, detailing a thinly fictionalized account of their love affair, and began asking questions. The American production was a big chunky book, and the sensationalized cover showed a woman at a cocktail party talking to a man who looked like Algren. Nelson had known that the book, dedicated to him, was about to be published; he may have even read it, but he hadn't seen the cover or anticipated the publicity. When a reporter asked if he had any comment on the book, Algren said, "Yes, I think Madame de Beauvoir has invaded her own privacy," and laughed. But he was far from happy about it. "She must have taken notes every time we made love," he later complained to Lou and Martha Lou Gilbert; he did not like having his personal life exposed and judged.

Lacking money to spend more than a few nights at the Hotel Gramercy, he stayed with actor Lou "Gigi" Gilbert, his wife, Martha Lou, and their children on 97th Street. He arrived in the night, calling from the sidewalk, and was very agitated throughout his stay. "He was miserable," said Martha Lou. "He couldn't rest, he was walking around muttering, pacing up and down, he had to see a publisher and couldn't get an appointment. He was insomniac, unresponsive, in a funk, another world." The Gilberts would have liked to help him, but Algren created an unhappy atmosphere, and the kids were scared of him. Gigi finally asked him to find another place, and a distracted Algren moved to a sublet in the Village for the month of June.

Despite the reviews, while in New York Algren noted that *A Walk on the Wild Side* was among the top fifteen best-sellers in June, right above "Frenchy's thing," as he called it. He was wined and dined constantly, giving interviews over the radio and for the print media, attention he both craved and needed. Moreover, the play of *Man with the Golden Arm* had received unqualified smash reviews. Preminger had sought only to make a "problem" film, as Delmore Schwartz put it in *The New Republic,* sacrificing the complexity and tragedy of the "really first-rate novel" for a diluted story in which Frankie and Molly walked off into the sunet. Kirkland, however, had created a tautly woven script which, psychologically complex and dramatically graphic, adhered closely to the novel. The *New York Post* found the play "impressive, absorbing, and excellently acted." In the *Herald Tribune* Walter Kerr agreed, crediting the consistently engrossing performances to the faultless direction of Louis Macmillan. The stern play moved inexorably toward tragedy without comic relief, and the tiny Cherry Lane, with only 189 seats, gave the audience the feeling of being crowded in by the circumstances trapping Frankie Machine.

And yet, like *Rebecca* and *Laura,* which had also gone the novel-to-movie-to-stage route, the play was not a commercial success. It didn't find an audience, and the theater was only half full every night.

Now Algren's history repeats itself, for if he was able to look happy around town, he was increasingly emotionally unstable, frustrated, and financially desperate—in fact, his circumstances were remarkably similar to those he had faced following the reception of *Somebody in Boots* twenty-one years earlier. In the thirties he had looked to writing for social acceptance and self-affirmation; in the fifties his need was the same. After the breakup with Simone, his disastrous marriage, and the damage Preminger and the Doubleday rejection had inflicted on his self-esteem, he really needed a successful book. Yet with the exception of Max Geismar, all the serious critics—and, at the time, to Algren they were the only ones who mattered—had tossed the novel aside. He took the criticism so seriously that he had even begun apologizing for the book, until, he wrote later, Herb Alexander told him, "If you can't say anything good for it, just don't say anything."

And as in the thirties, his future hinged on the book's success. While *A Walk on the Wild Side* was selling, it hardly came close to the high expectations he had had for it. Now he laid some of the blame on the publishing industry. He believed a Doubleday rumor mill was trying to dampen the book's success and was still angry that the book had not been sold to Bill Targ: World had published Simone's novel, and Targ could have promoted the two books together. He didn't trust Straus, and his agents—Ingersoll, who had tuberculosis, and Brennan, who was known as a heavy drinker—seem to have encouraged the deal with Farrar, Straus because it paid off old debts: they had done business with Straus for years, and Straus, in his oral-history interviews, said that for a while he exerted a strong influence over the affairs of Ingersoll and Brennan.

In order to regain his house, pay Pilpel her four and a half grand, and give the government the seven it now demanded, Algren needed to profit handsomely on the reprint rights; this would happen only if the book was a hit. But he had turned down Herb Alexander's pre-publication offer of $32,500 because Straus, he wrote later, thought they might get more. With a sick feeling, he soon saw that that mistake had made the writing of *Wild Side* all for nothing: no one else was biting. Brennan hadn't wanted to tell him what to do after the Preminger fiasco, and there had been no Art Shay to advise him on financial matters. He was still broke and waiting for deliverance. And the months of endless waiting for money and running into dead ends, of living in furnished rooms and hotels and planes and trains and taxis and not knowing when, if ever, it was all going to end, had exhausted him.

Now he caught a case of the blues so deep he called Margo and told her he wasn't well. She urged him to find a doctor, but he said it wasn't that kind of illness—it was an illness of regret, an illness of what might have been, and the first real sign that he might never be able to return to the life he had once had. He felt a bad, bad pang for not holding on to the people and emotions of "Entrapment," for throwing them away on a relationship that never should have happened at all. "All I had to do was to be willing to live lonely— the way I prefer—for a couple of years," he wrote Max Geismar in the saddest letter of his life:

> Up to that time I did everything right—blindly, but in some way becoming somebody. Only one little thing, very deep, was wrong— and that was the shadow of guilt toward the girl I got married to a long time ago, and who wanted to try again. I tried every way of getting out of letting this happen—but I never quite cut the knot. I never said "No." I let it happen.
>
> . . . In my hands was the luckiest chance ever given an American writer—I mean that without exaggeration, for this reason: I made myself a voice for those who are counted out, and I did this because of compassion and not for what was in it. All I had to do was to keep my nose clean. I didn't. My devotion was to the outcasts, that was the real thing—the girl was just a kind of obligation I thought I was supposed to fill. By so supposing I began trying to do two things at once—trying to live her kind of life, being a conventional husband with a house and car. When I saw that by doing this I was going against my true needs, I began trying desperately to get out of it in time. That was why I began racing all over the country. . . . I had to write a book in flight—Montana, Saranac Lake, New York, Baltimore, Havana, East St. Louis. . . .
>
> When I got it done in this mid-air fashion, I knew it would have an enormous push from the publicity about "The Golden Arm"— it would come in on the best-seller lists, I would get cash for the reprint rights, buy my house back, try not to regret so much time taken from the book I'd begun, and get back to my lonely life, and do the book I'd begun before. I wanted to take years to do

it, you see. I wanted to have footing while doing it. I had a hundred pages, and still have of it. . . .

I had control of this situation, albeit by remote control, up till the time of Herb's offer. Had I said "Yes" I would have been off the limb and had my house back and the same situation I'd had before I began the furious business of writing a book to get out of a marriage that was really destroying me.

I almost made it. In fact, I did. But I didn't pick up the money. I played poker with it, hoping for 40. Roger [Straus] said he didn't need the money, in publication week we might get a competitive bidder, so I said, "Let's wait." . . . Since then I've counted that $32,500, divided it with Roger, paid off in a fantasy world, and saved my life with it. My life as a writer with it.

Still he struggled to save himself. Unable to get Amanda out of the house, his thoughts returned to Paris, although his enthusiasm for going, he wrote Amanda, had waned. The press was still badgering him about his affair with Simone. He told *Time* magazine, "A good female novelist ought to have enough to write about without digging up her own private garden. For me, it was just a routine relationship, and she's blown it up." Exposed, he sought to portray himself as a tough guy; with life crowding in on him, he needed to be strong. But his comments were for the public, not Simone. He placed a call to Paris to explain himself, but did not call back at the appointed time. Instead, Simone recalled receiving a lighthearted letter from him saying that the novel made him look like a great lover and that lots of women were propositioning him. But there was also anger in his letter. Simone's revelation of their affair had ended something for him.

Simone nonetheless remained the one to whom he turned. She told him she was not disturbed by his remarks about digging up one's own garden: she seemed to realize he was probably referring to his belief that the artist should be connected to the outside world. And she understood why he couldn't call—it would have been too emotional for her too, after all the time gone, to hear his disembodied voice. "Well, you say *it* was hard to die," she wrote, "it was hard for me too and in a way it will never fade away. . . . I'll always care for you deeply, with a warm, living, wonderfully important feeling." If love was dead, an intimate friendship awaited him.

Paris seemed his last and only chance for peace and escape, but on June 26 his passport was again denied. He realized now that signing the statement saying he'd never been a Communist had been a bad, impulsive mistake. In order to contest the refusal, he'd have to have a hearing, and if the passport office had evidence linking him to the Party, they could get him for perjury. Somewhere, Neal Rowland recalled, he heard of a Washington lawyer who could get into the files and pull his falsified statement: then, of course, he'd be in the clear. What Algren thought the lawyer would actually do is a mystery—was he going to roam the passport office after hours with a flashlight or distract the secretary as in the movies? It was an absurd scheme, but as he kept failing in ventures with the business world, he was increasingly drawn to the illegal way of doing things, with its comforting savor of the underworld. He was desperate enough to have his divorce lawyer ask Amanda for a thousand dollars of the settlement to pay the new lawyer. She agreed.

Correspondence between the passport office and Algren's lawyer suggests, however, that the lawyer was a legitimate and eminently respectable man who prudently questioned Nelson about his past, was surprised at his client's rather flippant answers, and then wrote the passport office suggesting that there was a large gap between what Algren thought constituted membership in the CP and what the passport office thought. Hoping to construct a defense against the affidavit in this way, the lawyer began proceedings to set up a hearing, while Algren went to Baltimore to "live off the horses" with Jesse Blue. But his insomnia, sadness, irritability, anger, indecision, and inability to concentrate were by now so pronounced that Blue called Amanda; and Nelson showed up in Gary pathetically asking to be taken into his own house.

In August 1956, he went to the wedding of Margo's daughter, but at the reception he was constantly moving about and perspiring. At home he was increasingly hostile to Amanda, furious over her insistence upon staying in the house. His condition did not improve. He had, briefly, been to a doctor Peltz recommended, someone Neal Rowland once met. "He was a discomforting man who came into the living room barking like a seal—Peltz said don't pay any attention—that is to distract from a deformed leg." "I think you have a depression on top of a depression," the doctor noted astutely. But Algren knew that the source of his creativity lay in his unconscious, and he did not want to disturb that; there were, of course, other reasons, such as fear, that made him resist psychoanalysis. Hanging his head, he just said, "Come on, Dave, let's go," and they left the doctor's office. His condition deteriorated. He could hardly sleep at all, and he'd sit in his room, depressed and often weeping, until Amanda saw he'd have to go to a hospital.

Neal Rowland came over to help. "Nelson was pacing, pulling his hair, in a bathrobe and slippers, round and round the house through the rooms. He said he hadn't slept for days, for weeks. I said, 'Why don't you go to a hospital and get some tranquilizers? This is a dead end. You can't work.' I stressed that he needed to do it for his writing." All the while, like many compulsive gamblers who have exhausted all avenues for funds, he kept talking about money, money, money, and each time he went around, Neal would try another tack of persuasion until Nelson began getting dressed. "In one trip he'd put on pants, another circle and he'd put on socks, then shoes and shirt" until finally he was dressed, remembered Neal, who went home when Peltz appeared to drive Nelson to the hospital. Although Nelson got into the car of his own volition, the two-hour trip to the North Shore was marked by his indecision. He knew he had to go, yet he didn't want to. He wanted to go home, then he wanted treatment. At one point they turned the car around and headed back, but Peltz kept assuring him that they should go to the hospital and if he didn't want to go in that was fine.

"There was a lobby, like a hotel lobby, and he had to sign himself in," Peltz recalled. "He wouldn't sign, and they wouldn't accept him unless he signed. The deal was, he would stay for two weeks—maybe a week; if at the end of the week he felt better and wanted to continue he'd have to sign himself in. If he didn't want to sign himself in he didn't have to stay.

"I said, 'Come on, Nelson, sign.' He walked over and signed a loop—an *l* or an *e*. Then he walked away. I said, 'OK, come on back and sign your name.' He walked over and did another letter on the 'Algren'—an *n*—and it took about a half an hour of him walking up, putting down one more letter and walking away. Amanda sat down not interfering, knowing that if she tried to assert herself . . . she was very anxious that they take him and that he sign himself in. And no sooner had he signed himself in than two guys come out of this door in white coats. When he saw them he resisted and they grabbed him and turned him around and muscled him— *muscled* him right through the corridor and the door slammed and he was hollering, 'Dave! Da-a-ave! Da-a-ave!' I heard that 'Da-a-ave!' . . . and I still hear it."

*

As was true to his luck, the hospital was able to do nothing for him. The barking seal was out of town for a few days, and he couldn't even be given a sedative without his doctor's consent. A few days later, when Amanda went to visit him to see how he was, the staff told her he'd left and they had no idea where he'd gone. He had walked out through a window or down a fire escape and headed for Chicago. He visited Mary Jane Ward, the author of *The Snake Pit,* the celebrated novel about life in an insane asylum, whom he'd known since the forties and had always liked; he wanted to talk about the depression with her. "She's a nice lady," he later told Dave Peltz seriously. "She's been there. She's been down there."

Eventually he came home. "He was not subdued and we did not discuss it," said Peltz. "He could not deal with it as an experience." Amanda finally found her own house in Gary. During those months he wrote only two brief notes to Max; Simone wrote, but he did not write back. He'd missed the deadline for a passport hearing, but he wasn't going anywhere. Seeing very few people, he was still rehashing the very problems that had been bothering him before the breakdown. One day, walking the beach with Peltz, he seemed haunted by Simone. He boasted to Jack Conroy and other friends that he'd never read *The Mandarins,* but he felt she had betrayed him, and this idea was connected not only with what she had exposed in the novel but also with the fact that it was a big best-seller and *Wild Side*'s sales were not even steady. "He felt connected to her and she had reached rarefied heights and he wanted to share in that—he felt entitled to that," Dave recalled. Moreover, he was still bemoaning the fate of *Wild Side,* still believing both books should have been published by World. Peltz remembered that he had an image of her book and his book, "married" side by side in the same volume. Though Peltz felt that this was only because he wanted money, the word "married," especially connected to Simone, cannot be dismissed so easily.

One evening the divorcee he'd been seeing in Chicago came to Miller, but when her train arrived he wasn't there to meet her, and dark was falling. She crossed the tracks to a phone booth but had no change to call him and didn't know what to do. Suddenly Algren emerged from the shadows: he'd been watching her in her dilemma. He greeted her in a monotone; his voice had no animation. They went to his house, and he turned on Studs Terkel's radio show on

WFMT, then put the fights on TV and began pacing. He plopped a frozen piece of meat in a pan. The house was a mess; the toilet was dripping. Communication with him was impossible, so she asked to see his photographs of Simone and Sartre in Paris. He brought them out—in a heap—and she asked if she could have a couple. He didn't say yes or no, and she put them in her purse. Although he asked her to spend the night, he was so distant and morose she wanted only to leave, and looking in her purse for bus fare, she realized that, without saying a word, he had opened it and removed the snapshots.

One day he saw Frank Sandiford at the offices of the doomed *New Chicago Magazine* to pick up a story he'd written on Preminger the magazine had rejected as sour grapes and possibly anti-Semitic. "He came into the offices a distraught person," Sandiford remembered, "suspicious and strangely unsure of himself. . . . He was there but obviously didn't want to be there though he made no attempt to leave. . . . Then, with a suddenness that surprised me, he bolted out of the place and I saw him through the window walking rapidly down the street, then stopping uncertainly before a small coffee shop. I went there to pay for his coffee; he seemed not to have any money. Perhaps he had lost at gambling, I thought. . . . It was out of character for him to be beholden to anyone for anything, even a cup of coffee. He was nervous, agitated, and disheveled, and acting as though he had committed a crime for which he was being hunted." Another time, when Peltz had driven him to the station, Algren was so indecisive that he stood with one foot on the train and one foot on the platform, completely unable to choose whether to go to Chicago or stay.

Many times, however, he seemed like his own self. In December of 1956, he met Geraldine Page, whom he considered one of the finest actresses on the stage, a great artist able to affect thousands. Page, then thirty-two, was playing in *The Immoralist* at Chicago's Studebaker Theater, and she recalled feeling an immediate affinity with Algren. She was staying in a suite at the Clarendon Court on North State Street, and Art Shay remembered dropping Nelson off there in the evenings and picking him up the next morning. Algren would emerge starry-eyed. "Everything is so clean up there," he said in awe. "We had breakfast on this heavy linen, and even the lid on the marmalade jar was polished. And there were these red flowers. Even they were clean." Algren took Page on his by now legendary tour of Chicago dives, but her limited engagement made their time together brief.

Besides, he was too emotionally preoccupied to start a serious relationship. He called Amanda almost every day to bitch and blame her for his problems, telling her she was the reason he hadn't had more success with Page. He did not want to recognize his responsibility for the whole fiasco, Amanda recalled: he did not want to see her pain, did not want to see her weep. His response to what happened would no longer be guilt—an emotion that, since it was at the heart of his writing, had always moved him deeply. If before he had been constantly obsessed, even in his dreams, by guilt, this was an emotion he now seemed to consider dangerous. Amanda, who would develop Reynaud's disease, a circulatory ailment, as a result of the stress she endured at his hands, tolerated his calls as a kind of therapy for a sick man until she finally told him that if he didn't have anything good to say not to call at all.

That lost fall of 1956, Margo came out to the dunes for extended visits, and Algren took a roll of pictures of her walking in the now barren woods by the lagoon, wearing his jacket. "She was his true muse," Peltz would later conjecture, "more like his inner self than his other relationships. She was raggedy, a stray cat, and so was he. She corresponded to all the sad lonely things that were Algren." So when Algren, in a macho attitude Peltz never took seriously—"he was delicate, sensitive"—told him, "I think I'll marry the broad," Peltz saw that it represented new hope, new life, for Algren, but still felt it was a crazy idea: "They're going to be two happy people settling down into a conventional marriage and she's going to be keeping house while he's out earning the bread? It was sick." Still, Algren may have merely been seeking the comfort of a human relationship from someone to whom he felt close.

But Margo didn't want him. One snowy day Margo and Caesar were taking Algren to a studio where he was going to make a television appearance, and there in the cab he asked her to marry him. Margo was angry—perhaps because he had asked her in front of Tabet. He got out of the car with her and she didn't want to see or talk to him: the proposal made her mad. Tabet thought she could do worse. "I don't want to not do worse," said Margo, who had been off narcotics for four years and aspired to a marriage where she could be safe and secure. She wanted to do better.

In fact, in December Margo called to tell Nelson she was marrying a workingman with a steady job, and she wanted the two to meet. It was unlike him to be so cold with her, but he told her he wasn't that unselfish, and hung up. Over the next two decades Nelson would keep up with her through Tabet, but they never saw each other again.

Earlier that year, Algren had edited some of James Blake's letters for *The Paris Review.* Blake had returned to jail in Florida, and some of his words detail an alienation that Algren too was feeling:

> I am increasingly disenchanted with the world outside. When I left the joint I came out with a brand-new fresh eye, and I was appalled and infinitely wearied to see the dull, mindless, crippling enmity the Good people feel for one another and for all men, the sullen truce they live under,
>
> The routine of working to eat doesn't make much sense to me any more. I want to work at something that will be an end in itself. And since I do most of my living inside my head anyway, it shouldn't make much difference where I am.

Algren's own efforts to remain whole in the legitimate world had failed miserably. Since he had been unable to pay Harriet Pilpel with the reprint-rights income, she had put a $4,500 lien on the movie rights to *Wild Side* and would soon drop the case against Preminger for lack of funds. Algren seems to have mortgaged his place to buy Amanda's house; he still owed the government $7,050. He felt that if he'd had some protection—from an agent, say—he wouldn't have been in such a mess. He had become convinced that Ingersoll and Brennan cared for nothing but their percentage, and he told Max that with Roger Straus he felt he'd gotten into "a quick-buck grinder beyond description. Sometimes Harriet [Pilpel] turns the crank, sometimes Roger [Straus]." He said they were trying to get hold of the rights to *Somebody in Boots,* and all kinds of ancient material, to produce extra money: "I don't like it in the least—but there I am." It soon became clear that Straus didn't have faith in Algren as a novelist: in December, Straus rejected an advance on "Entrapment." Nelson asked to be released from his contract, but it was a crushing, crushing blow. The couple of hundred manuscript pages that remain among Algren's papers indicate that this would have been a significant work. Of an unfinished version of "Entrapment," Algren's subsequent editor William Targ said, "In it he seemed to reach the deep-down essence of the blackest lower depths:

drugs, pimping, prostitution, at their most grim level. . . . It would have been an extraordinary achievement . . . it could have been his major opus."

In December Algren wrote to Simone that a light had gone out of him. He was depressed and very hard on himself, and he apparently told her he was having difficulty writing. She reassured him that he would write anew, he still had things to say and he would write a very good book and feel pleased again. She believed these things, but she could have been a million miles away: she had no idea what was happening.

On December 31, 1956, Algren went to buy groceries at a small store on the other side of the frozen lagoon. To get there, he walked across the ice, a tremendous shortcut, but a dangerous business all the same—Neal Rowland had forbidden his children to play there. It was a typical Algren move: once he had driven a friend's roadster so recklessly that he'd flipped it over. Another time Amanda was driving him past the Gary train tracks, and the warning bell began ringing and the arm of the gate swinging down. "Go on ahead," Algren had commanded her, and she had floored it across the tracks a split second before the arm on the other side swung down and had sat there with her heart in her throat wondering what kind of man she was living with.

There was probably nothing deliberate in what happened as he returned across the ice with his groceries, but Peltz believed that he was toying with the idea of not caring and letting it happen. When the ice broke, Nelson plunged into the dark freezing water of the lagoon, surrounded by lonely dunes on a desolate winter morning, and, suddenly confronted with death, he started screaming. Each time he tried to grab on to the ice around him it broke in his hands. Fortunately, workmen nearby heard his cries for help and rushed to rescue him. He warned them not to walk on the ice; they pitched him a rope, which his hands were too numb to hold. Finally he wrapped it around his body and was dragged across the ice to safety.

Wet and freezing, he called a man named Robert Jordan from a nearby phone booth. But Jordan lived on Chicago's North Shore, almost two hours away, and was not really a close friend. Why didn't he call Peltz? Or Neal? Or somebody local? Because, even in such a condition, his emotional guard was up: they would have asked too many questions. He was taken to a nearby hospital, treated for exposure, and released.

A short while later Peltz happened to stop by Nelson's. As he neared the front door, he saw Algren's clothes lying in a solid frozen heap on the ground, as if he had just dropped them there and stumbled inside. Peltz walked into the house and called out. There was a voice from the bedroom, and Nelson told him he'd taken the shortcut across the ice. Peltz immediately saw more to it. "You mother-fucker, did you really try to do it?" he accused him, but Algren would neither confirm nor deny that it was a suicide attempt. He would neither confirm nor deny: he probably knew that it didn't make a damn bit of difference whether the motivation was conscious or not.

When Max Geismar read about it in *The New York Times,* he immediately wondered if Algren had tried to kill himself; but strangely, Simone was shocked when this possibility was suggested to her later: she seemed to know only the vibrant Nelson of the past. That night Nelson went to a New Year's party at the Kogans'—why sit at home thinking about it?—but something had indeed died. Just as he had discarded the old lost self of Nelson Abraham after his hospitalization in 1935, after his fall through the ice, the man he was as a writer would change completely. "Entrapment," conceived in the spirit of *Never Come Morning* and *The Man with the Golden Arm,* would never be finished, and the naturalistic writer in the tradition of Wright and Sandburg and Dreiser was gone.

17.

The Past Is a Bucket of Ashes

IN EARLY 1957, theater producer Arthur Langer, who thought *Golden Arm* was "like Flaubert in English," wanted to mount a stage production of an Algren novel and made plans to meet Algren one weekend in Gary. "I phoned all day Friday, Saturday, and I had just about given up and I decided to call on Sunday and I got him, and he said, 'Omigod, I forgot, I've been playing cards all weekend' "—he must have been gambling with the $2,500 he'd finally received for the reprint rights. At any rate, Langer came out to the house in Gary. "I thought his cottage was an ideal place for a writer—a retreat," Langer remembered, "but he said he was there because he couldn't afford anything better. He made beef stew. We talked about *Man with the Golden Arm*—and I was startled. I found him naive—he could be taken. He was talking about his poverty, and there was a lot of self-pity. He said, 'I wrote a big American novel. Where's the hi-fi? Where's the stereo?' "

Langer got the impression that Ingersoll and Brennan had dissolved the contract with Roberts to effect the sale to Preminger, and in fact Algren had already severed his bond with his agents, calling them irresponsible and demented. "The files, it seems, were kept at the bottom of gin bottles and the records lost when the sheets were changed," he now told a friend. Free from Straus, he was eager to sign with World Publishing and did so without an agent in early February. But he did not contract for "Entrapment" and did not yet show it to Bill Targ. Instead, he promised to deliver a collection of eight to ten stories called "Love in an Iron Rain." With its name changed, the title story would be "The Man in the Hotel Mirror," which he now saw as a short novel.

With Shay's encouragement, Nelson was soon represented by Shirley Fisher of MacIntosh and Otis, but it was the friendly, direct Langer whose advice he sought when Marion "Joe" Lebworth offered him $25,000 for the movie rights to *A Walk on the Wild Side.* "Truthfully, I don't think he had money for carfare, but he came to New York with Art Shay," said Langer, who made reservations at Sardi's. They had lunch with Edward Kook, president of Century Lighting, and the well-known Herman Shumlin, who had produced and directed many of Lillian Hellman's plays and had been asking questions about Algren. "Shumlin was in absolute awe of Nelson," Langer recalled, "and for Nelson it was star time. I had never seen such a complete change in his personality. It was as if the spotlights from heaven had opened up. Shumlin looked at the contract and said, 'I think it's a front deal.' " It looked as if Lebworth might be looking to get it cheap and then sell it. "When Nelson left the lunch all these guys were saying he should send the contract back along with the check, that it was a no-good deal."

While in New York Algren met the artist Lily Harmon, a close friend of the Geismars' who was having a show of paintings in a gallery in White Plains. Recently divorced and raising two daughters, Harmon was also struggling with her career: the show in White Plains had been a real comedown from the New York galleries where her work was usually presented. After a party at Max and Anne's, she drove Nelson back to New York; along the river he kept recalling earlier trips to Babylon, when he'd won the National Book Award and felt like the toast of the town. They ended up at Lily's apartment overlooking Central Park West and became lovers.

Naturally, Langer, Lily, and Shay were stunned when Nelson signed the contract with Lebworth within the next few days. Shay had explicitly instructed him not to do anything without consulting him first, but Nelson, who had sidestepped his agent and her $2,500 fee, said, "Aw, I just wanted to get rid of the guy." Outraged, Lily immediately made him call his agent, but the deed was done. Perhaps the easy money, the attractive, agentless deal through which he might avoid Pilpel's lien were seductive, and as he'd learned by rejecting Herb Alexander's paperback offer, he couldn't be sure there'd be a better one. Yet he must have known it was wrong, or he wouldn't have tried so lamely to justify himself to Shay. And for almost a year he couldn't face Langer: "The reason I didn't write you for such a spell was that I let the film rights to WILDSIDE go and didn't have the heart to admit it to myself, far less anyone else." Langer later heard that Lebworth had sold the rights to producer Charles Feldman for $75,000; the sale resulted in the film starring Jane Fonda, which Algren claimed he didn't even bother to see.

That spring he nudged students at the University of Illinois at Urbana to laughter with a witty lecture called "The Wild Side of American Fiction," but he was not really writing. Instead of finishing the collection for Targ, he wrote charming love letters to "Lily-O," who that spring found his house on the dunes exactly as Simone had described it in *The Mandarins.* He'd told her not to bring any fancy clothes, that they wouldn't be going anywhere, then took her to a Chicago bar and announced a party that night at the home of editor and journalist A. C. Spectorsky, author of *The Exurbanites.* So they went to a very fancy party, Algren style: he in a T-shirt and she in a cotton dress. Here was his love of contrast, his conflicting desire to touch success and thumb his nose at it at the same time.

In the summer he visited Lily in her new house on Cape Cod, loving the sand and the sea and the light and a crippled man named Jimmy Thomas, who was building a bulkhead for Lily. A gentler version of the legless man in *Wild Side,* Thomas had built his own house, with a ramp leading up to it. "I think too of your wonderful, terrible friend, the little crippled man who holds back the sea with his hammer," Nelson would write in the kind of letter that made Lily love his sensitivity and romanticism. But Lily said that although Nelson suggested it, there was never any serious discussion of marriage. Nelson's constant pacing scared her daughters, whom he jokingly suggested putting in an orphanage so he and Lily could travel to Marseilles. He was very guarded about his feelings, and she had no idea that he gambled.

He couldn't bring himself to cash Lebworth's check. For weeks it sat on his breakfast table, gathering butter and coffee stains and being stared at until Nelson called Peltz to drive him to the bank. There, he cashed the entire twenty-five thousand and jammed it into a paper sack. His plans for the money seemed completely reasonable yet ridiculously out of character: he wanted to buy an apartment building in Chicago and become a landlord. Earlier he had voiced a desire to become a pimp, "but that was when he was already demented," as Peltz excuses him gently. At any rate, he found a lovely building with a carriage house in a pleasant section of the city. But as soon as he bought the place he realized he couldn't handle it. One night he called Art Shay to borrow eighty dollars for a refrigerator: he was having an affair with the woman living in the carriage house, and he felt if he didn't come up with a refrigerator she wouldn't sleep with him again. Clearly the responsibility was just too much, and he quickly sold the place back to the real estate agent at a loss. Then he gambled away the rest of the money. Every few days he would come to the office of his lawyer, "Fearless" Sam Freifeld, who was holding the money, and ask for three or four thousand. Within about sixty days it was all gone. Had he hung on to the building, now worth many hundreds of thousands, he could have had a pleasant income into his old age, but it seemed that as soon as Algren approached bourgeois respectability, he had to get rid of it.

The urge to gamble was surely exacerbated by anxiety about his work: that summer or fall, Targ also refused him an advance on "Entrapment," part of which had just been published in *Playboy*. Not only was the book not far enough along or in any shape to be presented, but Algren had yet to deliver the story collection, and there was little reason to give advances on two uncompleted projects. But once Targ refused the advance, Algren lost the motivation to finish the stories. In October, Stuart Brent told Bennett Cerf at Random House about the rejection, and Cerf was excited about a new Algren novel. But he was disappointed with what he received, jotting a harsh "NO!"—which Algren would never see—on the cover letter which "poignantly" asked for backing. Cerf was firm: "The scattered sheets you sent me (including one episode that is duplicated) are very interesting, but utterly insufficient to establish any idea of where you are going or what you are planning to accomplish. Very frankly, we would have to see a lot more before we could decide whether or not we would want to talk terms of a contract with you," said the man Algren would hereafter refer to as "Bennett Surface."

Despite the sloppy presentation of "Entrapment," the fact that he was showing it around suggests he was still trying to get back to it. But increasingly, fiction for magazines now took precedence over all else since it earned immediate payment and could be recycled into Targ's collection. More and more he seemed to be incapable of producing sustained work, and his frustration may have been taken out on his agent, whom he suspected of doing little for him, because he switched agents to work with Alice Bridge Jackson from Armitage

Watkins. Jackson, a longtime friend, was a warm, sensitive woman very concerned about getting Nelson back to work. She told him his last *Esquire* article, "G-String Gomorrah," about Calumet City, was not up to his potential. Having himself been disappointed in the piece, he liked her honesty and felt comfortable working with her. But instead of steadily producing new work, he was obsessed with protecting old properties. For a stage adaptation of *Never Come Morning* that Langer arranged, Algren insisted on an unheard-of 66 percent, instead of the author's customary 45 percent. Langer managed to get him 60 percent, but Algren's refusal to take it made Langer feel he was just too difficult to work with.

This insistence on getting his share or more was surely a result of the exploitation by Preminger, the long-term effects of which were now apparent. "The film was a loss to people who are addicts, who are helpless, and to me it was a loss of influence," Algren realized. And the fact that *A Walk on the Wild Side,* whose hero didn't even try for the American dream, was the bawdy antithesis of current American propaganda, helped foster the growing idea that he was a grade-B writer. That the conservatism of the fifties had made him seem more like a freak than a serious novelist became clear to him when a *Chicago Tribune* profile of him appeared in the fall of 1958. "It's a bit bewildering, to one who began in Sandburg's league, to find himself pitching to Kim Novak or picking existential violets," he complained to himself, the editor, and others; it had indeed been a rather astonishing feat. Moreover, the debacle at Farrar, Straus and his new leap to World had made him seem unstable in the eyes of publishers, in whose rumor mill the rejection of "Entrapment" was apparently known.

For instance, there could have been no better writer than Algren to cover the Kentucky Derby for *Sports Illustrated.* Algren was thrilled with the assignment to avoid the swells and cover the crowds, bars, and seedy nightclubs; and his natural enthusiasm for Silky Sullivan, a horse that always came from far behind, was so great that he sent notes to editors Dick Johnston and Sidney James drawing an analogy among Sullivan, Jesse James, and various gangsters. After this seemed ridiculously complicated to James, Algren stuck faithfully to Sullivan, producing a story that made his new agent, who died later that year, think he was back in the sure writing slot. He was proud of the piece, and its quality was such that Johnston felt obliged to pay him the full $1,250 for acceptance. But, it was Johnston's theory, James's early dissatisfaction kept him from seeing the finished story in a fresh light. Later *Sports Illustrated* admitted it might have been a "prizewinner," but in 1958 wouldn't run it.

For it was becoming increasingly evident that the main threat to Algren's fragile grasp on his career came from the critics. In winter 1957, Larry Lipton wrote a persuasive and eloquent defense of *Wild Side* in *The Chicago Review*, linking the post-1950 critical attacks against Algren with the suppression of all radical thought in the cold-war era. Algren was glad to read it. In addition to Podhoretz, Kazin, and Fiedler, academics like Edmund Fuller, who called Algren, Bellow, Mailer, and others "destroyers of the social order," and liberal critics like Charles Walcutt were, by the late 1950s, jumping aboard an anti-Algren bandwagon that directly attacked the whole idea of the writer as the compassionate social conscience and defender of the accused. In fact, as Carla Capetti, a professor of American literature who has researched the cold-war attacks on Algren, has noted: "The remarks directed against Algren's work during the fifties . . . succinctly evoke the critical landscape during the cold war, one dominated by conservative ideology . . . [and] in them one finds not merely the specific contentions that marginalized Nelson Algren but just as importantly the larger dispute that exiled the whole urban-sociological tradition from the hall of fame of American letters."

For, propelled by academia, American intellectual life was being made to serve the establishment. The loyalty oaths that had flooded American educational institutions during the fifties had weeded out radicals while providing security and prosperity to those who remained. Literary intellectuals came under the spell of the New Critics, men like Lionel Trilling, Jacques Barzun, and Mark Van Doren, whose literary ideas were committed to formalism and opposition to political ideology, seeing literature as something removed from the turbulence of life, above social and historical forces. Their orientation was white, European, and elitist; they searched for imagery, symbolism, secret codes. Algren believed that, in its concern for defined symbols and easy patterns, American criticism "left unheeded the truth that the proper study of mankind is man. . . . It mistook the uses of literature for literature." He particularly loathed Alfred Kazin, who had trashed *Wild Side* and whom he dubbed Elvis Zircon, the Footnote King. Over dinner in New York, Kazin had apparently questioned his ancestry. "I don't feel I'm any closer to being Jewish than I am to being a Viking," he wrote Max, who was also Jewish but nonreligious, "and I resent the period of cross-questioning by people using the tone that, if I give the right answers I can still get in. If Elvis and his old lady are Chosen People, deal around me." He had already taken a stand, not with his own ethnic group but with a far larger spectrum of humanity, and the New Critics were not going to direct his allegiance.

He saw little effective counterculture. Even the beatniks, who had their roots in a genuine literary movement, had been boosted by the media into a useless fad. When a beatnik trio headed by Allen Ginsberg passed through Chicago, Algren called them an "aid and comfort to complacency, to people who take it for granted that the proper function of the artist is to amuse, that his job is to expose himself as a gin-struck eccentric isolated from the lives of ordinary Americans. . . . They remind me of an ad I saw in a Greenwich Village window: Classes in Non-Conformity Wednesday at 9. Please be on time." This bitter, uncharitable attitude toward the only visible protest movement was perhaps rooted in his disappointment at the radicals of his own generation, who had failed to have any real effect on American life. He often found himself wondering where everyone from the thirties had gone, as if they'd all gone into hiding or sold out, while he alone was left completely alienated.

Algren believed that "literature is made upon any occasion when a challenge is put to the legal apparatus by conscience in touch with humanity," and throughout the late 1950s, he defended the literature of social protest in book reviews and articles with a voice that was effectively drowned out by the approaching tide. His remarks, often satirical, seemed too vehement next to the smooth self-confidence of the New Criticism, which was to dominate American literature for the next two decades. In describing the "new owners" of literature, Algren would write in 1960:

> They arrived directly from their respective campuses armed with blueprints to which the novel and the short story would have to conform, were a passing grade to be awarded. . . .
>
> Prewar mottos still hung on the walls, ancestral homilies offering obsolescent mysteries: "No Man is An Island." "I Have Always Depended Upon the Kindness of Strangers." "While There is a Soul in Prison I Am Not Free." Their names were something like "Leslie Fleacure," "Elvis Zircon," "Lionel Thrillingly," and "Justin Poodlespitz"—it was plain the old mottoes would have to come down. . . .

They formed a loose federation, between the literary quarterlies, publishers' offices and book review columns, presenting a view of American letters untouched by American life.

"It would be a serious mistake," writes Capetti, "to dismiss this as the private quarrel between Nelson Algren—the 'Grand Odd-Ball' of American letters, to use Norman Mailer's words—and a couple of conservative critics. Although a favorite target, Algren was not the only victim of this inquisition which purged American letters of social criticism and erased from memory the very tradition . . . to which Algren hails. The object of the campaign was less Algren himself than that long tradition of politically engaged novels which European intellectuals so admired, a tradition that had peaked during the 1930s and had found in Algren one of its most gifted interpreters. By the same token, Algren was not simply aiming at a few ill-disposed critics." Algren was in fact remaining true to his definition of the artist in taking the kind of risk by which, if one succeeds, one succeeds for all, and by which, if one fails, one fails alone. Continues Capetti: "He was attempting to stall the transformation of the literary institution in America into the formalist fortress of New Criticism."

It was a task doomed to failure.

Saying he was tired of his house in Gary, in September 1958 Algren moved back to Chicago's Northwest Side. The legal status of the house was terribly confused. Algren had transferred the title a couple of times and finally sold it to friends who wanted to help him, clearly in an attempt to cut his losses with his creditors, though he was not allowed to receive money from the sale. He still owed money on Amanda's mortgage, and in addition to the various Chicago lawyers to whom he owed thousands and the telephone companies and book-supply houses that never received payment, Harriet Pilpel was still trying to collect. Though Algren later claimed he thought she was working on a contingency basis, his willingness to pay before blowing the Pocket Books deal on *Wild Side* suggests otherwise. Pilpel claims he no longer remembers the details of the case, but Algren's loathing of her suggests she was relentless. Algren told Max she'd sent a posse after him, and a marshal with an eviction notice sent by a lady lawyer would soon appear in fiction pieces. But even if Pilpel did nothing more than threaten, it made things ripe for a move to Chicago. He offered the house to Jesse Blue and Totsie, but later changed his mind, retaining occasional access to the house until the early sixties.

For six months Algren lived in a "lightless cave off a loveless hall" on North Noble Street, then found an apartment he loved, a third-story floor-through at 1958 West Evergreen. The move back to the neighborhood where he'd written *Never Come Morning* seemed an attempt to recapture a once successful formula for self-renewal. In the last two years he'd put on a big paunch, yet at forty-seven, he told Peltz, he was going to get down to fighting weight—the only shape to be in for writing—just as in the old days.

But from his back-porch fire escape, he looked onto a world remarkably changed from the tightly woven European community he had known. Either the Chicago he knew, the neighborhood he knew, was gone, or he wasn't with it, he told a friend. He saw the same neon signs he used to see, but he didn't see them in the same way: now he just looked, and that was it. The difference was not only in himself. As in most American cities, a way of life was being lost. With Bernice's daughter, Ruth Joffe, now a grown woman, Algren went out to the dunes to see Bernice's cabin: it had just been leveled, sacrificed to the steel industry colonizing the Indiana lakeshore, and there remained only a heartrending rubble of old bedsprings and pieces of dolls. In Chicago, neighborhood after neighborhood would be razed for the interstate highway system; the house on Wabansia where he had spent the best years of his life would be demolished. Downtown, the city was building what Algren saw as "an enormous facade, a Trojan wall of steel . . . [that] will sell insurance, automobiles, booze, hi-fi." Organized crime was booming, and at the same time, surrounded by manicured suburbs and gaily decorated shopping marts, "great restless masses of Puerto Ricans, Negroes and Mountain People" were trapped in an almost visibly growing slum more lawless and dangerous than anything he'd seen in Marseilles or Naples.

The unspoken motto of America's new power brokers, Algren felt, was that there wasn't anyone who couldn't be bought. If it was distasteful to see Frank Lloyd Wright refrain from unmasking the New Chicago, it was far sadder to see Carl Sandburg selling out. When U.S. Steel staged a public-relations extravaganza called "Chicago Dynamic," it apparently paid Sandburg ten grand to be led to the new steel Prudential skyscraper, heart of "Carl Sandburg's Chicago," and parrot the meaningless city slogan, "I will." Algren felt they'd done everything but paint the old man's cheeks, trotting him around in an obscene routine driven by a boundless enthusiasm for loot. And it wasn't just that the man who said the slums take their revenge and that some men couldn't be bought had repudiated himself but that the PR men were presenting a city that wasn't there, a plastic mannequin instead of a living being. And Algren knew he had touched the real Chicago. "I married the real girl, slept with her, battled her, made up, caught her lying, forgave her, betrayed her myself but never quit feeling she belonged to me," he told Max, and he didn't like seeing the dummy marched out as Chicago while the real woman waited in the alley.

He sensed that eight years in Gary had drawn him irrevocably away from the underworld; he'd have been closer to home had he lived in New York. "It's as if, beginning in 1940, I started building a life-size drama," he wrote Max, "using the neighborhood people for all people, and kept casting and recasting, picking up props out of women's court or in a hotel and locking everything up in '42 and dusting it off again in '45 and finding then the parts began fitting more easily, until I had the marquis [*sic*] lit and the doors open and a few early comers looking curiously in and the actors wrangling in the wings—and then moved to the little house in the country. Wow. I still get letters, almost always from young people asking, 'Is that *all*?' with a challenging, yet really let-down feeling."

The new times felt empty, meaningless; and more than other writers, Algren was—and had always been—extremely sensitive to the social climate and dependent upon it for his writing. "Twenty years ago people were asking, 'What is going to happen to Man?' " Algren felt. "They used to talk like that, as if they were connected to one another." Literature now seemed a commodity; the endless cold-war propaganda that touted America and its people as the best had done its job. "I thought I'd make a dent," he told an interviewer about his earlier work. "I didn't make the least dent, because there is no way of convincing or even making the slightest impression on the American middle class that there are people who have no alternative, that there are people who live in horror, that there are people whose lives are nightmares. . . . The world of the drug addict doesn't exist. . . . The world of the murderer doesn't exist. Nothing that does not touch the person individually exists. . . . I thought there was a certain sentience. I thought there was something you could reach. Now I don't think it can be reached."

It was a combination of all these factors that made Nelson Algren finally abandon serious literature: a sense that society no longer had any interest in the ideas that had formed the heart of his work; a sense that he would be innocently offering them to a world that would merely slap them down; and a sense that to present more such books would be an invitation, and an acquiescence, to the kind of exploitation worked upon him by Preminger. Algren had wanted a reward for the years of emotional effort he put into his novels; he had instead received rejection. And he was not the kind of artist who could sit in his room and continue producing regardless of how the world felt about his work.

"The past is a bucket of ashes," he told a young woman who came out to visit him in Gary, and indeed he made it so. As if deliberately thumbing his nose at the New Critics, he now found his last novel superior to *Golden Arm* "by sixteen furlongs and eleven lengths." But to do this he had to self-destructively insult his best work: "*Arm* was a solid job which humanized and personalized an American streetcorner," he now said. "In a decade of books written by ribbon salesmen it appeared almost a great book." When a hooker in the back of a bar told him that in *Wild Side* he'd gotten the life just right, he knew that the publishers and Kazin had been too uptight to catch that it really *was* an American ballet, and a surefire bet for a musical. "*A Walk on the Wild Side* is a kind of novel that, so far as I know, has never been written before," he said now. "It is an American fantasy written to a beat as true as *Huckleberry Finn*." His new love for *Wild Side*—if it was real—was founded out of the belief, it seems, that the novel's farcical tone fit very well these times everyone took so seriously, and his new affection for the book surely made it easier to cope with the fact that the kind of writing he considered serious was regarded as anachronistic.

Over and over again he would remark that nobody wanted serious fiction, that to write it was a loser's game. He now offered the first National Book Award up for sale, saying its purpose was merely to unify the publishing industry's publicity departments. With the loss of the old Chicago, "Entrapment" would have been almost impossible to write anyway, and he abandoned it, though he occasionally looked at it in the years to follow. In the October 1958 issue of *Esquire,* "Goodbye to Old Rio," an evocation of the gas-station fiasco that had so long before started him writing, was a kind of farewell to his career as a serious novelist. For there would be no new novel, he assured a friend. "Who *for*? I used to think it was for some vague assemblage called readers. I used to think it was for some people named Cowley and Sartre and such too. But all it turns out it is for is someone like Rapietta Greensponge, girl counselor," a reference to Pilpel, whose apparent threat to take his house had been the last straw. "Maybe she did me a lefthanded favor at that," he wrote Max, "because she cured me of taking writing, mine or anybody else's, seriously."

But before the attacks of the New Critics, writing had always been for him a source of love from the outside world; and though he seems to have believed that in giving it up he was getting back at the world, he was really only hurting himself. This self-destructive force was evident in the way he began inexplicably cutting off old friends. Now, after twenty-five years of friendship, he cut Jack Conroy off completely by ridiculing him in print as "J. C. Kornpoen." With an equal lack of apparent reason, Algren would soon cut off the Rowlands in particular Chris, saying that if she came to a party at Studs Terkel's, where he was, he would leave. He would shortly drop work on a picture book he'd started with Shay because he wasn't permitted to publish the text beforehand, then mimicked Shay at a party the photographer missed. When Art heard about it later on the street, their friendship cooled.

Increasingly, he alienated others through self-centered and inconsiderate behavior. Though he religiously repaid gambling losses and debts to Studs and other friends, he seemed to be constantly trying to get even with a world he felt had ripped him off financially. Once, after being paid $500 to lecture at Wayne State University, he told Art Shay and suggested in a letter to Max Geismar that he went to the home of a rich professor to chat with students over coffee and refreshments, answered questions politely, but when it was time to go discreetly cleared his throat. "Uh, I think you owe me a hundred bucks," he said he told his host, receiving it without an argument. And he may have swindled a man out of three thousand dollars for rights to *Wild Side* that had already been sold—or at least he shamefully admitted so to Peltz, who merely asked why, if he was going to be a crook, hadn't he tried for a hundred grand? Nelson acted as if he just hadn't thought of it. "You figure him out," Peltz said in exasperation.

And there were times when such actions became pathetic. Charles Gold, a student at the University of Missouri at Columbia, recalled how Algren came there to give a reading and teach a small series of seminars during the 1959–1960 academic year. "Nelson was drunk a good deal of the time, or acted drunk, which I suspect amounts to the same thing," Gold remembered. "He talked at great length about having seen someone's ruined shoes in a shaft of sunlight in a dirty basement. He also talked about either a friend or a character whose name was, I think, Stahouska." This was indeed Nelson's "Lostball" Stahouska, the fictional batter who secretly caught the ball in play, ran the bases while the bewildered fielders searched for it, then pulled it out of his pocket between third and home because he had a guilty conscience—though he could steal for the Chicago cops with impunity.

Among the students was a friendly young woman with an "exuberant figure" and breasts that were the talk of the men in the department. "Algren moved in with her," Gold recalled, "stayed for several days, and gave every indication of having settled in for the long haul. Once the novelty wore off, she complained that he was drinking and eating her out of house and home and asked for some help in getting rid of him.

"He had, as I recall, no money at all. We bought him a train ticket from Columbia to St. Louis, and from St. Louis to Chicago, and poured him on the train, tucking some meal money in his pockets as well."

There were of course, good times. Before their split, he and Art Shay had clowned around town with Marcel Marceau when the mime was in Chicago, and in early 1960, *A Walk on the Wild Side* became a musical staged by Jay and Fran Landesman at the Crystal Palace, a plush cabaret in St. Louis. Algren and Fran wrote the lyrics, Tommy Wolfe wrote the score, and Dave Peltz directed the show and produced it with Jay Landesman. Peltz did most of the work while Nelson watched rehearsals, played a lot of poker, and drank and socialized at the Crystal Palace, where he met his longtime friend Joan Kerckhoff, a pretty, young, street-wise "cracker with a poetic streak," as Algren described her, who wanted to write. Fran Landesman remembered Nelson as charming but difficult, loyal but quick to take offense, with a contribution more confusing than helpful. About the play itself, Algren's opinion was, "Music—excellent, direction solid, lyrics fine, story mine." The show didn't make it to Broadway, but it was successful in St. Louis, and one of the songs was later recorded by Carol Lawrence, of *West Side Story* fame.

Even more pleasantly, Algren began seeing Geraldine Page again.

Shay and Marilou Kogan both remember how crazy Algren was about Page, who once pretended to be a retiring English teacher at a holiday party at the Geismars'. Page and Algren admired each other's work and were, Page said, somewhat in awe of each other. And Algren loved her celebrity status. Once, when Page was appearing in *Sweet Bird of Youth,* he met her after the show at Downey's, a show business hangout. Shelley Winters was there, and Paul Newman and Joanne Woodward took the table across from them. Algren was "droll, faintly sardonic," a friend remembered, "like a big butter and egg man with a famous actress on his arm."

In the fall of 1959, Algren had met the writer and novelist John Clellon Holmes, who had written a *Chicago Review* article on Existentialism and the novel that referred to Algren as "the only American novelist, whose point of view matured during the Depression, that we can read today." At Algren's invitation, they had drinks at the Oak Bar at New York's Plaza Hotel, where Algren, either a recent winner at the track or in a mood to be good to himself, was staying. "When I first met Nelson Algren, he was fifty years old, and he was wearing the loud, checked jacket and wide, Day-Glo tie of the short-odds bettor at the two-dollar window of a downstate Midwest racetrack," Holmes wrote later. Algren was playing the hick, his eyes boggling at the check, hands fumbling for his wallet. "He could be infectiously funny if you got on his wavelength, his savvy eyes aglow, his drawling delivery a little theatrical," and Holmes warmed to him. But as the evening wore on and they discussed Nathanael West and Richard Wright, Holmes sensed that Algren's getup and mannerism were part of "an elaborate put-on, the act of a man secretly bored, secretly aggravated by most things around him, and trying to amuse himself."

He would, of course, have to continue writing, to keep himself intellectually occupied and to make a living, but he could do so painlessly by selling articles to the glossy magazines and then collecting them into books. For this, his new agent, Candida Donadio, was an absolute godsend. "I happen to have had an agent who hung a very low price tag on herself—which was appropriate for herself," Algren said later of Maddy Brennan, "but she wrapped me into her crackerjack box. . . . James Jones gets three-quarters of a million dollars, Algren gets a free train-ride to New York. They know what the price is." He felt Donadio understood right away that the problem was to get him out of the free-train-ride league. For a while, any low-class skin magazine could pick up an Algren story by paying a token sum to Doubleday, since Ingersoll and Brennan had sold off those rights years before. Donadio got all these back.

Now when he wrote he turned increasingly to evoking nostalgia for the past or satirizing the present. In 1959, when the White Sox won the pennant for the first time in forty years, Algren covered the World Series for the *Sun-Times*. Woven into the stories he turned in were remembrances of the rigged 1919 series he'd bet on as a child, and as the years went by he would write more and more pieces that harked back to the past. But for describing the present, satire seemed the perfect genre. The literary scene, standing on the space the businessmen had bought, was a bit too absurd to take seriously: alongside a mean-spirited and homophobic caricature of James Baldwin would come a memorable if petty depiction of Norman Mailer, whose recent book, *Advertisements for Myself,* had a title that fit the times. Gracing a New York cocktail party, the self-aggrandizing Norman Manlifellow sported a self-promotional sandwich board and one sock that said, "Look at me!" while the other urged, "*Keep* looking!" A fan of the confrontational comedian Lenny Bruce, Algren was one of a number of American actors and artists beginning to explore satire as the 1960s dawned.

By late February 1960, he was back in New York, where he met Herbert Mitgang, whose novel *The Return* he had favorably reviewed, and began work on a travel book that would combine both nostalgia and satire. He had at long last been granted a passport. Though Nelson had known nothing about it, the FBI had finally given up its more than two-year effort to prosecute him for fraud against the government, despite the fact that it had obtained a copy of Algren's signed confession to typewriter theft from the Brewster County Jail and had tricked him into providing a handwriting sample by sending agents to his home to accuse him of writing pornographic letters. The bureau had never gotten anything that would stand up in court; and because Algren had refrained from political activity for five years, he was deleted from the Security Index. Moreover, after various court challenges, the State Department could no longer withhold passports without good reason. After a bon-voyage party in a cramped apartment, filled with "knots of antagonistic people from different parts of his life" including Norman and Adele Mailer, the Landesmans, gamblers, prizefighters, literary agents, and book reviewers, Algren boarded the first-class section of an ocean liner bound for Europe. After a two-year lapse between their letters, he and Simone had decided they ought to see each other again before they died.

Reading Simone's *Memoirs of a Dutiful Daughter* in the summer of 1959, Algren felt that as a teenager, Beauvoir had naively decided, I *will* be of service to humanity!—and that she had succeeded. "There never seems to be a moment when she was diverted or let herself falter," he wrote Max wistfully. "If she got sidetracked, she found her way back or made a new road." Algren was not that strong. From now on he would deliberately call himself a journalist, a totally different creature from the artist he had been. On the one hand, he wanted to protect himself; on the other, to spite the world. He was never going to write a big book again; he was never going to go all out. Yet in so doing he was robbing himself of the art that had consistently made his life meaningful. Through his writing he had always sought connection to the great mass of humanity; but this was a turning away, a closing of the heart. He had made a new road; but it would never be as important as the old one.

IV

This headlong flight from living, toward making believe that one is alive . . .

—NELSON ALGREN

© *Stephen Deutch*

18.
Who Lost an American?

AFTER A WEEK IN LONDON meeting old friends, and a few days in Ireland meeting Brendan Behan and the poet Patrick Kavanaugh, in March 1960, Algren arrived in Paris, the city that had been a haven in his mind for more than eight years. He and Simone were surely delighted to see each other, yet Simone's recollection that they immediately felt as close as in 1949 was hardly the truth. The intervening years had sent their lives in different directions. Simone's reputation as a writer and champion of women's rights had grown with each passing year. In 1949 she had been mocked, cartooned, vilified, and ridiculed by the French press; in 1960 Algren would write respectfully, "She was feared. She had broken through the defenses of the bourgeoisie, of the church, the businessmen, the right-wing defenders of Napoleonic glory, and the hired press. She was, at once, the most hated and the most loved woman in France. It had become plain: she *meant* it." In 1949 Algren had been heralded as a major talent in American literature; but now he couldn't even get an advance on a novel. Every morning he woke up angry, saying he'd been devoured, betrayed, made into a sucker; once he had lived in America, but now he just lived on American-occupied land.

Though he'd been given only a temporary passport and had to ask the U.S. Embassy three times before it was finally extended, Algren, having always wanted more time with Simone, decided to stay for six months. But according to her biographer, Deirdre Bair, Simone was upset because so long a visit would interfere with her work—which at the time was, as usual, Sartre's editing, research, writing, or any other chores he had for her. Throughout Algren's stay, according to Bair, she would drop whatever she was doing whenever she was needed to help Sartre. However, according to Simone's memoirs, she and Nelson lived together once again, saw Paris, took long walks, made a pilgrimage to the Rue de la Bûcherie. Algren had a movie camera and on the Rue Saint-Denis filmed prostitutes from a car window as they heckled and threatened him; he teased friends with a battery-lit bow tie and night after night dined with Simone on steak and Beaujolais. But Algren's bitterness remained. Her friends recalled that he drank a lot and ranted about how Preminger and the publishing world had screwed him. Simone, who had a reputation for being insensitive to others' needs and feelings, may not have been too sympathetic. When she asked him about his next novel he said that big books took too long; he wasn't going to put in four years on one—his latest explanation for his abandonment of serious fiction, but in its superficiality suggesting he was not really confiding in her or that she was not probing too deeply. It was undoubtedly not easy living with Algren's bitterness or his dependence on her (he would not learn French). When Simone took to spending mornings and several evenings a week with Sartre, it was surely to escape Algren's moods as much as to work.

Algren also had work to do—his travel book—but he wasn't particularly productive. He wrote scads of humorous, lighthearted, even silly letters to friends at home and preoccupied himself with all kinds of "business." He tried to interest the German publisher Rowohlt, Spearman in London, and Gallimard in Paris in his work and in books by Holmes, Geismar, and Kogan, and eventually arranged German publication of Holmes's *The Horn*. He was also fascinated by the idea of seeing the musical of *Wild Side* staged in Europe and urged Peltz to come to Paris so they could work on the script. Peltz felt this was an act of desperation, that Algren was trying to sell everybody on a great play that didn't even belong to him: the rights had already been sold.

In late April Algren traveled alone to Spain to attend an International Congress of Writers in Mallorca. He fell in love with Barcelona, spending most of his three days there among the poor people living in shanties on the city's rooftops. At the writers' conference he gave a speech on American literature, suggesting that the true spirit of America could be found in revolutionary Cuba. Then, after meeting Simone and writer Juan Goytisolo in Madrid, he and Simone set off for Seville, Tiana, Malaga, Torremolinos, and Almería. Algren loved Spain, and they spent three more days in Granada before returning to Paris.

There were many Americans in Paris in 1960, and Algren had no lack of friends. Studs "Transatlantic" Terkel arrived that summer, bringing Bessie Smith records and interviewing Simone on her recent trip to Cuba. The resourceful Terkel located Marcel Marceau, and he and Nelson saw the mime once more; they visited the Musée Grevin, a children's fun house of mirrors that Nelson adored with a childlike wonder; and Studs remembered a spirited Algren, attired in fatigue jacket, leading him through the dining room and kitchen of a fancy Parisian eatery, insisting it was a shortcut to Les Halles, while the maître d', waiters, and cooks chased after them, shaking their fists and shouting. James Jones, whom Algren found irksome, was also in town. "I should think he would be proud of making a million bucks out of the worst writing of the decade," was Algren's view, "but he doesn't see it that way." Jones's wife, Gloria, however, was "real fine." But among the Americans he met, Algren could not stand those who formed cliques among themselves: Algren felt they'd left small American towns they found unendurable, "so they had immediately set up small Fort Dodges and East Jesuses on the Left Bank in order to Keep Paris Away," complaining all the while about the lack of cheeseburgers and bacon and eggs; they didn't socialize with the French or want to learn the language.

Though he spent a lot of time with them, Algren did not seem to see himself as such an American. Simone disliked this enclave and was vexed by the amount of time Algren spent with the people in it. She felt that they too had grudges with America that had brought them to France, and that they reinforced the negative feelings Algren had brought with him. Relations were further strained when the willful, imperious de Beauvoir decided to go on a summer vacation with Sartre for several weeks, leaving Algren alone in her apartment.

That summer Nelson and Simone spent a few days in a no-longer-wild Marseilles and took a two-week jet trip to Istanbul and Greece. Istanbul was crowded and noisy and unbearably sexist, and after three days they flew to Greece, saw Athens, and arrived on Crete. They spent a week in the ancient fishing port of Herakleion, where Algren enjoyed watching the docks and accompanied the fishermen on one of their nightly trips. Then he and Simone returned to Paris, Simone preparing to depart for Cuba with Sartre, and again leaving Nelson stranded.

Algren stayed on in her apartment, spending time with Jacques Bost, who remembered that Algren was deeply upset at being abandoned and drank a lot. After so many warm invitations from Simone to come and live in Paris, Algren had finally received a passport and come to her, but she was too busy for him, he was no longer important to her. Earlier Algren had told Simone that he had once found himself walking without thinking toward the apartment they shared in 1949, as if his body were still living in the past. When Simone asked if the past had been so much better, he blurted that when he was forty, he hadn't realized he was middle-aged—he'd thought life was just beginning. But now the past was gone.

After winning handsomely at the Deauville track, he left France on September 5. He wrote Holmes that he wanted to take a slow boat back to America. He'd been in Europe long enough, but he wasn't eager to go home. There was no love left and no meaningful work.

Back in the United States, after a pleasant weekend with a young woman named Judy and John Clellon Holmes and his wife, Shirley, in Connecticut, Algren "arrived in the city of the big flannel shoulders . . . and mounted mechanically into the deep gloom of a flat where the calendar stopped in February." Seven months of *The New York Times Book Review* blocked the door and the landlady followed him up the stairs. "I felt like telling her I had never left the flat, because that was how I began to feel."

By spring 1961, he had made a few decisions about his future. For one thing, he would write what he wanted. Although he owed the short-story book to William Targ, the travel book would come first. When Targ didn't want it, Candida Donadio sold it to Macmillan, even though this apparently meant giving Macmillan an option on his next fiction after Targ's book. Beyond publishing one or two stories a year, and writing poems sometimes picked up by *The Nation,* he was now writing primarily nonfiction: the travel book, essays, memoirs, and book reviews—he was an early supporter of *Catch-22.* For a new edition of *The Neon Wilderness,* he wrote a challenging introduction mocking the New Critics; in 1961 a well-received reissue of *City on the Make,* dedicated to the Kogans, also carried an Algren introduction on the state of American letters, and in the next two years he would brilliantly introduce a new edition of *Never Come Morning* and an anthology of short stories by other authors. He wrote moving tributes to Richard Wright and Ernest Hemingway, who died that year. But he mocked his own efforts. "Pried open the door to a new field with a tribute to Richard Wright," he reported to Holmes.

"Now have a tape on Hemingway on the market." For a $650 speaking engagement at the University of Washington, he had, by his own account, "sucked and smiled and wheedled and lapped and meached and dandled and fondled and whinnied."

It was difficult to leave behind the Chicago he'd once felt so connected to, and it haunted him those first years after he gave up being a serious novelist. In his imagination, lost people he'd seen so often on Wabansia kept approaching from the shadows, and he wrote a sad farewell to them in a poem called "Tricks Out of Time Long Gone," in which, in an atmosphere strikingly similar to his old work, the lost came forward from a mist of dreams. Revealingly, after the poem appeared in *The Nation*, he also included it in the travel book *Who Lost an American?*; over the next ten years he revised it again and again and included it in his final collection of stories, *The Last Carousel.*

Ironically, like another remnant from his past, letters from Paris arrived signed "Your own Simone," as if everything had been renewed. Complaining that his letters didn't tell her anything, she urged him to write, and asked if she could come to Chicago. He was unenthusiastic and noncommittal enough to discourage her. In a bitter, unpublished poem, he determined to free himself of his old, dead love, but he did not tell Simone this. He had sent her three letters before returning to the States, had left her a poem. He no longer expected as much from her, and he was not going to pretend a grand passion, but they were still friends.

In the early 1960s, Algren was quite sociable. He often threw parties in his Evergreen Avenue apartment, making lasagne while his housekeeper, Mary Corley, fried chicken for the festivities, which lasted into the morning and spilled onto the back porch. He found a new friend in the photographer Stephen Deutch, who was putting together a book about Chicago with Herman Kogan and photographed Nelson for a book jacket. "I would go and look at places with Nelson—bars, taverns, wrestling matches, the races, boxing—just for the fun of it, and I was making photographs," said Deutch. Every couple of weeks Algren and Deutch had lunch at Riccardo, a newspaper hangout, with journalist Mike Royko or Herman Kogan or Studs Terkel, with whom Algren also spent a lot of time. "My idea of a redundant sentence," Nelson once wrote: "Terkel phoned excitedly." These two lively, witty, irreverent cigar-smoking Chicago pals played weekly poker, went to blues clubs and to Jazz Limited. Algren fictionalized a Terkel interview into a story, "Star and Garter," about a couple of married midwest shysters who become rich in legitimate business, and in early 1960, Terkel put on a radio show, *Come In at the Door,* for which Algren read from his unpublished works. Algren encouraged Terkel in compiling the kind of oral-history interviews for which he would eventually win the Pulitzer Prize.

In the spring of 1961, Madeleine Gobeil, a French-Canadian student writing a thesis about de Beauvoir, wrote to Algren asking him to show her America. Simone, whom she'd met the summer before in Paris, had encouraged her to look him up. In her early twenties, bright, sensitive, Gobeil would enjoy success in the next few years interviewing writers for *Playboy, The Paris Review,* and other magazines, but she wrote Algren that she felt trapped in Canada. When she came to Chicago in August, he was immediately smitten. "Hey, that was a goddamn *girl,*" he wrote Dave Peltz, "a real honest-to-god *girl*. You talk about surprised, I'm still in shock. A Canuck of pure gold." Not long afterward, Madeleine met Studs, the Kogans, Holmes, Peltz, Deutch, all his closest friends, and he took her to the races, to swim at the house in Gary, to Jazz Limited; he showed her sections of the travel book as he finished them. When she was in Montreal, they wrote frequently; sometimes he sent her money or plane tickets. They planned to spend Christmas in Chicago, but were invited for two weeks at a villa in Palm Beach and took full advantage. Then they spent two days in New York, going to the theater and then to Spanish Harlem with Joseph Heller. At the end of the two weeks Nelson was still bubbling with enthusiasm for her.

On one occasion, Madeleine went with him to meet James Baldwin in a South Side motel, but the meeting turned uneasy. Algren admired Baldwin as an essayist, and had brought along a gift of *City on the Make*. But a tense conversation ranging from the Reverend Martin Luther King, Jr., to Malcolm X made Algren feel he was being held to account for crimes against the Negro race simply because he was white. One of the "young studs" there, as Nelson described them, "all young guys . . . with a very hostile air," picked up his gift, looked at Algren's picture, said, "That man's dead!" and threw it into a corner. Another talked about throwing out the by now huffy Algren, who turned toward the one who'd threatened him and said, "Listen, *boy* . . ."

"That broke it up," Algren said, laughing about it later. "Baldwin jumped up, shaking, waggling his finger and said, 'You *said* it! You *said* it! You *said* it! You *said* it! You *said* "*boy*"!' "

"I said, 'Yeah, I'm a white supremacist, but it took you six hours to get it out of me. That's what you wanted me to say. That's all you've been driving at.' " Suprisingly, the evening ended with handshakes and good luck, and Baldwin sarcastically told Algren he was "an honorable, well-meaning white square;" he had become quite friendly with Madeleine, who seemed very pleased with the whole scene. "But I sort of watched it going down the stairs," Algren said, chuckling.

In July 1961, eighty-five-year-old Goldie died of heart disease in the private Chicago nursing home where Algren had put her because she was too proud to go to the county hospital. The day before she had heard a murmur of steam from the radiator. "Voices are coming up from below," she kept repeating rhythmically, and Nelson, surprised, felt she'd put her last strength into making a poem: he later said he thought this was a sort of final acknowledgment of his poetry.

He did not seem troubled by his mother's death, beyond its strain on his financial resources. The home threatened to hold Goldie's body until he paid up, but at Dave's suggestion, Algren told them to keep it: Goldie was quickly released. The undertaker shamed Algren into buying a top-of-the-line casket and expensive roses; later he was furious at the way he'd been conned à la Mitford's *American Way of Death*. Nelson vowed to give the mortician less than the full amount, and the dispute dragged on for years. And when Morris Joffe wanted him to pay for the upkeep of Goldie's grave, Algren refused: he'd already been helping to support her for almost twenty years.

No one remained of his immediate family, as his sister Irene, to whom he'd never been close, had died in 1960. Although he claimed to put the whole thing out of his mind, Goldie's death reawakened feelings of his childhood which he put to nostalgic use, writing an especially sympathetic portrait of his long-dead father. Published as "The Father and Son Cigar" in *Playboy* and included in the travel book as one of four sections on Chicago, it was highly praised, and he later revised it for his last collection of short stories.

With the travel book finished, he now began to expand the long tribute to Hemingway he'd written for *The Nation*. He couldn't believe the critics, especially Dwight Macdonald, had seen in Hemingway only an extroverted naturalistic writer, the man on the front lines or the safari. Algren saw him as a nocturnal writer, closer to Poe and Hawthorne than to the adventurer he had projected himself as. "He was not an athletic young man from Oak Park," Algren disputed the critics, "he was a soldier whose life had been broken in two." And Algren knew all about being different from one's image.

Once a week he played poker with Peltz, Studs, future moviemaker William Friedkin, a tall man known as Big Chief, and a man named Frank, who owned a chain of check-cashing stores and whose two brothers, both Chicago cops, were doing time for murder while he supported their families. Frank often won, and after losing especially badly one night, Nelson called Peltz the next morning and told him not to pay, that Frank and Big Chief were in cahoots. Studs also heard the story, but he paid. Out of friendship to Nelson, however, Peltz withheld payment, but called Frank and suggested they all get together and talk about it. The meeting never materialized, and one day Peltz went over to the house on Evergreen. Algren didn't answer the door. Peltz gained access and climbed the stairs to find Nelson pressed against the wall clutching a baseball bat, sure Peltz's steps were those of the gamblers coming to collect. "He was terrified," Peltz said, laughing. "I said, 'Nelson, you're going to have a heart attack.' " But Algren wasn't going to pay, because he had plans for that money.

For, with the book finished, he was going to travel before his passport expired, and not to the prosperity of Europe but to the Third World. When he told Candida he needed money to go abroad, she thought of getting an advance for an anthology of short stories selected by Nelson, published that year as *Nelson Algren's Own Book of Lonesome Monsters*. All he had to do was write a provocative little introduction whose theme was that "in order to make Man free, we must first understand what Man is"—even if he is a monster. Money in hand, Nelson went to an Indiana travel agent who found that for twelve hundred dollars he could make a three-month tour of the Far East. He invited Madeleine to come along, but she wanted to work on her degree. (Later she seemed annoyed that he had gone without her: "*You* figure them out," he wrote Holmes.) He booked passage. The ship would travel from Seattle to Japan, Korea, Hong Kong, Malaysia, India, Pakistan, and the Philippines. Though he naturally told Targ he was planning to use the leisure time to work on the stories, he was actually planning to develop the Hemingway essay into a book. He slipped down to Columbia, Missouri, picked up a little lecture money, and left for Seattle.

The ship was a freighter, the only other passenger a Chinese woman, and during the tedious landless weeks aboard he read Hemingway and his critics, working out ideas on the typewriter. He played poker regularly with the ship's crew, and when he lost he learned he could get the roll back by smuggling transistors. As the weeks passed, he came to see the vessel as a kind of traveling prison full of "very submerged men," some of whom never went ashore. The American crew isolated itself from the people in the ports and, confident that Asians were inferior to them, eyed them with contempt. At every port the docks were crowded with prostitutes, merchants, and servants waiting for the American sailors to spend money. If the sailors didn't come at least once a month, one mama-san said, they had to sell their clothes. Thus, Algren felt, in a small-scale model of U.S. foreign policy, the Asians were obliged to do whatever the Americans wanted.

As for the prostitution, the women were so desperate that Joes could pay whatever they liked. In the port of Pusan, he wrote later, he spent the night with a woman named Po-Tin in an earthen shack. With Nelson, such a liaison included basic human kindness; in the morning they had instant coffee because that was all she had. Later he found that her pimp had taken the ten dollars he'd left and split her lip. "Girls, I thought, those with hair like light and those with hair darkly piled; girls, I thought, with smiles still expectant and those with no smile at all; girls, I thought, whether in sleep or waking, lips parted in wonder or suddenly laughing: girls have a hard time of it everywhere."

In the heat, rain, and horror that was the parkless, liquorless city of Bombay, the women "are kept in cages," he wrote Lily Harmon, "they really are. Mothers, sweethearts, wives, [and] daughters go into a great cage and live in it, trying to screw their fathers, husbands, and lovers out of debt. They are from ten years old to great age, are barred in as animals are barred, except that they die in there of starvation if they are not chosen; whereas an animal would be fed." From this experience he would fashion "Kalyani-of-the-Four-Hundred," a powerful indictment of prostitution constructed of a sequence of narratives, each a numbered cage describing how the woman inside had come to live there. No other commentary was necessary.

While in Asia, Algren experienced a moment of insight into himself, but revealingly claimed not to see its full significance. In Calcutta he stayed for a week with a prostitute who had an apartment with books and records and supported a mother, a son, and a servant, though she did not like to sell her "bud-*dee*." One night when she was out working, two men from the ship came by to visit Algren and got drunk. A fight broke out, and Algren suddenly found himself chased by a knife-wielding sailor, wondering, he later told an interviewer, why didn't this happen to Saul Bellow? Or Alfred Kazin? Why should *he* be running down the corridor of a Calcutta tenement chased by a homicidal sailor? He should have been asleep in his quiet little nest in Chicago, and instead he was halfway around the world facing imminent death. If he had been self-destructive, he said, Hart Crane or Dylan Thomas or somebody, he could have understood it—but he wasn't he told his listeners, and perhaps he really believed it.

Meanwhile, Peltz had received a series of threatening phone calls and had been sitting in the living room of his house on the beach at about one-thirty A.M. when an enormous concrete block came crashing through the window. Then came another through the bedroom window. He heard the heavy, flatfooted steps of Big Chief running away, and a half hour later Frank called: "Dave, pay up, mother-fucker, or get killed." Peltz told him he'd broken the wrong window. "I know, but he's on a slow boat to China," replied Frank.

"We met at the Russian Baths on Division Street," Peltz remembered. "I was waiting—it was a Sunday around noon—and he pulls up in a big-assed Lincoln. He took a baseball bat out of the trunk: 'Are you alone?' I said yes." They went to the baths, and when they came out Dave gave Frank the $250, but Frank wasn't through with him. "He said now we had to go spend it," Dave remembered, "and we went from tavern to tavern to tavern drinking and spending, while I heard all about his family, his wife, everything." Friendship had been fully restored.

How Nelson settled this debt upon return to the States is not clear, but the reviews for *Lonesome Monsters,* which included stories by Bellow, James Blake, Bruce Jay Friedman, Joseph Heller, and Nelson's young protégée Joan Kerckhoff, were not bad at all. And in November, Madeleine came down from Montreal to see him.

*

Who Lost an American?—a tour of New York, various European cities, Istanbul, Crete, and Chicago—appeared in May 1963, dedicated to Simone. In a disingenuously innocent though hilarious first-person narrative, Algren had made his literary enemies into caricatures, although his gibes at James "Giovanni Johnson" Baldwin's homosexuality, which Madeleine urged him to delete, were rather tasteless. The account of his first-class transatlantic crossing was also funny but a little cheap. But despite its lighthearted meandering through de Beauvoir's Paris and Europe, the book grew increasingly serious as it reached the Chicago sections, which contained the best writing. Aside from the moving piece on his childhood, he had included one essay on Chicago corruption and another on the decline of the arts in the Second City. The final section was a lengthy, well-researched essay on *Playboy*. Algren felt that in its preoccupation with material wealth and women who could not be touched, *Playboy* was symptomatic of an America that had moved from what he called a "first person" country to a "third person" country, a world full of people who lived vicariously instead of being connected to humanity, "more at ease with a depiction of passion than with passion itself." The magazine and key clubs, flourishing in an era when dancers were careful not to touch each other, objectified women, generating feelings of contempt toward them to avoid intimacy and coming to terms with their humanity.

Although the Chicago sections were well received, the reviews were mixed. John Clellon Holmes thought that at times it was "an embarrassment," and critics almost invariably asked why Algren was not working on something significant, like a novel. It was difficult to judge a book that leaped from utter satire to serious essay. Some critics found the overall tone "surrealist and grotesque," edged with "venom and sourness," and *Time*'s review, "Intellectual as Ape Man," couldn't be beat for nastiness. One reviewer, cutting in close, saw the book as a record of Algren's anxieties as a writer. "Caught between his own past, in which a deep identification with the social outcast and the working class was all but inseparable from his sense of literary vocation, and the present, in which money seems to brutalize equally those who have too much and those who have too little, Algren seems to have lost all sense of what useful literary tasks might remain open to him."

Algren never fooled himself that he was writing great literature and undoubtedly felt the book was being taken too seriously. He himself may not have been in love with it. Discussing her forthcoming autobiography, Simone—who still wrote longer letters to his short ones—remarked, "I guess, like the Lost American, it had no right to be written," as if he had already said this. For the first time, the critics didn't seem to bother him too much, probably because attacks on Algren by formalist critics and in academic studies were still continuing in the early sixties and he had learned not to take them seriously. He was more concerned that the book wasn't selling, and, as if he still had faith in an audience, his relations with Macmillan soured accordingly.

The previous year he had begun giving a series of interviews to a young New York writer named H. E. F. "Shag" Donohue. A national magazine had been interested in them, and Shag had come twice to Chicago to talk with him about his childhood, beginnings as a writer, and experiences in Hollywood. Stephen Deutch recalled that, though Nelson pooh-poohed the interviews, he actually seemed to have mixed feelings about them. He didn't like exposing himself, but enjoyed the attention and found reminiscing stimulating. In the spring of 1963, Candida sold the interviews as a book to Hill & Wang, so Algren returned to New York for more interviews and met Madeleine for a weekend.

In August, however, Madeleine was planning to leave for Paris. Her letters to him suggest that Algren had probably asked her to stay with him, perhaps even to marry him, but Madeleine always felt anxious in the United States and Canada, and in Paris she would have access to de Beauvoir while completing her thesis. Shortly before they met for the last time at the Hotel Chelsea in New York, she wrote him, hoping that final meeting would be one of joy. Algren told her often that she had given him joy, and she too seemed grateful for their time together. Algren, supportive of her plans for Paris, told her she might find her roots there; his deeper feelings remain unknown.

In the middle of August, Algren arrived, brimming with tales of poker games en route, at the Bread Loaf Writers' Conference, near Middlebury, Vermont. Carolyn Gaiser, a journalist posing as an aspiring poet while covering the conference for *Glamour* magazine, met him there and remembered his huge stack of letters, his talk of leaving a steak nailed to his door as a reproach for the dining hall's lack of decent beef, and his generosity to young talent. "Algren emerged as the hero of Bread Loaf," Gaiser recalled, "a kind of Christ figure from Chicago with boundless compassion." He referred the then unknown novelist Russell Banks to Candida Donadio and arranged for the young folk singer Cornelia Hall to make her debut on FM radio. Meanwhile the witty Gaiser, in her early twenties, caught Nelson's eye. Just back from three years in Italy on a Fulbright scholarship, she had the youth and European flair of Madeleine. Toward the end of the conference she and Algren became lovers.

They exchanged letters throughout September, and in October met again in New York. They explored jazz clubs and Harlem bars and saw Woody Allen at The Bitter End, Nelson later writing the jokes down on index cards for possible future use in lectures. Their feelings for each other were intense, and Carolyn stayed with him at the Chelsea—except on the nights when he was playing poker. This was her first real love affair, and she thought Nelson was the funniest man she had ever met. But she was baffled at his constant letter-writing to James Blake and Joan Kerckhoff and other budding writers and soon realized that her role in the affair was to be consistently funny, an effort that quickly grew tedious. Although it became clear that Algren's feeling for her was not so strongly romantic, they remained friends. She accompanied him to a debate with William Buckley, to which he brought Sartre's book on Cuba, sure he was going to be the first left-winger to triumph over the master debater. However, the highly articulate and quick-witted Buckley reduced Algren to humming "Tea for Two" through clenched teeth and heading directly for a bar after the show. Naturally, in the following weeks Algren would reinvent the story to show that it was *he* who had kayoed *Buckley*.

That fall Algren's friend writer Earl Shorris arranged for him to be the featured speaker at the first—and only—Annual Roos Atkins Literary Award dinner in San Francisco. Algren had lectured in San Francisco the year before, had liked the city, and was happy to accept the lucrative assignment; later, he even tried to collect unemployment insurance from it. Blithely, Algren told Shorris he couldn't provide him with a copy of the speech beforehand, and the truth of the matter was that Algren didn't go to great lengths to prepare. Before two hundred local authors, he gave a humorous, but rambling and finally embarrassing talk on the state of American letters. The sponsors of the event were annoyed, but Algren enjoyed himself: Ken Kesey, Allen Ginsberg, and Herbert Gold later gathered around him in the bar while a beautiful dark-haired woman waited in the background. And Algren left, John Van der Zee remembered, "fresh from an evening of jokes and honors, with a lovely, runaway young lady on his arm, headed for his hotel. Located, with a sort of Algrenesque purity, on the edge of the Tenderloin."

That was Nelson Algren in 1963, a man who tried not to take life too seriously and who did what he pleased. When asked to write an introduction for *Erik Dorn* by Ben Hecht, whom he considered third-rate, instead of declining the thousand-dollar assignment he accepted it and felt that for that money he certainly couldn't do a whitewash. So he wrote what he had always thought: that *Erik Dorn* was a book that began as a brilliant naturalistic novel and ended as a grade B scenario. "It wasn't gas [Hecht] ran out of and it surely wasn't brass. It was belief," wrote Algren, who had run out of the very same thing. "For he came, too young, to a time when, like Dorn, he had to ask himself: 'What the hell am I talking about?' And heard no answer at all." Hecht, outraged, couldn't believe any editor would put such an introduction in front of his book, but it was published.

He was fiercely loyal to Donadio, who, in Shag Donohue's words, had "completely reorganized his professional life." At a *Paris Review* party in 1963, a literary critic seems to have suggested in a rather disparaging and sexist way that Candida might be trying to manipulate him. "Nelson got a sickly grin and my heart stopped," said Shag. Obliviously, the critic kept running on about how much he admired Nelson's work, while Nelson was frozen with this funny grin. "I'm saying, 'Let's go,'" Donohue said, "and he's saying, 'Yeah, we'll go in a minute but first I have to tell this goddamn mother-fucking son of a horse's ass who doesn't know any fucking thing that what I really think is that his fucking teeth should be shoved down his fucking throat so he can't talk anymore.'" Fortunately, Shag hustled Algren outside. Another time, after *Conversations* was published, Donohue remembered that Nelson started acting up at a party. "Candida went up and tapped him on the cheek and said, 'Shut up, Bubula.' He said, 'See? She runs my life.' Now, no one tells Nelson Algren what to do. That's how much he admired and respected her personally."

He liked his frequent radio and TV appearances and enjoyed acting and the theater, occasionally getting a walk-on part in productions at Chicago's Second City Theatre. To good reviews, he appeared as himself in Philip Kaufman's underground Chicago film

Goldstein, and critics singled out his cameo performance as one of the best in the film. He was such a masterful storyteller he could easily lure back a straying member of his audience, and the worst insult he could offer was humorlessness. "In his manner of relating stories everything was *funny,*" recalled Deutch, who was troubled by Nelson's absolute insistence on humor.

Because everything was *not* funny.

Conversations with Nelson Algren, published in the spring of 1964, was a fairly candid oral autobiography. Donohue acted the knee-jerk conservative to Algren's rebel, but the book caught, in a sense, the true Nelson Algren — direct, naive, contradictory, politically principled, yet a bit confused, functioning more on gut response than on reason. Algren emerged as human and vulnerable even as he stuck to his convictions. When Donohue asked him if his lack of a big book was a sellout, Algren answered that it was a sellout only if he was considered an artist and not a person, because he thought it would be a sellout of himself.

Algren did not seem to know where he was headed. The journalistic books he was writing were one-shot affairs—they didn't give an overall purpose to life as serious writing had once done. He felt now that the only way to get respect was to have money, and his feelings about money—the desire for lots of it and the deep belief that it was an unsatisfying reward—were too conflicting to be coherent. He stayed with Lou and Martha Gilbert when he came to New York to promote *Conversations,* and he seemed aloof, preoccupied with himself.

That summer he renewed his friendship with novelist Bruce Jay Friedman, who had wanted to write a play of *Never Come Morning,* a project abandoned for lack of funds. Friedman had a place on Fire Island, where Algren spent part of the summer in a rental house, the place in Gary having been sold two years before. Friedman had children, a wife, a housekeeper, and a home by the sea: the exact image of family life that Algren said he wanted, and he often wandered over to Friedman's house to solemnly give the children advice about life. He was trying to find something real in that summer, he wrote Dave Peltz. The dunes on Fire Island were not, like the ones in Gary, connected to the stacks of mills or to his past. The surf kept breaking and the grasses blowing in the wind, but the only connection he could make was with his typewriter. At a wild, all-night party he had seen that the Friedmans' life, the cozy family and the house by the sea, what he had wanted but could never achieve, was not as tranquil as he'd thought. The next morning Friedman, aching, hung over, his hand cut, walked him down to the ferry, and Algren asked him ruefully why people had to destroy themselves.

In *Conversations* Algren had attacked Simone with a bitter, sexist attitude, insisting that despite her reputation as a feminist, she had accepted an inferior position in their relationship. Moreover, he claimed that her revelation of their affair had destroyed it, that it "could never have meant a great deal in the first place, if its ultimate use has so little to do with love. . . . When you share the relationship with everybody who can afford a book, you reduce it. It no longer has meaning. It's good for the book trade, I guess, but you certainly lose interest in the other party." In the summer or fall of 1964, Bill Targ of World, who was bringing out the English translation of Simone's autobiography, *Force of Circumstance,* asked Nelson for permission for Simone to quote from his letters. Algren had no desire whatsoever to grant it, but cajoled by Targ, who told him he would be serving the cause of literature, he agreed. He was not happy about it, but it did, in some sense, prepare him for what was coming.

In November and December, excerpts from the autobiography appeared in *Harper's* under the titles "A Question of Fidelity" and "An American Rendezvous," and Algren must have been appalled to read Simone's "non-fictional" account of their affair. Their love as she presented it was merely an interlude in her life with Sartre; Algren read that her vows of deep undying love were but "the passion of a moment only." It was bad enough that she had put a pleasant, nostalgic gloss on his 1960 trip, but truly incredible was the way she offered him as proof positive of her theory of "contingent love," Simone's term for relationships outside of her pact with Sartre. The description of their affair was almost grotesquely self-serving. To read about it was, he felt, to read about a woman who had lived vicariously: a woman who wanted a taste of what she had, in choosing Sartre, already dedicated her life to living without.

Algren could not forgive being used to prove a theory, any more than he could forgive her for having publicized a private part of his life without concern for his feelings. It was certainly true that he could not, as de Beauvoir rather egocentrically and high-handedly put it, tolerate being number two. She would never have accepted such a position herself, yet she knew that in becoming involved with him she had put him there, no matter how bad she felt about it.

She had wanted love without commitment, and all this confirmed to Nelson Algren that he must rid himself of her publicly and put an end to all the pretense. They obviously had very different ideas of what love was, and he now felt that she had urged him to be unfaithful in 1948 because she did not want to risk her own freedom. Even if he had never been able to sustain a love relationship, Algren felt that the risk one took in declaring true love to another person was *precisely* the loss of one's own freedom; and if one couldn't risk that, one could not really experience love. About de Beauvoir's assertion that with him she had experienced "contingent love," Algren felt unequivocally that this was a contradiction in terms. "Anyone who can experience love contingently has a mind that has recently snapped. How can love ever be *contingent*?" he asked. "Contingent upon *what*?"

His reaction was a devastating critique in *Harper's*. In "The Question of Simone de Beauvoir," Algren describes her as a writer whose message is largely so true and unswerving in its commitment to social justice that we cannot help but listen to her. She is "a writer who has moved millions of women, leading submerged lives, toward lives of their own," he wrote. But when Algren discusses her writing, one can't help recalling their long-standing feud over who was the better writer: "No chronicler of our lives since Theodore Dreiser has combined so steadfast a passion for human justice with a dullness so asphyxiating as Mme. de Beauvoir," Algren wrote. "All the characters from her novels, although drawn from life, have no life on the printed page. These people are rememberable only if one has happened to have known them; from her books one remembers not one." About Madame's personal life, "procurers are more honest than philosophers," he wrote succinctly, about the "how-about-a-quickie gambit" he now felt his love had been to her. The review ended with a wonderful image of the end of the world, with Simone's voice alone burbling up from the ocean's depths: " 'In this matter man's sexuality may be modified. The dead are better adapted to the earth than the living. Sartre needs peace and quiet. Bost is on the Cinema Vigilance Committee. I want to go skiing. Merleau-Ponty—'

"Will she ever quit talking?" Algren demanded to know. As far as he was concerned, "Mme. Utter Driveleau" had reached "com-

plete pomposity." Twenty years later de Beauvoir was still outraged that anyone close to her had dared to disavow the life she had worked so hard to create. After the spring of 1965, no more letters passed between them, and they never saw each other again.

Simone de Beauvoir had been an important part of Algren's life for over seventeen years, and in turning away from her so completely, he severed yet another relationship that had given him satisfaction and a profound sense of connection with the outside world. And just as he had done after exiling himself from the world of serious literature, he ended more relationships with friends, a practice that had become, by now, an Algren trademark. Though the Hemingway essay would be dedicated to Max Geismar, who had also innocently become an outcast from the new literary establishment after writing an unflattering study of Henry James, Algren would soon inexplicably cut off connections with the critic. Dave Peltz and Herman Kogan, John Clellon Holmes and Bruce Jay Friedman would also be abandoned. But most of the friends he rejected sensed that his forsaking of them had little to do with themselves and everything to do with Nelson Algren. That is why, from Amanda and Chris Rowland to Jack Conroy, Peltz, Holmes, Kogan, and de Beauvoir, almost no one Nelson alienated was unwilling to talk about him, even though they still felt the pain he'd caused; moreover, they were often fiercely protective of him. "I kept my distance and we didn't break off," said Studs Terkel, summing it up best when he said Algren's friends knew he was essentially alone and terribly vulnerable. Algren's need to destroy love had to be accepted, finally, as a tragic but undeniable part of his personality.

19.
The Last Carousel

AFTER PERMANENTLY cutting off Simone and receiving news that Madeleine had met another man, Algren set in motion a familiar series of events. He began dating Betty Ann Jones, a widowed New York actress in her early thirties who had sent him a fan letter about *Wild Side*. In December 1964, they went out for dinner and drinks, and Nelson wanted to show her the electric chair; five or six dates later he suggested they get married. In Milwaukee, where her parents lived, he proposed again; this time she accepted and gave up her apartment in New York. "He said he wanted to be married," Stephen Deutch remembered, "and Betty corresponded to his fantasy of marriage." Sadly, even before the ceremony, Deutch had the feeling that Algren knew it wouldn't work but felt "too far along" to back out. This impulsive relationship was a psychological rerun of his second marriage to Amanda.

Deutch felt they were incompatible. "I met Betty and I couldn't understand what was going on—these were two totally different personalities." Still, "Betty seemed pleased that she had a famous author, and he seemed pleased that he had an attractive young woman as his wife." For her part, Betty walked into the marriage knowing little of Nelson's financial troubles, gambling, or insomnia.

A Chicago halfway-house priest and civil rights activist, James Jones, married them in a small ceremony attended by Betty's entire family. Friend and surgeon Leonard Kolb, who had treated Algren for a hernia, remembered that Nelson was not enthusiastic at the ceremony, and at a celebration dinner after the service, Deutch's fears for their future were confirmed. "Nelson was very defiant when it came to conventionalism," Deutch explained. "It actually bothered him—the formality of getting married. Anyway, Nelson was a sloppy eater. He got some juice or gravy on his necktie, and Betty said, 'Dear, you have gravy on your tie,' and reached over with her napkin. Nelson took the saltshaker and threw some salt on the tie, then some more gravy, and he kept smearing himself up to defy her. . . . Betty laughed, embarrassed, and it passed."

Still, as if their first week of married life were sacred, Algren refrained from gambling; but after the second week he began again, and it became obvious that he had no money, even if once he did stay out all night and win five hundred dollars. She found a job at Time-Life and for a short time helped Nelson with money. From early on, they had separate bedrooms and rarely ate dinner together. Betty would prepare food and leave it in the refrigerator so he could eat when he wanted. He'd break off from anything at anytime to add to whatever was in the typewriter: writing was a twenty-four-hour activity broken up by daily trips to the Luxor Baths. At fifty-four, Algren was stuck in his ways, used to living alone in a house kept by Mary Corley. As in his earlier marriage he was upset when his wife tried to throw out his old junk. Betty felt that he had no insight into himself and could not change.

At first Nelson said he wanted children and, as he had done in 1953, tried briefly to bring money into the house. Through an intermediary, he had been trying to sell his papers to Ohio State University and now began direct negotiations for manuscripts including *The Man with the Golden Arm* and Beauvoir's love letters. The literary man who came from Ohio to arrange a deal found Algren soft-spoken and polite, a lean man with a potbelly who looked much younger than his age, dressed in a polo shirt, slippers, and tight pants with the fly open. The apartment was filled with books and strewn with notes and papers: an inscribed early edition of *In Our Time* was jammed with Hemingway's letters—uncared for and folded—into a plastic bag, which was kept in an open suitcase with a heap of assorted belongings. Talking about writers, Algren was incisive: Jones was worthless, he didn't like Bellow or Farrell, he was fond of Dickens and liked O'Hara's ear. When they talked about the manuscripts, Algren seemed to have no business sense at all. He said he'd offered Simone's letters to Gallimard and a figure of $9,500 had been discussed—but he didn't want French funds. He asked for a price he himself described as much too high, then began to think he ought to keep the manuscripts as an investment. He wasn't interested in the suggestion that he take OSU's twenty grand and invest it in

AT&T. The intermediary got the impression that Algren frittered away his money, because there was nothing of any value in the house except a big console television. They finally decided on $20,000 for all the materials except the de Beauvoir letters, a substantial deal for Algren.

Nelson had wanted to take Betty on a steamboat cruise down the Mississippi—another attempt at evoking his past—but settled for a trip to East St. Louis and the Cahokia Downs racetrack. They stayed with Nelson's friend Leonard, apparently a former pimp whose mother had owned a whorehouse. Leonard lived in a suburban villa with dogs chained up out back and a pack of lively Chihuahuas dashing through the house. Nelson was soon smoking pot and drinking brandy as if Betty weren't around, just as Leonard did not recognize the presence of any woman except his own. To Betty, Nelson seemed to be imitating Leonard's macho attitude, although he may have merely been shifting gears into the underworld. Algren's friendship with Leonard was long-standing, and he stored things for Leonard in Chicago—probably marijuana, though Betty didn't want to know what. After three or four days they spent time with Joan Kerckhoff, who now had a wealthy new husband and a child and lived in grand style in the posh suburb of Clayton.

Algren had been visiting Cahokia Downs for years and had published a number of racetrack stories, most recently in *The Saturday Evening Post*. In the summer of 1964, when he had been trying to find meaning, he had begun a racetrack novel he called "Moon of the Arfy-Darfy" or "Get All the Money," despite his claim that he would never write another big book. Manuscripts at Ohio State University reveal characters in a tightly constructed circumscribed world like that at the Tug and Maul in *Golden Arm:* Mulconnery, a crooked track owner by night and a besotted, hypocritical judge by day; Hollis Floweree, a has-been jockey supported by the older horse owner Kate, who has betrayed him with the victorious Mexican jockey Casaflores. Complex psychological relationships between characters were established early on, and the fifty-odd pages of the earliest version concern throwing a race. The submerged world of losing gamblers and fading jockeys living in trailers was Algren's territory. His emphasis was on vivid description and dialogue: the jockeys in their silks, the sweating, skittish horses being calmed and cooled by water and electric fans, the smell of hay and manure, the double-dealing and odds-setting.

Algren was perhaps strengthened by the belief that the newly completed Hemingway essay would help to discredit formalist criticism. He had signed a contract for the Hemingway essay, the long-overdue story collection, and a novel, with G. P. Putnam's Sons, where Bill Targ was now working. Algren certainly had the financing for the new novel. Six to seven grand was coming annually from Ohio State University for three years, and the Writers' Workshop at the University of Iowa had made him yet another teaching offer, this time so lucrative that Betty, hoping to save *some* of the roughly $14,000 salary, urged him not to turn it down. Money might also be coming from the Hemingway essay: before moving to Iowa, the Algrens spent a week in New York for the August 11 publication of *Notes from a Sea Diary: Hemingway All the Way*.

Another travel book, *Sea Diary* was a vast improvement over *Who Lost an American?* Algren-as-narrator seemed less bitter, more relaxed and full of goodwill than in the earlier book. He had successfully merged the unlikely combination of Hemingway criticism and Far East adventures into a travel narrative studded with seafaring tales and nostalgia, climaxed by a ship officer's suicide after being caught smuggling watches and American currency. Amid the ocean's meditative calm, in and out of Asian ports, Algren alternately pondered the crewmen, the rampant prostitution, the port people, and the way Hemingway was perceived in his own land, his thesis being that the critic was now on the side of the establishment rather than that of the artist.

In New York, Algren was wined and dined and fussed over. There were radio interviews, a *Merv Griffin Show* appearance, and a Putnam publication party at which Algren met Roger Groening, a young fan with whom he'd been carrying on a lively correspondence for over a year. Nelson and Betty stayed with Robert Gover, the author of *One Hundred Dollar Misunderstanding,* in his large, modern apartment. Unfortunately, Gover asked Algren to read his as yet unpublished novel, and when Algren was not enthusiastic, he and Betty began to feel unwelcome and moved out.

Algren's expectations for *Sea Diary* had been raised by a pleasant early notice in *The Atlantic* and Conrad Knickerbocker's insightful and appreciative piece, one of the best ever written on Algren, in *Book Week;* even *The New Yorker* had carried a respectful note. So he was completely unprepared for the piece in *The New York Times Book Review*. In it, Arno Karlen, who'd been with Algren at Bread

Loaf, described him as a "tough-sentimental literary lush with whisky-courage whose breath is stronger than his brains," a man whose "small but unique talent" was now merely a habit, and whose critical statements were "clichés," "inanities," "rant." Betty remembered that Algren felt the *Times* had an animus against him and chose antagonistic reviewers; Karlen, with his totally irrelevant shot at the "literary communist of the thirties," was, at the very least, anti-left. Algren was not alone in being shocked at the review: John Cheever wrote Donadio that it had been "obscene and irrelevant."

Though the book also received disappointing coverage in Chicago, later reviewers remarked about how alive the book was, how it leapt off the page. In *The Nation,* Sol Yurick wrote that *Sea Diary* had to be understood as the product of a man who in *The Man with the Golden Arm* had written a great book—"Are there ten living American writers who have written a great book? Five?" Yurick dismissed Algren's diatribe against corruption in American letters as "silly" because he should have known it was corrupt, but predicted that more writers would be, "in the long run, influenced by Algren" than by Hemingway. Heartening words; but sales were not plentiful. The spectrum of people interested in his reflections on Hemingway and the Far East was much smaller than he might have reached with novels of more universal concern.

In 1965 Algren was an alert, hilarious, and sharp-witted man with an amused contempt for many things and a deep bitterness over the Preminger affair that he would never overcome. He made his living teaching at summer writers' conferences and giving eight to ten lectures a year at $500 each. In March 1965, Algren reported that all of his major works were in paperback in every country in Europe as far east as Romania and Yugoslavia and that one had made it to Japan; still, as Conrad Knickerbocker described his fall from grace with the American literary establishment, "he had become the man whose name everybody forgot to mention in the same breath . . . with Norman and Saul and Jimmy and Terry. He walked and talked with a sort of pre-war style, tough but not mean, when by now it should have been the other way around." Knickerbocker mocked the New York view of Algren: "He knew great numbers of the poor. He had hitchhiked around the country, quaint, and Chicago, I mean, really." Tom Dardis of Berkley Books, trying to acquire paperback rights to Algren's novels in the belief that his stature was similar to Faulkner's, agreed that the New York intellectuals had never had much to say favorably about Nelson Algren. "By the mid-sixties," Dardis said, "the view was that he was a literary whiner, hopeless, passé, belonging in the thirties and forties. This belief firmed up in New York literary circles. Nelson felt he was a man of integrity. He had the Nelson Algren stance, but as time went on it became more difficult to defend. The stance was comfortable in early years—later it was harder."

Nelson was the star attraction at a reception for new faculty in Iowa City, and he basked in the attention. The Workshop, long known as a haven for broke writers, had been very eager to recruit him, and Betty had been offered a job in the speech department, taking over for a professor on sabbatical and helping direct a play. The Algrens had the spacious top floor of a house at 1730 Muscatine. But Algren didn't really want to be there. Till now, he had taught summer workshops or appeared at conferences for a couple of days or weeks; he had never taught for more than a semester and had never had to move from Chicago. This September-to-May stint looked like an indeterminate sentence in academia.

He had never felt comfortable as a teacher because he didn't believe writing could be taught; a writer had first to live in order to write. And art was a solitary process, not a group effort or a picnic among friends. He listened to his students cite justifications for being at Iowa that had nothing to do with literature. "The longer I hang on here the longer I stay out of Vietnam." "I had to find a school where I wouldn't get kicked out for bad grades—either that or go to work for my old man." "It may lead to teaching creative writing somewhere else." They were mostly sheltered kids worried about what their parents would think of them, and they confirmed Algren's belief that Iowa "provides sanctuary from those very pressures in which creativity is forged." Only two of his students, both immigrants who had fled political repression, one of them the fiction writer Hua-Ling Nieh, seemed to show promise. It was no wonder he offered his services once a week to the writers in the Men's Reformatory at Anamosa, Iowa, encouraging writers who *were* under pressure.

His arrival after classes had started, combined with the way he passed out stories by Terry Southern and Joseph Heller and James Leo Herlihy instead of those of his students, didn't earn him high marks as a teacher. Burns Ellison, a student in Algren's spring 1966 workshop who played poker with him, remembered that Algren would arrive in class with stacks of magazines, newspapers, and book reviews from which students could help themselves. "The classes often started late and ended early. He obviously wasn't comfortable presiding over a class, discussing Literature or the Art of Fiction," said Ellison. "The only times he felt at ease were when he . . . told his stories, his anecdotes about hookers and pimps, junkies and barflies, gamblers and racetrack touts. . . . As the weeks went by, classroom attendance fell off. Students stopped coming or switched to other workshop sections. They had enjoyed hearing his stories about Life's Losers, but only up to a point; they were, after all, Life's Winners. What did any of them have in common with Roman Orlov, the biggest drunk on Division Street?" Kurt Vonnegut, Jr., also at Iowa that year, remembered Algren's teaching more charitably. The most important part of the workshop was the individual story conference, and Vonnegut recalled that although Algren found the classes incongenial and finally stopped holding them, students could and did regularly find him in the student union, where he was always available to discuss stories. Though the union was a hotbed of gambling activity (Ellison remembered that these conferences often degenerated into gambling tales), Vonnegut felt Algren was doing 90 percent of what he should have been doing but just couldn't hack the conventional classroom. Vonnegut recalled that he and Algren once taught a joint class. "I spoke for about twenty minutes and then Algren got up and said about three words and sat down. Then there was a voice from the back of the room—a woman—it was Betty. She said, 'I have a question, Mr. Algren. Are you happy in your new profession?' and Algren laughed."

Far more consuming than the workshops were the weekly all-night poker games in the basement of a bald shoe salesman named Gilroy. Other players included the lucky but rumpled and unshaven Lepp; Burns Ellison; another graduate student named Pablo; John the Barber; the nattily dressed Thede; and the Cincinnati Kid, who later outraged Nelson by putting his name down as a reference for a job as a *cop*. The stakes rose considerably once Algren became a regular player, and so did his losses, often three or four hundred a night, sometimes twice a week. On Burns Ellison's first night at the games Algren lost twelve hundred. Betty estimated that during the year Algren lost about five thousand dollars; Ellison thought it was more like ten. "Once I tried to talk to him about his play," Burns remembered. "I told him he had to protect himself, change his style, that he didn't have a chance against those sharks; that they were just waiting to carve him up. That was a mistake on my part. . . . He thanked me for my advice, but there was a distinct edge to his voice."

Iowa put him on a more frequent lecture circuit, which he called "The Ho Chi Minh Trail," since, except when teaching in the prisons, he now used these occasions almost invariably to speak out against the war in Vietnam. Encouraged by his new friend and correspondent, the politically active novelist Kay Boyle, he traveled to seventeen states and fourteen campus locations that spring with a humorous speech that made the White House staff look like characters out of *Batman*. But Algren was dead serious about his early and vehement opposition to the war, which seemed to embody for him everything that was wrong with the United States. He saw the war as the logical outcome for a country whose economy was built upon fifty billion dollars in defense spending, because such a nation needed enemies more than allies. He felt the Vietnamese peasant was fighting the kind of war Americans had fought for self-determination and that Lyndon Johnson should have been brought to public trial for crimes against humanity. In 1966, after a drifter named Richard Speck slaughtered eight Chicago student nurses, a Boston newspaper called Algren and asked him to cover "The Crime of the Century." He replied simply, "I don't want to go to Vietnam."

Algren was busy reviewing books for the *New York Herald Tribune* and had finished "Ticket on Skoronski," a short story about a man who dies of a coronary playing poker in a Chicago bar, but Vonnegut, who saw Algren every day, sensed correctly that Algren's work was not going well. Indeed, although he had his mornings free to write, Algren felt he wouldn't be able even to touch the racetrack novel till summer. Vonnegut, noting that the mood of Algren's great body of work was of the thirties and forties, felt that he somehow wanted to modernize himself. "There he was, a master storyteller, blasted beyond all reason with admiration for and envy of a moderately innovative crime story then appearing in serial form in *The New Yorker,* Truman Capote's *In Cold Blood.* For a while at Iowa he talked of little else." Algren was indeed fascinated by the story of the murder of a Kansas family. "It's just a hell of a poetic job of reporting," he wrote Roger Groening. "Moreover, the man deserved a big round of applause for breaking out of the Literature-bound in-group of . . . Sontag, Mary McCarthy, and all, who would never, never *never* take the risks he took. Nor would Mailer. Nor would Bellow. I think it's downright heroic for a party like Capote—who has enough loot to have breakfast at Tiffany's every morning for a hundred years, to take the chance he did, simply to write something new."

Meanwhile, he and Betty did little together. Vonnegut could not understand how Algren could simply ignore Betty, who was pleasant, attractive, and doing well in her job. But the destruction of love relationships was by now a deeply set psychological pattern for Algren. Comparing himself to Bruno Bicek, calling himself a loveless man, he continued to act on impulse, expecting events to follow the pattern so closely that he assumed Betty would want, as Amanda had, a significant financial and property settlement. In June, when she finally said she did want a divorce, he acted shocked, seemed angry and proud, but agreed that the marriage was over. She stayed at 1958 West Evergreen for the summer, while Algren, leaving behind an Iowa phone bill he had no intention of paying, took off for Cahokia Downs.

His three-month stay with Leonard was an escape from marriage, a warmongering country, and his own lost dreams; in the underworld he felt comfortable, relaxed, accepted. In Leonard's house gambling was normal, and his host, once apparently involved in a murder, introduced Nelson to a number of racketeers. Together they bought a racing mare named Jellious Widow, a far from consistent winner. For Algren the horse—alternatively called Jealous Widow and Algren's Folly—provided access to behind-the-scenes life at the racetrack, less connected to his gambling and desire to be a big shot than to what it could contribute to "Moon of the Arfy-Darfy." Although sustaining a novel was another matter entirely, Algren's intent at least was serious.

He returned to Chicago in September, and Betty stayed on for a few weeks. One day when Dave Peltz met him at the baths, Algren was guilt-ridden and filled with remorse, and confessed that he had become violent toward Betty. By November she had found an apartment in New York; a divorce witnessed by Mary Corley and neighborhood friend Stuart McCarrell followed a few months later. They had lived together for fifteen months. Salvaging something from the marriage, they remained friends until the early 1970s, an accomplishment that seemed to make Algren proud.

By 1967, Algren's interest in the racetrack novel had more or less died, surely affected by the attack on *Sea Diary* and its lack of sales or effect on the formalist critics. In between book reviews and an introduction to *The True Story of Bonnie and Clyde,* he did, however, write a wonderful fight story, "Home to Shawneetown," published the following year in *The Atlantic Monthly.*

But the story had been inspired by *Ring* magazine, and not by the streets of the city around him. Increasingly, Daley's Chicago seemed to him a dead city, a vicious, petty, bought city. His apartment seems to have been broken into, and the man who had never avoided dangerous streets got a permit for a .38 Smith & Wesson revolver. In early 1967, the once respected author had made headlines when the cops picked him up with a couple of friends from St. Louis and found a joint of marijuana in the car. Preminger's film was on TV around the same time, and after Chicago gossip columnist Maggie Daly capitalized on the story of the author of *The Man with the Golden Arm* in Narcotics Court, other newspapers and television stations followed suit, though the charges were dropped and the driver found guilty only of running a stoplight. In Mike Royko's column, Algren wrote a spirited rebuttal to Daly, "the woman in mink who feeds the city's insatiable appetite for nastiness." But his increasing disenchantment with Chicago was also reflected in a new epilogue to a 1968 edition of *City on the Make,* whose title, "Ode to Lower Finksville," he changed to the stronger "Ode to Kissass-ville." The editor refused to alter the entire printing, but Algren was able to obtain, for his personal use, a hundred copies of the book with the new title.

By the time the book appeared in March 1968, Algren, who had earlier written a fan that he was apprehensive about not fulfilling himself, was already thinking of leaving town, and when he returned from a trip to New York in late spring he had made up his mind to go to Vietnam, having continued to speak out against the war on his lecture junkets. In 1968, the war was at its height, and perhaps, in seeing the war as the "Crime of the Century," Algren thought he could find material for a book of reportage like *In Cold Blood.* Miraculously, financing for the trip simply appeared: in May he was awarded $6,000 from the Illinois Arts Council; he won handsomely at Arlington in June, picked up a nice fee at a writers' conference in Colorado, and later that summer learned that *The Atlantic* would provide press credentials and advance money for four pieces on Saigon.

He returned from Cahokia Downs in time for the August 1968 Democratic Convention in Chicago. The Democratic Party was split wide open on the Vietnam issue, and Mayor Daley, fearful of the long-haired protesters who flocked to the convention, had turned Chicago into a garrison. In addition to the Chicago police force, Daley had on hand 6,000 National Guardsmen and 7,500 army troops, a show of force that outnumbered the actual protesters two to one. The inevitable bloodbath, without question instigated by the authorities, increased in its ferocity night after night, as the Chicago police brutally beat protesters in the head, stomach, and groin with their nightsticks and filled the summer air with tear gas. At week's end, more than 700 civilians and 83 policemen had been injured, and 653 jailed; and after Eugene McCarthy had turned part of the Conrad Hilton into an emergency medical clinic and his offices had been hit in a predawn raid by police, Hubert Humphrey was somehow nominated. Given the relentless skull-bashing, it was a miracle no one had been killed.

The week stunned the city and the nation and would go down in Chicago's history of violence alongside the Haymarket Riots and the St. Valentine's Day Massacre. For Algren, the brutality was as much a result of Mayor Daley's policies as of what the city had become: an ugly capital of greed, "the only major city in the country where you can easily buy your way out of a murder rap." "I don't think the clubbing represents one man," he said of Daley, who had continued to be re-elected since 1955. "I think it represents a majority of the people of Chicago. If an election were held today, he'd win." Fantastically, Herbert Mitgang's favorable review of *City on the Make* appeared in *The New York Times* on the very morning of Daley's disgrace. But as for the convention violence, he could only have agreed with his friend the British journalist James Cameron, who unconsciously echoed Algren's earlier assessment of Chicago as the city built out of man's ceaseless failure to overcome himself: "It will take many years to disinfect Chicago from the sour smell of human failure," Cameron wrote. "The city quivers with a kind of corporate bitterness. The place sings with a kind of hate."

San Francisco, his first stop on the way to Southeast Asia, was a welcome change after the cold blank faces he complained of constantly seeing in Chicago. On his many lecture junkets there he had made friends in the city, including Kay Boyle, whom he now visited; he thought increasingly about buying a house in the Bay Area. Naturally, he was having trouble with his passport. In September he had sent it, with check and application, to the embassy of the Republic of South Vietnam for a visa, and although the application had been received, check and passport had not. He'd gotten another passport, sent it by registered mail, and been assured that the new, now visaed passport was on its way to Chicago. It still hadn't arrived before he left for San Francisco, however, and now he waited for it to be forwarded to his hotel. "American shenanigans," was Kay Boyle's view of "L'Affaire du Passeport." It finally arrived, eight hours before his boat sailed.

Japan, where he spent two weeks, was an absolute wonder. Tokyo was alive like Paris, an explosion that made New York seem slow: lots of neon, good-natured crowds, and an incredible sense of personal dignity—"no tipping, no kissing, no handshaking, no hauling, mauling, yanking or back-slapping," Algren noted, and no pickpockets either, because the Japanese just didn't seem to steal. Everybody was working, and everybody seemed immaculate—even take-out sandwiches came with a moist hand napkin. The Japanese had an intense interest in the arts, and he was shown around town by novelist and dramatist Suji Terayama. Through their interpreter, Terayama assured Algren that the Japanese look of contentment wasn't entirely sincere—the people were bored and sad. Still, on a Tokyo slum tour, Algren felt Terayama didn't know what slums were, for even the streets of the poorer sections were clean and tidy.

Algren was charmed by Japanese women, and what he wrote about them revealed much about his own conflicts. Fundamentally, he thought women should lead rich, interesting lives; indeed, the women who had held his interest had been successful, independent, and strong: Simone, Margo, Lily Harmon, Geraldine Page, and Madeleine Gobeil. However, he saw the women he had married as domineering, probably because they disliked his gambling. Generalizing from his own experience, as he tended to do increasingly as he got older, he thus felt that Western man was woman-dominated. But he could not reconcile his beliefs. At his most disgustingly sexist, for instance, Algren stated that the fact that Japanese men were allowed to strike their women, while the women could not strike back, "accounts, in part, for the relative contentment of Japanese women, compared to the dissatisfied, irritable, unresponsive, and boring American female"; the observation was especially out of touch in the age of women's liberation. At the same time he thought this submissiveness bored Japanese men, and suspected that beneath the women's air of silent contentment lay resignation, or even despair. Curiously, when he read Kate Millett's *Sexual Politics* eighteen months later, he thought it was the most important book of the year and much better than *The Second Sex:* he felt that Millett wrote from the experience of women, while de Beauvoir deduced theories from other theories.

He didn't dwell on the women's issue, however, since Terayama owned a racehorse and took him to races and the Fuji-Locche world junior welterweight title fight, where Algren asked Terayama to get him down for ten thousand yen, twenty-eight American dollars, on Locche. And after Fuji was declared the loser and pelted with tangerines and half-eaten sandwiches, Algren was more than a hundred dollars richer for his tour in Vietnam.

He arrived in Saigon, a city expecting combat for Christmas, on December 15, 1968. "It's a mean, sick city," he wrote Roger Groening. It was a run-down French provincial capital with Versailles buildings, chauffeured cars, French restaurants, American wives, and pimps, poverty, pushers, moneychangers. There was no public transit. Honda, Suzuki, and Yamaha riders cruised the boulevards day and night, tangling in hideous accidents, their bloody remains splattered on the street until policemen nonchalantly phoned for help. Haggling wildly for a crummy, expensive room in the heart of town, Algren was assured of "perfect security," although the building next door had been shot to hell and couldn't be used. It was safe only because the Vietnam War was fought not in the cities but in the jungles and countryside, leaving the city a booming black market full of short-term investors.

Poverty-stricken, Saigon lacked pretense, but its chaos dismayed him, and the anti-American feeling was overwhelming. Algren could not have expected the Vietnamese to regard the Americans with gratitude; but as another reporter noted, there was hardly even the most basic kind of respect: Americans were seen simply as better off, able to afford decent food or a woman's body. Underlying most transactions between the two peoples was a sense of deceit which made any real contact impossible. When Algren could pass for French, the hostility diminished, but only by a degree. "Pity has escaped the soul of this city's people," the same journalist described the tragedy of Saigon. "You can buy pity from them; but they will never give it to you." Sometimes Algren felt the Vietnamese lack of concern extended even to themselves; and his inability to penetrate their seeming indifference made him less sympathetic to them as a people, although there were many Vietnamese whom he liked personally.

If Algren thought his experiences as a medic in Germany would prepare him for seeing the carnage of battle, he was mistaken. During his first contact with the war, in an airplane over the jungle observing troop activities, shots were apparently fired and his plane damaged; this ended any thought of covering the war directly. He retreated to Saigon's Chinese ghetto of Cholon, where he could observe the city's underworld, for which his life had better prepared him.

But opportunities to exploit the black market were too tempting to miss. Cigarettes, toothpaste, cameras, tape recorders, record players—the Cholon PX had them all for cheap, and Nelson decided to set up shop. Roger Groening and Studs Terkel responded to his request for C-notes hidden in carbon paper and blank, unpersonalized checks; Algren exchanged the dollars for Vietnamese money at a high rate of exchange, then converted this into Military Payment Certificates—the only money negotiable at the PX. He saved up about a thousand bucks in MPCs, and all he needed was the card identifying him as a major, which he soon acquired: a pleasing promotion, he felt, since he'd never made higher than private before. "Nelson wanted only to out-guile the Orient and raise money to buy a not so little house somewhere by the ocean, a wish he frequently expressed, and which he innocently believed this opportunity in Vietnam was heaven-sent to make concrete," Roger remembered. Algren seemed to think he was still the shrewd marketeer he'd been twenty-five years before in Marseilles.

"Whistles kept shrilling, sirens kept warning, horns kept squawking, ducks kept quacking, and toy-tanks kept zapping chopchop eaters at their chopstick bowls, a girl with a basket on her head came crying, among charcoal fires and children squatting to pee, 'Ay vit lon! Ay vit lon!' like a querulous bird," Nelson remembered the streets of Saigon in 1969. "The woman getting a chirping cry out of coca-cola tops strung on a wire was offering to massage me, on the street, for fifty piastres. The boy beating a pair of strung balls with a pair of drumsticks . . . [announced] the coming of steamed rice. . . . If the beat was slower, it wasn't steamed rice. It was a woman who'd dye your trousers while you waited." Steam baths, massage parlors, cricket fights, and pickpockets—into it all plunged Nelson Algren, who spent off-hours hammering at his typewriter or

reading modern novels in an air-conditioned room. The war became
so remote, he wrote a friend, that he'd have been closer to it watching
TV on Evergreen.

Roger, now in for two more C-notes, knew it sounded too good
to last. Saigon was not Marseilles, and Algren was not a thirty-five-
year-old man physically fit from two years in the army. He was a
sixty-year-old with a potbelly, gray hair, and a longing for the peace
and quiet of a house on the beach. The easy money didn't last more
than a month or so. Then, after some kind of a price dispute with
two men, one apparently held Algren while the other beat him up
and kicked his teeth in.

Aching, broke, probably needing dentures, and with only forty
pages to show for five months' work, he fled Saigon. And almost as
soon as he found refuge in Hong Kong he was suggesting that his
failure in Cholon had had nothing to do with himself and everything
to do with the Vietnamese. "They don't have *original* personalities,"
he complained. "They keep saying, 'Numba One, Give me Money,
Numba Ten, Zippo lighta, give a cigarette, coca-cola, me wuv you
too much' and on and on." It took two weeks before he felt like a
human being again, he wrote later, and then he seems to have spent
another month in a pleasant tourist home overlooking Hong Kong
Harbor, watching a carnival of ships and junks surrounded by mountains that rose into mist. But already he looked like an old man, and
it couldn't have made him feel any younger.

Soon he was ready to bounce back, overly optimistic as ever. At
a stop in Taipei he received word that Universal Studios was thinking
of offering him $5,000 for one of his racetrack stories; there was also
interest in *Never Come Morning*. After arriving in San Francisco the
day the astronauts landed on the moon, Nelson seems to have borrowed against his good fortune and headed directly for Los Angeles.
Two producers, including Abe Polonsky, were competing for the
racetrack story, which Phil Kaufman wanted to direct, but when,
after a few days, neither bought it, Algren went home. A week later
Kaufman phoned to tell him that it might come through as a TV
deal, but it never did. Algren's debts, combined with the Saigon
disaster, made his financial situation bleak.

Candida pulled him out of the hole by selling a section of the
abandoned racetrack novel to *Playboy* for $3,000; this seemed to
patch up all bad feelings between Algren and the enterprise. She

had also sold "The Decline and Fall of Ding-Dong Daddyland," the story of two heroin-heads in a condom factory, to *Commentary,* and a piece on Tokyo went to *Holiday*. He had sent one piece on Saigon to *The Atlantic* and was working on two more, but was surprised when the magazine didn't buy them, for he felt they were too topical not to be taken. However, as Max Geismar later commented, since Algren "always ends up in the slums of any society he visits, and usually makes his sociological discoveries in the brothels of those slums, he is not always the best guide to contemporary history."

At a party, Algren met *Playboy* fiction editor Sue McNear, a much younger woman with three daughters who was beginning to write fiction. McNear found Algren kind, loving, and compassionate, and they were soon having dinner together two or three times a week. "He liked to be taken care of and he wanted to be loved," McNear remembered. Algren, generous about helping her with her work, told Targ about her forthcoming story in *Redbook* and suggested he take a look at her novel; he introduced her to John Blades, of the *Chicago Tribune,* where she was soon reviewing books. McNear let him be himself. She loved the rebel in him, laughed at the way he stole a book whenever he went into Brentano's because he thought it was good for them, and if he became too boisterous or acted up at a party, she could get him to calm down. Nelson was also drawn to McNear's daughters, aged four, eight, and ten, taking them to Chinatown and the circus each year; he sent books and records every Christmas. But the relationship with McNear was not perfect. He wanted to believe it was a big romantic love story, but their warm attachment was more emotional than physically passionate. Somehow it was Algren's luck; but this distance between them may have helped the friendship last until his death.

During the early seventies, Algren published a substantial number of articles and enjoyed working on stories. In early 1970, *New Orleans Review* carried an interview with Algren, following it with his story of a man with an incredible nose for sniffing out gas leaks; that fall Algren wrote a weekly column, on subjects ranging from nostalgia to the police, for the antiestablishment *Chicago Free Press*. Some of the Saigon pieces that, aside from one published in *Rolling Stone,* had never found a home appeared in the intellectual magazine *The Critic*. An expanded story about his Depression gas-station days, "The Last Carousel," won second prize in an annual *Playboy* fiction contest; "I Never Hollered Cheezit the Cops" appeared in *The At-*

lantic and other stories in *Audience.* He wrote a number of articles for the *Chicago Tribune Magazine,* including a piece of art criticism on Edward Hopper, five poems, and some nostalgia pieces. Another reminiscence of Simone de Beauvoir—sardonic, of course—wound up at *Playboy.*

But by now his way of working had completely changed. Little was left of his earlier sociological method of walking the streets, observing humanity, and taking notes. He had withdrawn, and now he fed off himself. Many of his stories were based on incidents from his past, or tales told to him by others, or ideas gleaned from written sources, all filtered through his tremendous imagination. It was work that, like book reviewing, could be done primarily in his apartment. "I have this curious knack," he wrote Roger of his work habits. "I'll toss scraps, pieces, odd comments, an interesting fact from Helsinki or a complaint from Mozambique into drawers until the accumulation amounts to a fire hazard; and then, years later, will grope (with only the vaguest notion of what I'm groping for) and will find a yellowed and torn dateline of a couple of lines with some silly observation that fits right into some current dilemma. I don't know how I do it."

Algren had always been a steady book reviewer and from 1969 to 1974 published some thirty book reviews and a couple of movie reviews, mostly in *The Critic* and in the *Los Angeles Times Book Review,* less frequently in *Rolling Stone, Chicago Free Press,* and the *Tribune.* Algren's tastes were eclectic. He read widely among contemporary novelists and world literature, often polishing off a book on the way to Sportsman's Park racetrack. "I don't know anyone who read more," said Sue McNear, recalling Algren's absorption for weeks in a three-volume history of the Civil War. "When he reviewed a book he would always go back and reread all of an author's work." Algren thought enough of his reviews to have them all retyped for a never-to-be-published seven-hundred-page collection of his criticism, and he appreciated a good review. "If there's a better reviewer than Styron I don't know who it is unless it's Elizabeth Hardwick; until she gets too cerebral," he wrote Roger after reading Styron's *New York Times* review of James Blake's *The Joint,* a novelistic collection of prison letters, which Algren had just reviewed for the *Los Angeles Times.* Styron's review had renewed some of his lost faith in *The New York Times Book Review.*

As a reviewer, Algren was rarely neutral. He was very appreciative of *The Joint,* had nothing but praise for Christopher Davis's *A Peek into the Twentieth Century,* the story of Edison and Westinghouse's rivalry to produce the electric chair. He knew of no more original writer than Donald Barthelme, and greatly enjoyed Lloyd Zimpel's *Meeting the Bear.* Favorite writers included Don DeLillo, John Cheever, and Joan Didion; the honesty of Hunter S. Thompson's *Fear and Loathing in Las Vegas* was worth more to him than Bellow, Barth, Updike, Gass, and Pynchon put together. When he disliked a book he could be vicious. "I shafted Mme. Utter Driveleau pretty good in the *LA Times,*" he told Targ of his review of de Beauvoir's *Coming of Age,* which accused Simone of obsessive detail, obvious truths, an inaccurate memory, and a gullibility he personally had witnessed. A review could nicely serve the revenge motive, though after finishing this piece, he wrote to a friend that even he was through with de Beauvoir.

But mostly Algren reviewed books for money. Lecture income had been falling off, and the $200 from LA was a handy item, given his weekly trips to Sportsman's Park. *The Critic* didn't pay that well, so he gave them reviews padded with quotes and plot summaries. He was sometimes bitter that someone of his talent should have to read tedious books for very modest sums, but he didn't complain much. For by now he considered himself a workingman whose trade happened to be writing, and like most workingmen, his trade was not the most important thing to him. "If I could get by without writing, I'd be very happy," Algren told an interviewer in the early 1970s. "I write for financial reasons. I don't figure I'm changing the world. Some people get a lot of laughs out of what I write, and that's good. I'm satisfied with this trade, which I do very easily—and because there's really nothing else I can do."

The fear of exploitation never left him. He always tried to publish parts of a book before it appeared in its full version so he could get the maximum payment before the publishers owned it, and he did not write on spec or to please an editor. When *The New York Review of Books* asked for a review and then wanted him to rewrite it, he sold it to *The Critic.* When Digby Diehl of the *Los Angeles Times* refused Algren's scathing review of a James Jones Book-of-the-Month Club selection, backed as it was by a quarter-million dollars of advertising, Algren refused to accept the offered fifty-dollar consolation prize and told Digby to pay up. Diehl did, though noting, apparently, that extortion and intimidation had won the day. "I thought it was the *LA Times Book Review* doing the exploiting and here it was *me* all along!" Nelson exclaimed to Roger. He had never gotten over the way the novel of *Golden Arm* had been lost, and even in 1971 he was peddling a story called "Otto Preminger's Strange Suspenjers."

Algren was a confirmed bachelor. Mary Corley still kept his house, working against the clutter of his books and an eccentric collection of typewriters kept in case his current one broke down—he rarely handwrote even the shortest letter. He still went weekly to Sportsman's and daily to the Luxor Baths. He was a regular moviegoer and liked to watch TV with a remote-control channel changer, hooked on *Laugh-In, The Carol Burnett Show,* talk shows, and public television. And he was an excellent host. When people came over, he welcomed them graciously, quick to fetch a pitcher of martinis or drip Italian coffee through a paper towel; interviewers were always made comfortable before any serious conversation could begin. Twice yearly he would throw terrific parties, and early guests to a summer affair would find Mary frying chicken in hundred-degree heat while electric fans blew hot air and paper napkins all about. Hospitable, courtly, Algren would serve up egg rolls, ravioli, chicken and potato chips, offering napkins and bringing more drinks. People spilled from one room to the next and onto the porch, invariably staying until late into the morning. The back porch was festooned with Christmas lights: "It was a crummy flat," said Studs, "but Nelson made it seem like the Dakota."

Many people thought that Algren looked years younger than his age. "It's striking how the man can move," remarked one journalist. "As he talks . . . his hands lead a life of their own, gesturing, tapping, raking his fringe of hair up the nape of his neck and into a peaked thicket." He could not endure fools, but he was easy to talk to, hilariously funny, and unintimidating. "One moment he's talking about some guy back in the old neighborhood who used to crib drinks by performing weird tricks on top of the bar, and half a second later he's discussing Mikhail Sholokov and his influence on French and Russian literature," wrote another observer. It was his energy and humor that people noticed.

But friends who hadn't seen him in a while were often shocked at the way he'd aged, and photographs of Algren in his early sixties reveal that his lack of ambition had taken a visible toll. Dressing in cheap polyester pants and polo shirts, he looked a bit like Art

Carney—and he liked the comparison—only Algren was fatter. Rarely sedentary, he nonetheless seemed to put on five pounds a year: he liked steaks, potatoes, wine, rich foods, and fancy desserts. His thinning hair was gray-white, his face jowly and sallow, his belly round and fat.

This was the individual who was becoming, as Studs noted, a sort of "nonperson" in Chicago, treated with benign neglect. One of his books was soon to appear in a new edition in Italy, but he couldn't find it on the shelves of the Chicago Public Library. In October 1971, *Playboy* had held a big conference of writers in Chicago without inviting him. Everyone from Alberto Moravia to Bruce Jay Friedman, John Clellon Holmes, Calvin Trillin, Arthur C. Clarke, and Jean Shepherd was there, but Studs had had to sneak Nelson in.

For a while Algren toyed with the idea of combining his Vietnam and Japan pieces into another travelogue on the Pacific, but the payoffs from his last two efforts didn't justify the time. Having decided to complete the story collection for Targ, he now wanted it to include poems, articles, and book introductions. Targ was amenable, and in early 1971, Algren set a date of January 1, 1973, for delivery of the manuscript. In the meantime, he reached into his "magpie drawer." "Algren sent me a huge box of clippings, scraps, junk mini-manuscripts, stuff going back to his early high school days," Targ remembered. "Book reviews, sports sketches, interviews, casuals, etc. I spent a week reading, sifting, sorting out the wheat from the chaff. Damned little wheat. We battled for weeks on the long-distance phone. He was reluctant to part with anything." Preliminary decisions were finally made, and Algren sent much of the manuscript to the typist, but the haggling and additions continued over the next two years.

He wanted a big, five-hundred-page book, and when Targ suggested something half that size, Algren insisted that this was exactly what he wished to avoid. Perhaps he thought a long book would get more attention and be taken seriously, but Roger Groening remembered that Algren also simply liked big books. Once Algren picked up a 99-cent hardcover in a supermarket and told Groening earnestly that he knew it would be good just by its weight. Roger tried to persuade him that he'd get more money, more sales, and probably a better critical reception by splitting the book in two, but Algren was adamant.

"Love in an Iron Rain" would no longer work as a title, and the story—the last of his old style—would be omitted. Algren called the collection *The Last Carousel,* after his prizewinning *Playboy* story, and sent Targ a Stephen Deutch photograph of a carousel for the front cover. Targ went along with the title, liked the photograph, and put a book jacket into production. Algren missed his January 1 deadline, set a new one for three weeks later, missed that one and told Targ to wait till late March. His letter seems to have been in the mail when Targ, who had been taking Algren's deadlines seriously, called long-distance. He was upset. Planning to publish in spring, he had sent salesmen out with the jacket to sell the book. "My God, Nelson, my heart just *stopped,*" Algren quoted Targ as saying when he heard the manuscript still wasn't ready. Algren thought Targ ridiculous for jumping the gun, never apparently feeling that *he* ought to have tried harder to meet his deadlines—though he seems to have been punctual with magazine articles. Publication was put off till fall.

In the manuscript Targ did finally receive, almost all the pieces had been published previously; he sent it back to Algren, who promptly returned it, asserting that permissions were the publisher's responsibility. By this point, Targ must have been irritated. "Something tells me he's salty at me," Algren wrote Roger. "Because he didn't even send me the fall catalog listing the book." Moreover, the manuscript Targ received was far from a final draft. Deleting the book introductions was easy enough, but because Algren constantly recycled old material, there were often duplications in scene or plot, some of which were still being sorted out of the galleys in July. Some were never sorted out at all.

But this didn't prevent the collection of thirty-seven pieces of prose and poetry from being highly entertaining—not because of Algren's self-described but hardly noticeable efforts to arrange the stories to give the overall impact of a novel but because his view of the world was so original. Many of the stories were memorable, especially "Home to Shawneetown," retitled "Dark Came Early in that Country," and "The Mad Laundress of Ding-Dong Daddyland" and "The Last Carousel." The volume also contained nostalgia from his adulthood as well as childhood pieces recycled from *Who Lost an American?,* historical pieces on Bonnie and Clyde, the Black Sox scandal, and Gregorio Cortez, the last begun as a screen treatment. There were glimpses into the world of the racetrack, carnival, Saigon street life, and Chicago: material that set off Algren's wild humor and wide curiosity. Sure, it was a hodgepodge, an omnibus, a big grab-bag to which Algren had added material for reasons as unliterary as revenge: "You're right about the Kazin and de Beauvoir, and a couple of other pieces—also the Preminger, being spiteful," he wrote Roger after publication. "You're also wrong about omitting them. Your feeling is based upon a false assumption, that the writer is a literary dude of great detachment, intent upon producing *Literature*." The cost to his reputation, especially in its current state, of trying to drive a wedge into Simone's belief in her infallibility or knocking the smiles off Kazin and Preminger was negligible. And despite its length and the occasional repetitions in scene or good lines, the collection succeeded; the variety of genres was not a problem at all. "Algren's journalism is a little hard to tell from his fiction," wrote one reviewer. "Algren puts himself right in the middle of his non-fiction, too, sets scenes beautifully, and tells it all with dialogue and colorful details . . . in other words . . . it's New Journalism, and Nelson Algren was writing it this way when Tom Wolfe was still at Yale working on his Ph.D. in American Studies." The advance reviews, especially from Max Geismar, were very enthusiastic, and Nelson looked forward to good sales, since the collection would clearly make a wonderful Christmas item.

The original publication date was apparently in late October, and in early September Algren requested a hundred copies from Targ—three times. When he received the book on October 23, the pages were out of order. Then things really began to go wrong. On October 27, Henry Kisor, book editor of the Chicago *Daily News,* devoted the cover of the weekly *Panorama* to the book, Algren recalled, along with a long article and a highly favorable review. The Monday after it ran, Kisor remembered, "I received a nice note from Nelson thanking me for the piece and offhandedly mentioning that the publication date had been moved back six weeks. Now it's a book editor's nightmare to review a book before it's in the stores— readers do take the trouble to go to a bookstore on the strength of a review, and they get mighty angry if a book's not in yet. So I had someone call Putnam's and find out what the hell was going on. Nobody'd told me the book had been delayed." The publicity person at Putnam's lamely explained that she'd told the *Sun-Times* and expected them to pass the word along—though why they'd be expected to do a competitor a favor is anybody's guess. The new pub-

lication date was November 28, and on November 10 Algren wrote
Targ that Studs Terkel, who wanted to devote a week of his radio
show to the book, couldn't seem to get a copy. This was rectified,
but the problem persisted. On November 26, Kroch's & Brentano's
still didn't have copies, and the *Tribune* and *Sun-Times* reviewed the
book favorably in time for November 28. "The reviews came out
and the books were not in the bookstores—none whatsoever,"
Deutch recalled. "Some finally came, in about ten days or two
weeks—but they sold out within two days. We were outraged, Nelson, Studs, Kogan, and myself. I called the publisher and so did
Studs. They apologized and books started trickling in before Christmas."

According to Algren, Putnam's saw "no reason to spend five
hundred dollars to promote a book out in the sticks. A Detroit reader
volunteered to underwrite a reception and Van Allen Bradley, a
Chicago bookman, offered to organize it. He ordered books but
none arrived. Authors are not permitted, by contract, to sell their
own books. Nevertheless I took fifty of my own copies and sold them
all within a half an hour. I could have sold the full hundred. The
book was not available elsewhere." By December 1, just three days
after the official publication date, Algren was quite frosty with Targ.
"The question of my next novel—which apparently troubles you—
isn't the question," he told Bill. "The question is whether I earn
money, or don't, on *Last Carousel*." It was easy enough to surmise
that he would not. Ironically, Algren had predicted the whole fiasco
in May, when he confided to Roger the uneasy suspicion that Putnam's was going to mishandle the book. "How I don't know. Probably by taking a full-page ad in the *Times* the week it comes out but
failing to distribute it until three months later."

With the holidays and the Modern Language Association convention, a dozen or so people converged on Nelson, perhaps helping to
distract him from the *Carousel* fiasco. Betty, Jess Ritter and his
girlfriend, and Malcolm Cowley were all in town, and Algren and
Terkel had drinks with Douglas Day, the pleasantly direct and non-
academic biographer of Malcolm Lowry. But the disappointment
over *The Last Carousel* remained. "Putnam's stopped distributing
the book two weeks before Christmas," Algren wrote Groening in
January, "and I haven't seen it on display anywhere since. The way
people buy it is to demand the bookstore order it, that's all. Or order
it themselves. You have to want it pretty badly to go to the trouble.

One ad in the Sunday *Times,* two small ones in the local press and that's it for G. P. Putnam's." For a time Algren liked to complain that the book wasn't reviewed anywhere, but it was reviewed fairly widely, and on the whole quite favorably. Yet many of the reviews had appeared before the book was available or after the first of the year, and with the distribution problem, it in effect missed the Christmas season. "Books started coming in quantities after the holidays," Deutch recalled, "and they were remaindered."

In early 1974, Kurt Vonnegut, Jr., nominated Nelson for the American Academy and Institute of Arts and Letters' Award of Merit for the novel, a prestigious honor, consisting of a medal and a thousand dollars, that had been awarded exclusively to Thomas Mann, Theodore Dreiser, Ernest Hemingway, Aldous Huxley, John O'Hara, and Vladimir Nabokov. "The other members thought it was a swell idea," Vonnegut remembered. "The respect was immediate. There was no campaigning because everyone agreed."

When Algren learned of the award, his correspondence with the Academy was unfailingly cordial, but he didn't seem as thrilled as Vonnegut had hoped he would be. Perhaps, as Vonnegut suspected, he was miffed at not already being a member of the Academy, the nation's highest honor society in the arts. Also, the award followed too closely the failure of *The Last Carousel,* which, as with all his unsuccessful books, Algren seemed to see as a rejection of himself. Besides, he had long before been vociferously excluded and had long since withdrawn himself from the first rank of the literary world. He had needed such an award twenty years before, when it might have helped him get a contract for "Entrapment." Now he was just a journalist, a professional writer working for a barely middle-class living, and no medal was going to change that. Having mocked a *Playboy* fiction medallion and offered the National Book Award for sale, he could hardly have been excited about the medal, and the thousand dollars, while pleasant, wasn't an incredible amount of money. He may well have felt gratified, but in a practical sense, what did it really mean? Was it suddenly going to sell *The Last Carousel,* the way such awards boosted sales in France? Of course not.

Algren believed—and believed with contempt—that awards could not generate respect because the only real way to gain respect in America was to make a lot of money. Book editors judged books on their potential profits, with no thought toward encouraging or supporting an artist worthy of the Award of Merit. He had once noted that the hostility of the local Poles toward *Never Come Morning* had subsided when he'd received the thousand-dollar fellowship in 1947, and that when word came out that Sinatra would star in *Golden Arm,* it had practically vanished. If he still correctly believed that Preminger and the formalist critics had been his enemies, with each setback his animosity extended, now to the American people, who allowed their opinions to be shaped, he felt, by *Time* magazine, in his eyes the quintessential purveyor of this moneygrubbing attitude.

Thus his acceptance speech was an attack on the weekly news magazine. Noting that in its pages he had been called an ape and a dog leaping for a bone, he was glad at least to have been in the company of Tennessee Williams, "whose plays were denounced in *Time* as too nauseating to serve as food for swine," he wrote. "*Filet mignon avec sauce bernaise* [sic] was hardly good enough, once *Time* learned his plays had earned Williams eighteen million dollars [where Algren got his figures is unclear]. His picture then appeared on the cover, accompanied by a long, respectful, even flattering interview. The present honor, however more solid, will not, I'm afraid, get me out of *Time*'s Children's Zoo. For I'm still on my first million."

His tortuous logic was, of course, more obvious to himself than to others. Reading it in advance of the ceremony, Vonnegut found Algren's acceptance speech not only inappropriate but "not sane," even "batty." He was able to cut it to a gracious "thank you," for Algren apparently couldn't see spending a chunk of the grand just to pick up the award: he hadn't attended the ceremony for the 1947 fellowship either, when a thousand dollars had meant a lot more. Perversely telling Vonnegut, whom he actually liked a great deal, that he had to lecture to a garden club, Algren became the first recipient in the history of the award not to claim it personally.

20.
The Devil's Stocking

IN EARLY 1974, *Esquire* offered Algren $1,250 for an article on boxer Rubin "Hurricane" Carter, who had been convicted, along with his friend John Artis, of triple murder in 1967. A ruthless, aggressive fighter, Carter had often appeared on televised Friday-night fights in the early 1960s, and Algren had seen him at St. Nick's Arena in New York. At the time of his arrest, Carter was the number-one contender for the middleweight title. The story, combining boxing, murder, and prisons, seemed perfect for Algren.

Carter and Artis's trouble began at around two-thirty A.M. on June 17, 1966, when two black men walked into the all-white Lafayette Bar and Grill in Paterson, New Jersey, and shot three people to death and wounded another man in the eye. Within minutes, police chased and lost a white car speeding toward New York. They then stopped a white car driving quietly through Paterson, carrying Rubin Carter, John Artis, and John "Bucks" Royster, but let it go, since they were looking for *two* blacks in a white car. The trio continued on, stopping briefly at Carter's house and dropping off Royster. A quarter hour or so later, their car was stopped again, this time by five squad cars loaded with shotgun-bearing cops. Artis and Carter were taken to the Lafayette Bar, where about seventy-five people had gathered. No one could identify them. Aside from being black, they did not match the description of the killers, and even the man who had been shot in one eye studied them from his hospital bed before emphatically declaring they were not the men. Nevertheless, the pair was taken downtown and grilled for seventeen hours without counsel. Carter even took a lie detector test, and was allowed to go.

Hurricane Carter was no stranger to the American penal system. A juvenile offender sentenced to a reformatory for stabbing a homosexual who attacked him, he escaped, joined the Marines, and discovered boxing. In his early twenties, after serving four years in Trenton State Prison for snatching a pocketbook, he became a professional boxer and went straight. At the time of the shootings, Carter was an established and respected prizefighter who often won by knockout; he had previously missed the middleweight title only by a controversial decision and was planning to fight Dick Tiger for it again. An outspoken man who drove a custom Eldorado, he was a militant spokesman for black civil rights and against police brutality. Perhaps because of this, by the mid-1960s he began to be harassed by the police.

Four months after the shootings, when he returned from a fight in Argentina, Carter, along with Artis, was charged with triple murder. The prosecution's main witnesses were two habitual criminals, Bello and Bradley, who claimed they'd been trying to break into a nearby sheet metal company at the time of the shootings. The night of the murder, Bello had been unable to identify Carter, but four months later, when on separate charges he and Bradley faced many decades in prison, he changed his story and fingered the boxer. Two grand juries refused to believe him, but a third handed down indictments. Though the prosecution had no other witnesses, no motive, and no murder weapon, police now claimed to have found two bullets during a search of Carter's car.

Firearms experts testified to no similarities of the two bullets to the ones used in the shootings, other than caliber; one bullet was nonetheless entered as evidence. Carter and Artis, steadfastly proclaiming their innocence, were found guilty by an all-white jury that recommended mercy instead of the electric chair: Carter would serve two consecutive life terms, and the twenty-one-year-old Artis, who had been offered athletic scholarships and had never been in any trouble, received three concurrent life terms.

Carter had served seven years when Algren sought out Fred Hogan, an investigator for the New Jersey Public Defender's Office who was convinced that Carter and Artis had been framed. Hogan and Algren liked each other. Algren had come to the case thinking Carter was guilty, but Hogan told him that Bradley had bragged to cellmates about lying in the Carter case; Bello also revealed he had lied. Since the statute of limitations for perjury had run out, Hogan was sure both would recant their testimony. It became obvious to

Algren that Carter's and Artis's convictions had been a serious miscarriage of justice. Hogan, eager to publicize the case, expedited Algren's work, arranging for him to visit Carter, then in Newark Hospital for an eye operation.

Algren liked Carter immediately. "A very forthright man, coherent, deeply moral, and determined," he wrote Roger Groening; and in another letter continued, "Carter is the *sanest* man I've ever met." Feeling he shouldn't have been in there, Carter would neither wear a prison uniform nor join the work detail for eighty cents a day. According to Sue McNear, Algren admired the way Carter just let his anger *pour* out.

That summer Algren's original article on Carter was rejected. "*Esquire* wanted their own commercial piece—and they went to the wrong man," explained Hy Cohen, who then worked for Candida Donadio. Raising the question of Carter's innocence seemed taboo, but both McNear and Cohen remembered that after a rejection at *Playboy,* Algren felt he was really on to something. "He needed a project," McNear said, "and there it was."

He financed it by speaking at Michigan State University, running a summer workshop in Boulder, and teaching a ten-week creative writing class for ten grand at the University of Florida in the fall. But he was eager to return to Paterson. Bello and Bradley's recantations, revealing that they had committed perjury following threats, promises of leniency, and appeals to racism from Passaic County law officers, made *The New York Times'* front page, and Algren's *Esquire* editor probably could have kicked himself as Selwyn Raab, downplaying Hogan's efforts, got the glory. However, Judge Larner, who had presided at the Carter-Artis trial, ruled that such recantations were notoriously unreliable and could not be used as a basis for a new trial: "The entire judicial process would be frustrated by the whim of a witness recanting his testimony." Nevertheless, along with Carter's just published autobiography, *The Sixteenth Round,* legal efforts to free him continued.

By mid-December, Algren had found an apartment in a Sicilian neighborhood one block from the Passaic River in Paterson. He met John Artis, and his friendship with Hogan, who had given him the trial transcripts, was deepening. He spent Christmas with Hogan and his parents on the Jersey Shore; he saw Brooklyn across the bay the way he'd once seen Chicago from the beaches at Gary. A small city of ethnic neighborhoods much like the Chicago he had lost, Paterson made him realize how little he had in his own city. There, his career was in a rut, and his life was stagnating; his friend Stuart McCarrell felt that Mary Corley's recent death had unnerved him and disrupted his domestic life. Ostensibly because he needed more time to understand the complexities of the murder case, Algren decided to move to Paterson and leave Chicago for good.

"I don't know why you, or anyone should be surprised at my moving to Paterson," he wrote Steve Deutch lightheartedly. "I've been telling you, for at least a decade, that I planned to move to San Francisco, and Paterson is directly on the way. I'm only two hours from New York Harbor now, where I can get a ship to Barcelona or Marseilles, and from there to a Greek or Cretan port, thence to the Persian Gulf and down through the Indian Ocean and around to Yokohama and Tokyo (I won't stop in Korea because that would be going out of my way). And from Japan, Manila is a comparatively short distance. Any freight ship can make San Diego, from Manila or Luzon, in two weeks. Then I'm only about forty-five minutes, by air, from San Francisco. So it all fits in exactly as I planned."

When he returned to Chicago in February to pack up, there were farewell lunches, interviews, and television appearances to herald his departure. But after longer than sixteen years in the apartment, moving proved more difficult than he had imagined. After dispatching seventy-five twenty-pound cartons of books by the postal system, he ran into three suburban women who ran house sales and instantly solved his moving problem. He would auction off everything except things of value like Simone's letters, hoping to pick up as much as three grand.

So on a Saturday in March, Algren began auctioning off the possessions of his Chicago life with seemingly little sentimentality, though for his friends, the sale created an air of finality, a sense that past was past. Art Shay bought the oak desk on which Algren had written *Golden Arm,* remembering Nelson and Simone leaning against it, sipping tea. As collectors, fans, hangers-on, old friends, reporters, and photographers descended on the Evergreen apartment, asking, How much for the signed *Playboy*s? Was the dishwasher for sale? Algren gloried in his own swindles: he'd fetched a tidy sum for a table he said was the very one on which he'd played poker with the neighborhood guys while writing *Golden Arm.* Actually, it was just an old table. But other moments of acquisitiveness weren't funny. "He was a very strange individual," said Stephen

Deutch. "He liked me and I loved him—I thought he would offer me a memento—I wanted to have something. There was a photo of Nelson in his living room, and I said I wanted that photo, and he said, 'OK—it's three and a half bucks.' I paid it, but this says something about the strange combination of things that was Nelson. I don't resent it—it was that his personality was so complicated."

Deutch sensed correctly that for Algren, the sale represented a clean break with Chicago. When Algren severed a relationship, it was nearly always completely. He had long been saying that he wanted to move, and now he had found a place to go, but the fiasco with what he hoped would be his big comeback book, *The Last Carousel,* had probably precipitated his departure, as such rejections always forced him to withdraw. In 1974, the year following *Carousel*'s publication, Algren had spent at least seven months out of town, in Gainesville, Boulder, Paterson, Cahokia Downs, and in other cities for lecture stops. In his mind he may have already made the break. He told reporters that Chicago had never done anything for him and that he had never been able to find his books in the libraries there the way he had in other cities. "This is all worthwhile," Algren told reporters, motioning to the sale. "For the first time in my life—now that I'm leaving—Chicago is finally saying some nice things about me. You know, the kind of praise I wouldn't be getting unless I had just died."

By the end of the weekend, everything including manuscripts, knickknacks and furniture, even the refrigerator, had been auctioned off. For the week or so before he left town, he stayed with Sue McNear. "He was anxious and upset," she recalled. "He needed to calm down. He wasn't sleeping. He didn't look well, and he knew he wasn't." Master as he was at leaving his past behind, it was not easy. He was almost sixty-six. Even if the Wabansia nest had been torn down long before, Chicago had been the backdrop for his entire life, the place where Bruno Bicek and Frankie Machine had lived and died, where he had fallen in love with Simone, where he had once felt so profoundly connected to humanity. Before he left he called Caesar Tabet to say he was leaving. Tabet hadn't heard from him in years, and after some small talk wished him well in Paterson. But Algren had really called about the woman inextricably tied to the lost, half-finished work that had died with his own ambition.

"How's Margo, Caesar?"

"She's fine, Nelson, just fine. You'd be surprised. She's got a job, her daughter's with her, her grandchildren."

Nelson seemed very pleased. Then he left town.

He wrote to a friend in Chicago that there were moments when he sat among his cartons wondering what the hell he was doing in Paterson. For he was a man who was cut off—he had no family and no love relationship, and he had left the city where he had lived for more than sixty years.

Yet he was soon socializing with friends in New York, and that summer the attractive and savvy Joan Kerckhoff Hammond, in town to see her ex-husband about money, visited Nelson with her two daughters, eight and fourteen, and brought his apartment alive. Roger Groening, who phoned frequently and periodically, came down from upstate, introduced Algren to Roy Finer, a tall, careworn New York City homicide detective. Algren loved to listen to Finer talk about his cases, and Roy took him to the morgue, where he saw a doctor cut a scalp, pull the face down like a mask, saw through the skull, and pull out the brains. Algren was revolted, but also toured the Parts Department, a repository for body parts found citywide, and the Black Museum, with its sample victims of drowning, electrocution, gassing, and so on which help pathologists and coroners determine cause of death. "It is strange how fragile this man-creature is," Nelson wrote Roger. "In one second he's just garbage. Garbage, that's all."

Algren warmed to the old-time local fight programs that flourished in the industrial towns around Paterson. A longtime fight fan, he knew all about faking injuries, slowing down, saving oneself, keeping the opponent bewildered, the blitzkrieg. He had even liked the movie *Rocky,* despite its obviousness. He'd always wanted to own a fighter and had a natural nostalgia for old-fashioned gyms with peeling paint, swinging wood doors, faded linoleum. In Paterson, he hung around Lou Duva's Gym; in Manhattan, he went to Gleason's; sometimes he would get on buses to Elizabeth, Bayonne, even Philadelphia. His apartment was covered with pictures of Stanley Ketchel, Hurricane Carter, and other fighters pasted together into collages, his latest way of displaying memorabilia.

At the same time he pored over old newspaper accounts of the Carter case and copies of *Ring* magazine in the New York Public Library; he met Hogan often and visited Carter in Rahway, New

Jersey. He planned an extended article based on the trial transcripts, the type of investigative reporting that could be serialized. Although he had strong doubts about Carter's guilt, he would not focus on Carter's innocence, but would merely show the nefarious process by which the verdict had been reached. By summer he had more than two hundred pages of manuscript.

By then several articles had appeared in the local press about Algren, and he began having trouble with his landlady, a woman he claimed had prevented two telephone workers, both black, from entering her basement to install his desk phone. As Hogan saw it, she was conservative and didn't appreciate his work on the Carter-Artis case or his free-spirited attitude. She served Algren, who had no intention of moving, with an eviction notice, and the court ruled in her favor. There may have been justification: letters from Nelson's lawyers suggest a dispute over payment of rent.

In addition to a small Social Security check, Algren lived on modest foreign and paperback royalties and an occasional $250 from *Chicago Tribune* book reviews. His income was erratic, but he often bet at OTB and, unwilling to scrimp on pleasure, took Hogan out to expensive lunches with four or five drinks each. "He had certain patterns," Roy Finer explained, "certain things he had to do. When I went over there he would insist on going out to a sit-down dinner. He'd have a couple of martinis and start crackling with a roller-coaster delivery of ideas and witticisms." He very likely had occasion to pay for dinner with the rent money.

Unwilling to fight the eviction, Algren moved to the tamer nearby town of Hackensack, only thirty minutes from Manhattan. His new landlord was Matt Panczyk, a young history professor who didn't mind his work on the Carter-Artis case and laughed at the trouble it had caused his landlady. His new apartment was a duplex in a rambling Victorian on a dead-end street between a railroad track and a Sears. A sanitation worker and an ex-con helped Nelson move his books and furniture, and once again he felt he could make a new start, this time paying his rent on time.

Algren spent Thanksgiving with Hogan and that winter invited the investigator to Chicago for a week. Algren stayed with friends; and Sue McNear, who put up Hogan, threw a party in their honor. Hogan remembered her as a great hostess, but Algren was in a foul mood. He was rude, brusquely trying to cut off talk of the Carter case; McNear remembered a fight. Journalists and everyone else wanted to talk to the much-younger Hogan about his work on the case, and Studs Terkel interviewed him on the radio. Nelson was jealous; *he* had wanted the attention.

In early 1976, the Carter-Artis convictions were struck down because the prosecution had suppressed tapes surrounding the interrogations of Bello and Bradley. With a new trial pending in the fall, Carter and Artis were freed. By his own account, Algren received a $6,000 grant from the National Endowment for the Arts for his work on the case, and if the previous summer he had denied writing a book, now he was eagerly trying to market one. The timing couldn't have been better: public opinion seemed increasingly favorable, and Artis and the former fighter were bound to be exonerated in the second trial.

Four major magazines including *The New Yorker* turned down Algren's lengthy article on Carter, but he refused to believe the trouble was with his writing or the subject matter. In early 1976, he tried working with another agent, Joan Daves, but their relationship was so brief they never even met. As he explained to Donadio when he humbly asked to be taken back, "We differ upon my obligation to Targ." Targ would not let him go. It was indeed strange, since Algren was no money-maker for Putnam's: *Last Carousel*'s paperback rights had been sold for what was described as "the weensiest sum ever heard." As Putnam's read the manuscript, Algren was crudely insulting Targ in Chicago and New Jersey newspaper interviews. Infuriated, Targ wrote Algren that he wanted no more to do with him, that he "could no longer cope with his psychosis." He may have also threatened to sue. Nelson found this letter hilarious, and carried it in his pocket to show interested parties.

Putnam's rejected "Carter," though probably not because of the Targ-Algren feud. The first fifty pages, about Carter's rise in the world of prizefighting, were underwritten. Neither Roger Groening nor Stephen Deutch liked them. "I was bored with this section," said Deutch, who felt it could interest only fight fans; Roger agreed, surprised at how completely it lacked the vivid storytelling Nelson had earlier brought to his fight scenes. The second half of the book relied almost exclusively on trial transcripts, with little embellishment or interpretation. The consensus, including that of the editors who saw it, was that it contained too much trial testimony and not enough Algren. Nelson did revise the first fifty pages, but his response to this criticism, Roger recalled, was to say that putting in more Algren wasn't the point: he was trying to do an objective, journalistic job. "He wanted to do it at arm's length," said Roger, "with as little emotional involvement as possible." He wasn't even attempting to create poetic reporting. He introduced himself as a journalist, and he thought of himself as an excellent one, but he had moved away from a commitment to good prose.

For he felt with a gambler's certainty that the subject alone was bound to make him a lot of money, and Putnam's rejection didn't discourage him in the least. "He thought he was going to the World Series," Roy recalled; Algren felt sure he could sell the book for at least fifty thousand. In an interview with Henry Kisor of the *Sun-Times,* he was ridiculously cocky: he said he was glad to be free of Putnam's, that the book was now going to Random House. Kisor asked if anyone there had read the manuscript or any part of it. "No, they haven't seen it," Algren admitted, but "they'd take it anyway."

Luck at the track seemed to sustain his enthusiasm that summer of 1976. In late July he had a winning streak, one day picking up $236 of track money. He headed home, he wrote Roger, "so drenched in sweat I can hardly make the subway platform . . . with token in hand, I hear the train coming and start to run and my goddamned pants start falling. I have only one pair I can get into and they don't zip. I hold them together with a horse-size safety pin and wear my shirt outside to cover the pin. I've got to run holding my wallet in my left hand and my pants up with my right and the token too." He made the train and took a room at a Times Square hotel with a Japanese health club on the third floor. He got into a wonderful tub in an air-conditioned room, emerged for veal scaloppine, martinis, and red wine at Sardi's, and had a massage. His good luck at the track continued: a few days later, he had another ninety-nine coming from an off-track bet.

He was also entertaining. One party attended by Geraldine Page and Rip Torn was wall to wall with people, and Nelson, with no one to cook for him, had catered it with pizza and plenty of liquor. Some parties, however, were smaller and not as cheerful. New York artist Richard Merkin, a fan who'd been writing to Nelson since 1969, remembered a small birthday celebration Nelson threw around 1976. "It was hopeless. There was Roy Finer and his girl, me and my girl, and Algren. It was a most bizarre party. Algren was leading this older-bachelor thing with this enormous paunch. . . . There were several plates of the richest, most expensive German cookies, around twelve pizzas for the six people, and cheap sweet wine. Finer brought over two porno movies. . . . One was like seventeen guys and a girl. My girlfriend and the other girl were talking. It was like a stag party but there were women there—a kind of a forties thing." Another friend remembered a breakfast at Algren's: a bunch of rolls dumped onto the kitchen table.

By now, Algren's relationships with women were casual, uncommitted, and mostly paid for. The big-money Times Square area was an enormous revelation. It was hard to afford, but he visited dance shows, spas, health clubs, massage parlors, and tropical lounges, for a while seeing a Japanese woman regularly, for another period a multilingual Eastern European. In response to Mayor Koch's sweeping crackdown on Times Square prostitution, Algren sent the mayor a letter with his name and address, indicating that he visited a woman in a place on West 45th Street every two weeks or so—should he call before he went next time, so they could arrest him? When his girlfriend had to take an unexpected trip home to Japan, he was lonely until she returned. Algren looked older than his sixty-seven years. He was overweight, and this, along with his gravy-stained shirts and other signs that he didn't care about his appearance, kept other women at a distance.

He was somewhat eccentric. Once, visiting one of Roger's friends, Algren took a shower after being told to make himself at home; at one of Roy's parties, he went to sleep. Roy and Nelson once drove up to Saratoga to visit Roger, who had just opened a bookstore. Nelson browsed among the books, birdlike head down. "Got any Algren?" he barked. "I don't know, is he important?" Roger shot back. Nelson couldn't resist pointing out that there was no Alberto Moravia, but assured Roger there would be lots of money there—he could smell it. (Six months later the store was failing.) They met Roger's wife for a fancy meal Roger naturally paid for, and everyone was in fine spirits. But Nelson and Roy were staying at a country farmhouse a few miles away, and Algren couldn't stand the solitude. The next morning he was pacing like a caged lion; he had heard *owls*. "So. You come up here, you see the sights, and that's it; there's nothing else to do," he complained, so irritated and agitated that Roy took him back to Roger's and then to Hackensack.

Nelson's landlord, Matt, was an old friend of Joe Pintauro, a novelist who had a house on Long Island, and that summer Nelson said he'd like to meet him and see the Hamptons. He still imagined living where he could look out to miles of water, and on a lovely July day he and Matt and Joe headed out the Long Island Expressway. In Southampton, they ate shrimp near the Atlantic, surrounded by ficus trees, Nelson pouring glass after glass of wine and feeling he was in paradise. "I'm not on Long Island," he exclaimed. "This is Cuba! The Virgin Islands!" But things turned gloomy when Algren made no move to pick up the tab. The reason was simple, Roger later explained. "He worked on a turf policy. When you were on his turf, he always paid. When he was on your turf, you paid." Uneasily, his companions took care of the check. Later Algren took an instant dislike to Joe's roommate, and after a tour of the Hamptons and a sumptuous dinner at the American Hotel which he again refused to help pay for, he wanted to go home. Pintauro felt that Algren disliked him, but most likely Algren had simply seen what he wanted to see.

He'd still had no luck placing the Carter manuscript: Random House and a number of other publishers had rejected it. Scores of celebrities including Muhammad Ali and Bob Dylan were organizing a benefit fund-raiser for Carter at Madison Square Garden, and Hogan and Algren viewed this celebrity circus with disdain. Algren was worried about the way Carter, out on bail, was offending people. The more he learned about the case, the more he gave up trying to come to a clear conclusion about Carter's innocence, but on the basis of the evidence he expected an acquittal. As the new trial approached, Algren told Donadio not to submit the book anymore: he'd add an update after the verdict.

That fall of 1976, Algren agreed with Hogan that it would have been better for the local Office of the Public Defender to represent Carter and Artis than the New York team of Beldock and Steel, who might not sit well with a small-town jury: Algren called Myron Beldock "an abrasive New York Jew." The prosecutor did indeed play on the jury's resentment of the New York media and its coverage of the Garden fund-raiser. And former defense witnesses now testified for the state. Hogan, it was claimed, had bribed Bello to obtain his recantation (a charge for which Hogan was later prosecuted and exonerated). Bello recanted his recantation and now testified for the prosecution, and, in the state's most blatantly unjust move, a motive of "racial revenge" was introduced, suggesting that the Lafayette murders avenged the slaying of a black bartender earlier the same day. This motive suggested, basically, that the crime could be explained by the fact that the victims were white and the accused black. When Judge Leopizzi, who had been excluded from the first trial because he had represented another suspect in this case, allowed the motive's introduction, attorney Lewis Steel accused him of "turning the trial into a racial nightmare" and was charged with contempt for his "idiotic remarks." Even the prosecutor expected the jury, which began deliberating before lunch after hearing six weeks of testimony from over seventy witnesses, to take a day to reach a decision, but they were ready after dinner: Carter and Artis were again found guilty.

Algren was shocked. He simply couldn't believe that the jury had been taken in by the racial innuendo and the implausibility of so much of the evidence. In frustration and disappointment he briefly believed Carter had been sent back to jail to be murdered, but after he had calmed down, what bothered him most was that Carter had not taken the stand on his own behalf. Carter had not wanted to be cross-examined on his attitudes toward police in his autobiography, but Algren felt that too many people, especially Hogan, had put themselves on the line for Carter, and that he should have been willing to do the same. Hogan knew there had been enough irregularities in the second trial to bring about a third, but it was over.

Carter was now passé. Algren's book had been retitled "The Other Carter," and Candida continued to send it around, but without success. "I'm not disappointed, however," Nelson said. "I liked the three years I put into it, and know it's a good book. And so long as Carter remains alive, the story remains alive." He would finish it anyway, though he tiredly told an interviewer, "It's possible, I suppose, that I'll never publish another book, but so what? . . . I've seen a lot of writers who didn't know when to stop."

In May 1977, after the book was rejected at Pantheon, the house that published Studs Terkel, Algren went to the Midwest for a six-week trip, the longest since he'd left Chicago. Candida had been suggesting he fictionalize the book to salvage something, and Deutch and Terkel encouraged him to do so. Algren realized that it was either make it a novel or abandon it altogether, but fictionalization meant going back on his own promise to himself not to write another novel, a deliberate choice adhered to for many years. He was not happy as he set about revising it that fall.

He changed the title to "The Fighter" and turned Carter into a boxer named Ruby Calhoun, extending the action beyond the second conviction and adding a wholly fictional character, a young black woman named Dovie-Jean Dawkins, who enters a kind of living death as a prostitute in Times Square after Calhoun's second conviction. It became clear that the novel needed expansion and more characters, and Algren revised it, placing Dovie-Jean in Times Square earlier and including more scenes of the life there. But even with the new material, Roy Finer felt Algren was sporadic in his intention. "One day he'd think, 'The hell with it, I'm not gonna work on it anymore,' and then a few days later he'd find himself thinking, 'Well what the hell else am I doing? I might as well give it a shot.' . . . He was ambivalent about it. He'd get disgusted." Roger agreed. "It was the loss in belief. He didn't really think the novel mattered. So he worked on it, but beneath it all it didn't matter."

In spring 1978, after a rejection from Viking, he began revising it again. In May, Jimmy Breslin devoted a highly laudatory column to his underrated career, and Algren soon applied for a Guggenheim grant, listing Breslin, Royko, Terkel, and John Blades, book editor of the *Tribune,* as references. But like all such applications, the effort did not succeed. In August he spent a month's vacation in the south of France with Joan Hammond and her two daughters, of whom he was extremely fond. Hammond was now in permanent exile. Algren wrote a friend that he too would have liked to exile himself—as if he had not already done so. But he had no money, and could not retire until he finished and sold "The Fighter."

That he was trapped by his financially precarious life Algren would never admit. "I'm not in debt. I don't have a family. I'm not afraid of not having money," he said publicly. But he wanted the security of owning a house. He was getting old, and he was terrified of dying in a nursing home. Once Finer, back from an operation in the hospital, told Nelson he'd seen a guy paralyzed from the neck down. Nelson was chilled. " 'If I get that bad, I just want to go,' " Finer remembered him saying. "That was his term for death—'just go.' "

Algren's belly had reached huge proportions. He knew it was a burden on the heart and didn't like to talk about health. "I don't want to call down some curse—you know, fall down tomorrow with a cardiac thing." But he hated the stomach, which didn't match his mental image of himself as sexy and alive. "He had always been an exerciser," said Richard Merkin, "you know, the light bag, the heavy bag, but he seemed to have thrown in the towel. I found it astonishing." Lou and Martha Lou Gilbert had also been shocked when they saw him in late 1976; they asked him if he'd been drinking, but Algren told them seriously that he just couldn't get rid of it. He wasn't sedentary; he liked to walk, worked out at the Hackensack Y, and even bought a bicycle. But he seemed to think he could work off the stomach by exercise alone, without cutting down on the rich foods, martinis, and sweet desserts, and this was not a realistic approach to the problem.

Outside of seeing Roy and Roger and Hogan occasionally, Algren's life was solitary. The excitement, optimism, and sense of purpose he had felt while involved in the Carter case were gone. "He would answer the phone like someone from the morgue," Roger remembered. "I got the impression it was really bleak." Once Roger came down and set up a color TV, leaving the wires draped around the room for Nelson to make a more permanent arrangement, and they had some scotch. "When I came down six weeks later, the wires had not been touched and the same amount of scotch was in the bottle, so I knew he hadn't seen anyone," Groening said.

There were other signs that he was estranged from the world around him. His sexist remarks that American women were expensive and uncooperative reflected the *Playboy* objectification of women he had so harshly criticized in the early sixties. And his keen observation sometimes deserted him. One time at the fights a friend couldn't help but notice Algren's inability to tell a right hand from a left hook, as if the fight he was "seeing" was as much in his imagination as in the ring. Another time he and Roy had gone to the South Bronx and looked over the devastation. Nelson said, "This is the kind of place where good fighters come from." But it was completely blasted out. "This was not the neighborhood he was thinking about, the rough neighborhoods of the thirties and forties that were still neighborhoods," Roy said. "He wasn't in touch."

And he could be forgetful, disorganized. Once he and Roy's girlfriend, Naomi, had a date for the racetrack, Roy remembered. "He says, 'Meet me at Penn Station.' Now I don't have to tell you what Penn Station is—it's a helluva big place—but this is the kind of fuck-up he was. Things got lost . . . [were] chaotic, incomplete. He didn't like organization: it was a departure from freedom, it was conformist." Of course, he didn't conceive of himself as disorganized. When Steve Deutch's daughter was an executive producer of the movie *Heartland,* Deutch invited Nelson to the premiere in New York. But Nelson had confused the name of the theater with another one, and arrived at the right theater just in time. "He accused me," said Deutch, who had written him with all the information. "It was my fault."

This was the man who, in April 1979, after throwing a bash to celebrate his seventieth birthday, handed Donadio what he considered the final version of the novel he called "Chinatown." He had added a prison uprising, taking details from the report of the New York State Special Commission on Attica, and while it was ostensibly a novel about the boxer Calhoun, it focused significantly on Dovie-Jean Dawkins and her lover, Red Holloways, who resembles the other suspect in the Carter case. After the murders, Dovie-Jean and Red flee to New York, where she becomes a Times Square hooker. Like Sophie in *Golden Arm,* Red ends up in a psychiatric hospital; and Calhoun is reconvicted in the second trial.

It was approximately the sixth version of a book that he had thought was going to be an easy money-maker, something he could put together at little emotional cost to himself. Instead, Algren's last work, a "non-fiction novel" as Donadio described it, was one he had not even wanted to write, one that had been created merely out of an attempt to salvage a property. "Chinatown," published after a number of revisions as *The Devil's Stocking,* portrayed outcast people, but without a deep identification with them, and it seems curiously flat and dead. There are some memorable scenes, especially those of an older man like Algren himself, who bets on the horses and patronizes Times Square whorehouses. But in general there is little rhythm between sentences, no poetry at all. Characters are "breathless with surprise and wonder"; the sex scenes, in which Dovie-Jean "[brings] the organ up hugely," are the work of a man who has substituted stock phrases for description, who has refused to give of himself. *The Devil's Stocking* is the creation of an act of will, the same furious will that once made Algren mold himself into one of the great American novelists of the twentieth century. But it is a novel written from the head, with almost nothing from the heart.

Algren did not really want to see the book's many problems, or that these were the result of years of his withholding of self. Stephen Deutch, who spoke to him often, remembered that he became much more enthusiastic as he worked. "He'd say, 'You know, Steve, I think I've got a *book*.' " He had a great feeling of accomplishment, encouraged by recent German interest in his work. In late 1978, Algren had become friends with journalist Jan Herman, who put him in touch with Carl Weissner, a top German translator who had served as German agent for Charles Bukowski and William Burroughs.

German literary people had unfailingly treated Algren with the respect due an important novelist, and Weissner was no exception. He told Algren an author of his reputation could afford to insist on new translations and assured Algren that he could find a publisher who would offer a straight 10 percent royalty. Sales suddenly began to appear. When German *Playboy* paid hefty prices for "Dark Came Early in That Country" and "Topless in Gaza," a Times Square bar piece from *New York* magazine, Nelson dove into the magpie drawer for other possible sales. One German publisher even offered him an advance, sight unseen, on the new novel.

Algren wanted big money, and, fantasizing about this, he now told Donadio he thought a reprint of *The Neon Wilderness* would sell a million copies. The German sales and his own vanity encouraged him to believe that the first Algren novel in more than twenty years had to be worth a hundred thousand dollars, and on the basis of this, he began looking for a house. Wanting to be by the sea, he pulled out a map of Long Island and picked out Oyster Bay, an unspoiled, New England–like community on the Sound, many of whose residents were millionaires. Roy Finer knew the town well. A real estate agent showed them houses in the $125,000 range, one of which Amy Vanderbilt had lived in. Nelson especially liked one house in the middle of town, near the beach and the old-fashioned train station, but although the agent kept calling him about it, he had nothing with which to make a down payment.

For Donadio was trying assiduously to place "Chinatown," without arousing much interest. "I would speak to young people in big positions," Donadio remembered, "and they would say,'Who's Nelson Algren?' " Hy Cohen remembered that Algren once called up furious about a lunch date with an editor at Viking. When Nelson arrived at the restaurant the editor had been seated in another room. Waiting for her up front, Nelson hadn't bothered to give his name to the maître d': he was Nelson Algren, he was a celebrity, he should have been recognized! His expectations of a hundred grand were completely out of proportion to reality.

*

In mid-1979, Donald Fine, then at Arbor House, found many memorable scenes in the new novel and sent Algren a long, single-spaced letter suggesting changes. Roger Groening, who had read the manuscript, had never read such a perceptive, intelligent letter. "The kind of editor you'd be delighted to have," Roger said, but Algren was furious: the gall of this guy Fine, suggesting such changes in a hundred-thousand-dollar property. However, Algren did get the message that he was the only interested buyer. On October 31, 1979, Algren gave Candida a copy of the novel, now called "The Devil's Stocking" after a character who is "knitted backwards." He had revised it in accordance with Fine's suggestions, discarding large, undigested chunks of trial testimony. Fine wanted to publish it and began trying to find a paperback buyer to sweeten the deal. But he offered only $15,000, and Algren was furious and insulted.

The day after Christmas, Roy and a detective friend wanted to get together with Nelson. "I called and he wasn't home, and you know he was home three-quarters of the time," said Roy. "So I got a little worried—you know, he's an old guy, and he's overweight, and he might have a heart attack or something." Roy was concerned enough to drive from the Bronx to Hackensack. "I went over there and he wasn't home. I asked a kid on the street what happened to the old man who lived in that house, and he said he went to the hospital. There were big H signs, so I just followed them to Hackensack Hospital. Is there a Nelson Algren there? Yes. So I went up."

"How the hell did you find me?" Algren growled on seeing him.

"I'm a detective," Roy said. "What do you expect?"

The heart attack may have started on Christmas, with a feeling of extreme anxiety. Sweating and nervous, he hadn't been able to sleep, and this intense agitation had continued for hours while he tried to relax in the apartment, all the while utterly terrified. Finally he'd called his downstairs neighbor and was whisked away in an ambulance. The attack had been mild; the doctors had put in a pacemaker.

Roger came within days. "Nelson was terrified, dispossessed of his cool," he recalled, remembering how the old man had turned the story of his hernia operation into a Homeric tale, making it funny, Roger felt, to overcome his fears. But a heart attack was ten times worse, and Algren swore Roy and Roger to secrecy: if anyone learned of the attack it would affect the price of the book—and he *had to have that money.* "They won't pay me anything—they'll think

I'm going to die so they'll wait and get it for nothing," he declared from his hospital bed. He had no desire for people to know his body was failing, and the pacemaker felt like a violation. He was convinced that it would drive him crazy. "His landlady in Paterson had had a pacemaker," Roger explained, "and he thought *she* was crazy. He saw a direct connection. He had evidence." As Roger left, he hoped Algren would get used to the device.

When he returned a week later, he saw that a neighbor had brought over Nelson's mail. "It was then that I discovered that he was a terrible mail thief," Roger said, chuckling. "There were cartons of books from all these book clubs, addressed to F. Machine and all kinds of wild names. Norman Mailer's book on Gary Gilmore had arrived." Nelson seemed much better. He'd made those doctors take out that pacemaker. "I don't need that shit," was his attitude. "The docs say I should keep it in, but I'll take care of myself." "There was no sense arguing with him," said Roger, who feels certain that once out of the hospital Nelson didn't even go back for checkups.

By February 15, 1980, Algren handed Donadio yet another revision of "The Devil's Stocking"; by March 1, though he still wanted to publish it, Fine had not yet found a single paperback house interested in Nelson's book. But Algren was not about to accept $15,000 after six years of work. "As for Donald Fine—No, we won't 'work something out,' " he assured Donadio. "That's the answer I anticipated from him and it's an answer that doesn't work. Get the ms. back from him and say Goodbye. That's it."

A week later he was suggesting possibilities for income to Donadio. "The sooner we can nail some money down, the faster I'll be able to cut loose," he said, having determined to move to Long Island. Apparently, the house in Hackensack had been sold and his lease was up; besides, he could no longer plan his life by the vagaries of the publishing world. That spring he spent a week with Stephen Deutch in Chicago, and when he returned opened the magpie drawer and pulled out a few stories and nostalgia pieces to rustle up a couple thousand. He sold a reminiscence of de Beauvoir and Sartre to *Chicago* magazine. He also seems to have put his name on a friend's manuscript, sent it out, and sold it, though not necessarily without permission; manuscripts at Ohio State University reveal he may have done this more than once, a terrible sign of how little literary pride he had left, how cynical he had become, how mercenary. At the same time, Jan Herman had put a German writer named Wolf Wondratschek and his photographer girlfriend in touch with Nelson. The photographer, who had already put together a photo book on prostitutes, wanted to do a picture story on a New York homicide detective for a German magazine. She took the pictures, and Nelson earned $1,500 for writing the story "Meow, Baby" about Roy Finer. He had not forgotten the beauty of eastern Long Island and found an apartment in Southampton in June. When the deutsche marks arrived at the bank he called the movers.

21.
Sag Harbor

ACCORDING TO NELSON, his new landlady liked him so much she bought him a box of strawberries. But trouble arrived a few days later with the moving van and the bulk of his belongings. He had far too much furniture for the small five-room apartment; the staircase was too narrow for his desk, and it sat, with a leather couch, eight bookshelves, and various smaller items, strewn across the front porch and lawn. The landlady stopped the movers: it looked like a fire hazard, and Nelson had been hammering huge nails in the wall to hang paintings; worse, his check for $2,000 had bounced. She threatened to call the police. Nelson found a pay phone and called Roy, who assured him he couldn't be taken to jail for a civil matter and that he'd done nothing criminal. Nelson went back to the house, but his landlady told him to move. "I was stunned," wrote the white-haired seventy-one-year-old, who'd probably mismanaged his checkbook. "I couldn't make the transition between packing and unpacking that fast. But I realized that when in a bad situation don't make it worse by grieving. I began repacking."

The only person he knew out this way was Joe Pintauro, from that miserable weekend in '76. With cars whizzing past the phone booth, he called Matt Panczyk, who encouraged him to call Joe. Short of breath, his voice shaky, Algren dialed. Pintauro was happy to hear from him, invited him over, and gave him the number of a storage company that would pick up his things. Nelson took a cab to Sag Harbor.

Nelson arrived gray, nervous, disheveled, and sincerely thankful. Joe already had a real estate agent looking for an inexpensive rental and now made up the guest room and settled Algren, with a drink, into a comfortable chair. Nelson insisted on reading Joe's novel and after praising it lavishly, they had dinner with a potter who arrived from across town. The real estate agent found a neat studio apartment on Concord Street in Sag Harbor, available right away, and Nelson toasted Joe and expansively told his old tales of de Beauvoir and Hemingway as they celebrated by the fire.

While his ex-landlady dickered over the security deposit with the real estate agent, Jan Herman wired Nelson $500 to rent the new apartment. "It was a point of pride with Algren that he always repaid his loans in full, and quickly," Jan said. Indeed, the day after he moved, Nelson invited Pintauro to lunch at the Bridgeview Diner, an old building with a big woodstove overlooking the water. Nelson picked up the tab, and despite their completely different temperaments, the two writers became friends.

From the beginning, Nelson loved Sag Harbor. The old whaling town was easy to live in, neighborly and unpretentious—unlike Southampton, which he now called a "bank managers' town." He could get around on his bicycle, there was a good public library, and New York was just a train trip away. It was summer, the air was lovely and the water serene; and as he relaxed and began acquiring a tan, it all must have felt similar to childhood summers on the Indiana dunes, to the good days in Gary. Roy and Jan Herman and other friends came out to visit; Wolf Wondratschek, who had a German arts grant, decided to make a short film about Algren and came out to Sag Harbor to shoot it, paying Algren $1,500. That summer, Studs Terkel dedicated his new book to him, and Algren reconnected with Herbert Mitgang of *The New York Times*. They had lunch at the Bridgeview Diner and swam in Little Noyack Bay, Nelson chatting about books with Mitgang's daughter and telling yet again the Otto Preminger story. Soon after, Mitgang wrote a piece on Algren and his newly finished novel in the *Times Book Review,* just the kind of publicity Nelson needed. As the summer progressed, Algren seemed delirious, giddy, Pintauro remembered, "as if the gods of good fortune were at last paying attention to him."

Around September, Algren finally got his house near the ocean. A small saltbox house on Glover Street, a short walk from the water, it was only $375 a month. It had a small backyard, a fireplace, and plenty of room to display all the things he'd had in storage for years. He began decorating, painting his roadside mailbox, buying a red-and-yellow rug. At the bottom of the stairs he hung a huge blowup of the well-known photograph of a napalm-covered Vietnamese girl running toward the camera, and that was only the beginning. "Almost every inch of wall space was covered with heavy, framed home-made collages consisting of old headlines, letters, clippings, and photos depicting the recent history of the world in terms of rape, war, sports, violence, literature and art," Pintauro noted. There were photographs of Lawrence, Proust, Lincoln, Dostoevsky; drawings, art posters, and a painting by Jan Herman's small daughter Olivia. In the upstairs bedrooms he hung pre-Columbian figures on the wall; the shelves held a lifelong collection of books including sets of Dickens and Orwell. With a clear corner for his desk and typewriter, Algren finally retired. He had no serious writing plans.

There were a number of writers in the east end of Long Island. Algren had already met the playwright Lanford Wilson, and, alerted by Candida Donadio that he was in town, Peter and Maria Matthiessen had him over for dinner. E. L. Doctorow lived nearby; Betty Friedan was across the street; he also met Irwin Shaw. Kurt Vonnegut, Jr., lived in a neighboring town, and although he wasn't happy that Nelson thought the Academy's Medal of Merit had "rolled under the sofa somewhere," they remained friends. Vonnegut introduced Nelson to John Irving, and the three of them had a meal at the American Hotel. Algren's winks and wisecracks mystified Vonnegut and Irving until they later realized Nelson thought he was talking to *Clifford* Irving.

He renewed ties with James Jones's widow, Gloria, now living in an impressive house in Sagaponack. Algren had always liked the attractive and direct Gloria, and they became eating and drinking buddies, seeing each other once a week or so. She noticed that he looked pale, and worried about his heart: James Jones had also had heart trouble. She wondered about his circumstances, was curious about the lack of interest in the Carter book, and offered him money to fix up his house because she knew he was broke. But he wouldn't take it, nor would he join a poker game she played in with friends. Instead, she picked up the tabs for their lunches at the American Hotel, where he limited himself to one martini and restrained his opinions about her husband's literary worth.

It is strange to imagine Nelson living where everyone seemed to have money, and there were times when he couldn't stomach the bourgeois refinement of the Hamptons set. Pintauro was shocked when the old man took out his dentures at a dinner party, rinsed them in his water glass, and returned them to his mouth, though at the Bridgeview Diner Mitgang had taken this as a sign of openness. Algren simply may have liked to go nude in the house, but he apparently flashed his neighbor, an elderly woman already disgusted with his housekeeping. And he took great pleasure in telling Donald Fine he was "a cheap SOB" in a crowd of guests at Gloria's. "Nelson had a tendency to misbehave at parties," Donadio explained. Especially parties where less talented writers and literary people were living in luxury.

A more pleasant surprise in Sag Harbor was the opening of Canio's Books directly around the corner from his house. Algren went in and started poking around. "You call this a bookshop?" he barked. "I got more books than this in my bedroom." Despite Canio Pavone's assurance of a larger selection to come, he left unassuaged, but a woman just coming into the shop told Pavone that that had been Nelson Algren. The bookseller unearthed an early paperback of *Walk on the Wild Side,* thinking he'd be prepared the next time Algren came in. "The next Saturday at ten A.M. Algren was the first person in the shop, a bag of books in his arms," Canio remembered. " 'Thought you could use these,' he said, and I was very glad to be able to say, 'Thank you, Mr. Algren.' He seemed to appreciate being recognized." Canio gave him the copy of *Wild Side,* and after that, Nelson was always first in the shop on Saturday mornings. Canio made coffee and Algren brought rolls and they talked about American writing; Nelson would tell boxing and horseracing stories and dare Ronald Reagan to cut *his* Social Security check. Soon a small group, including a feminist writer who was always clashing with Algren, came to hang out there on Saturday mornings, as Nelson the storyteller held forth from a green armchair, a literary figure once again.

Nelson had never lived in a house with a fireplace, and as the cold weather came on he was eager to use it. Lacking wood, he balled up newspapers. Pintauro was shocked that Algren might actually light them, but Algren told him to mind his own business. The next time Joe returned, he saw a long tongue of black carbon running up the mantel and onto the wall. Algren then turned to collecting twigs on his bicycle, and once when Roy was over he went out and came back dragging a huge fifteen-foot tree limb. "Are you going to saw it?" Roy naturally asked. "Naw, it's all right," Algren said, putting one end of the limb into the fireplace and letting the other fourteen feet stick out into the room. Roy couldn't believe it, but Algren lit it. As the flames began to lick out into the room, however, he realized he'd better put it out.

Thus he settled into his new home. He threw a Christmas party, mailing invitations, ordering in from the deli, and stringing up old-fashioned Christmas lights over all the ceilings and walls: the brightly colored bulbs were the only illumination, and Roger thought it was wonderful—Nelson had transformed the place. As people arrived, he served a fine champagne, baked ziti, and sliced ham, orchestrating an elaborate yet chaotic seating arrangement throughout the living and dining rooms. When everyone was seated to his satisfaction, he toasted Joe for having put an end to his losing streak and later entertained his guests with the best of his many yarns.

That evening he told Roger and Roy he'd been thinking of doing something for Joan Hammond's girls, of leaving something for them. "Why don't you draw up a will?" Roger suggested practically, but the very thought made Nelson uncomfortable: he wasn't going to die. "Well, you know I had that little trouble last year, but that was just a cold," he told the only people who had visited him in the hospital. Roy and Roger just looked at each other: he had completely talked himself out of the heart attack.

In February he learned that he had been voted, however belatedly, into the American Academy and Institute of Arts and Letters, nominated by Donald Barthelme and seconded by Malcolm Cowley and Jacques Barzun. At first, when he told Canio about it, he seemed bitter about having been locked out for so long—should he even answer, could he hock the membership pin? Canio also remembered that Saul Bellow was mentioned, as if Algren believed that Bellow, who was rumored to have dismissed him as a tavern writer, had kept him out. But Pavone encouraged him to accept the nomination because he deserved it. In 1974, when he'd received the Award of Merit, he'd been cynical, but now Algren was happy, flattered, deeply satisfied. Heretofore he'd felt he was on some kind of American blacklist: his books sold abroad, and it was only in his own country that he was treated so badly. Suddenly he was being welcomed back into the literary world. It was *community* and being included that Algren craved; and that was what he found in Sag Harbor after all those lonely years in New Jersey and Chicago.

Moreover, election to the Academy could only help in finding an American publisher for "The Devil's Stocking." By early spring the novel, under the title *Calhoun,* was already scheduled for fall publication by Zweitausendeins in Germany, to be followed by editions of all his major works. For this he would receive a twelve-thousand-dollar advance. "Why did we ever go to war with Krauts?" a delighted Algren asked Jan Herman. He felt Germany was a fabulous launching place for the book, sure to revive interest in his Italian editions, which paid modest but steady royalties.

It was as if he were suddenly a writer again after all those years as a self-described "free-lance journalist," a label so conveniently supporting his role as an outcast from the literary establishment. "I'm going on half a century in this ridiculous business," he was now quoted as saying, allying himself with working writers. "You know, Hemingway said the main point is to last. And I guess I'm still here." The day before his birthday he was the opening speaker at the Small Press Book Fair held at New York University. His first New York reading in years was a good chance for publicity, made even more attractive when the literary organization Poets and Writers came through with two hundred dollars. Despite being worried about speaking—he had cracked his dentures on the train—he arrived at the fair looking robust and vigorous in a checked plaid sports jacket and chatted with events coordinator Susan Mernit about his recent move to Sag Harbor. "I thought he had money," Mernit recalled. "He seemed so proud and talked about what a great place he had. . . . He acted like he was a big success." He was in such good spirits that he even began flirting with a well-dressed woman in designer clothes and jewelry who chanced to be Susan's mother. Yet journalist Carolyn Gaiser, who hadn't seen Algren since 1974, was shocked at how old he looked, walking up to the podium with small, almost mincing steps, when he had once had such an exuberant stride.

"He was spontaneous—almost deliberately antiliterary," Mernit remembered Algren's reading. "He was arrogant and very confident." At the end of one of his long and extremely funny shaggy-dog stories, he talked about how nobody in America wanted to publish "The Devil's Stocking," although it would soon appear in Germany. Even as he was trying to sell it, Mernit got the distinct impression that it was not a good book; yet for Nelson the reading was an unqualified success. Afterward, Carolyn Gaiser came up and, with Nohra and Canio Pavone, they ate dinner at a Spanish restaurant, Algren relaxing with a few martinis and "holding court and feeling good," Canio remembered.

A week later Algren invited Carolyn to the Academy of Arts and

Letters' dinner for new members. "Here we are. Meeting the elite," he confided to her in mock awe after he'd been introduced to the Academy. Muriel Cowley almost didn't recognize him because of his potbelly, but he gallantly assured her that he was still 168 pounds, that he and the stomach were not on speaking terms. After dinner, Carolyn dropped him off in a cab at the Chelsea Hotel. Though he said he was tired, he began walking in the opposite direction, and Carolyn wondered whether he was going to place a bet, find a prostitute, or buy a newspaper.

His election to the Academy brought sudden publicity, including interviews in *The New York Times* and *Newsday,* and all spring he was in great spirits. At parties he was the expansive, confident raconteur, hamming it up, making passes at women. Canio had invited him to give a reading at the bookstore, and on principle Nelson had insisted on being paid—the same principle that made him ask a local lawyer to send Mernit a threatening pay-up letter thirty one days after the book fair. He and Canio decided to charge two dollars a head. When Nelson mentioned the reading in the *Times* article, Canio had to hastily find chairs; Nelson brought some outdoor cushions. The little bookstore's festive wine-and-cheese party was packed with people from as far as Manhattan. Nelson read stories from *Last Carousel,* material from index cards, and the poem "Tricks Out of Time Long Gone" with visible emotion. At the evening's end, he was beaming with pride, and took Canio, Nohra, and a few other friends out for a good dinner on the $120 or so that had been collected. Drinking his martinis, he kept exclaiming that he thought he'd done pretty well, and all agreed. The next morning he walked into Canio's so absolutely ecstatic over the way everything was working out that he fell down on his cushions and began rolling like a puppy.

The following Friday, Algren consulted Dr. Robert Semmler in Sag Harbor about pains in his chest. Recognizing a cardiac problem, the doctor recommended he check into Southampton Hospital, but Nelson wouldn't hear of it. The next day, Saturday, May 9, he was having an afternoon party to celebrate his induction into the Academy, he told the doctor, so he couldn't go to the hospital even if he wanted to. Semmler felt that Algren simply refused to believe that this was a life-threatening condition. Later that day W. J. Weatherby came out to interview him, and Algren complained of a heaviness in his chest. Weatherby tried to avoid stressful topics, but Algren was eager to talk about "The Devil's Stocking," Rubin Carter, and New Jersey; and he spoke furiously about de Beauvoir, whose biographer was coming within days to interview him.

Roy Finer called in the evening to say the trains weren't running at convenient times and that he would arrive around noon, rather than later in the afternoon after the party had started. A neighbor noticed that Algren returned from a bike ride shortly before midnight and that the lights in his house were still on after daybreak.

The next morning was the first Saturday Nelson did not show up at the bookstore, and although he was somewhat surprised, Canio assumed he was getting ready for his party. But when Roy arrived at Nelson's locked front door he knew immediately that something was wrong. He entered through the back door and found Algren lying faceup on the bathroom floor.

Algren had had another heart attack. Roy felt the stomach, the last place that gets cold, but Nelson was already beginning to turn blue; his pupils were dilated. Roy figured he'd been dead about twelve hours.

A small ceremony was held a few days later, in Sag Harbor's Oakland Cemetery, arranged by Pintauro and attended by Roy Finer, Carolyn Gaiser, Stephen Deutch, and friends from Sag Harbor, who brought spring flowers from their gardens. Candida insisted that Nelson be buried in a plain morgue box. For his eulogy, she chose, fittingly, lines from his own elegiac "Tricks Out of Time Long Gone," a farewell poem to the lost.

Epilogue

ALTHOUGH SIMONE DE BEAUVOIR did not love Algren the way he wanted to be loved, she was buried wearing his ring.

More than a year after Algren's death, an American publisher for "The Devil's Stocking" had still not been found, and when Herbert Mitgang mentioned this in *The New York Times Book Review*, Donald Fine renewed his offer to publish the last Nelson Algren novel, paying about half what he had originally offered. The novel appeared in 1983.

Algren's tombstone arrived with his name misspelled and had to be recut. And when the City of Chicago changed West Evergreen Street to West Algren Street, residents complained that the new address caused too much trouble. So the City changed it back again.

Books by Nelson Algren

Somebody in Boots, Vanguard, 1935

Never Come Morning, Harper and Brothers, 1942

The Neon Wilderness, Doubleday, 1947

The Man with the Golden Arm, Doubleday, 1949

Chicago: City on the Make, Doubleday, 1951

A Walk on the Wild Side, Farrar, Straus and Cudahy, 1956

Nelson Algren's Own Book of Lonesome Monsters,
    Lancer Books, 1962

Who Lost An American? Macmillan, 1963

Conversations with Nelson Algren, Hill & Wang, 1964

Notes From a Sea Diary: Hemingway All the Way,
    G. P. Putnam's Sons, 1965

The Last Carousel, G. P. Putnam's Sons, 1973

The Devil's Stocking, Arbor House, 1983

Notes

1. CHICAGO CHILDHOOD 11–24

Account of Isaac Abraham's life compiled from NA's accounts in *Conversations with Nelson Algren* (Hill & Wang, 1964), 6–10; in *Nelson Algren* by Martha Cox and Wayne Chatterton (Twayne, 1975), 17 18; from the death certificate of Gerson Abraham; from unpublished autobiographical fragments in the Ohio State U. Division of Rare Books and Manuscripts; and from the recollections of relatives.
"good on the con," "to cook and sew," and **"Hey!"** *Conversations*, 8–9.
"But it's always interested me" Ibid., 9.
"He always put it" Ibid., 10.
Information on Goldie's background from interview with Evelyn Rupprecht, June 10, 1987.
"calling him and he" Caption on photograph. Courtesy Ruth Sherman.
"green gem," "blue flutter," "roll-a-hoop," and **"fly-a-kite"** *Who Lost an American?* (Macmillan, 1963), 233, 244.
" 'You're so damned smart' " Ibid., 226–227.
Account of Goldie's behavior from interview with Robert Joffe, July 28, 1984.
"But you got her" Ibid.
"chased up and down" *Who Lost*, 231.
"My father was a working man" *The Last Carousel* (G. P. Putnam's Sons, 1973), 248.

"a physics shark" Descriptions of Bernice from her diary, yearbooks, other memorabilia. Courtesy Ruth Sherman.
"NEVADA COWBOYS FORM UNION" and **"intercourse with the world"** *Chicago Evening News.* Courtesy Ohio State U. Libraries.
"feeling nothing save some" *Chicago: City on the Make* (McGraw-Hill, 1983), 33.
"We were very conservative" Interview with Benton Curtis, Jan. 4, 1987.
"Anything Bernice said" *Conversations*, 17.
"moon," "pregrant," etc. are discussed in *Conversations*, 17–18, and *Algren*, 19.
"Other men wished" *Who Lost*, 226.
"That's different" Unpublished autobiographical fragment. OSU.
"*the* gamblers of the city" Interview with Curtis, Jan. 4, 1987.
"That's crazy" *Conversations*, 18.
"Contemptuous of his hands" Unpublished autobiographical fragment. OSU.
"There was a man downstairs" Interview with Curtis, Jan. 4, 1987.
"Joe sent me" Ibid.
"more than just a guarantee" *Conversations*, 58.
"Even in high school" Interview with Curtis, Jan. 4, 1987.

"**staggered**" *Conversations,* 21.
"**The old man never went**" Ibid., 22.

2. URBANA–CHAMPAIGN 25–31

"**I never knew anybody**" *Conversations with Nelson Algren* (Hill & Wang, 1964), 26.
"**spiritual phase**" *Nelson Algren* (Twayne, 1975), 20.
"**To be a man**" Ibid.
NA's austerity program is discussed in *Conversations,* 23–31, and in *Algren,* 19–20.
"**walking down Walnut Street**" *Conversations,* 28.
Description of NA in the ROTC from interview with Amanda Algren, July 31, 1984.
"**Outside the ranks**" Prof. Donald R. Taft, *Daily Illini,* April 17, 1930, 1.
"**taverns and clubhouses**" Interview with Ralph Zwick, Jan. 4, 1987.
"**We kind of drifted**" Interview with Benton Curtis, July 24, 1987.
"**the shamed women**" and "**vast legions**" "The Shamed Women," unpublished MS. Courtesy Ohio State U. Libraries.
Algren's affair with the landlady is mentioned in *Conversations,* 29.
"**Huge barriers of buying orders**" *Daily Illini,* Oct. 29, 1929, 1.
"**STOCK PRICES RALLY**" Ibid., Oct. 31, 1929, 1.
"**The stories of the bankers**" Prof. H. M. Gray, *Daily Illini,* Nov. 14, 1929, 1.
All short stories by NA mentioned here can be found at OSU.
"**You have an insight**" Grades and comments written on unpublished MS. OSU.
"**This is one of the most vivid sketches**" Ibid.

"**stands on the prairie**" and "**economic accident**" "The Vendreyevs," unpublished MS. OSU.
"**a writer in the literary sense**" *Conversations,* 54.
"**It was just something**" Ibid., 53.

3. DRIFTING INTO A CAREER 32–45

"**editor, columnist**" *Conversations with Nelson Algren* (Hill & Wang, 1964), 30.
"**I think you're a nice girl**" Unpublished autobiographical fragment. Courtesy Ohio State U. Libraries.
"**Well, then I have to leave**" *Conversations,* 31.
"News Flash," "Escape—or the Woman," "A Woman Called Mary," and "Sweat" are unpublished MSs. OSU.
"**neither Jew nor Gentile**" Early handwritten poem. OSU.
"**flat, ugly sound**" Note on draft of "The Vendreyevs." OSU.
"**acrawl with the living smells**" *A Walk on the Wild Side* (Penguin, 1984), 111.
"**I remember a girl**" Unpublished autobiographical fragment. OSU.
"**It was hot**" Unpublished autobiographical fragment. OSU.
"**just a promoter**" *Conversations,* 52.
"**sitting around a little kitchen**" Ibid., 55.
"**We've just done turned**" *Walk,* 146.
"**So she says**" *Conversations,* 32–33.
"**Please try and get this young man**" Letter from Isidor Achinofsky, Aug. 16, 1932. OSU.
"**It was just his way**" NA's comment written on bottom of Achinofsky's letter. OSU.
"**And so we got**" *Conversations,* 33.
"**I was always getting**" Ibid., 52.

"**It was all falling apart**" Ibid., 33.

"**They would move**" This and all subsequent Benton Curtis quotes from interview with Curtis, Jan. 4, 1987.

"**I'm packing black-eyed peas**" *Conversations,* 35.

"**Everything I'd been told**" Ibid., 55–56.

"**It was a curious hotel**" Ibid., 48.

"**Then almost everybody would win**" Ibid., 49.

"**a new social dimension**" Eric Sevareid, "Hitchhiker," in *The Thirties: A Time to Remember* (Simon & Schuster, 1962), 109.

"**He moved, moved**" *Somebody in Boots* (Vanguard, 1935), 93.

"**I remember eating**" *Conversations,* 51.

4. SO HELP ME 46–58

"**a fine, gentle person**" This and all subsequent Murray Gitlin quotes from interview with Gitlin, June 21, 1986.

"**big-league lawyer,**" "**Jew-kid,**" and "**wrangle a meal out of him**" "So Help Me," *The Neon Wilderness* (Writers & Readers, 1986), 272, 273.

"**his lack of sentiments**" James T. Farrell, "The Short Story," in League of American Writers, *American Writers' Congress,* ed. Henry Hart (International Publishers, 1935), 109.

"**O' course, I wouldn't never**" "So Help Me," 273.

"**Now . . . maybe you will**" Ibid., 272.

"**didn't figure . . . could**" *Conversations with Nelson Algren* (Hill & Wang, 1964), 11.

"**We have been very favorably impressed**" Whit Burnett to NA, May 22, 1933. Courtesy Ohio State U. Libraries.

"**Nelson was a tall, gangly**" and all subsequent Abe Aaron quotes from interview with Aaron, Aug. 4, 1984. The story about discrimination against Richard Wright at the Troy Lane hotel from interview with Aaron, Aug. 4, 1984.

"**You'd buy a string of tickets**" Interview with Benton Curtis, Jan. 4, 1987.

"**because of the pain**" Unpublished MS. OSU.

"**flower child**" Term used by Albert Bein to describe his sister, in letter to the author, Nov. 9, 1984.

"**bearing in mind**" Milton (last name unknown) to NA, Oct. 15, 1933. OSU.

"**I was twenty-four**" *Conversations,* 60–61.

"**the colored spray of Niagara**" "Rail Rod Notes" notebook. OSU.

"**It soon developed**" Bein to author, Nov. 9, 1984. Description of NA's trip through the South derived primarily from his notebook of the journey, called "Rail Rod Notes." OSU. Unless otherwise specified, all quotes are from this notebook.

"**The colored guys**" *Conversations,* 47.

"**utterly displaced**" Unpublished draft of foreword to 1965 edition of *Somebody in Boots.* OSU.

5. ALPINE, TEXAS 59–74

"**a deteriorated ranch**" *Conversations with Nelson Algren* (Hill & Wang, 1964), 37.

"**I would simply walk in**" Ibid.

"**burros and Baptists**" "As Walt Might Have Put It," a mercifully unpublished poem. Courtesy Ohio State U. Libraries.

"**ten ranting millions**" Ibid.

"**I sing my country**" Ibid.

"millions are fighting" Milton (last name unknown) to NA, Oct. 15, 1933. OSU.

"proletarian novel" For a discussion of the genre, see Walter Rideout, *The Radical Novel in the United States 1900–1950* (Harvard U. Press, 1956), esp. 129, 144–147, 153, 155, 166, 167, 169, 313.

"poverty, bleak and blind" *Somebody in Boots* (Vanguard, 1935), 5.

"broad dust-road" Ibid.

"An American Diary" Unpublished MS. OSU.

"Nazi" Fragment of poem. OSU.

"She ate more than any" Undated autobiographical fragment. OSU.

For incidents concerning NA's relationships with students at Sul Ross, I have relied on interviews with Paul Forchheimer, Sept. 14, 1984, and Jan. 6, 1985.

"The Culture of the Proletariat" "Novelist Talks on Proletarian Culture," Sul Ross *Skyline*, XI, 8 (Jan. 1934), 4.

"It is Mr. Abraham's opinion" Ibid.

"the working-class" "Young Novelist to Speak at Writers' Club," Sul Ross *Skyline*, XI, 6 (Dec. 1933), 3.

"I think I told them" NA to William Targ, Oct. 8 (early 1960s). OSU.

"almost a compulsive attachment" *Conversations*, 37.

"the train slowed up" Ibid., 38.

"Dear Ma" Alpine/Jail notebook. OSU.

"Dear Mr. Henle" Ibid.

"Lumpenproletariat, me" Ibid.

"troughs," "wet filth," and **"thundermug"** Ibid.

Algren's deposition from records of Brewster County Sheriff's Office, Alpine, TX.

"play-pretend of underdogs" *Somebody*, 168.

"They made Piedmonts" Alpine/Jail notebook. OSU.

"Charlotte the harlot" Ibid.

The belt-beating game is discussed in *Conversations*, 42.

Rules of Court text from a handwritten copy Algren took when he left jail. OSU.

"highly feigned hatred" *Somebody*, 153.

"a legal hangover" "El Presidente de Mejico," *The Neon Wilderness* (Writers & Readers, 1986), 166.

"They hit the Mex's head" Alpine/Jail notebook. OSU.

"His face was grayer" "Presidente de Mejico," 175–176.

"It was a very sparse diet" *Conversations*, 39–40.

"Hunger our enemy" Alpine/Jail notebook. OSU.

"brought me up a can of insecticide" *Conversations*, 43.

"One terror: being alone" Alpine/Jail notebook. OSU.

"Very few people" Interview with Forchheimer, Sept. 14, 1984.

"Dear Mr. Henle" A draft of this letter is in the Alpine/Jail notebook. OSU. It is doubtful NA sent it.

Description of Judge Van Sickle is taken from a draft of an unpublished article by Prof. J. Allen Briggs, formerly of the English faculty, Sul Ross State U., made available to me by Dr. Elton Miles of Sul Ross.

"militant, defiant man" Sul Ross *Skyline*, XI, 10 (Feb. 1934), 3.

"the youth with the mysterious brain" Ibid.

"What is a carpenter without his tools?" The account of NA's attorney's speech is from notes by Dr. Elton Miles following an interview with Forchheimer, late 1950s. The quote it-

self is from Miles's notes, which he made available to me. That this was the substance of the speech was confirmed to me by Forchheimer in an interview, Sept. 14, 1984. Prof. J. Allen Briggs also confirmed the defense attorney's oration.
"Then I got on the witness stand" *Conversations*, 45.
NA's visit to the evening session of the Brewster County Court recounted in Sul Ross *Skyline*, XI, 10 (Feb. 1934), 3.
"glutton for punishment" Ibid.
Draft of letter to Henle from Alpine/ Jail notebook. OSU.
Description of NA's departure from interview with Forchheimer, Sept. 14, 1984.
"Had I been black" Letter from NA to H. Allen Smith, Aug. 22, 1975, made available to me by Dr. Elton Miles.

6. THE NEAR NORTH SIDE 75–97

"little cloudy-yellow swimming spells" "Lest the Traplock Click," *Calithump*, June 1934, 25.
"all the time . . . I thought " Ibid., 28.
"tremendous promise" Notes from correspondence between James Henle and James T. Farrell, July 9, 1934. Files of Edgar M. Branch.
"Oppressed man will rise up!" Canadian *Masses*, March–April 1934, 4.
"was originally intended" NA to Kenneth McCollum, May 17, 1973, *Dictionary of Literary Biography*, vol. 9 (Gale Research, 1981), 11.
"I don't think any of us" Meridel Le Sueur to the author, undated (spring 1985).

"Going to a meeting" Interview with Le Sueur, Nov. 19, 1985.
"Those who came to the house" Lawrence Lipton oral history transcripts (unpublished), recorded early 1960s, 773. Lawrence Lipton Trust, U. of Southern California.
"zigzag riot of fakery" *Somebody in Boots* (Vanguard, 1935), 297.
"college-trained men" Ibid.
"But these were only the few" Ibid., 301.
"when a few were driven off" Ibid.
"He expected [the book]" Farrell to John Switalski, Jan. 17, 1943. James T. Farrell Collection, Van Pelt Library, U. of Pennsylvania archives.
"very bad shape" Ibid.
"Algren has little concern" Farrell to Henle, July 5, 1934. Branch files.
"almost incredibly bad" Henle to Farrell, July 9, 1934. Branch files.
"damn good things in it" Ibid. (quotes Farrell).
"Algren resented" Interview with Sam Ross, April 27, 1985.
"as if it were not an extraordinary union" Farrell to Switalski, Jan. 17, 1943. Farrell Collection, U. of Pennsylvania.
"putting in the party line" Ibid.
"We are having a great deal of trouble" Henle to Farrell, Nov. 12, 1934. Branch files.
"just as surely as the young executives" Maxwell Geismar, *American Moderns* (Hill & Wang, 1958), 188.
"He shrugged off self-consciousness" *Somebody*, 237.
"What good's it do" Ibid., 74.
"After dark they met" Ibid., 75.
"A woman with furred shoulders" Ibid., 147.
"The red day will come" Ibid., 300.
"In the latter portions" Jack Conroy,

"Somebody in Boots," New Masses, April 16, 1935, 21–22.

"Could no one else" *Somebody,* 31.

"social criticism so violent" Review of *Somebody, Chicago Tribune,* May 11, 1935.

"a violent and brutal book" Conroy, *"Somebody in Boots,"* 22.

"powerful and disturbing book" Edith H. Walton, *"Somebody in Boots," NY Sun,* April 6, 1935. Typed MS. Courtesy Ohio State U. Libraries.

"cannot be accepted" *"Somebody in Boots* and Other Recent Works," *NY Times Book Review,* April 7, 1935, 6.

"bitterness not of revolutionary fervor" Ibid.

"If I can write" NA's deposition, Alpine, TX, Jan. 26, 1934.

"like a thermometer" Le Sueur to the author, undated (spring 1985).

"Put him in a cab" Lipton oral history transcripts, 811. Lawrence Lipton Trust, USC.

"He was broke and dispirited" Ibid.

"I don't have any parents" Ibid., 812.

"They said, 'It just shows' " Ibid.

"assessing the costs" James T. Farrell, "The Short Story," in League of American Writers, *American Writers' Congress,* ed. Henry Hart (International Publishers, 1935), 109.

May Day parade incidents from interview with Jack Conroy, Aug. 31, 1984.

"It was the first time" Le Sueur to the author, undated (spring 1985).

"Nelson was always shy" Interview with Ross, Aug. 2, 1984.

"Frankly, he was in terrible shape" Farrell to Switalski, Jan. 17, 1943. Farrell Collection, U. of Pennsylvania.

"almost insane" and **"if he will go"** Notes from Farrell's diary, May 5, 1935. Branch files.

"never stopping talking" Farrell to Switalski, Jan. 17, 1943.

"Nelson wasn't doing anything" Interview with Dorothy Farrell, April 22, 1985.

"His condition got worse" Lipton oral history transcripts, 816. Lawrence Lipton Trust, USC.

"I sought out" Ibid., 817.

"Whore! Get out" Interview with Amanda Algren, July 31, 1984.

"What I tried to do" Interview with Ross, Aug. 2, 1984.

"an uneven novel" Preface to *Somebody* (Berkley Medallion, 1965).

Account of party at John Reed Club and NA's subsequent meeting with Amanda from interviews with Amanda, July 31 and August 1, 1984.

"Somehow his Jewish origin" Lipton oral history transcripts, 818. Lawrence Lipton Trust, USC.

Harry Hansen's telegram is at OSU.

"Nelson Algren . . . is equipped" "The Proletarian Short Story," *New Masses,* July 2, 1935, 17–19.

"Dear Alan Calmer" Fragment. OSU.

"that it would make a fair book" *"Somebody in Boots," New Republic,* July 17, 1935, 286–287.

"An American Obituary," *Partisan Review,* Oct. 1935.

7. THE LITERARY LEFT 98–121

Description of NA's early life with Amanda Algren from interview with her, July 31, 1984.

"accepted a job" and **"felt obliged to abandon"** NA's application to the Guggenheim Foundation, 1940. Courtesy John Simon Guggenheim Foundation.

"Volume One was to deal" NA's application to the Guggenheim Foundation, 1941. Courtesy John Simon Guggenheim Foundation.

"Had it not been for [the Writers' Project]" NA to Jerre Mangione, Aug. 11, 1969. Courtesy Jerre Mangione.

"It served to humanize people" *Conversations with Nelson Algren* (Hill & Wang, 1964), 64.

"trained writers to record" B. A. Botkin, "WPA and Folklore Research: 'Bread and Song,'" *Southern Folklore Quarterly,* March 1939, 7; and "Living Lore of the New York City Writers' Project, *New York Folklore Quarterly,* 2 (Nov 1946), 258.

"Spain . . . was a war" *Conversations,* 73.

"I don't think I've been" Ibid., 71.

"We move in a world" NA to Kerker Quinn, Feb. 20, 1938. U. of Illinois, Urbana, archives.

"The loss to American" "Federal Arts Projects: WPA: Literature," *Chicago Artist,* Dec.–Jan. 1937–38, 10. Kent State U. Library.

"Commerce in Illinois" Original MS. OSU.

"a minor trilogist" Jack Conroy, introduction to *Writers in Revolt,* eds. Jack Conroy and Curt Johnson (Lawrence Hill, 1973), xix.

"Algren grew impatient" Ibid.

"This went against me" *Conversations,* 87.

"called onto the carpet" Interview with Conroy, Aug. 31, 1984.

"whenever we could get someone" Ibid.

"We had little to do" Saul Bellow to Mangione, Oct. 1968. Courtesy Jerre Mangione.

"investigated the lore" William McDonald, *Federal Relief Administration and the Arts* (Ohio State U. Press, 1969), 715.

"You call this efficiency?" "Hank, the Free Wheeler," *Treasury of Amer-*

ican Folk-Lore, ed. Benjamin Botkin (Crown Publishers, 1944), 542.

"We thought he was gorgeous" Interview with Lil Frankel, Oct. 6, 1985.

"dames who didn't know" Interview with Margaret Walker, Nov. 11, 1985.

"Oh, yeah, he had a feeling" Interview with Theodora Pikowski, Oct. 6, 1985.

"serious arthurs" Interview with Conroy, Aug. 31, 1984.

"working-class people" Interview with Dorothy Farrell, April 22, 1985.

"The Fallonites were a gold mine" Interview with Conroy, Aug. 31, 1984.

"He always believed" Ibid.

"And the slender brunette" Unpublished MS. Courtesy Ohio State U. Libraries.

"I belong to this city" Unpublished MS (notebook). OSU.

"Being a loser" Unpublished MS (notebook). OSU.

"This sense of imminent death" MS by George Bluestone, 2–3. OSU. (Published as "Nelson Algren," *Western Review,* 22 [Autumn 1957].)

"Rather it is some" Blanche Gelfant, quoted ibid., 7.

"Barefoot with Shoes On," or "No Shoes for Novak," is an unpublished MS. OSU.

"in a world where social relations" Bluestone, 10.

"Nelson always gave the impression" Interview with Frank Sandiford, Dec. 20, 1986.

"He was always behind" Ibid.

"He kept a large part of himself" Interview with Conroy, Aug. 31, 1984.

"It's very nice" Interview with Amanda, July 31, 1984.

"omnivorous—a tom cat" Interview with Conroy, Aug. 31, 1984.

"pale Americans stricken with pale blue sleep" "Travelog," *Poetry,* Nov. 1939.

"**Nelson never spoke**" Interview with Abe Aaron, Aug. 4, 1984.

"**ultimate purpose**" NA's application to the Guggenheim Foundation, 1940. Courtesy John Simon Guggenheim Foundation.

"**Sometimes, though, a sharp break**" NA to Millen Brand, Oct. 25, 1939. Millen Brand Collection, Rare Book and Manuscript Library, Columbia U.

"**without an inkling of self-doubt**" NA to Brand, Oct. 9, 1939. Brand Collection, Columbia.

"**He was a compulsive gambler**" Interview with Conroy, Aug. 31, 1984.

"**Amanda's gone with Lynch**" Interview with Conroy, Aug. 31, 1984.

"**Nelson was not an easy person**" Interview with Pikowski, Oct. 6, 1985.

"**To—My old friend Nelson**" Inscription in NA's copy of *Native Son*. OSU.

"**Dear Dick, Native Son arrived** " NA to Richard Wright, March 9, 1940. Collection of American Literature, Beinecke Rare Book and Manuscript Library, Yale.

8. WHITE HOPE 125–141

"**When I come to**" NA to Richard Wright, March 12, 1940. Collection of American Literature, Beinecke Rare Book and Manuscript Library, Yale.

"**surface look**" Ibid.

"**It was the thing to write**" NA to Wright, May 25, 1940. Beinecke.

"**always asked with something like**" Ibid.

"**the Petersburg of Dostoevsky**" NA to Wright, Oct. 22, 1940. Beinecke.

"**Hey, you wanta go 'n drink**" Algren notebook. Courtesy Ohio State U. Libraries.

"**I hate t' see the Spring**" "Do It the Hard Way," *Writer,* March 1943, 69.

"**tremendous, downright crushing**" Alexander Kuprin, *Yama* (Hyperion Press, 1977), 91.

"**Do you understand**" Ibid.

"**all set ways**" and "**feel**" "Do It the Hard Way," 69.

"**Proust of the Proletariat**" NA to Wright, Aug. 15, 1940. Beinecke.

"**the poor man's Dostoevsky**" Ibid.

"**use of the printed word**" "Do It the Hard Way," 68.

"**Trouble and tribulation**" NA to Wright, undated (mid-August 1940). Beinecke.

"**You have a sure sense**" Wright to NA, Sept. 7, 1940. OSU.

"**integrated, center of the stage struggle**" NA to Wright, Sept. 8, 1940. Beinecke.

"**is only a very slight variation**" NA to Elizabeth Ingersoll, Dec. 19, 1940. Beinecke.

"**pavement-colored**" is a favorite Algren description.

"**Chicago gets bigger**" NA to Wright, Feb. 12, 1941. Beinecke.

"**Edith Lloyd is dead**" Ibid.

"**all the way through**" Alexander Bergman to NA, undated (May 1941). OSU.

"**It's all up with me**" Ibid.

"**They saw his right**" *The Last Carousel* (G. P. Putnam's Sons, 1973), 249.

"**an American classic**" Bergman to NA, undated (May 1941). OSU.

"**conceptual structure**" Wright to NA, Sept. 7, 1940. OSU.

"**moral imbecile**" "Killer of the Four Bet He'd Burn," *St. Louis Star-Times,* Sept. 27, 1941.

"**I'm nuts**" Ibid.

"**The hell with you**" "Illinois Executes Youngest Convict," NY *Sun,* Jan. 17, 1942.

"never expected to be" "Killer of the Four."

"roast" and "burn" Ibid.

"a crumby relief station" *Never Come Morning* (Harper Colophon, 1963), 34.

"Next, next" Ibid., 74.

"disgust coming up" Ibid., 72.

"as he hoped" Ibid., 12.

"The thought broke" Ibid., 57.

"At seventeen" Ibid., 26.

"possession of one thing" Ibid., 53.

"Steffi's fingers" Ibid.

"uselessly for the sound" Ibid., 28.

"animals" Ibid., 64.

"too old to understand" Ibid., 3.

"When the thunder kills" Ibid.

"hunters" and "hunted" Ibid., 163.

"Ever'thin's crooked, Widow" Ibid., 26.

"Always pay off" Ibid., 101.

"murmurous with poverty" Ibid., 135.

"with a low slow pall" Ibid., 136.

"men watch the weather" Ibid.

"stumblin' block" Ibid., 141.

"Go it, guy" Ibid., 159.

"hardened to a burnished" Ibid., 209.

"The enormity of being accessible" Ibid., 190.

"Everyone went through the streets" Ibid., 194.

"making the same endless plans" Ibid., 215.

"She ceased to go" Ibid., 208–209.

"A book, a true book" "Do It the Hard Way," 67.

"where his clumsiness" *Never Come Morning*, 199.

"feeling troubled to learn" Ibid., 200.

"without developing" *Yama*, 100.

"he had other sins" *Never Come Morning*, 199.

"I was constantly reminded" Richard Wright to Edward Aswell, Sept. 21, 1941. Richard Wright Collection, Schomburg Center for Research in Black Culture, New York Public Library. Astor, Lenox, Tilden Foundations.

"I know I overdo" NA to Wright, Sept. 27, 1941. Beinecke.

"morning would never come again" *Never Come Morning*, 223.

"*Never Come Morning* depicts" Wright, introduction to first ed. of *Never Come Morning* (Harper and Brothers, 1942).

"It's a book of great integrity" Aswell to NA, Nov. 26, 1941. OSU.

9 THE GREAT CITY'S NIGHTTIME STREETS 142–156

"brilliant book" Fred T. Marsh, *NY Times Book Review,* May 10, 1942, 6.

"knockout," "head and shoulders," and "powerful achievements" Benjamin Appel, *Saturday Review of Literature,* April 18, 1942.

"utter sincerity" Philip Rahv, *Nation,* April 18, 1942, 466–467.

"I, for one" Clifton Fadiman, *New Yorker,* April 18, 1942, 15.

"The girls sitting around" Malcolm Cowley, *New Republic,* May 4, 1942, 613–614.

"It is the most solid" Granville Hicks to NA, April 27, 1942. Courtesy Ohio State U. Libraries. Reprinted by permission of Stephanie Hicks Craib, Estate of Granville Hicks.

"*Never Come Morning* is not merely" James T. Farrell, quoted in Edward Aswell to NA, May 12, 1942. OSU.

"it would do a good deal" Lawrence Lipton to Aswell, April 18, 1942. Lawrence Lipton Trust, U. of Southern California.

"first rate" Martha Gellhorn to NA, July 11, 1942. OSU.

"I think it very, very good" Ernest Hemingway to Maxwell Perkins, July 8, 1942. Reprinted with permission of Charles Scribner's Sons, an imprint of Macmillan Publishing Co., from Carlos Baker, ed., *Ernest Hemingway: Selected Letters 1917–1961* (Scribner's, 1981), 533. © 1981 by Mary Hemingway.

"about the best book" Hemingway to Evan Shipman, Aug. 25, 1942, ibid., 538.

"Great rewards" "Do It the Hard Way," *Writer,* March 1943, 66.

"The happy truth" Ibid., 68.

"The average American" Ibid.

"a lead-pipe cinch" NA to Millen Brand, June 9, 1942 (postcard). Millen Brand Collection, Rare Book and Manuscript Library, Columbia U.

"veil of sophistication" NA to Richard Wright, March 29, 1942. Collection of American Literature, Beinecke Rare Book and Manuscript Library, Yale.

"the furious logic" Introduction to *Never Come Morning* (Harper Colophon, 1963), xi.

"without the assistance" Ibid., x.

"Herr Goebbels' devilishly cunning mind" Polish protester to Harper and Bros., May 29, 1942. OSU.

"strictly an insulting falsehood" Undated clipping (probably from *Zgoda*). OSU.

"If the book was written" Aswell to John J. Olejniczak, June 3, 1942. OSU.

"all wrong, strictly wrong" Czech to NA, June 10, 1942. OSU.

"the crocodilism of minds" Introduction to *Never Come Morning,* xii.

"Any sane man" Polish protester to Harper and Bros., May 29, 1942. OSU.

"anything less" Introduction to *Never Come Morning,* xiii.

"a comprehensive list" Neil J. Welch and David W. Marston, *Inside Hoover's FBI* (Doubleday, 1984), 55.

"a search was made" FBI report, released under Freedom of Information Act, dated Sept. 8, 1941, and made at the New York City office. NY file no. 100-1409, 2.

"timid bookkeeper" Letter from Lillian Friedman to the author, July 28, 1986.

"Once when we were out" Ibid.

"I may get drunk" NA's Board of Health Journal. OSU.

"Those shots give me a chill" Ibid.

"I was born that way" Ibid.

"It involved some detective work" Interview with Jack Conroy, Aug. 31, 1984.

"one feels life" "Design for Departure," *The Neon Wilderness* (Writers & Readers, 1986), 243.

"he liked the whole atmosphere" Interview with Conroy, Aug. 31, 1984.

"The gates of his soul" Ibid.

"I had a very ambitious hope" *Nelson Algren* (Twayne, 1975), 41.

"no noise, no fighting" "Design for Departure," 240.

"twilit land" Ibid., 243.

"She drifted" Ibid., 251.

"Veronal. Allonal" Ibid., 257.

"he had spent" Ibid., 262.

"Her fingers learned" Ibid., 244.

"I felt that if" Introduction to *Never Come Morning,* xiii.

"He had an idea" Interview with Christine Rowland, Nov. 21, 1985.

"wants to use" *Conversations with Nelson Algren* (Hill & Wang, 1964), 63.

"You thought nothing" Interview with Christine Roland, Nov. 21, 1985.

"When we lived on Evergreen" NA to Amanda, summer 1955. Courtesy Amanda Algren.

"I've got some dough" Interview with Amanda, Aug. 1, 1984.

"Watch your language" Ibid.

"You'll have to find" Ibid.

"To Mrs. A with love" Inscription in Amanda's copy of Woody Guthrie's *Bound for Glory*.

"he was a reluctant conscript" Interview with Conroy, Aug. 31, 1984.

10. PRIVATE ALGREN 157–169

"They never had any right" *Who Lost an American?* (Macmillan, 1963), 149.

"They couldn't wait" Unpublished MS, "Me and My Big Mouth" (also called "Mein Kampf"). Courtesy Ohio State U. Libraries.

"Somehow those dumb" Ibid.

"I was an officer" Letter from Herbert Aptheker to the author, Aug. 6, 1986.

"in the big stuff" NA to Richard Wright, Oct. 8, 1944. Collection of American Literature, Beinecke Rare Book and Manuscript Library, Yale.

"I didn't know" Ibid.

"Transfers are froze" Ibid.

"The Shame of the Nation" Interview with Herbert Gross, July 12, 1987.

"Get Algren to do it" Ibid.

"would wake up" Autobiographical fragment. OSU.

"put on the ball" NA to Wright, Oct. 8, 1944. Beinecke.

"I told him" Ibid.

"goof-off country" *Conversations with Nelson Algren* (Hill & Wang, 1964), 69.

"The days, like the sky" "That's the Way It's Always Been," *The Neon Wilderness* (Writers & Readers, 1986), 188.

"Officers were using" Ibid., 189–190.

"strutting stage prop" and **"Bull"** Ibid., 189.

"The most comical" Ibid., 190–192.

"The people were lively" NA to Lou Gilbert, April 16, 1945 (postcard). Courtesy Martha Lou Gilbert.

"They were looking for us" "That's the Way It's Always Been," 193.

The official army history of Algren's unit, "History of the 125th Evacuation Hospital" (Passau, Germany: Ablass-mayer and Penninger, 1945), aside from providing interviews of men who served with Algren, confirms the accuracy of "That's the Way It's Always Been."

"Nobody wanted to leave" *Conversations*, 80–81.

"This wasn't an infantry outfit" Ibid., 82.

"There's nothing wrong" Interview with Amanda Algren, Aug. 1, 1984.

"Saw a ghost" NA to Gilbert, June 8, 1945. Courtesy Martha Lou Gilbert.

"The terrible part" Ibid.

"and who wants to" NA to Gilbert, April 16, 1945 (postcard). Courtesy Martha Lou Gilbert.

"You people have a bill" NA to Gilbert, May 12, 1945. Courtesy Martha Lou Gilbert.

"But this wasn't protest" *Conversations*, 59.

"[The] arrival of VE day" NA to Gilbert, May 12, 1945. Courtesy Martha Lou Gilbert.

"always the children" *Neon Wilderness*, 96.

"Wild West town" *Conversations*, 83.

"Hey, Joe! MP!" Ibid., 84.

"very easy to push" Ibid.

"the guys would be" Ibid., 83.

"Combien?" "Love on the Rue," unpublished MS. OSU.

"for such a cheap item" Ibid.

"They called her" Ibid.

"she was so thin" Ibid.

"I was the anonymous man" NA to Maxwell Geismar, undated (1954). Maxwell Geismar Collection, Mugar Memorial Library, Boston U.

"He came out" Interview with Dorothy Farrell, April 22, 1985.

11. THE NEON WILDERNESS 170–191

"life-size drama" NA to Maxwell Geismar, undated (1959). Maxwell Geismar Collection, Mugar Memorial Library, Boston U.

"The last of Chicago's gaslamps" Introduction to *The Neon Wilderness* (Hill & Wang, 1960), 10.

"They fought—not because" "The Face on the Barroom Floor," *The Neon Wilderness* (Writers & Readers, 1986), 129.

"Somebody died in my room" and the quotes that follow are from "Show-up Notes." Courtesy Ohio State U. Libraries.

"Neither God, war" *The Man with the Golden Arm* (Penguin, 1984), 7.

"And the minute" Interview with Ken McCormick, March 3, 1987.

"Céline" *Conversations with Nelson Algren* (Hill & Wang, 1964), 95.

"Let's Research Around" NA to Mary Guggenheim, Oct. 15, 1946. This and all letters to Guggenheim courtesy Mary Guggenheim.

"bad" Interview with NA in Malcolm Cowley, ed., *Writers at Work:* The Paris Review *Interviews* (Viking, 1958), 241.

"the most representative" and **"characterless and remote"** "Dreiser's Despair Reaffirmed in the Stoic," *Philadelphia Inquirer Book Review,* Nov. 23, 1947.

"I heard a dead sound" Blue notebook with entries from 1946. OSU.

"I just had an over-all *feeling***"** Interview with NA in *Paris Review,* Winter 1955, 52.

"I've always figured" Ibid., 45.

"He is determined" *NY Times Book Review,* Feb. 2, 1947, 16.

"an excellent collection" Maxwell Geismar, *American Moderns* (Hill & Wang, 1958), 190.

"There is enough horror" *Saturday Review of Literature,* Feb. 8, 1947, 14.

"Algren's world" *NY Times Book Review,* Feb. 2, 1947.

"unfortunate sales confusion" McCormick to NA, May 5, 1948. OSU.

"like being up" NA to Guggenheim, Feb. 10, 1947.

"Far from being ashamed" NA to Guggenheim, Nov. 11, 1946.

"My idea of money" *Conversations*, 155.

"If you get anything" Interview with Amanda Algren, Aug. 1, 1984.

"I wrote you" NA to Amanda, March 27, 1947. This and all letters to Amanda courtesy Amanda Algren.

"He had a lot of one-night stands" Interview with Ted Liss, Nov. 1987.

"the hope of French literature" Francis and Gontier, *Simone de Beauvoir: A Life, a Love Story* (St. Martin's Press, 1985), 201.

"the whole human being" Ibid., 228.

"must commit himself" Ibid., 233.

"That Simone de Budoir" NA to Guggenheim, Feb. 10, 1947.

"Often when it rang" *Conversations*, 180–181.

"Where I thought *she'd* **been"** Ibid., 181.

"Simone de Beauvoir's eyes" *Who Lost an American?* (Macmillan, 1963), 96.

" 'It's beautiful' " Simone de Beauvoir, *America Day by Day* (London: Duckworth, 1952), 81.

"Everything I know" Ibid.
"I think he initially" SdB quoted in Deirdre Bair, "A Man and The Woman," *Lear's*, March 1989, 132.
"I showed her the electric chair" *Conversations*, 182.
"I was happy" SdB to NA, Feb. 23, 1947. OSU.
"disobeyed" SdB to NA, Oct. 3, 1947. OSU.
"Nelson constantly got angry" Interview with Liss, Nov. 1987.
"He was a bit of a misogynist" Ibid.
"Haven't seen the Rowlands" NA to Amanda, March 27, 1947.
"Just like all the American women" "A Man and The Woman," 133.
"furious curiosity" *Conversations*, 180.
"the Petersburg of Dostoevsky" NA to Richard Wright, Oct. 22, 1940. Collection of American Literature, Beinecke Rare Book and Manuscript Library, Yale.
"Algren totally bowled me over" "A Man and The Woman," 132.
"My beloved husband" and **"Your own Simone"** Common greetings in letters from SdB to NA. OSU.
"I did not think" NA, quoted by SdB to NA, July 19, 1947. OSU.
"Do you think we" NA, quoted ibid.
"I tried to explain" SdB to NA, July 22, 1947. OSU.
"deep intimacy" SdB to NA, June 2, 1947. OSU.
"the fulfillment of love" SdB to NA, Oct. 3, 1947. OSU.
"fine lover" SdB to NA, March 25, 1948. OSU.
"something broke up" SdB to NA, Sept. 26, 1947. OSU.
"Rich is having trouble" *Paris Review*, Winter 1955, 41.
"They would come in" Ibid.
"He came out" Ibid., 42.

"These were people" Ibid., 44.
"striking example" *America Day by Day*, 85.
"The national climate" ACLU statement quoted in Fred J. Cook, *The Nightmare Decade* (Random House, 1971), 64.
"We no longer laugh well" "Laughter in Jars, Not as Sandburg Wrote of It," *Chicago Sun-Times Book Week*, July 20, 1947, 2.
"The cult of money" "Laughter in Jars."
"the tide of war" "American Message: A Reply to Open Letter of Soviet Writers," *Daily Worker*, May 10, 1948.
"frog wife" and **"crocodile"** SdB to NA, passim, late 1947–1948. OSU.
"mastered [the] language" Ken McCormick to NA, May 5, 1948. OSU.
"The frog would give everything" SdB to NA, April 19, 1948.
"Love's promises" Simone de Beauvoir, *Force of Circumstance* (Penguin, 1983), 136.

12. THE MAN WITH THE GOLDEN ARM
192–208

"found each other" NA and SdB's joint diary. Courtesy Ohio State U. Libraries.
"that is, women" Ibid.
"While we gorged ourselves" Ibid.
"a punchdrunk fighter" Ibid.
"sat in the lost sunny Yucatán" Ibid.
"finally saw the wonderful ruins" Ibid.
"Nelson *very bad*" Ibid.
"phony Broadway" Ibid.
"the only two people" Ibid.
"carpets of candles" Ibid.
"We didn't even have time" Ibid.
"native dancing" Ibid.

"Real bad night" Ibid.
"You can't love someone" Simone de Beauvoir, *The Mandarins* (London: Flamingo/Fontana, 1982), 589.
"It comes in lumps" NA to Joseph Haas, March 1, 1952. Courtesy The Fiery Clockface Bookstore, Chicago.
"with whether it would *say* anything" Ibid.
"kind of innocence" *Conversations with Nelson Algren* (Hill & Wang, 1964), 132.
"No matter what you hear" Interview with Robert McCullough, Nov. 20, 1985.
"Nelson looked at the picture" Interview with Arthur Shay, July 10, 1986.
"I'm stuck here" Quoted in Simone de Beauvoir, *Force of Circumstance* (Penguin, 1983), 176.
"I judge that I rewrote" NA to Haas, March 1, 1952. Courtesy Joseph Haas.
"the poetry of Faulkner" Telegram from Ken McCormick to NA, Oct. 21, 1948. OSU.
"I suppose there were" NA to Haas, March 1, 1952. Courtesy Joseph Haas.
"It does so because" NA to McCormick, Feb. 18, 1949. OSU.
"The great, secret" *The Man with the Golden Arm* (Penguin, 1984), 17.
"These were the luckless" Ibid., 18.
"mouth at the end" Ibid., 30.
"Anything that pays" Ibid., 93.
"monkey on his back" Ibid., 56 and passim.
"a heart-shaped face" Ibid., 30.
"from monkey to zero" Ibid., 59.
"the retentiveness" Ibid., 1.
"honest copper's duty" Ibid., 296.
"the sentence hanging" Ibid., 200.
"we are all members" Ibid., 198.
"I don't say my characters" Quoted in Dick Bauer, "States Ideas and Ideals—Has No Social Solutions," *Roosevelt Torch,* Oct. 24, 1949, 5.
"Frankie's destruction of Zosh" George Bluestone, "Nelson Algren," *Western Review,* 22 (Autumn 1957), 36.
"love is the only way" Ibid., 34.
"there was no escape" *Golden Arm,* 187.
"From early manhood" Fragment. OSU.
"For Amanda—who helped write" Dedication, Amanda Algren's copy of *Golden Arm.*
"without consciously wanting to" *Force of Circumstance*, 176.
"What occurs to me now" NA to Ken McCormick, Oct. 30, 1948. OSU.
"The only things that last" *Conversations*, 134.
"and the lights" *Who Lost an American?* (Macmillan, 1963), 92.
"It's like eating cardboard" Arthur Shay, "Author on the Make," *Sunday, The Chicago Tribune Magazine,* Sept. 14, 1986, 10.
"She couldn't write a scene" Interview with Carolyn Gaiser, Dec. 18, 1988.
"I never really thought" SdB to NA, June 6, 1950. OSU.
"He was not an intellectual" Interview with SdB, June 26, 1985.
"somehow assumed" NA to Michel Fabre, March 22, 1963. Courtesy Michel Fabre.
"women who were not serious" "Brave Bulls of Sidi Yahya," *The Last Carousel* (G. P. Putnam's Sons, 1973), 109.
"I knew we were in the wrong neighborhood" Ibid., 107.
"See, she has one too!" Ibid., 108.
"It's just huge, warm" *Force of Circumstance,* 194–195.

13. "You Are Going to Be a Champion" 209–228

"a true novelist's triumph" *Time*, Sept. 12, 1949, 104.
"Algren [is] an artist" *Chicago Sun-Times Book Week*, Sept. 11, 1949, 6X.
"virtually nothing more" *NY Times Book Review*, Sept. 11, 1949, 8.
"broad compassion," "unforgettable," and "overwhelmed" *New Yorker*, Sept. 11, 1949, 105–106.
"Now add the name" Full-page *NY Times Book Review* ads, fall 1949. NA's scrapbooks. Courtesy Ohio State U. Libraries.
"Into a world of letters" Ernest Hemingway to NA, 1949, OSU.
"probably the best writer under 50" Hemingway to Maxwell Perkins, Oct. 11, 1949. Reprinted with permission of Charles Scribner's Sons, an imprint of Macmillan Publishing Co., from Carlos Baker, ed., *Ernest Hemingway: Selected Letters 1917–1961* (Scribner's, 1981), 681. © 1981 by Mary Hemingway.
"OK, kid, you beat Dostoevsky" Hemingway quoted in Norberto Fuentes, *Hemingway in Cuba* (Lyle Stuart, 1984), 266.
"When I get a few bucks" NA to Amanda Algren, Dec. 4, 1949.
"What stopped me till now" NA to Ken McCormick, Nov. 18, 1949. OSU.
"He was still wearing" A. J. Liebling, "The Second City," *New Yorker*, Jan. 19, 1952, 50.
"bushy-tails" NA to Amanda, Dec. 4, 1949.
"ball of fire" NA to McCormick, Dec. 18, 1949. OSU.
"We shot on the streets" Arthur Shay, "Remembering Nelson Algren," *Sunday, The Chicago Tribune Magazine*, Sept. 14, 1986, 14.
"an exact and candid representation" NA's application to the Guggenheim Foundation, Oct. 10, 1950. Courtesy John Simon Guggenheim Foundation.
"just feel around" "Headliners and Bestsellers," *NY Times Book Review*, June 11, 1950, 5.
"a country girl who'd become" "Previous Days," *The Last Carousel* (G. P. Putnam's Sons, 1973), 214.
"that he was very, very troubled" *Conversations with Nelson Algren* (Hill & Wang, 1964), 104.
"Acker looked very spurty" Ibid., 107.
"Nelson was like a bull" Interview with Tiba Willner, June 20, 1987.
"flying saucer" *Chicago: City on the Make* (McGraw-Hill, 1983), 46.
"The Ten-Day-Hollywood-Hospitality Treatment" "A Walk on the Wild Side," unpublished MS (essay). OSU.
"Roberts was very salty" NA to McCormick, March 22, 1950. OSU.
"his whole manner" *Conversations*, 112.
"we had reached" "Walk." OSU.
"might be regarded as a message" *NY Times*, as quoted in Cedric Belfrage, *The American Inquisition, 1945–1960* (Bobbs-Merrill, 1973), 130.
"out of an almost Christlike feeling" *Conversations*, 157.
"At a time when everyone" Interview with Albert Maltz, June 10, 1984.
"Sartre *has* to go away" SdB to NA, Jan. 3, 1950. OSU.
"I had no family" Quoted in Dick Bauer, "States Ideas and Ideals—Has No Social Solutions," *Roosevelt Torch*, Oct. 24, 1949, 1.
"That's the kind of house" Interview with Amanda, Aug. 1, 1984.

"I'm telling them" Interview with Arthur Shay, July 10, 1986.

"from every bum" "Remembering Nelson Algren," 39.

"It would have *made* Nelson" Interview with Shay, Feb. 16, 1988.

"He had to protect himself" *Conversations,* 111.

"definitely washed out" NA to McCormick, March 22, 1950. OSU.

"What did you buy that house for?" Interview with Christine Rowland, Nov. 1985.

"What about this sand" and **"Well, there's this"** Interview with Shay, July 10, 1986.

"It seems ridiculous" Simone de Beauvoir, *The Mandarins* (London: Flamingo/Fontana, 1982), 698.

"quite athletically loving" "Remembering Nelson Algren," 10.

"I was always afraid" *Mandarins,* 685–686.

"I never met anyone" Photograph caption, Francis and Gontier, *Simone de Beauvoir* (St. Martin's Press, 1987), between 204 and 205.

"Nelson was always saying" Interview with Neal Rowland, Nov. 1985.

"In 1950, after a break" Interview with SdB, June 26, 1985.

"I think I'm not" *Mandarins,* 678.

"We had a party" Interview with Christine Rowland, Nov. 1985.

"living together without baby-raisin' " NA to Amanda, Oct. 30, 1950.

"the marked-down derelicts" *Chicago: City on the Make,* 10.

"two outs to the inning" Ibid., 14.

"silver-colored yesterday" Ibid., 29.

"The Black Sox were the Reds" Ibid., 36–38.

"the place built out of" Ibid., 73.

"psychological nerve" Ibid., 58.

"stuck out their stubborn" Ibid., 66.

"You can't make an arsenal" Ibid., 55.

"plastic masks of an icy-cold despair" Ibid., 59.

"He was a prey" Simone de Beauvoir, *Force of Circumstance* (Penguin, 1983), 171.

"Café Flore intellectual" *Chicago: City on the Make,* 53.

"tough it out" Ibid., 54.

"the whole great American tradition" Quoted in Natalie Robins, "Hoover and American Literature: The Defiling of Writers," *Nation,* Oct. 10, 1987, 369.

14. RUMORS OF EVENING 231–243

"The way I see Chicago" Interview with Arthur Shay, July 10, 1986.

"Don't let any of this" Harry Nickles to NA, May 24, 1951. Courtesy Ohio State U. Libraries.

"I'd be less disappointed" NA to Nickles, May 27, 1951. OSU.

"complete composure" NA to Ken McCormick, undated (Sept. 1951). OSU.

"You don't know me" Interview with Shay, July 10, 1986.

"I've never been afraid" *Conversations with Nelson Algren* (Hill & Wang, 1964), 150.

"the finest thing on the city" *Chicago Sun-Times,* undated clipping, Algren's scrapbook. OSU.

"therein lies its strength" "Heartbeat of a City," *NY Times Book Review,* Oct. 21, 1951, 3.

"Jekyll-and-Hyde sort of burg" Ibid.

"Nothing can stop sales now" McCormick to NA, Oct. 1951 (telegram). OSU.

" 'It's not friendship' " Simone de

Beauvoir, *Force of Circumstance* (Penguin, 1983), 262.

"To love a woman" Ibid.

"that old thing" A familiar Algren reference to *Somebody in Boots*.

"It's so bo-o-o-oring" Charlie Chaplin interview with Cedric Belfrage, 1955, in Belfrage, *The American Inquisition, 1945–1960* (Bobbs-Merrill, 1973), 179.

"The out-loud kind of doubting" "A Walk on the Wild Side," unpublished MS (essay), 12. OSU.

"Speak up for freedom!" "What Are You Doing Out There?" Public statement, *NY Times*, Jan. 15, 1951, 9.

"The whole thing is straight" NA, quoted in *Daily Worker*, March 7, 1952, 9. FBI files on NA.

"Whether he's in writing" "Walk," 9. OSU.

"A certain ruthlessness" Ibid., 23.

"We live today" Ibid., 46–48.

"small-boy-got-to-have" NA to Ellen Borden Stevenson, undated (April 1952). Harry Ransom Humanities Research Center, U. of Texas, Austin.

"perhaps the only great man" "An Intimate Look at Dylan Thomas," *Chicago Sun-Times Book Week*, Jan. 1, 1956, 4.

"In one place in Italy" *Conversations*, 90.

"We were kind" From unpublished 25-page poem by Algren. Courtesy David Peltz.

"the little whore" SdB to NA, passim. OSU.

"Why don't you marry" SdB to NA, April 2, 1952. OSU.

"It's funny" From "Show-up Notes," Nov. 28–29, 1949. OSU.

"When she'd withdraw" Interview with Caesar Tabet, Feb. 19, 1988.

"If you hang onto me" Ibid.

"Darling poor old ugly" SdB to NA, May 4, 1952. OSU.

"I think my affair" Interview with SdB, June 26, 1985.

15. ENTRAPMENT 244–272

"Hi, Amanda" Interview with Amanda Algren, November 23, 1985.

"It has been alleged" R. B. Shipley, passport office, to NA, March 3, 1953. Freedom of Information Act files.

"This will be one of the first" Maxwell Geismar to NA, June 3, 1953. Courtesy Ohio State U. Libraries.

"I'd like to be raided" NA to Geismar, March 15, 1954. Maxwell Geismar Collection, Mugar Memorial Library, Boston U.

"For $100 I plummet" NA to Geismar, undated (September 1953). Mugar.

"Do you have pine-scented" NA to Geismar, undated (August 1954). Mugar.

"gifted misfit" and **"walled Yaddo"** William Styron, *NY Times Book Review,* April 25, 1971, 1.

"a kind of death" and **"too much"** SdB to NA, July 22, 1953. OSU. (She refers to his letter.)

"a real pangish pang" Ibid.

"So you see" Ibid.

"line by line" *Conversations with Nelson Algren* (Hill & Wang, 1964), 143.

"turns from his fumbling" Fragment from "Entrapment." OSU.

"whirlpool of regret" Ibid.

"you didn't have to get lucky" Ibid.

"In that land" Ibid.

"It was fall" Ibid.

"His legs went suddenly weak" Ibid.

"It had been the sort of thing" Ibid.

"Baby, I thought" Ibid.

"And though I close up" Ibid.

"Polishing is a polite phrase" NA to Geismar, Aug. 6, 1953. Mugar.

"I put too much work in it" NA to Geismar, undated (fall 1953). Mugar.

"I don't have as much heart" NA to Geismar, Jan. 18, 1954. Mugar.

"Currently I support a wife" NA to Millen Brand, Oct. 2, 1953. Millen Brand Collection, Rare Book and Manuscript Library, Columbia U.

"I think that the writers" NA to Geismar, April 7, 1954. Mugar.

"House-car-cat" NA to Geismar, June 22, 1954. Mugar.

"I thought that by seeing again" NA to Geismar, undated (summer 1954). Mugar.

"seeing nothing but" Ibid.

"reeling around Louisiana" NA to Amanda, Feb. 25, 1955.

"Max, I can't tell you" NA to Geismar, undated (Dec. 1954–Jan. 1955). Mugar.

"she is the most" Ibid.

"the cards kept the everlasting" *The Man with the Golden Arm* (Penguin, 1984), 119.

"Frankie would sit back" *Golden Arm,* 115.

"Yeah—but tonight" Interview with Neal Rowland, Nov. 1985.

"It's the only game in town" Interview with Caesar Tabet, Feb. 20, 1988.

"deeply a gambler" Interview with SdB, June 26, 1985.

"Algren came alive" Interview with David Peltz, July 1988.

"rigged ball game" *Chicago: City on the Make* (McGraw-Hill, 1983), 14.

"Either you win" *Conversations,* 153.

"Asking producers for work" Interview with Robert Goldfarb, Dec. 2, 1985.

"between a pretzel-shaped swimming pool" NA to Amanda, Feb. 1, 1955.

"but like most things" NA to Amanda, Sunday (February 1955).

"politically clear" Ibid.

"[Preminger] told Mary Baker" Ibid.

"One of the first questions" *Conversations,* 136–137.

"Be nice to Otto" Ibid., 120.

"If I took *him* seriously" Ibid.

"Thank you for letting me" Ibid.

"I think the idea" NA to Amanda, Feb. 8, 1955.

"Actually, I've never cared" NA to Geismar, April 15, 1955. Mugar.

"Although I did not find" NA to Otto Preminger, Feb. 10, 1955. OSU.

"Nelson was typical" Interview with Goldfarb, Dec. 2, 1985.

"Nelson felt that everyone" Interview with Clancy Sigal, July 26, 1985.

"When Preminger took" Interview with Peltz, July 20, 1986.

"I remember him sitting" Ibid.

"Lionel Lardass" NA to Geismar, undated (summer 1955). Mugar.

"suddenly announced" Ibid.

"deadly . . . such schoolboy poetry" *Nelson Algren* (Twayne, 1975), 33.

"In every chapter" Ibid.

"big silly stud" and "clown-town" Autobiographical fragment. OSU.

"It was a goofed-up book" Ibid.

"You're more inclined" *Paris Review,* Winter 1955, 55.

"Algren [had] found" Maxwell Geismar, review of *A Walk on the Wild Side, Nation,* June 2, 1956.

"of all the major works" *Algren,* 34.

"comic-strip vitality" Ibid., 80.

"of far greater than" Ibid.

"I don't think his book" Alfred Kazin, *NY Times Book Review,* May 20, 1956.

"[Seldes] told me" NA to Geismar, Nov. 15, 1955. Mugar.

"Don't embarrass me" Ibid.

"He sat among [the guests]" *Notes*

from a Sea Diary (G. P. Putnam's Sons, 1965), 35.

16. A WALK ON THE WILD SIDE
273–287

"I feel that, in working" NA to William Targ, undated (early 1956). Courtesy Ohio State U. Libraries.

"immense vitality" Milton Rugoff, *"A Walk on the Wild Side," NY Herald-Tribune,* May 20, 1956.

"an American ballet" Autobiographical fragment. OSU.

"[he] finds bums" Norman Podhoretz, "The Man with the Golden Beef," *New Yorker,* June 2, 1965, 2.

"the bard of the stumblebum" and **"museum piece"** Leslie Fiedler, "The Novel in the Post-Political World, *Partisan Review,* 23 (Summer 1956), 360–361; and "The Noble Savage of Skid Row," *Reporter,* July 12, 1956, 43–44.

"He never got over" Interview with Tom Dardis, Aug. 4, 1986.

"Yes, I think Madame de Beauvoir" " 'Golden Arm' Author Has Mean Elbow" *NY World Telegram and Sun,* June 22, 1956, 17.

"She must have taken notes" Interview with Martha Lou Gilbert, Nov. 23, 1985.

"He was miserable" Ibid.

"Frenchy's thing" NA to Amanda Algren, undated (June 1956).

"problem" and **"really first-rate novel"** Delmore Schwartz, "Films," undated clipping, *New Republic* (late 1955–1956), 22. OSU.

"impressive, absorbing" *NY Post,* May 22, 1956.

"If you can't say anything" Autobiographical fragment. OSU.

"All I had to do" NA to Maxwell Geismar, July 2, 1956. Maxwell Geismar

Collection, Mugar Memorial Library, Boston U.

"A good female novelist" "People," *Time,* July 2, 1956. Maxwell Geismar Collection, Mugar Memorial Library, Boston U.

"Well, you say *it* was hard" SdB to NA, July 12, 1956.

"live off the horses" NA to Amanda, undated (summer 1956).

"He was a discomforting man" Interview with Neal Rowland, Nov. 23, 1985.

"I think you have a depression" Interview with David Peltz, July 20, 1986.

"Come on, Dave" Ibid

"Nelson was pacing" Interview with Rowland, Nov. 23, 1985.

"In one trip" Ibid.

"There was a lobby" Interview with Peltz, July 20, 1986.

"I said, 'Come on, Nelson, sign' " Ibid.

"She's a nice lady" Ibid.

"He was not subdued" Ibid.

"He felt connected" Interview with Peltz, Aug. 7, 1988.

"married" Ibid.

"He came into the offices" Interview with Frank Sandiford, Dec. 20, 1986.

"Everything is so clean" Arthur Shay, "Remembering Nelson Algren," *Sunday, The Chicago Tribune Magazine,* Sept. 14, 1986, 14.

"She was his true muse" Interview with Peltz, Aug. 7, 1988.

"he was delicate" Ibid.

"I think I'll marry the broad" Ibid.

"They're going to be" Ibid.

"I don't want to not do worse" Interview with Caesar Tabet, Feb. 20, 1988.

"And I am increasingly disenchanted" James Blake to NA, Dec. 5, 1956, in *The Joint* (London: Secker and

Warburg, 1972), 98. Reprinted by permission of International Creative Management, Inc. © 1970 by James Blake.

"a quick-buck grinder" NA to Geismar, Dec. 11, 1956. Mugar.

"In it he seemed" William Targ to the author, July 2, 1987.

"Go on ahead" Interview with Amanda, Aug. 1, 1984.

"You mother-fucker" Interview with Peltz, July 20, 1986.

17. THE PAST IS A BUCKET OF ASHES
288–303

"like Flaubert in English" Interview with Arthur Langer, Aug. 13, 1986.

"I phoned all day Friday" Ibid.

"The files, it seems" NA to Simon Michael Bessie, April 27, 1957. Random House Archives, Rare Book and Manuscript Library, Columbia U.

"Truthfully, I don't think he had the money" Interview with Langer, Aug. 13, 1986.

"Shumlin was in absolute awe" Ibid.

"Aw, I just wanted" Interview with Arthur Shay, July 10, 1986.

"The reason I didn't write" NA to Langer, Feb. 5, 1958. Courtesy Arthur Langer.

"I think too of your wonderful" NA to Lily Harmon, undated (1957). Courtesy Lily Harmon.

"But that was when he was already" Interview with David Peltz, July 20, 1986.

"NO!" and **"poignantly"** NA to Bennett Cerf, Oct. 27, 1957. Random House Archives, Columbia.

"The scattered sheets you sent" Cerf to NA, Oct. 24, 1957. Random House Archives, Columbia.

"The film was a loss" *Conversations*

with Nelson Algren (Hill & Wang, 1964), 296.

"It's a bit bewildering" NA to Lloyd Wendt, March 22, 1958. Files of the *Chicago Tribune*. Courtesy John Blades.

"prizewinner" Whitney Tower, "Prose for the Roses," *Sports Illustrated,* April 25, 1986, 45.

"destroyers of the social order" Edmund Fuller, *Man in Modern Fiction* (Random House, 1958), 43–44.

"The remarks directed against Algren's work" Carla Capetti, "A Walk on the Other Side: *Never Come Morning* by Nelson Algren," in "Urbanism as a Way of Writing: Chicago Urban Sociology and Chicago Urban Literature, 1915–1945," Ph.D. dissertation, Columbia U., 1989, 5. © 1984 by Carla Capetti. Reprinted by permission. I am indebted to Capetti's discussion.

"left unheeded the truth that" "Ride on an Elephant," *Nation*, May 19, 1962, 449.

"I don't feel I'm any closer" NA to Maxwell Geismar, undated (Jan.–Feb. 1959). Maxwell Geismar Collection, Mugar Memorial Library, Boston U.

"aid and comfort to complacency" David Ray, "A Talk on the Wild Side," *Reporter,* June 11, 1959, 32.

"literature is made upon any occasion" Afterword to *Chicago: City on the Make* (McGraw-Hill, 1983), 81.

"They arrived directly" Introduction to *The Neon Wilderness* (Hill & Wang, 1960), 10–11.

"It would be a serious mistake" "Urbanism as a Way of Writing," 9–10.

"lightless cave off a loveless hall" NA to Geismar, Feb. 20, 1959. Mugar.

"an enormous facade" NA to Geismar, Dec. 23 (1957). Mugar.

"great restless masses" Ibid.

"Carl Sandburg's Chicago" and **"I will"** Ibid.

"I married the real girl" Ibid.

"It's as if, beginning in 1940" NA to Geismar, undated (1959). Mugar.

"Twenty years ago" Ibid.

"I thought I'd make" *Conversations,* 94.

"The past is a bucket of ashes" Interview with Paula Rheingold, Aug. 1984.

"by sixteen furlongs" "A Talk on the Wild Side," 32.

"*Arm* was a solid job" Ibid.

"*A Walk on the Wild Side* is the kind of novel" Ibid.

"Who *for?*" NA to John Clellon Holmes, Jan. 20, 1960. Collection of Alfred Hirsch, Jr., c/o Pharos Books, New Haven, CT.

"Maybe she did me a lefthanded favor" NA to Geismar, undated (1959?). Mugar.

"J. C. Kornpoen" "A Talk on the Wild Side," 32.

"Uh, I think you owe me" Interview with Shay, July 10, 1986. Nelson also reports the incident in a letter to Geismar.

"You figure him out" Interview with Peltz, July 20, 1986.

"Nelson was drunk" Charles Gold to the author, Aug. 6, 1986.

"a cracker with a poetic streak" Interview with Fran Landesman, Oct. 22, 1986.

"Music—excellent" NA to Holmes, Jan. 20, 1960. Hirsch collection.

"droll, faintly sardonic" John Clellon Holmes. "Arm: A Memoir," in *Representative Men* (U. of Arkansas Press, 1988), 249.

"the only American novelist" Ibid., 246.

"When I first met Nelson Algren" Ibid., 243.

"He could be infectiously funny" Ibid., 248.

"an elaborate put-on" Ibid., 246.

"I happen to have had an agent" *Conversations,* 151.

"Look at me!" and **"*Keep* looking!"** *Who Lost an American?* (Macmillan, 1963), 24.

"knots of antagonistic people" *Representative Men,* 252.

"There never seems to be" NA to Geismar, undated (1959). Mugar.

18. WHO LOST AN AMERICAN?
307–324

For the section on NA's 1960 European trip, I am indebted to discussions with SdB's biographer Deirdre Bair, April and May 1989.

"She was feared" *Who Lost an American?* (Macmillan, 1963), 97.

" 'Transatlantic' Terkel" NA to David Peltz, summer 1960.

"I should think" NA to Maxwell Geismar, April 7, 1960. Maxwell Geismar Collection, Mugar Memorial Library, Boston U.

"so they had immediately" *Who Lost,* 102.

"arrived in the city" NA to John Clellon Holmes, Sept. 26, 1960. Collection of Alfred Hirsch, Jr., c/o Pharos Books, New Haven, CT.

"Pried open the door" NA to Holmes, Aug. 23, 1961. Hirsch collection.

"sucked and smiled" Ibid.

"I would go and look" Interview with Stephen Deutch, July 15, 1986.

"My idea of a redundant sentence" NA to Herman Kogan, undated. Courtesy Ohio State U. Libraries.

"Star and Garter" is an unpublished MS. OSU.

"Hey, that was a goddamned *girl*" NA to Peltz, undated (1961).

Account of NA's meeting with Baldwin from *Conversations with Nelson Algren* (Hill & Wang, 1964), 236–240, and interview, "Nelson Algren Off the Cuff," *Cavalier*, Nov. 1963, 82.

"Voices are coming" *Conversations*, 328.

"He was not an athletic" *Notes from a Sea Diary* (G. P. Putnam's Sons, 1965), 90.

"He was terrified" Interview with Peltz, Aug. 7, 1988.

"in order to make Man free" Introduction to *Nelson Algren's Own Book of Lonesome Monsters* (Lancer Books, 1962), 9.

"*You* figure them out" NA to Holmes, June 30, 1962. Hirsch collection.

"very submerged men" *Conversations*, 176.

"Girls, I thought" *Sea Diary*, 54.

"are kept in cages" NA to Lily Harmon, Aug. 3, 1962. Courtesy Lily Harmon.

"bud-*dee*" *Sea Diary*, 221.

"Dave, pay up" Interview with Peltz, Aug. 7, 1988.

"I know" Ibid.

"We met" Ibid.

"first person" and **"third person"** *Who Lost*, 317 and passim.

"more at ease" Ibid., 326.

"an embarrassment" John Clellon Holmes, *Representative Men* (U. of Arkansas Press, 1988), 251.

"surrealist and grotesque" Robert Lowry, "Algren Stuffs a Book Like a Barracks Bag," *Chicago Sun-Times Book Week*, May 12, 1963, 2.

"venom and sourness" Larry McMurtry, "Algren's Venomous Views," *Houston Post*, May 19, 1963.

"Intellectual as Ape Man" Review of *Who Lost, Time,* May 31, 1963.

"Caught between his own past" Hilton Kramer, "He Never Left Home," *Reporter*, June 30, 1963, 46.

"I guess, like the Lost American" SdB to NA, undated (Sept. 1963). OSU.

"Algren emerged" Carolyn Gaiser, "Remembering Nelson Algren," unpublished MS made available by Gaiser.

"fresh from an evening" John Van der Zee, "The Man with the Golden Pen," unidentified source. Courtesy Jack Conroy.

"It wasn't gas" Nelson Algren, "Erik Dorn: A Thousand and One Afternoons in Nada," introduction to *Erik Dorn* (U. of Chicago Press, 1963), xvii.

"completely reorganized" Interview with H. E. F. Donohue, June 30, 1984.

"Nelson got a sickly grin" Ibid.

"Candida went up and tapped" Ibid.

"In his manner of relating" Interview with Stephen Deutch, July 15, 1986.

"could never have meant" *Conversations*, 269.

"the passion of a moment only" Simone de Beauvoir, *Force of Circumstance* (Penguin, 1983), 136.

"contingent love" Ibid., passim.

"Anyone who can experience" Nelson Algren, "The Question of Simone de Beauvoir," *Harper's*, May 1965, 136.

"A writer who has moved" Ibid., 134.

"No chronicler of our lives" Ibid.

"procurers are more honest" Ibid., 136.

" 'In this matter' " Ibid.

"Mme. Utter Driveleau" and **"complete pomposity"** NA to Joel Wells, undated. OSU.

"I kept my distance" Interview with Studs Terkel, July 14, 1986.

19. THE LAST CAROUSEL 325–349

"He said he wanted" Interview with Stephen Deutch, July 15, 1986.

"too far along" Ibid.

"I met Betty" Ibid.

"Nelson was very defiant" Ibid.

"tough-sentimental literary lush" Arno Karlen, "Hard Shell, Soft Center," *NY Times Book Review,* Aug. 12, 1965.

"literary communist" Ibid.

"obscene and irrelevant" Cheever, quoted by NA to William Targ, undated (fall 1965).

"Are there ten living American writers" Sol Yurick, "Correspondent to the Underworld," *Nation,* Oct. 25, 1965, 263.

"in the long run" Ibid

"he had become the man" Conrad Knickerbocker, "Scraping the Barnacles off Papa," *Book Week,* Aug. 15, 1965, 3.

"By the mid-sixties" Interview with Tom Dardis, Aug. 4, 1986.

"The longer I hang on" and the following student quotes from "Hand in Hand Through the Greenery," *The Last Carousel* (G. P. Putnam's Sons, 1973), 77.

"provides sanctuary" Ibid., 76.

"The classes often started late" Burns Ellison, "First Annual Nelson Algren Memorial Poker Game," MS version, 17. Courtesy Burns Ellison.

"I spoke for about twenty minutes" Interview with Kurt Vonnegut, Jr., Oct. 31, 1988.

"Once I tried" "First Annual," 27–28.

"The Ho Chi Minh Trail" NA to Roger Groening, April 28, 1965, and elsewhere. This and all letters to Groening courtesy Roger Groening.

"I don't want to go to Vietnam" "Letter to Joel Wells," *Critic,* Feb.–March 1967, 25.

"There he was" Kurt Vonnegut, Jr., introduction to *Never Come Morning* (Four Walls, Eight Windows Press, 1987), xix.

"It's just a hell of a poetic job" NA to Groening, Feb. 1, 1966.

"the woman in mink" Mike Royko, "Nelson Algren Takes Dim View of Girl Scribblers," *Chicago Tribune,* undated clipping (March 1967). Courtesy Roger Groening.

"The only major city" Vonnegut, introduction to *Never Come Morning.*

"I don't think the clubbing" "McCarthy Offices Raided at Dawn by Chicago Police," *NY Times,* Aug. 31, 1968, 11.

"It will take many years" James Cameron, quoted ibid.

"American shenanigans" "I Know They'll Like Me," *Last Carousel,* 112.

"no tipping, no kissing" "Letter from Saigon," Ibid., 134.

"accounts, in part" Ibid., 137.

"It's a mean, sick city" NA to Roger Groening, Dec. 21, 1968.

"perfect security" Ibid.

"Pity has escaped" Dean Enclis, *The Face of South Vietnam* (Houghton Mifflin, 1968), 18.

"Nelson wanted only to out-guile" Roger Groening, "Amateur Night Way Out East," *Writing in the First Person: Nelson Algren 1909–1981* (Chicago Public Library, 1988).

"Whistles kept shrilling" "What Country?," *Last Carousel,* 140.

"They don't have *original*" NA to Groening, May 11, 1969.

"always ends up" Maxwell Geismar, "Algren Shows Us How Good American Fiction Can Be," review of *Last*

Carousel, photocopy from unidentified source. Courtesy Ohio State U. Libraries.

"He liked to be taken care of" Interview with Sue McNear, Oct. 30, 1988.

"I have this curious knack" NA to Groening, Dec. 13, 1970.

"I don't know anyone" Interview with McNear, Oct. 30, 1988.

"If there's a better reviewer" NA to Groening, April 26, 1971.

"I shafted Mme. Utter Driveleau" NA to William Targ, Aug. 17, 1972. OSU.

"If I could get by" Henry Kisor, "Nelson Algren, Hale and Salty at 64," *Chicago Daily News,* Oct. 27, 1973.

"I thought it was the *LA Times Book Review*" NA to Groening, undated (1971).

"It was a crummy flat" Interview with Studs Terkel, Nov. 11, 1988.

"It's striking how the man" "Nelson Algren: Sixty Years from Mack Avenue," *Detroit Free Press,* May 26, 1974, 6.

"One moment he's talking" Phil Tracy, "Nelson Algren: One with His Own," *National Catholic Reporter,* April 1, 1970, 6.

"nonperson" Studs Terkel, introduction to *Chicago: City on the Make* (McGraw-Hill, 1983), 6.

"Algren sent me" Targ to the author, July 2, 1987.

"My God, Nelson" NA to Groening, April 8, 1973.

"Something tells me" NA to Groening, June 22, 1973.

"You're right about the Kazin" NA to Groening, Dec. 30, 1973.

"Algren's journalism" Bruce Cook, review of *Last Carousel, Commonweal,* Feb. 8, 1974, 469.

"I received a nice note" Henry Kisor to the author, Nov. 7, 1988.

"The reviews came out" Interview with Deutch, July 15, 1986.

"no reason to spend" Autobiographical fragment. OSU.

"The question of my next novel" NA to Targ, Dec. 1, 1973. OSU.

"How I don't know" NA to Groening, May 7, 1973.

"Putnam's stopped distributing" NA to Groening, Jan. 25, 1974.

"Books started coming" Interview with Deutch, July 15, 1986.

"The other members" Interview with Vonnegut, Oct. 31, 1988.

"whose plays were denounced" Algren's acceptance speech for the Award of Merit. OSU.

"not sane" and **"batty"** Interview with Vonnegut, Oct 31, 1988.

20. THE DEVIL'S STOCKING 350–368

"A very forthright man" NA to Roger Groening, undated postcard (Feb.–March 1974).

"Carter is the *sanest* man" NA to Groening, March 31, 1974.

"*Esquire* wanted" Interview with Hy Cohen, Dec. 6, 1988.

"He needed a project" Interview with Sue McNear, Oct. 30, 1988.

"The entire judicial process" Publisher's note to Rubin "Hurricane" Carter, *The Sixteenth Round* (Warner, 1975), 412.

"I don't know why" NA to Stephen Deutch, Jan. 11, 1975. Courtesy Stephen Deutch.

"He was a very strange individual" Interview with Deutch, July 15, 1986.

"This is all worthwhile" Rick Soll, "Nelson Algren Bids Final Farewell," *Chicago Tribune,* March 10, 1975, 2.

"He was anxious" Interview with McNear, Oct. 30, 1988.

"How's Margo, Caesar?" Interview with Caesar Tabet, Feb. 20, 1988.

"It is strange" NA to Groening, June 10, 1975.

"He had certain patterns" Interview with Roy Finer, Feb. 24, 1987.

"We differ upon my obligation" NA to Candida Donadio, March 20, 1976. Courtesy Ohio State U. Libraries.

"the weensiest sum" NA to Groening, Aug. 8, 1974.

"could no longer cope" William Targ to the author, July 2, 1987.

"I was bored" Interview with Deutch, July 15, 1986.

"He wanted to do it" Interview with Groening, May 7, 1989.

"He thought he was going" Interview with Finer, Feb. 24, 1987.

"No, they haven't seen it" Henry Kisor, "Nelson Algren, That Hackensack Homebody," *Chicago Daily News,* June 12, 1976.

"so drenched in sweat" NA to Groening, Aug. 1, 1976.

"It was hopeless" Interview with Richard Merkin, June 2, 1987.

"Got any Algren?" Interview with Finer, Feb. 24, 1987.

"So. You come up here" Ibid.

"I'm not on Long Island" Joe Pintauro, "Algren in Exile," *Chicago Magazine,* Feb. 1988, 94.

"He worked on a turf policy" Interview with Groening, summer 1988.

"an abrasive New York Jew" Interview with Finer, Feb. 24, 1987.

"turning the trial" and "idiotic remarks" James B. Lieber, " 'Hurricane' Carter's Second Trial," *Nation,* April 2, 1977, 397.

"I'm not disappointed" NA to Deutch, Aug. 27, 1977. Courtesy Stephen Deutch.

"It's possible, I suppose" Jim Gallagher, " 'Literary Exile' Is Pleasant for Algren," *Chicago Tribune,* March 29, 1977, sec. 2, p. 1.

"One day he'd think" Interview with Finer, Feb. 24, 1987.

"It was the loss in belief" Interview with Groening, July 9, 1987.

"I'm not in debt" Jan Herman, "Nelson Algren: The Angry Author," *Chicago Sun-Times,* Jan 21, 1979, 10.

"If I get that bad" Interview with Finer, Feb. 24, 1987.

"I don't want to call" " 'Literary Exile' Is Pleasant."

"He had always been an exerciser" Interview with Merkin, June 2, 1987.

"He would answer the phone" Interview with Groening, summer 1988.

"This is the kind of place" Interview with Finer, Feb. 24, 1987.

"This was not the neighborhood" Ibid.

"He says meet me" Ibid.

"He accused me" Interview with Deutch, July 15, 1986.

"non-fiction novel" Donadio, quoted in John Blades, "The Novel Nelson Algren Didn't Want to Write," *Chicago Tribune Book World,* Aug. 21, 1983, sec. 13, p. 37.

"breathless with surprise" *The Devil's Stocking* (Arbor House, 1983), 37.

"brought the organ up hugely" Ibid. 36.

"He'd say, 'You know, Steve' " Interview with Deutch, Dec. 5, 1988.

"I would speak to young people" Interview with Donadio, June 23, 1987.

"The kind of editor" Interview with Groening, summer 1988.

"knitted backwards" *Devil's Stocking,* 25.

"I called and he wasn't home" Interview with Finer, Feb. 24, 1987.

"Nelson was terrified" Interview with Groening, Dec. 1988.

"They won't pay me anything" Ibid.
"His landlady in Paterson" Ibid.
"It was then that I discovered" Ibid.
"I don't need that shit" Ibid.
"There was no sense" Ibid.
"As for Donald Fine" NA to Donadio, March 1, 1980. OSU.
"The sooner we can nail" NA to Donadio, March 8, 1980. OSU.

21. SAG HARBOR 369–376

"I was stunned" Late notebook. Courtesy Ohio State U. Libraries.
"It was a point of pride" Jan Herman, "In at Last: Nelson Algren's Final Happy Days," *Chicago Sun-Times Book Week,* May 17, 1981, 1, 31.
"bank managers' town" Dallas Gatewood, "Respite from the Wild Side," *Newsday,* Jan. 22, 1981, part 2, p. 3.
"as if the gods" Joe Pintauro, "Algren in Exile," *Chicago,* Feb. 1988, 99.
"Almost every inch" Ibid., 100.
"rolled under the sofa" Interview with Kurt Vonnegut, Jr., Oct. 31, 1988.
"a cheap SOB" Budd Schulberg, *"The Devil's Stocking:* Algren's Last Look at the Inner Circle of Outcasts," *Chicago Tribune Book World,* Aug. 21, 1983, sec. 13, p. 37.
"Nelson had a tendency" Candida Donadio, quoted ibid.
"You call this a bookshop?" Interview with Canio Pavone, Jan. 8, 1989.
"The next Saturday" Ibid.
"Are you going to saw it?" Interview with Roy Finer, Feb. 24, 1987.
"Why don't you draw a up a will?" Interview with Roger Groening, Dec. 1988.
"Well, you know" Ibid.
"Why did we ever go to war" "In at Last," 31.
"I'm going on half a century" "Nelson Algren, Novelist Who Wrote of Slums, Dies," *NY Times,* May 10, 1981.
"I thought he had money" Interview with Susan Mernit, Aug. 31, 1986.
"He was spontaneous" Ibid.
"holding court" Interview with Pavone, Jan. 8, 1986.
"Here we are" Carolyn Gaiser, "Nelson Algren Meets the Literary Establishment," *Newsday,* June 7, 1981, 20.

Index